LIBERALISM AND TRADITION

LIBERALISM AND TRADITION

ASPECTS OF CATHOLIC THOUGHT IN NINETEENTH-CENTURY FRANCE

BERNARD REARDON

Head of the Department of Religious Studies, University of Newcastle upon Tyne

CAMBRIDGE UNIVERSITY PRESS

CAMBRIDGE
LONDON · NEW YORK · MELBOURNE

Published by the Syndics of the Cambridge University Press
The Pitt Building, Trumpington Street, Cambridge, CB2 1RP
Bentley House, 200 Euston Road, London NW1 2DB
32 East 57th Street, New York, NY 10022, USA
296 Beaconsfield Parade, Middle Park, Melbourne 3206, Australia

© Cambridge University Press 1975

Library of Congress Catalogue Card Number: 75-7214

ISBN: 0 521 20776 2

First published 1975

Photoset and printed in Malta
by St Paul's Press Ltd

CONTENTS

PREFACE

'The nineteenth century is with the seventeenth the greatest in the literary history of France. The two periods, despite their many differences, are not without their points of resemblance. Both of them are great centuries alike in philosophy and in poetry; and perhaps for this very reason, in religion also, in the sense that religious questions were seen by both as of chief importance and by both searchingly explored from every angle. Together they attained the loftiest heights of thought and of art.' This judgment of Émile Faguet's has long seemed to me a just one. French culture during the last century achieved excellence and variety to a degree worthy of comparison with the *grand siècle* of Descartes and Pascal, of Racine and Molière, of Bossuet and Fénelon. In particular the religious as well as the literary influence of René de Chateaubriand left a deep mark upon it. For whatever value may be placed on *Le Génie du Christianisme* as apologetic, and to the modern reader its deficiencies in this regard are only too patent, its author was in large measure responsible for the changed attitude of public opinion towards religion which the nineteenth century, by contrast with its predecessor, at once began to register. This first became apparent in the earlier years of the century, when the place and function of religion in society were of express concern, Catholicism being viewed as the counterpart either — as with Maistre and Bonald — of the political restoration, or — with Lamennais and his disciples — of a new liberalism under papal patronage. However, the advance of the sciences, both natural and historical, was bound sooner or later to re-open the question of the credibility of the faith, an issue as to which, so it increasingly was felt, the traditional scholasticism offered no satisfactory guide. Thus a new type of religious philosophy was to be sought, capable of sustaining belief in an increasingly secular age on the grounds less of external authority or abstract logic than of the moral experience of the 'whole man'. This development, extending from Bautain to Blondel and Laberthonnière, is the outstanding feature of French religious thought throughout the period, drawing nutriment from the parallel movement in French philosophy from Maine de Biran to Renouvier, Boutroux and Henri Bergson. On the other hand scholasticism itself, especially in its Thomistic form, was far from being eclipsed, and in the later decades underwent vigorous revival. And here again we find

vii

a parallel, in the neo-ultramontanism which reached its apogee in the years following the infallibility definition of 1870. Nevertheless the apologetic enterprise continued, though in a manner which official Catholicism was less and less disposed to approve, inasmuch as the growing pressure whether of scientific naturalism or historical positivism had seriously to be faced. Unfortunately the so-called Modernist movement, in which it culminated, made its appearance at a time when the triumph of ultramontane forces and the 'integralism' for which these stood could only render its efforts unavailing. Finally, as the second *grand siècle* began with the *Génie* and the Napoleonic Concordat so it may be said to have concluded with the Separation Law and *Pascendi*.

It has been my aim in the present volume to trace the course of this tension between liberalism and tradition, taking as it does a variety of shapes, political and social, philosophical and biblical. To study each of its successive phases in real depth, however, would have been impossible in a work designed to furnish the reader with a general survey; but sufficient information is to be found in the bibliographical references to enable him to pursue his inquiries a good deal further, should he so desire. What I have endeavoured to do is to offer a history of the age, in respect of the development of Catholic religious philosophy, such as will bring to light a diversity and complexity that has not always been recognized or admitted by those who at least until recently have professed to represent the standpoint of ecclesiastical authority. For Catholicism has rarely been the monolithic system which either its defenders or its critics frequently wish to portray. Completeness, no doubt, I have not achieved, nor indeed striven for. Rather have I concentrated on the movements and tendencies which have best typified their time; and I am not aware of any single book hitherto published that has undertaken to do this in a comprehensive way. Studies of individual persons, periods and episodes within the century abound, but a more panoramic view, of a kind likely — as I hope — to interest readers on this side of the English Channel (or the hither side of the Atlantic) is less easy to point to. I have tried, as a responsible historian should, to be objective; but my assessments are my own and I have not attempted quite to conceal my personal angle of vision.

I would like here to acknowledge the help I received from Miss Madeleine Knight in the preparation of the index and also my thanks to the staff of the publisher for all the care they have bestowed on the book's production.

University of Newcastle upon Tyne   BERNARD REARDON
October 1974

1

INTRODUCTION: THE NEW CENTURY

The Concordat

On Easter Day, 18 April 1802, a solemn Te Deum was sung in Notre Dame de Paris in simultaneous celebration of peace with England and with the Catholic church. The papal legate, Caprara, presided and Bonaparte himself attended in state.

The peace with England had been secured by the recent Treaty of Amiens, that with the church by an agreement with the Holy See reached only after protracted and frequently acrimonious negotiations. But the latter had brought to an end, in principle at least, the schism in the French church created by the attempt of the Revolutionary governments to impose upon it, under oath, the ultra-Gallican Civil Constitution of the Clergy of 1790.[1] No such schism had indeed been intended, since basically the *Constitution Civile* was a compromise which did not require the separation of church and state nor any change in doctrine. But under it the pope, although acknowledged as the church's spiritual head and the focus and symbol of its unity, forfeited his administrative powers as these had hitherto been exercized in France. Thus the opposition of Rome was provoked from the first, with the result that the French clergy immediately found themselves in the dilemma of a divided loyalty the outcome of which was not only the virtual paralysis of the new ecclesiastical system but a widening gulf between Catholicism itself and the whole Revolutionary ideal – 'the principles of 1789' – such as was destined to persist for well over a century to come. For under the Reign of Terror the church suffered grievously. Hundreds of non-juring clergy, the *réfractaires*, as they were called, were put to death: two hundred and twenty-five priests, it was reported, in the capital alone in the massacres of September 1792. The climax of the persecution was reached when in November 1793 the Paris Commune abolished even the constitutional worship, thereby setting an example soon to be followed throughout France. This act was marked by a 'Feast of Reason' during which an opera dancer was enthroned on the cathedral's high altar as *la Déesse Raison* and received the adoring homage of the mob. With the inauguration

---

[1]On the French church during the Revolution see J. Leflon, 'La crise révolutionnaire', in A. Fliche and V. Martin (eds.), *Histoire de l'Église*, xx (1951), pp. 17–158.

1

of Robespierre's cult of the Supreme Being, however, the tide began to turn, and when the Directory gave way to the Consulate Catholics sensed a change to a more favourable atmosphere. Not that Napoleon's own religious convictions were a potent factor. Nominally a Catholic, he had latterly affected a modish 'atheism' and in Egypt had even disclosed Muslim sympathies. Of Christianity as a faith he understood little or nothing, but he was quite capable of recognizing the strength of religion as a social force. 'No society', he told the assembled clergy of Milan in June 1800, 'can exist without morality. But there is no good morality without religion. Religion alone therefore can give the state firm and lasting support.' He affected to deplore the church's persecution and expressed himself satisfied that the French had been cured of their delusion on this score. 'France', he declared, 'having learned from her misfortune, has brought back the Catholic religion into her midst.' It only remained to embody this change of heart in appropriate legal forms, and for that the authority of the pope was indispensable. 'If there had been no pope', the French dictator remarked, 'it would have been necessary to invent one.' This in practice meant that the Holy See was to be induced to bring pressure on *émigré* bishops, and through them on 'refractory' priests, to accept the Republic and therewith the church's own role, under suitable disguise, as the upholder of a *religion gendarme*. The Concordat, after eight months of tortuous discussions — it was re-drafted no fewer than twenty-five times — achieved Napoleon's purpose. Cardinal Ercole Consalvi, on behalf of Pius VII, had been driven to a hard bargain, but ostensibly the breach was healed. The government of the republic allowed that 'the Catholic, Apostolic and Roman religion' was 'the religion of the great majority of Frenchmen', whilst being careful not to affirm that Catholicism was the religion of the French state. Freedom of public worship was guaranteed, but only in conformity with such *règlements de police* as the government should deem 'necessary for public tranquillity'. Other provisions included a new delimitation of dioceses, the resignation of existing holders of sees 'for the sake of peace', the power of the First Consul to nominate to vacant bishoprics within three months (the pope authorizing canonical institution according to the ancient forms), an episcopal oath of fidelity to the state, episcopal nomination to parishes (subject to government approval), the preservation of the rights of existing owners in alienated church property, state payment of bishops and parish priests and confirmation of the First Consul in the same rights and privileges in regard to the Holy See as belonged to the prerevolutionary government. The pope's assent was embodied in the bull *Qui Christi Domini vices* of 29 November 1801, by which he 'suppressed, annulled, and for ever extinguished' all existing French sees and deprived the occupants of their canonical jurisdiction.[2]

---

[2] Forty-eight bishops tendered their resignations as demanded, but thirty-seven refused. See Leflon, 'La crise', pp. 203f.

The irony of the Concordat lay in the assertion of the ultramontane principle against the Gallican in order to secure to the new French state a plenitude of power over the national church exceeding that of the old monarchy.[3] The pope's temporal sovereignty was recognized and his spiritual authority reaffirmed, but Bonaparte's gratuitous and unilateral addition to the terms of agreement of certain *Articles organiques* virtually withdrew all that he had conceded. For by them not only papal decrees but those even of a general council were rendered unenforceable in France without the *placet* of the government. Moreover no ecclesiastical synods were to be held within the country unless with the prior authorization of government, and the four Gallican Articles of 1682 were imposed as obligatory teaching in seminaries.[4] The pope protested in vain; he could do nothing but hope, as he mildly put it, for 'change and amelioration'. In fact such changes as occurred during the next decade or so were only for the worse; of amelioration there was nothing. Pius attended the emperor's coronation in December 1804, his journey to France for the occasion being marked by great popular acclaim along its whole route. But the imperial will was unbending in its determination to use the papacy as an instrument of policy. In July 1809 the sovereign pontiff was abducted from the Quirinal and to all intents became Napoleon's prisoner, first at Avignon, then at Savona and lastly at Fontainebleau. Shorn of the temporal power, he was reduced to the status of a pensioner on two million francs *per annum*. For the future the Vicar of Christ was to be required, on election, to declare his adherence to the Gallican Articles. This public humiliation of the head of the Catholic church ended only with Bonaparte's fall.

Chateaubriand and 'Le Génie du Christianisme'.

But four days previous to the ritual celebration of the Concordat a young author, François-René, Vicomte de Chateaubriand (1768–1848), published a work that was to become a landmark in the literary and religious history of his country: *Le Génie du Christianisme*. A Breton of ancient lineage, he joined the *émigré* forces after a short sojourn in America, was wounded at Thionville and in the following year took refuge in London, where he eked out a livelihood as a hack-writer. His first book, an *Essai sur les Révolutions* steeped in the scepticism of the *philosophes*, appeared in 1797. Disillusioned however by the course of public events and saddened by the deaths in 1799 of both his mother and his sister he re-embraced the religion of his boyhood. 'I became', he says, 'a Christian. I did not yield, I admit, to any mighty supernatural illumination. My conviction came out of my heart. *J'ai pleuré et j'ai cru.*' A few months later he was back in Paris.

---

[3] On the effect of the Concordat as encouraging the growth of ultramontanism see *Cambridge Modern History*, ix, pp. 187ff.   [4] On Gallicanism see Appended Note, p. 18 below.

A token of its author's own conversion, the *Génie du Christianisme* was conceived as apologetic, a vindication of the historic role of Christianity in Western civilization. It was necessary to prove, he wrote in his introduction, that contrary to the prevalent view

the Christian religion is the most humane, the most favourable to liberty, and to the arts and sciences, of all the religions that have ever existed; that the modern world is indebted to it for every improvement, from agriculture to the abstract sciences; from hospitals for the reception of the unfortunate to the temples raised by Michaelangelo and embellished by Raphael. It was necessary to prove that nothing is more divine than its morality, that nothing is more lovely or sublime than its tenets, its doctrines and its worship; that it encourages genius, corrects taste, develops the virtuous passions, imparts energy to ideas, presents noble images to the writer and perfect models to the artist; that there is no disgrace in being a believer with Newton and Bossuet, with Pascal and Racine. In a word, it was necessary to summon all the charms of the imagination and all the interests of the heart to the assistance of that religion against which they had been set in array.[5]

As apologetic it had unfortunately one patent defect — that it made no use whatever of logical argument: its appeal was simply to the imagination and the heart. Nevertheless it was a portent; or in the words of Sainte-Beuve, a rainbow, a 'brilliant sign of a reconciliation and alliance between religion and French society'.[6] The author had spoken of the condition of France after the chaos of the Revolution. 'All the elements of society were in confusion; the dread hand which was beginning to separate them had not yet accomplished its task; order had not yet emerged from despotism and *la gloire*.' As he was to express it, long afterwards, in his *Memoirs*:

It was in the midst of the ruins of our temples that I published *The Genius of Christianity*. The faithful felt themselves saved; there was a craving after faith, a thirst for religious consolations, which sprang from the privation of these consolations for so many years. . . . The victims of our troubles (and how many they were!) sought a refuge at the foot of the altar, like shipwrecked mariners clinging to the rock on which they sought for safety from the stormy seas.[7]

Aptly subtitled 'The Beauties of the Christian Religion', the book's real intent was to justify Christianity aesthetically. For the latter, though derided by the age of Voltaire, Diderot and Condorcet, had inspired great art and created a noble civilization. In acknowledging as much therefore men might begin by wishing it were true and end by admitting that it was.[8]

[5] *Le Génie du Christianisme*, Première partie, i, 1.

[6] *Chateaubriand et son groupe littéraire* (1860), p. 275. But Sainte-Beuve's appreciation had also an astringent quality: '*Le Génie du Christianisme* fut utile en ce qu'il contribuera à rétablir le respect pour le christianisme considéré socialement et politiquement. Il le fut moins en ce qu'il engagea du premier jour la restauration religieuse dans une voie brillante et superficielle, toute littéraire et pittoresque, la plus éloignée de la vraie régénération du cœur.'

[7] *Mémoires d'Outre-Tombe*, Deuxième partie, (E.T., 1854, iii, p. 22).

[8] 'Devant le siècle se dressait une apologétique qui montrait le christianisme si beau que l'on commençait à souhaiter qu'il fût vrai et presque à l'admettre' (Georges Goyau, *Histoire religieuse de la nation française*, 1903, p. 537).

Le Génie du Christianisme was not of course the only indication of a new spirit abroad. There had been other pointers already: among them de Maistre's *Considérations sur la France* and Ballanche's *Du sentiment considéré dans ses rapports avec la littérature et les arts*. But it was Chateaubriand's work that first stirred the public imagination. As he himself claimed, not without justice, it 'threw the eighteenth century for ever out of the track upon which it had entered; men recommenced — or rather they commenced — to study Christianity at its source'. A draft of the book had actually been completed in 1799, but he wisely withheld publication until his return to France. Copies of a second draft appeared in Paris in 1800 or early in 1801, but were withdrawn.[9] Nor was its title an immediate choice. The author's final decision — and for the purposes of publicity it could hardly have been bettered — was first disclosed, it seems, in a letter to Madame de Staël.[10] Even the basic plan of the work underwent more than one alteration. At first it was divided into seven parts; later it became a sort of triptych: dogma, poetry, worship. In April 1801 the 'poetic' character of Christianity — its power to inspire literature and the fine arts — had evidently come to the forefront of Chateaubriand's mind. On the book's initial appearance it bore no dedication, but in 1803, when its success was evident, the name of 'General Bonaparte' or 'The Citizen First Consul' was placed at the head. Thus did the former *émigré* pay tribute to the new regime, not without an eye for possible advantage to himself.[11]

Le Génie du Christianisme consists of four parts. The first, devoted to 'Dogmas and Doctrine', is manifestly not the work of a theologian, professional or amateur; it treats of the Christian 'mysteries' and sacraments, morality, the scriptures (affirming the 'superiority of the Mosaic tradition over all other cosmogonies'), and the existence of God as testified by the wonders of nature. But the view taken is superficial and even perfunctory. In the second and third parts, however, on 'The Poetry of Christianity' and 'Fine Arts and Literature', the author finds himself on more congenial ground. Epic and drama, the life of the emotions ('le vague des passions'), music (Gregorian chant especially), architecture, and above all the great Gothic cathedrals of his native France, are made to present a splendid if somewhat chaotic tableau. Echoes of Pascal and Bossuet contribute to the effect. The fourth part, 'Worship', conjures up the beauties of the liturgy, along with church bells and festivals, tombs and solemn processions, the duties of the parish clergy, missions and the social benefits of religion. Once again ideas, images and poetic meditations jostle one another regard-

---

[9] Parts of this second draft were suppressed in the edition of 1802. *Atala* had already come out as a separate piece in 1800. See Victor Giraud, *Chateaubriand: Études littéraires* ('Le problème bibliographique du Génie du Christianisme'), 1904.

[10] See Pierre Moreau, *Chateaubriand* (1927), p. 90.

[11] But the dedication also necessitated a few discreet changes in the text. See Moreau, *Chateaubriand*, p. 91.

less of any precise objective. As interludes in this medley of rhetoric, piety and aestheticism are two short but exquisite novels of sensibility, *Atala* and *René*, which alone would justify the author's title of 'the father of Romanticism'.[12]

As serious apologetic, therefore, *Le Génie* may be dismissed. Its true purpose — in which it succeeded — was to create a new mood, one of sensitivity to mystery. There is nothing, Chateaubriand tells us, that is beautiful or great in life which is not also mysterious. The very obscurities of Christianity are to be preferred to the trite lucidities of the so-called age of Reason. And his appeal to mystery and imagination is enhanced by a superbly evocative style. That the book's erudition was largely second-hand is of slight account: Chateaubriand's friend, Joubert, and his current mistress, Pauline de Beaumont, were of help to him here. What mattered at the time was that his work seemed to carry with it the originality of a genuine personal experience. Sainte-Beuve's well-known judgment of its author as 'an Epicurean with a Catholic imagination, sensual in life and at bottom sceptical of heart' represents the reaction of a subsequent generation,[13] though the chapters on virginity and the permanence of marriage certainly do come oddly from a man living apart from his wife, of whom he wished to be rid as soon as possible, and with a woman who had only lately divorced her husband. But Chateaubriand's was a complex nature in which the sexual component was strong.

Yet *Le Génie du Christianisme* has a place of its own in the history of modern religious thought. Its author was no philosopher, and indeed he did not pose as one; but Catholic intellectuals in France throughout the first half of the ensuing century were invariably responsive to his influence, and not least, paradoxically enough, to his Rousseauism. For even when the *Génie* appeared the Savoyard Vicar was still being widely acclaimed. His ideas had become part of the ethos of the age, not only as a fount of revolutionary idealism but because of their opposition to rationalism and eloquent vindication of sentiment in life and in letters. Not that Rousseau could be enlisted as an upholder of traditional religion — far from it; but his attitudes were not without their usefulness to the defenders of Catholicism.[14] In the case of Chateaubriand, whose own debt to Rousseau was already plain in the *Essai sur les Révolutions*, this influence was carried a good deal further. He was now strongly critical of Rousseauism in its negative aspects, but he believed

---

[12]Their novelty was less apparent at the time. L. R. Furst observes that neither of them, nor *Le Génie du Christianisme* as a whole, 'was regarded by contemporaries as a serious menace to the Neo-classical tradition which still reigned unchallenged' (*Romanticism in Perspective*, 1969, p. 38).

[13]G. Bertin, in *La sincérité religieuse de Chateaubriand* (1900), laboriously strives to meet Sainte-Beuve's objections point by point, but hardly dispels the impression which the latter's view reflects.

[14]The evidence is collected in P. M. Masson, *La religion de Jean-Jacques Rousseau* (1916).

there was enough of religious feeling in it to make its author look a 'half-Christian', who had 'faith in something which, although not Christ, was nonetheless in the Gospel'.[15] What pervades Chateaubriand's own work is a vein of Rousseauseque *sentiment* not only for nature but for traditional religion as well, with all its rich and affecting historical associations. He shared, in fact, Rousseau's anti-rationalism and dislike of bloodless systems of 'philosophy', but he also needed food for the imagination such as historic Catholicism — or at least its externals — could alone give. René, unlike the earlier 'promeneur solitaire', is a Christian soul whose heart-sickness — a mark, perhaps, of original sin? — could only have arisen within the Christian tradition.[16]

The success of *Le Génie du Christianisme* at the bar of public opinion far surpassed its author's own hopes. It was warmly praised or keenly criticized, but everywhere discussed. He himself had done all he could to secure it the maximum of *réclame*. It was announced by Fontanes, Napoleon's minister for education, in a lengthy article in the *Mercure de France* for 25 Germinal, which in turn was reproduced in the government organ, *Le Moniteur*. New editions of the work came out in rapid succession. Meantime Chateaubriand had met the First Consul at a reception held by Lucien Bonaparte, Napoleon indeed going out of his way to speak to him, an occurrence which, along with the sudden rush to literary fame, stimulated ambitions for a life not only of letters but of action. In 1803 he was appointed first secretary at the Rome embassy under Bonaparte's uncle, Cardinal Fesch. But there his openly voiced contempt for his superior's intelligence led to his removal to La Valais, in the post of French minister. He immediately resigned, however, on hearing of the death of the Duc d'Enghien. The rising of his political star was clearly not yet.

The positive achievement of Chateaubriand's famous book lay in its having rendered traditional Christianity intellectually fashionable. In his own words: 'Il faut assez de mode de l'être chrétien, qu'il avait été de ne l'être pas'. Voltaireanism as a doctrine had received a mortal blow.[17] More, it helped to restore the confidence of Catholics in their own allegiance, tried as this had been during the long years of public derision and persecution. Naturally the work had its detractors. It was severely mauled by the journalist, Ginguené, in three articles in *La Décade*, while abbé Morellet, in a review redolent of the spirit of the *Encyclopædia*, was but little less un-

[15] See Masson, *La religion*, III, c. vi ('Rousseau et la préparation du Génie du Christianisme').

[16] In subsequent editions Chateaubriand sought to lighten his former stress on the *mélancolie* of the Christian consciousness. Thus the statement, 'c'est dans le génie du Christianisme qu'il faut surtout chercher la raison de ce vague des passions répandu chez les peuples modernes', was among those omitted. To his critics disenchantment with life was a trait more pagan than Christian. cf. Moreau, *Chateaubriand*, p. 93.

[17] Victor Giraud, 'Chateaubriand et le Génie du Christianisme', in *Revue des Deux Mondes*, 1926, p. 388.

sympathetic. Chateaubriand himself, stung by these criticisms, wrote an express *Defence* of his book, besides modifying its language in certain respects in later editions. But the original work, whatever its faults, had made its mark. The age had been surfeited with rationalism; what now was needed was play for the imagination, stimulated by a newly awakened sense of the romance and mystery of the past.[18] The verdict of Bonald, that '*Le Genie du Christianisme* is of the small number of fortunate productions which add to their sum of merits that of supreme opportuneness — works which belong at once to all ages and yet to a particular occasion', may stand.

Mme de Staël and her Circle

One whose influence upon her time in some respects paralleled that of Chateaubriand was Mme de Staël (1766–1817), today remembered chiefly as the author of *De l'Allemagne*. Daughter of the Genevan financier, Necker, Louis XVI's minister, and heiress to a fortune, she married in 1786 Baron de Staël-Holstein, the Swedish ambassador in Paris, from whom she later separated. Intellectually precocious almost from infancy, she drew great stimulus from the men whom she met in her father's drawing-room, among them Diderot, Marmontel, Grimm, Buffon, Raynal and Edward Gibbon, though the last-named thought her ill brought up and did not conceal the fact that he preferred her intelligence to her looks. A true child of the eighteenth century, she was an assiduous reader, even as a girl, of the works of Montesquieu and Rousseau. The Revolution she greeted with enthusiasm, although she condemned its excesses and crimes. She herself left France just before the massacres of September 1792 and settled on her father's estate at Coppet, on Lake Leman, where she soon attracted around her a circle of literary friends and personal admirers which included August von Schlegel, Sismondi, and in particular Benjamin Constant, who was to be for many years her intimate companion. Of a passionate, impulsive and romantic disposition, she was entirely convinced of the essential goodness of human nature and its capacity for social progress. She returned to Paris under the Directory, whose agents however kept an eye on her, and thereafter lived out her chosen role of *maîtresse de salon*. With the rise to power of the First Consul she aspired to play Cleopatra to his Caesar, but in vain: Napoleon disliked both her plainness and her intelligence, and in 1803 forbade her to live in or even near the capital.[19] Thus frustrated in her social ambition she sought fulfilment in authorship. Her *De la Littérature considérée dans ses rapports avec les institutions sociales* had appeared in 1800 and was to be

---

[18] In 1804 Chateaubriand published *Les Martyrs* as a kind of pendant to *Le Génie*. It has its moments of felicity but lacks on the whole the imaginative afflatus that carried the longer work to success. On his chosen subject in this instance the author's knowledge was simply inadequate.

[19] On her relations with Bonaparte see H. Guillemin, *Madame de Staël et Napoléon* (1966).

followed by a couple of novels, *Delphine* and *Corinne*, in 1802 and 1807 respectively. In 1808, during a stay at Weimar, she began work on *De l'Allemagne*, a task which occupied her for the next two years. But the first edition, of ten thousand copies, was immediately confiscated by the police on the grounds of its being 'unFrench' and the book did not in fact come before the public until 1813, and then only in London, where it was brought out by John Murray. But she still craved for emotional satisfaction, and when her estranged husband died she married a young Swiss cavalry officer twenty-three years her junior. Napoleon's consistent opponent until his final overthrow, she nevertheless was mortified to see France occupied by foreign troops. Her last years were darkened by failing health and the spent energies of an over-active life. Yet she managed to write two more books, which were published posthumously: *Dix années d'exil* (1821) and *Considérations sur les principaux événements de la Révolution française* (1818). Politically her hopes centred on a constitutional monarchy of the British type, her views in this respect being perpetuated after her death by the so-called *Doctrinaires* who frequented the house of her daughter Mme de Broglie. Guizot too was among her disciples.

Anne-Louise de Staël was possessed by an unquenchable thirst for ideas. Of Protestant upbringing, she was by nature a moralist, but she had an open mind and was in the van of intellectual fashion. Ardent and hospitable, she made it her aim to shine as the centre-piece in a circle of talents. Happily to her other qualities was added the gift of a considerable literary ability, even though her reputation, in her lifetime and since, was built up on rather more than her books. She had much of the sensibility of Rousseau, if with a dash of Voltaire's wit, and her first published writing — the work obviously of a devotee — was a series of *Letters* on Jean-Jacques, whose influence was to continue to dominate her thinking and outlook throughout life.

De la Littérature considérée dans ses rapports avec les institutions sociales applies Condorcet's theory, typical of its age, of the perfectibility of the human race. Of Christianity in its historic embodiments she takes a generally harsh view, but allows that religion has from time to time been the impetus to literary or artistic achievement. Her own literary idols were not so much those of classical antiquity or seventeenth century France as Shakespeare and Ossian, and she felt that the rather moribund classicism of the day needed new life. But she thought that this would come more from philosophy than religion, since Catholicism she looked on merely as a superstition, while her own Protestantism, vaguely latitudinarian or deistic, was scarcely a source of inspiration. Her book, however, was a success and widely praised, although Fontanes in *Le Mercure* was not too well pleased and concluded an article on it with a reference to a work then awaiting publication in which, as he claimed, the author had treated Mme de Staël's themes in a far more striking and novel way; what he had in mind being, of course,

Le Génie du Christianisme. She· herself replied to Fontanes's criticisms in the preface to a second edition of her book six months later, but when Chateaubriand interposed with the remark (in a letter to Fontanes) that where she saw only human virtues he saw the divine Christ his words signalled the beginning of what was to be a long-sustained rivalry between the two eminent precursors of the Romantic movement. Her own reaction to *Le Génie* was indeed appreciative, approving of much of it. With suitable cuts, she said, she could accept the work.

On the other hand her friends, especially Benjamin Constant, considered that Chateaubriand had filched her ideas, for all his difference of standpoint. Yet if the latter's book has any resemblance to hers it is much more obviously an implicit refutation of it. Chateaubriand's faith in the social benefits of religion rested on the historic Catholicism of France, not on a humanistic idealism the failure of which the whole course of the Revolution had demonstrated.

But to the good Genevoise the historical effects of Catholicism had been for the most part baneful, and Bonaparte's concordat she deplored, though she realized that Protestantism was never likely to become the religion of the French people. Yet *Delphine*, published only a few months after the appearance of *Le Génie*, was in its way a Protestant retort to *Atala* and *René* — taking Protestantism, that is, in her own broad and liberalist meaning. She noted the claim that what above all had contributed to the splendours of the classical age of French literature were the religious beliefs then held and that no great work of the imagination could be created apart from them. Her intention therefore was to counter this by example and to show that high art could be produced outside the classical and Catholic traditions. Her model, plainly enough, was the *Nouvelle Heloïse* of her favourite Rousseau. For like Rousseau she recognized the nutritive strength of religious ideas (in his case, those of 'natural' religion), but she insisted that 'the Protestant religion is far closer to the pure spirit of the Gospel than the Catholic'. She argued moreover for the legitimacy of divorce. To such opinions Chateaubriand was entirely opposed, even if in the matter of divorce his practice defied his principles, and his comment on *Delphine* was a fair *riposte* to hers on *Le Génie*: he could accept it 'avec des ciseaux'. He believed indeed that his own work had in some degree succeeded in modifying her views. Thus in a footnote to an article on Bonald he wrote:

Mme de Staël herself, in the preface to a novel, is clearly willing to concede us something and to allow that religious ideas are favourable to the development of genius. Nevertheless she has written her book in order to combat these very ideas and to prove that there is nothing either more arid than Christianity or more tender than philosophy. Has she attained or has she missed her goal? It is for the public to say.[20]

[20] *Oeuvres complètes*, vi, p. 449.

In justice, though, it was not Christianity as such but Roman Catholicism with which she had found fault, and if any change in her opinions had occurred it was simply a shift away from deism in the direction of a more orthodox-looking Protestantism.

In *Corinne* this tendency became more pronounced; or at any rate her confidence in the regenerative powers of philosophy seem to have weakened. The author's travels in Italy had worked on her imagination and she spoke eloquently of her impressions of Rome and especially St Peter's, a 'monument which is the emblem of so many notable and generous ideas'.

La prière seule, l'accent du malheur, de quelque faible voix qu'il parte, émeut profondément dans ces vastes lieux. Et quand, sous ces dômes immenses, on entend de loin venir un vieillard dont les pas tremblants se traînent sur ces beaux marbres arrosés par tant de pleurs, l'on sent que l'homme est imposant par cette infirmité même de sa nature qui soumet son âme divine à tant de souffrances, et que le culte de la douleur, le christianisme, contient le vrai secret du passage de l'homme sur la terre.[21]

The accents here are Chateaubriand's own. He himself wrote to congratulate her on having revealed the Italy he knew and loved.

The truth was that Anne-Louise de Staël had begun to feel the wear and tear of life. The death of her father, to whom she was deeply attached, was a grievous loss; her liaison with Benjamin Constant had brought regrets and disillusionment as well as bliss; her continued exile from Paris distressed her; and she was conscious of growing older. Not surprisingly her thoughts began to take a more serious turn. To speak of her experiencing a religious crisis would be an exaggeration, but her belief in the capacity of reason to solve all the ills of humanity was waning, to be replaced by the spirit if not the traditional dogmas of her inherited religion. It was in this frame of mind that, towards the end of 1807, she went to Germany, which she had already visited four years earlier. The outcome of this second stay was her most important book, *De l'Allemagne*, in the preparation of which she had the help and advice of such friends as Charles de Villers, Schlegel and Ancillon. Like *Le Génie du Christianisme* her work too was to prove an event in French literary history. Both the facts and the judgments may often be questionable and the point of view idealizing: the Germany she saw, or affected to see, was already in 1810 becoming more of a sentimental memory than a present reality; but *De l'Allemagne* was an enterprise of a kind scarcely again attempted since Voltaire's *Lettres philosophiques*.

The tone of the book was no longer an echo of the eighteenth century: the voice of the *idéologues* had fallen silent. Instead she had been reading Schiller and Fichte, and Teutonic *Schwärmerei* drew from her warmer praise than Gallic *esprit*. Germany was mediaeval, chivalrous, romantic, Christian.[22]

---

[21] *Corinne, ou l'Italie* (ed. N. de Saussure et Sainte-Beuve), p. 68.
[22] The Christian past had moreover been illuminated for her by Stolberg and the new

In Christianity she recognized 'the marvellous point at which positive law does not exclude the inspiration of the heart, nor the inspiration of the heart positive law'. In particular it was governed by two motifs — repentance and the sense of the infinite — which bring man to a truer apprehension both of himself and of that universe of nature of which he is an inhabitant. The German character, as she interpreted it, was Christian in its introspectiveness, its essential interiority. Romanticism and religion, as springs of imaginative vitality, went hand in hand.

Nevertheless the differences of attitude disclosed in *De l'Allemagne* and *Le Génie du Christianisme* respectively, are considerable, for all the romantic appeal to the past and reverence for immemorial religious tradition common to both. Thus the two writers diverge in their assessments of the literary inheritance itself. Chateaubriand was as much a classicist as a romantic, and to extol classicism as such was part of his purpose: a re-invigorated, Christianized and Catholicized classicism no doubt, but classicism all the same. Mme de Staël however found her inspiration not here but in the literature of a foreign tongue owing nothing to the great French tradition. German literature, deeply romantic by nature, was intrinsically alien to classicism, and from it, she was convinced, the literature of France could imbibe a wholly fresh creative energy. 'The sterility', she wrote, 'with which our literature is menaced makes one believe that the French spirit itself has need of renewal from a more vigorous sap; and as social elegance will always preserve us from certain faults, it is above all important to rediscover the source of true beauties.'[23] But the source of true beauties had become for her a basically religious one. 'To treat with jocosity what is serious, noble and divine is played out, and something of youthfulness will henceforth be restored to the human race only in a return to religion by way of philosophy and to sentiment by way of reason.' Such was the effect upon her of her German tour. The Germanic nations impressed her as being naturally religious. But it had also to be remembered that in Germany Christianity had undergone the reconstituting and fortifying experience of the Reformation, thus enabling it later to come to terms with reason and the *Aufklärung* in a manner not open to Catholicism. German literature was suffused with Protestant insight and idealism, — whence its strength. Nor was Protestantism less 'poetic' than Catholicism, even if its worship was less showy. In its philosophy, its literature, its art the German nation gave living proof that the Lutheran Reform, so far from checking the development of the soul's faculties, was on the contrary a condition of their further realization. For Protestantism allows a place equally to reason and to feeling, while its dogmas are less

generation of German Catholics, so that she even could hope, in God's good time, for a *rapprochement* between the Catholic and Protestant churches. On the German Catholic romanticists see Georges Goyau, *L'Allemagne religieuse: le Catholicisme 1800–1848* (1905).

[23] *De l'Allemagne* (Flammarion, 1917), i. pp. 14f.

restricting than the Catholic, since Protestantism stands for the freedom of the spirit. As a *via media* between the aridities of rationalism and the childish superstitions of popular Catholicism it continues to testify its worth as a religion for the modern mind.

In the execution of her task Mme de Staël had been aided, as we have noted, by members of her circle. Of these Schlegel was the most ready to encourage her in her romanticizing enthusiasm and in her criticisms of the French classical tradition.[24] Charles de Villers, a former *émigré*, had become a dedicated Germanophile and an exponent of the Kantian philosophy, which was still little known in France at that time. Strongly anti-Catholic in his religious views, he had in 1804 published an *Essai sur l'esprit et l'influence de la Réformation de Luther*, designed as an answer to Chateaubriand and an express apology for Protestantism.[25] But it was Constant who exercised the dominant, because a very personal, influence upon her. A Vaudois of French origin, he took an active part in French public life and ended his days as president of the Conseil d'État. A man of considerable intelligence, cosmopolitan in outlook, and a talented writer, he was also egotistical and devious, though Mme de Staël found his company and conversation fascinating. Not only did he stimulate her interest in Germany and German literature — he himself translated Schiller's *Wallenstein* purposely for her — but he helped shape her ideas generally. Their relationship is portrayed, under a thin disguise, in his novel *Adolphe*, a work of remarkable candour in the self-protraiture of its author. Curiously, perhaps, this disciple of Laclos was also genuinely interested in the question of religion, and his most ambitious literary work — it ran to five stout volumes — was a treatise *De la Religion considérée dans ses rapports avec la philosophie grecque et la religion chrétienne*. Brought up in Protestantism and preserving throughout life a streak of Protestant religious feeling, he disliked the brash rationalism of the *philosophes* and their followers, and although he would have been loath to admit it was himself by no means unmoved by *Le Génie du Christianisme*.[26] In scope *De la Religion* is a positive study of the religious phenomenon from the varying angles of history, sociology and psychology, and for its time is notable for the range of knowledge and understanding it displays. In so

[24] cf. J. de Pange, *Auguste-Guillaume Schlegel et Mme de Staël* (1938).

[25] For Villers Protestantism and intellectual progress meant one and the same thing. 'Quiconque aurait à cœur de s'instruire en histoire, en littérature classique, en philosophie, ne pouvait rien faire de mieux qu'un cours de théologie protestante' (*Essai sur l'esprit*, p. 218).

[26] 'Nous pensons que l'idée dominante de notre ouvrage n'ébranle aucune des bases de cette religion (i.e. Christianity), au moins telle que la conçoit le protestantisme que nous professons, et que nous avons le droit légal de préférer à toutes les autres communions chrétiennes' (*De la Religion*, i, p. 14). E. Faguet observes that Constant 'introduisait dans la pensée française un élément qui lui manquait tout à fait, c'est à savoir un peu, — je dis un peu — d'esprit protestant' (*Politiques et moralistes du xixe siècle*, i, 1891, p. 254). Constant was well versed in contemporary German theological thought, cf. J.-R., Derré, *Lamennais, ses amis et le mouvement des idées à l'époque romantique (1824—1834)* (1962), p. 96.

far as it has a thesis at all it is that 'religions of the spirit' are superior
to those which depend on sacerdotalism. Thus it is critical of Catholicism;
as, moreover, of Catholicism's most recent apologist, *Les Martyrs* in particular
coming in for disparaging comment, although its author's eloquence is
unstintingly admired. What Constant really values in religion is its ethical
idealism, not the quasi-political institutions into which it sooner or later
hardens. 'Let us', he concludes, 'regain religious freedom, boundless, infinite, individual; it will surround religion with an invincible strength, and
guarantee its perpetuity. It will create more and more religious forms, of
which each will become purer than its forerunner ... Divide the torrent, or,
better still, let it divide itself, into a thousand rivulets. They will fertilize
the earth which the torrent itself would only have devastated.' What, however, he desiderates is not a church, with its inevitable human imperfec-
tions, but an elevated sentiment.

A severe critic of Benjamin Constant's ideas was Baron Eckstein (1790–
1861), editor of *Le Catholique*. Of a Jewish family converted to Protestantism,
Ferdinand Eckstein was born in Copenhagen. In his youth he attended
Creuzer's lectures at Heidelberg and applied himself to learn Sanskrit, so
laying the foundations of his subsequent career as an orientalist and student
of religion. After visiting Rome in 1809 he became a Catholic, having been
repelled, as he later explained, by Protestantism's total lack of feeling for
history or sense of the mystery of religious doctrine, and he always reproached its theologians with 'not having sufficiently grasped the Holy
Spirit, which suffuses the pages of the Bible'.[27] While in Rome he met Hum-
boldt, through whom, in all probability, he struck up a friendship with
Friedrich Schlegel, who strongly influenced him, especially in his attitude
to historical criticism. But under the same influence he also became interested in politics and lent his support to the Holy Alliance. In 1816 Louis
XVIII's government appointed him commissioner-general of police for the
department of Bouches-du-Rhône, where he discharged his duties, which
were of a largely political nature, assiduously, although not to the neglect
of his scholarly researches. He resigned in 1818 and settled in Paris in an
administrative post that was little more than a sinecure. The leisure this
afforded him he devoted to journalism and further study, particularly of
'the mysterious obscurities of ancient India'. At the beginning of 1826 he
founded his review, the purpose of which was, as he put it. 'to give science
active entry into life', but which was more and more to turn into a show-
case for his own opinions.[28]

[27] *De l'Espagne* (1836), p. 307.
[28] This Eckstein admits: 'Là je dépose mes pensées et mes résultats, comme dans un magasin'
(*Le Catholique*, xiv, p. 337). It must be confessed that he exhibits little skill as a writer. Lamennais,
whom he came to know in 1823, seems to have regarded him lightly ('Il avait les clefs de tout,
mais n'ouvrait rien'). Nevertheless Eckstein was a man of erudition and considerable breadth of

Like Bonald, Eckstein aimed at a restoration or revivification of the great tradition of Catholic thought which the eighteenth century had so largely blighted. Christianity, he believed, 'had in some sense renewed the form of human existence', and in its Catholic shape at least alone had the answer to the metaphysical and moral problems by which mankind is perpetually vexed.

On the one hand we have science without action, without movement and without life; on the other, science united in supreme degree to a practical religion. There is today no other way open to the human spirit, no other means of replacing, in the conduct of life, the ideas and lessons of the philosophers of antiquity.[29]

But Christianity has its false apologists who completely misrepresent it, and one of these, in his view, was Constant. The latter no doubt had exposed the errors of the Enlightenment, but in the interest merely of the Reformation as now interpreted by the heirs and disciples of Lessing and Schleiermacher.

M. Benjamin Constant believes in the perpetuity of a Protestantism reconditioned in the light of modernity. He hopes for the dissolution of Catholicism, and hopes for it with all the frankness of utter dislike ... It is the sacerdotal system which he detests in Catholicism, it is the church as such which he attacks.[30]

Constant's notion of the religious sentiment also comes under fire for its individualistic pietism and subjectivism. Religion is not, as it were, a natural endowment of the human being, and to see it thus is to evacuate it of all solid content, dogmatic or social. A 'mysticism of enlightened feeling', as Eckstein calls it, is no different, however romanticized, from the deism of Locke and Rousseau.[31] His own intention was to show, rather, that beneath the diversity of their cults there exists a fundamental unity of religious belief among all men; indeed a 'Catholicism before Catholicism', he goes so far as to call it.

It is this which, from all antiquity, has been hailed in the name of natural religion. By that should not be understood a vague deism, but rather a primordial and positive doctrine, with its dogmas, its mysteries, its rites, its cultus and its future life, disfigured by the shadows of idolatry but still recognizable through this obscurity and forming the basis of the mission of the Son of God, determined entirely by the fall of degenerate man.[32]

In proof of his theory of a primitive revelation Eckstein appeals to philology as well as history, blaming Constant for having paid insufficient attention to the phenomenon of language. Natural religion, he contends, is not simply the product of a human instinct directing man towards God; some kind of aid was necessary, namely speech. 'Natural religion is thus a nomenclature,

mind. cf. Louis de Carné, *Souvenirs de ma jeunesse au temps de la Restauration* (1872), p. 162. See also N. Burtin, *Un semeur d'idées au temps de la Restauration: le Baron Eckstein* (1931).

[29] *Le Catholique*, vi, p. 439.   [30] *ibid.*, xv, p. 171.
[31] *ibid.*, xv, p. 174.   [32] *ibid.*, iii, p. 171.

a word, a hymn, an invocation, a liturgy, a language.'[33] Here of course he is at one with Bonald, by whose views he was a good deal affected. Analyse, he says, the ancient tongues and you will discover at the origins of human thought, as amongst the earliest documents of fable and history, a 'bedrock of sublime metaphysic' very different from the atomized fragments out of which it used to be supposed that the human intelligence could be built up.[34]

The End of the Age of Reason

Such, then, were the new tendencies, but the recent past was not without its surviving representatives. The great names of the previous century were now indeed only a memory: Condorcet, Chamfort and the poet André Chenier had been the last of them; but their disciples remained and during the first decade or so of the new century stubbornly resisted the ideas and beliefs that were beginning to gain a hold on the public mind. At the Institut they even maintained their sway, not only among philosophers, and they could count numerous supporters in the Senate. Their organs included *Le Journal de Paris, Le Citoyen français, Le Publiciste* and *La Décade*. The Paris suburb of Auteuil was their favoured *milieu*, in the *salons* of Mmes Helvétius and Condorcet and that genuine relic of the bygone century, Destutt de Tracy. The designation *encyclopédistes* had fallen out of fashion, but a new name, *idéologues*, coined by Tracy, imparted a certain stylishness to the deism and atheism of pre-Revolutionary days. For the *idéologues* too made a cult of 'reason' or (in Condillac's term) 'analysis'. Not only did they despise anything that reminded them of religion in its Christian form, but sentiment and imagination they held in almost equal contempt. In thought and in literature they were classicists and in politics republicans.

Ginguené and abbé Morellet, both regularly to be found *chez* Mme Helvétius, were also prominent among them, the latter an acute critic whose standards however were as narrow as they were exacting, the former a man of in some respects wider sympathies, but essentially backward-looking, prejudiced and cocksure. Tracy himself, an old soldier turned *philosophe*, was a dedicated Voltairean. Cabanis, physician, poet and *penseur*, and a kinsman by marriage of Condorcet's, professed an ideology compounded of materialism and stoicism.[35] Others of the group were Daunou, a learned 'classicist' of the straightest sect, who until he abandoned Christianity had been an Oratorian, and Volney, world traveller and author of a pretentious work bearing the title *Ruines*, who gained the esteem of Napoleon and was made a senator, although as a convinced *idéologue* he opposed the Concordat. Of

[33] *ibid.*, xi, p. 352.   [34] *ibid.*, viii, pp. 112f.
[35] His *Rapports du physique et du moral* (1802) places him among the pioneers of clinical psychology.

the Revolutionary figures still surviving Marie-Joseph Chénier, poet, drama-
tist and critic, was probably the most typical of his age. He had been a
member of successive Revolutionary assemblies and had voted for the
execution of the king. Replete with the spirit of Voltaire, whom he delighted
to describe as 'a veritable arbiter of taste, and the greatest man of letters
in Europe', he now ridiculed those whom he dubbed 'the new saints'. In
his *Tableau historique de l'état et des progrès de la littérature française depuis 1789*
he refers to *Le Génie du Christianisme* only to dismiss it for its 'poétique
extraordinaire', so contrary to the ideals of classicism. *Atala* he reviewed,
though with the same distaste as Morellet. The sort of work he regarded as a
masterpiece was Boileau's *Art poétique*, which, if it did not 'produce poets'
nevertheless 'formed and inspired them'.

Finally, beyond the *idéologues*, was a group of more or less militant atheists:
Diderot's friend, Naigeon, Sylvain Maréchal, author of a *Dictionnaire des
athées*,[36] Dupuis, with his *Origine des cultes*, and the physicist Laplace, whose
Exposition du système du monde could, as he assured Napoleon, dispense with
the hypothesis of God. For these men, who reduced the moral order to the
social and the psychological to the physical, science and religion were of
necessity foes and religion had already lost the battle. Theirs still was the
spirit of the *Encyclopædia*, self-confident and iconoclastic.

The intellectual condition of the French church in the years immediately
following the Concordat was, it need hardly be said, enfeebled. The up-
heavals of the preceding decade had left no time for scholarly pursuits.
Moreover although public education had not thrived under the Revolution
it had favoured the experimental sciences at the expense of the humanities.[37]
Even Kant's works were scouted, the Directory's censor judging a proposed
translation of the *Critique of Pure Reason* to be 'useless', a new scholasticism
as objectionable as the old. The church of course had lost all influence in the
educational sphere. For ten years the seminaries had been closed and
the more cultivated among the clergy had either fled the country or perished.
Not only had the religious houses been suppressed but some ancient universities as well, including the theological faculty of the Sorbonne. To repair
the damage would perforce be the task of years; nothing could be effected
by a mere stroke of the pen and in any case the church's most pressing need
was the reconstitution of its organizational life. Its only centres of intellectual
activity were the few newly-established seminaries necessary for recruiting
the depleted ranks of the parish clergy, itself a slow enough process. The
disarray in ecclesiastical affairs persisted indeed for a good many years

[36] See C.-A. Fusil, *Sylvain Maréchal, ou l'Homme sans Dieu* (1936).
[37] cf. Ernest Renan, *Essais de morale et de critique* (1860), p. 51: 'La société qui sortit immédiatement de la Revolution fut servile parce que toute aristocratie intellectuelle avait disparu, parce
que l'exercice le plus sérieux de la pensée se réduisait alors à des traductions d'Horace et à des
vers latines' (cited L. Foucher, *La Philosophie catholique en France au XIXe siècle*, 1955, p. 13).

and church education at all levels lagged far behind secular. Qualified professors were scarce and there was a serious shortage of books, those available
being no more than reprints of older works that by then were largely out-
dated. Attempts to establish institutes of higher education in the fields of
theology and philosophy, not only during the Empire but under the Restoration as well, all failed, mainly through lack of interest on the part of the
ecclesiastical authorities themselves. Thus when Cardinal Fesch tried in
1805 to set up just such a centre at St Denis, M Emery of St Sulpice showed
no enthusiasm, objecting (not without some reason) that there were tasks
more urgent.[38] At that time in fact throughout the whole of France (including Belgium) there were only some six hundred priests under the age of
forty. It was partly at least through lack of theological training on traditional
lines that the younger clergy were rendered so susceptible to the doctrines
of a man like Lamennais.[39] For what was most vital in French Catholic
thinking in the early years of the century was not its presentation of church
teaching, which was mediocre, but its free-lance apologetic, shaped with an
eye to contemporary needs and conditions.

Appended Note: Gallicanism

Gallicanism may be defined as the tendency, especially pronounced during the
seventeenth and eighteenth centuries, to stress on the one hand the French church's
relative independence of the Holy See, and on the other the ecclesiastical prerogative of the crown. As a doctrine it was strongly upheld at the Sorbonne, at first
in the form developed by Gerson and D'Ailly, later in that associated with the name
of Richer. Its classic formulation, consequent upon Louis XIV's differences with
Pope Innocent XI, is the Gallican Declaration, consisting of four main articles,
which was drawn up by Bishop Bossuet, accepted by the French episcopate on
19 March 1682, and thereafter imposed upon the clergy generally. The articles were
condemned by Alexander VIII in 1690 and three years later withdrawn by the
king himself, although they were widely invoked in the disputes over the bull
Unigenitus of 1713.

The first of them lays it down that kings and sovereigns are not by God's
command subject to any ecclesiastical power in temporal matters, that they cannot
be deposed, whether directly or indirectly, by the authority of the head of the
church, and that their subjects cannot be dispensed from their obedience or ab-
solved from any oath of allegiance. The second affirms that the plenitude of power
in spiritual matters possessed by St Peter and his successors nevertheless remains,
as laid down by the decrees of the Council of Constance. The third states that the

---

[38] cf. J. Leflon, *Monsieur Emery* (1946), ii, pp. 261f. Even some twenty-five years later, when
Mgr Frayssinous, by then minister for church affairs and public instruction, wished to found a
Catholic institute in a very convenient building placed at the church's disposal by the government he was opposed by the archbishop of Paris. The minister's plan was not indeed realized
until 1843.

[39] cf. H. de Lacordaire, *Considérations sur le système philosophique de M. de Lamennais* (1834), pp.
27f. Lamennais himself was to a considerable extent self-educated.

exercize of the apostolic power must be regulated 'by following the canons made by the Holy Spirit and sanctified by universal reverence', and adds that the rules, customs and constitutions accepted in the realm and church of France necessarily have their proper strength and virtue, 'since the greatness of the Holy See requires that the laws and customs established with its consent and that of the Churches remain invariable'. The fourth article insists that although the pope has the chief voice in questions of faith, and his decrees apply to all churches and to each particular church, yet 'his decision is not unalterable unless the consent of the Church is given'. An appended article demanded the assent of all the French bishops and churches. (For the original text see W. F. Reddaway, *Select Documents of European History*, p. 155.)

In 1802 Bonaparte re-asserted the substance of the articles in the so-called *Articles organiques* attached to the Concordat of the previous year.

Gallicanism was not a unitary system and its theological aspect has to be distinguished from its polical. The former maintains a doctrine of the church under which the Roman primacy is limited either by the episcopate as such — Bossuet's own view — or by the entire body of the faithful — Richer's theory; whereas political Gallicanism is more concerned with the subordination of the church to the state and the precise expression of this in legal and administrative instruments. The Richerian or 'democratic' type of Gallicanism, championed by the Revolution, had its outcome in the Constitutional Church; but with the subsequent Concordat it disappeared, although political Gallicanism was brutally enforced by Napoleon and perpetuated in essentials under the Restoration.

In the early decades of the nineteenth century the ultramontanist theory had few exponents in France, Lamennais being the most convinced as well as the most prominent of them. (On Joseph de Maistre's views see below, pp. 26–9). The teaching of the seminaries was consistently Gallican and adhered closely to the principles of Bossuet. The prevalence of the Gallican doctrine after the Restoration is not difficult to explain in view of the then widespread determination to return to the conditions of the *ancien régime*. Opposition to any limitation of the rights of the crown even in the ecclesiastical sphere was too strong, despite the new wave of Catholic fervour, and to most men altar and throne were of mutual support. (On Gallicanism generally see W. J. Sparrow Simpson, *A Study of Bossuet*, 1937, esp. cc. 7 and 8.)

2

A PROPHET OF THE PAST:
JOSEPH DE MAISTRE

The Meaning of Sovereignty

When Chateaubriand heralded the dawn of a new age with a magnificently rhetorical apology for the Catholicism which its predecessor had despised and rejected he expressly declared that his aim was not to attempt to reconcile to religion the 'sophists' who had attacked it but rather the public opinion which they had so consistently duped. Hence the success of *Le Génie du Christianisme* must be attributed in no small measure to its opportune encouragement to a change in the public mood. Others, however, there were who preferred to meet the sophists on their own ground and to fight them with their own weapons. This enterprise might be slower in producing results, but what it achieved could be expected to be intellectually more solid. Its beginning had indeed been marked as far back as 1796 with a work from the pen of a Savoyard nobleman, Comte Joseph de Maistre, the title of which we have already noted: *Considérations sur la France*.[1] The same author's later writings were all, moreover, directed to the same end, namely to mount a full-scale counter-attack upon the various philosophical influences which he regarded as noxious, whether the empiricism of Bacon and Locke, the rationalism of the Encyclopædists or the social doctrines of Rousseau, all of whom he denounced with a Voltairean zest. On the positive side he believed, seemingly with utter conviction, that traditional religion is the only sure foundation of society and political order. And traditional religion, he also went on to argue, had its bedrock in the Roman papacy. Of nineteenth-century ultramontanism he was in fact one of the founders.[2]

Born at Chambéry in 1753, the son of F.-X. de Maistre, president of the Savoy senate, Joseph-Marie was educated at the Collège Royal of his native town and afterwards at the university of Turin, where he graduated in law. He himself entered the Savoy public service at the age of twenty-one, but in his spare time he continued his studies, eagerly imbibing many of the current ideas, especially Rousseau's. He also became a freemason and an admirer of the theosophism of the *lyonnais* thinker Louis-Claude de Saint-

---

[1] The immediate occasion of the book was the appearance of a brochure by Benjamin Constant, *De la force du gouvernement actuel et de la nécessité de s'y rallier*. See the preface to the critical edition of *Considérations sur la France* by R. Johannet and F. Vermale (1937).

[2] See Appendix II, p. 290, below.

Martin.[3] On the strength of at least one of his speeches in the senate he even acquired a reputation for revolutionary opinions. But when the Revolution reached Savoy he denounced it and urged his fellow-countrymen to resist. In January 1793 he fled with his wife and children to Lausanne, where he published his *Considérations sur la France*; in the event anonymously, although it was not long before the secret of its authorship became common knowledge. Taking offence at the views expressed, the French government demanded his expulsion from Switzerland and in the following year he left for Turin to put himself at the disposal of the king of Sardinia, Charles Emmanuel IV. Meantime his property in Savoy had been confiscated, and the king having no use for his services he soon found himself in a state of penury. Lord Morley perhaps was right in noting that 'the student of de Maistre's philosophy may see in what crushing personal anguish some of its most sinister growths had their roots';[4] but Maistre himself was a man of courage not given to either self-pity or recrimination.

His fortunes changed only a little for the better when Charles Emmanuel's brother and successor, Victor Emmanuel I, sent him in 1802 as minister plenipotentiary to St Petersburg, a post he was to hold for the next fifteen years. For an ambassador his life in the Russian capital was modest in the extreme. He had to keep up appearances on an exiguous allowance and even his wardrobe contained no more than essentials. But the worst of his privations was separation from his family, to whom he was deeply attached. All the same he carried out his duties assiduously, made his mark on Russian society and withal managed to spend hours daily at his writing-table. Unfortunately his last days in Russia were somewhat clouded by the disfavour of the Tsar Alexander who objected to his religious opinions and accused him of proselytizing in behalf of Rome. But to Maistre religion was always of prime importance and it was only natural that he should correspond with friends and acquaintances on religious matters and that he even should have allowed his correspondence to be circulated privately.[5] In regard to the future charge of 'intrigue' with the Jesuits the Sardinian envoy made no secret of the high esteem in which he held the Society, although he seems never to have acted indiscreetly. The occasion however of the conversion to Catholicism of a young member of the Gallitzin family

---

[3] For Maistre's attitude to Saint-Martin see *Œuvres complètes*, ix, pp. 8f. and E. Dermenghem, *Joseph de Maistre mystique* (new ed. 1946), pp. 45f. Maistre met Saint-Martin at Chambéry in 1797 (*Œuvres complètes*, xiii, pp. 331f.). On the *lyonnais* school generally see J. Buche, *L'École mystique de Lyon, 1776—1817* (1936).

[4] 'Joseph de Maistre' in *Critical Miscellanies*, ii (ed. 1892), p. 272.

[5] See, e.g. his 'Lettre à une dame protestante sur la maxime qu'un honnête homme ne change jamais de religion' (9 December 1809) and 'Lettre à une dame russe sur la nature et les effets du schisme' (8 February 1810) (*Œuvres complètes*, viii, pp. 126—57). On Maistre as religious thinker see G. Goyau, *La pensée religieuse de Joseph de Maistre, d'après des documents inédits* (1921) and R. A. Lebrun, *Throne and Altar. The Political and Religious Thought of Joseph de Maistre* (Ottawa, 1965). And on Maistre generally see Jack Lively, *The Works of Joseph de Maistre*, 1965.

led to the banishment of the Jesuits from St Petersburg in December 1815 and some months later from all Russia.[6] Maistre returned to Piedmont in 1817, where the only reward for his constancy was a nominal government appointment. He died at Turin in February 1821, his final publications securing him the recompense of at any rate a posthumous European fame.

The works published during his lifetime include, besides the book on France, an *Essai sur le principe générateur des constitutions politiques* (1808) and *Du Pape* (1819), his best-known. *Les Soirées de Saint-Pétersbourg* and *De l'Église gallicane* came out in the year of his death, and his study of the philosophy of Bacon in 1826.[7]

For Joseph de Maistre the political upheaval of the French Revolution raised questions not only about the nature of civil government but as to the process and meaning of history itself. Indeed his interpretation of the Revolution is the induction to his philosophy as a whole; but that philosophy itself rests on a religious creed, not on the empirical data of history or politics, though its interest lies in the way empirical and pragmatic elements are combined with the theological to give it a distinctively Burkian character. For Maistre admired Burke and echoed him frequently.[8]

What, he begins by asking, was the real cause of the Revolution? There is, he is aware, a ready explanation at surface level, but to explain it simply in terms of human motivations and decisions is not enough, for the men who would appear to have shaped it were in reality much less controlling agents than instruments of a power far larger than themselves. In fact as soon as they aspired to dominate it they fell ignominiously. Likewise those who set up the republic did so without truly willing it and without comprehending what it was they were creating. They were simply led by events; no plan had achieved its intended end. Men are astonished at the outcome of their deeds only because great historical happenings have an impetus of their own; and in the case of the Revolution it can be said that no human event has ever revealed the divine purpose more clearly.[9] France, as the leading European power, had a mission to fulfil, but she proved un-

[6] See G. Goyau in *Revue des Deux Mondes*, 15 April 1971, pp. 612–16.
[7] *Examen de la philosophie de Bacon.* The *Œuvres complètes* in fourteen volumes (including six volumes of correspondence) were published 1884–7 (ed. Vitte), but a further collection of letters came out in 1908 and *Les Carnets du Comte Joseph de Maistre* (ed. X. de Maistre in 1923).
[8] As he wrote to a friend (Costa de Beauregard) in January 1791: 'Avez-vous lu ... l'admirable Burke? ... Pour moi, j'en ai été ravi, et je ne saurais vous exprimer combien il a renforcé mes idées antidémocrates et anti-gallicanes' (*Œuvres complètes*, ix, p. 11). It is odd, though, that an Irish Protestant should have afforded any encouragement of his ultramontanism. See Robert Triomphe, *Joseph de Maistre: étude sur la vie et sur la doctrine d'un matérialiste mystique* (Geneva, 1968), pp. 138–40.
[9] 'Ce qu'il y a de plus admirable dans l'ordre universel des choses, c'est l'action des êtres libres sous la main divine. Librement esclaves, ils opèrent tout à la fois volontairement et nécessairement: ils font ce qu'ils veulent, mais sans pouvoir déranger les plans généraux' (*Considérations sur la France*, c. i. *O.c.*, i.).

faithful to it. Thus having used her influence to pervert her vocation and to demoralize Europe it is not surprising that 'terrible means' had to be employed to put her on her true course again. The specific political, social and economic conditions that led to the cataclysm Maistre ignores; he is not concerned to analyse secondary causes but only to relate events to what he sees, mystically, as their ultimate ground. The reason why France herself had so suffered was that, having sinned (especially in renouncing Christianity), she had met with inevitable retribution.

All who have worked to separate the people from their religious beliefs; all who have opposed metaphysical sophistries to the laws of property; all who have said, 'Attack anything, so long as we gain by it'; all who have meddled with the fundamental laws of the state; all who have recommended, approved, favoured the violent methods used against the king: even our restricted vision can perceive that all these have willed the Revolution, and all who have willed it have most appropriately been its victims.[10]

Hence France's punishment, self-inflicted, has been providentially ordained; and if the innocent suffer with the guilty, then such (as Saint-Martin teaches) is the law of history: a grim philosophy, but one to be accepted uncomplainingly, the true facts of human existence being very different from what the facile optimists of modern times would have men believe.[11]

Nevertheless the world's evil will be turned by Providence to good account; a truth of which the Revolution provides the latest and a signal instance.[12]

In Maistre's view of history is prophetic his conception of the political order itself is scarcely less so. Here too destiny controls.

Man can modify everything in the sphere of his activity, but he creates nothing: such is the law binding him in the physical as in the moral world. Doubtless a man can plant a seed, raise a tree, perfect it by grafting, and prune it in a hundred ways, but never has he imagined he can make a tree. How far has he thought that he has the power to make a constitution?[13]

On the contrary all free constitutions known to the world have come about by one of two ways. 'Sometimes they have imperceptibly germinated, as it were, by the combination of a host of circumstances that we call fortuitous, and sometimes they have a single author who appears like a freak of nature and enforces obedience.' The implications, Maistre thinks, are obvious. No government is the product of deliberation: a written constitution is viable

---

[10] *Considérations sur la France*, c. ii.   [11] *ibid.*, c. iii.

[12] 'Si la Providence efface, sans doute c'est pour écrire.' *Considérations sur la France* had an instant success among the *émigrés*, who, in the words of Maistre's most recent biographer, 'y reconnurent avec joie, dans le miroir éclatant du style, leurs thèmes favoris'. See Triomphe, *op. cit.*, p. 170.

[13] *Considérations*, c. vi. 'Qu'est-ce qu'une constitution— n'est-ce pas la solution du problème suivant? Étant données la population, les mœurs, la religion, la situation géographique, les relations politiques, les richesses, les bonnes et les mauvaises qualités d'une certaine nation, trouver les lois qui lui conviennent' (*ibid.*).

only on condition of being the simple expression of an unwritten one already existing among the people for whom it is promulgated, as would be the case in England. In the forming of constitutions it is circumstances which are the determining factor, and men themselves are but part of those circumstances. Usually it is in pursuing one goal that they attain another.

The rights of the people may originate in a concession from the sovereign, in which event they can be established historically; but the fundamental rights, those of the sovereign himself and of the aristocracy, have neither date nor author. Hence no nation can confer liberty on itself if it does not possess it already. 'Its laws are made when it begins to reflect on itself. Human influence does not extend beyond the development of rights already in existence but disregarded or else disputed.' If there is to be innovation at all it can only be rare and must always be cautious and moderate. Nations themselves really are natural growths; they are not the creation of legislative assemblies: 'All the *Bedlams* in the world could not produce anything more absurd or extravagant than such an enterprise.' For it has to be remembered that legislators are not intellectuals and scholars but men acting basically from instinct and impulse. Between the theory of politics and its practice in government there is as much difference as between poetics and poetry.

Maistre is to be listed, along with Fichte and Mazzini, among the exponents of modern nationalism.[14] The specific forms of government are, he contends, determined by the differing characters of nations. The latter moreover, like individuals, are born and die. In a quite literal sense they have fathers, as they also have teachers more famous, in many instances, than the fathers themselves, since the supreme merit of such teachers is to have penetrated the character of the infant nation and created for it the circumstances in which it could develop all its capacities. 'Nations have a general *soul* and a true moral unity which makes them what they are', so that to speak of the 'spirit' of a people is no mere metaphor.[15] Every nation has its own traditions, disposition and mission, of which its religion is the appropriate expression and support.

Religion and political dogmas, mingled and merged with each other, should together form a *general* or *national mind* sufficiently strong to repress the aberrations of the individual reason, which of its nature is the mortal enemy of any association whatever, inasmuch as it gives birth only to conflicting opinions.[16]

Indeed Maistre goes even further than this. Government itself, he claims, 'is a true religion; it has its dogmas, its mysteries, its priests; to submit it to individual discussion is to destroy it; it has life only through the national mind, — that is to say, political faith, which is a *creed*'. Man's primary need is

[14] cf. H. J. Laski, *Studies in the Problem of Sovereignty* (1917), p. 212.
[15] *Étude sur la Souveraineté*, I, c. iv.
[16] *ibid.*, c. x.

the curbing of his nascent reason under the 'double yoke' of religion and the civil authority, thus transforming an individual existence into a communal one. Patriotism is the abnegation of self in acceptance of a political faith; its constituent forms are 'submission and belief'. Political faith, the national soul, a people's inherited traditions, are, like the heart and conscience of the individual, the work of God.

Exaggeration is an essential part of Maistre's style, but the inflation of his argument should not conceal the elements of truth which it contains and which the political doctrinaire or social engineer tends to overlook or deny. Not only is it an eloquent assertion of the conservative and historical spirit against the rationalist and innovating; change, he reminds us, must be gradual not precipitate if it is to be constructive; real amelioration of society will come by reform, not revolution. Radicalism, in destroying continuity, destroys the means by which society maintains its self-identity. Here again Maistre follows Burke, who also found the organic unity of a people to consist not in its conscious decisions but in the consolidating work of an 'habitual social discipline'.[17] To the question what is the best form of government Maistre's reply is simply that it is 'that which, in the territory occupied by a nation, is capable of producing the greatest possible sum of happiness and strength, for the greatest possible number of men, during the longest possible time'.[18]

But as the origin and growth of constitutions is spontaneous and natural so is that which lies behind them, namely *sovereignty* itself. For sovereignty is of divine foundation: it is because God wills society that he wills the authority and the laws without which there would be no society. Hence although the means for the exercise of sovereignty are human and fallible, sovereign power as such is absolute: ultimately the sovereign cannot be judged. The real problem is not in preventing him from willing without restriction but in preventing him from willing unjustly.

The most ancient and universal form of government, as history shows, is monarchy. So natural in fact does it appear that it may well be identified with sovereignty *per se*. God, Maistre tells us, prepares a 'royal race' which he brings to maturity 'in the midst of a cloud that hides their origin'.

They appear thereafter crowned with glory and honour. The greatest sign of their legitimacy is that they come forward as of themselves, on the one hand without violence, and on the other without any marked deliberation: there is about them a kind of splendid tranquillity which is not easy to express. *Legitimate usurpation* would seem to me the appropriate term, were it not too bold, to characterize this kind of origin, which time hastens to consecrate.[19]

In any case all governments, strictly speaking, are monarchical, differing

---

[17] Edmund Burke, 'Appeal from the New to the Old Whigs', in *Works* (ed. 1859), i. pp. 524f.

[18] *Étude sur la Souveraineté*, ii, c. vi.

[19] *Essai sur le Principe générateur des constitutions politiques*, Préface.

only in whether the monarchy is for life or for a term of years, whether hereditary or elective, or whether individual or corporate.[20] 'Avoiding all exaggeration, it is certain that the government of a single man is that wherein the
vices of the sovereign have the least effect upon the governed.' And Maistre
adds that of all monarchies 'the hardest, most despotic and most intolerable
is King People'. History, he claims, witnesses to the great truth that the
liberty of the minority is founded only on the slavery of the masses and that
republics have never been anything but multimember sovereigns whose
despotism, always harder and more capricious than that of kings, increases
in intensity with the numbers of their subjects. But if the strength of political
institutions depends on their coming ultimately not from man but from God,
the principle is even more manifest in respect of ecclesiastical institutions.
It is therefore to Maistre's theory of the church and in particular of the
papacy that we must next turn.

The Role of the Pope

This he sets out partly in his book on the Gallican church but mainly in *Du
Pape*.[21] The Roman pontiff, 'whose sublime prerogatives form part of revelation', is to be seen as a key-figure in the whole social order of Christendom.
Moreover, regarding the papacy there is also the question of infallibility,
which signifies in the spiritual order what the absoluteness of sovereignty
means in the temporal. 'Both give voice to that high power which rules
over all other powers, from which they derive, which governs and is not
governed, which judges and is not judged.'[22] Yet to hold that the church is
infallible is not to demand for it some unique privilege but merely to ask that
it should enjoy the right common to all sovereignties, each of which is bound
to act *as if* infallible. 'For every government is absolute, and the moment it can
be resisted under the pretext of error or injustice it no longer exists.' The question is simply that of deciding where sovereignty in the ecclesiastical sphere
resides, since once it is recognized it is no longer possible to appeal from its
decisions. Now nothing, Maistre believes, is more evident, to reason as to

---

[20] *ibid.*, c. vi.

[21] Maistre certainly regarded *Du Pape* as one of the most important of his works, and he
was naturally anxious that it should be well received in Rome. On this score however he did
not harbour too many illusions. (The nuncio at St Petersburg had already characterized him
as a man 'full of learning, but full also of vanity and false ideas'.) As he wrote to
Lamennais: 'Je suis étonné que Rome ait eu tant de peine à comprendre vos magnifiques
idées sur le pouvoir pontifical. J'ai vu en France des gens du monde, très étrangers assuré-
ment à la théologie, les saisir parfaitement après une première lecture. . . . S'il m'était permis
de juger des Romains par les livres qui nous viennent de leur pays, j'aurais quelque pen-
chant à croire qu'ils sont un peu en arrière de la société. On dirait, à les lire, que rien n'a
changé dans le monde depuis un demi-siècle. Ils défendent la religion comme ils l'auraient
défendre il y a quarante ans' (*Oeuvres complètes*, xiv, p. 370).

[22] *Du Pape*, Bk I, c. i.

faith, than the essentially monarchical character of the universal church. The very idea of universality presupposes it. But although the structure of the church is necessarily that of a monarchy 'it is sufficiently tempered by aristocracy [i.e. the episcopate] to be the best and most perfect of governments'. Thus infallibility, in Maistre's view, is inherent in the pope's supremacy as a property or attribute of his spiritual sovereignty. It has no need, that is, of any expressly theological sanction. 'By claiming unity to be necessary, logically if not in practice, error could not be opposed to the Supreme Pontiff, even as it cannot be opposed to temporal sovereigns who have never laid claim to infallibility.' Hence the pope must be infallible simply as the highest court of appeal. 'Whoever had the right to tell the pope he is mistaken could, for the same reason, have the right to disobey him, which would destroy infallibility and supremacy alike.' If the body politic is not to crumble there can be no appeal from a permanent and necessary government to some intermittent power. And of the pope's title to supremacy, Maistre concludes, there can be no serious question on grounds of the papacy's actual history: in the course of ages and by a natural process power was transmitted from the Roman empire to the Roman church.[23]

[23] Maistre is well aware of course that the papacy as it exists in modern times presents a very different appearance from what it did in antiquity. But in this it no more than conforms to the universal law of development, of which Christianity itself provides a signal instance. Christ wrote nothing; his apostles drew up no code of doctrine; their own method of preaching and teaching was determined by the needs of the moment. 'Si le dogme se présente sous la plume de l'écrivain sacré, il l'énonce simplement comme une chose anciennement connue. Les symboles qui parurent depuis, sont des professions de foi pour se reconnaître ou pour contredire les erreurs du moment' (*Essai sur le principe générateur des constitutions politiques*, c. xv). The fact that the papacy has grown up in this manner betokens its divine nature, 'car tout ce qui existe légitimement et pour les siècles, existe d'abord en germe et se développe successivement' (*Du Pape*, Bk i, c. iv). Nevertheless the development is not a logical deduction, nor is it necessarily even conscious. 'Jamais aucune institution importante n'a résulté d'une loi et plus elle est grande, moins elle écrit. Elle se forme d'elle-même par la conspiration de mille agents, qui presque toujours ignorent ce qu'ils font; en sorte que souvent ils ont l'air de ne pas s'apercevoir du droit qu'ils établissent eux-mêmes. L'institution végète ainsi insensiblement à travers les siècles; *crescit velut arbor aevo*: c'est la devise éternelle de toute grande création politique ou religieuse. Saint Pierre avait-il une connaissance distincte de l'étendue de sa prérogative et des questions qu'elle ferait naître dans l'avenir? Je l'ignore' (*ibid.*, Bk i, c. xiv).

At the same time the faith does not admit of innovations: 'Il n'y a rien de nouveau dans l'Église et jamais elle ne croira que ce qu'elle a toujours cru' (c. i). New dogmatic formularies arise because of fresh errors. To the Gallican objection that the doctrine of papal infallibility is of comparatively recent origin he replies: 'On ne comprend pas comment des hommes, d'ailleurs si distingués (he has Bossuet in mind), ont pu confondre deux idées aussi différentes que celle de *croire* et de *soutenir* un dogme. l'Église catholique n'est point argumentatrice de sa nature; elle croît sans disputer; car la foi est une *croyance par amour*, et l'amour n'argumente point. Le catholique sait qu'il ne peut se tromper, il n'y aurait plus de vérité révélée, ni d'assurance pour l'homme sur la terre, puisque toute société divinement instituée suppose l'infaillibilité.'

Maistre goes on to argue that the Catholic Church has no need of self-examination or self-explanation, in which respect she differs wholly from the sects. 'C'est le doute qui enfante les livres: pourquoi écrirait-elle donc, elle qui ne doute jamais?' When however a dogma of the faith is impugned, the church must make her mind explicit — reconsidering the basis of her

Although therefore the Donation of Constantine is a fable there is a sense in which it possesses genuine historicity, in that it was by a just Providence that the papacy came to exercise temporal sovereignty. But if this is so the supreme pontiff cannot remain indifferent to the authority exercised by other temporal sovereigns. In fact Maistre claims that the pope's authority transcends all temporal sovereignties and that he has power to release peoples from their duty of obedience to temporal rulers, an opinion not only in flat contradiction of Gallican principles but one which reasserts mediaeval pretensions at their highest. Such power must be judged as of right in view of the historical conditions under which the papacy developed. Nations then 'had *within themselves* only worthless or despised laws and *corrupt customs*. This indispensable *check* had therefore to be sought from *without*. It was found and could only be found, in papal authority. What happened, therefore, was only what ought to have happened'.[24] The authority of the popes was the *potestas* chosen and constituted under the mediaeval system to balance the temporal and make it bearable for men. Christendom had nothing to fear or complain of in this. There were times when the popes struggled with sovereigns, but never against sovereignty. 'The very act by which they released subjects from the oath of fidelity declared sovereignty inviolable.' Thus the social order suffers no disturbance; rather is sovereignty enhanced and fulfilled by the intervention of this unique representative of God, although such intervention has come about only in response to some great abuse or crime. As actually exercised papal authority is purely spiritual; and in any case there is nothing whatever shocking in the hypothesis of all the Christian sovereignties united by a religious fraternity in a kind of universal republic under a supreme spiritual sovereign – a truth which civil rulers would be wise to recognize, since history proves that the survival of the papacy has been in their own best interest.

For Maistre the vitality of Christendom itself depends on the pope.[25] Outside the papal obedience it is in a state of greater or less impotence through schism – and Maistre is thinking in particular of the Russian Orthodox Church, which he regards as no more effective than the Protestant communions of Luther and Calvin ('Every religion which bears the name of a man or of a people is necessarily false'[26]). He argues too that the real motives underlying schism are not always explained by the sort of reasons openly given. The breach caused by the Eastern church – the 'Photian', as he rather contemptuously calls it – was essentially an insurrection against the sov-

belief, questioning antiquity, and above all devising some formula (of which the faith itself has no need) wherewith to preclude all innovation or deviation. Fine words indeed, but is not Maistre's certitude not just a little too complete? The sceptic often compensates for his doubt of truth by an obsession with order.

[24] *ibid.*, Bk II, c. ix.
[25] The church and papacy are really, he considers, one. cf. *ibid.*, Bk III, c. ii.
[26] *ibid.*, Bk IV, c. iv.

ereignty represented by the papacy and has separated that church from the one to which alone 'belong the promises'. As for the Protestant bodies which have united with the Eastern churches only in a common detestation of the pope, they are now in visible dissolution, for the knowledge which comes with time will always expose error. Maistre brings his book to a close with an appeal for unity addressed to Protestants, and in particular, we may note, to Anglicans as those destined 'to set in motion the great religious movement that is in preparation'.[27] However, the French also must decide to abandon their Gallicanism, which not only is itself a species of Protestantism but in fact paved the way for the hated *philosophes* of the preceding century and thus, through them, for the Revolution. Finally let all the enemies of the Holy See who, in beholding the sovereign pontiff 'driven out, exiled, deprived of his States by a dominant and almost supernatural power *whilst the earth kept silence*', have so confidently announced its fall, now contemplate its resurrection, in which the operation of divine Providence may once again be seen.

The Nature of Man and the Problem of Evil

In Maistre's eyes human existence as exhibited in social relations contains an irresolvable paradox. On the one hand man is a naturally social animal, created so by God. The notion accordingly of a primal state of individual solitariness and isolation out of which man himself established society from conscious motives of convenience is a pure fiction. The unit, the embryo, of society is the family, granted; but if we would understand what man really is we must consider him in his historical record, which continuously reveals the existence of a multiplicity of different societies each with its own sovereign authority. In other words, there has never been a *pre*-social state of mankind, because before men existed in societies they were not properly human. In any case it is absurd in principle to look for the determining characteristics of a being only in its embryo. Rousseau's idea of a 'state of nature' in which a people formally deliberates on the advantages and disadvantages of the social state and decides to change from the one to the other is sheer nonsense.[28] Unhappily the word 'nature', so much in vogue among theorists,

[27] cf. his remarks on the Church of England in *Considérations sur la France* c. ii: 'Si jamais les chrétiens se rapprochent, comme tout les y invite, il semble que la *motion* doit partir de l'église d'Angleterre. Le presbytérianisme fut une œuvre française, et par conséquent une œuvre exagérée ... Mais l'église anglicane, qui nous touche d'une main, touche de l'autre ceux que nous ne pouvons toucher; et quoique, sous un certain point de vue, elle soit en butte aux coups des deux partis, et qu'elle présente le spectacle un peu ridicule d'un révolté qui prêche l'obéissance, cependant elle est très-précieuse sous d'autres aspects, et peut être considérée comme un de ces intermèdes chimiques, capables de rapprocher des éléments inassociables de leur nature.' But the spirit which Maistre shows here is more Gallican than ultramontane. Elsewhere he gibes at Anglicanism for assuming 'that God became incarnate for Englishmen'.

[28] For Maistre Rousseau's was one of the most noxious minds in a century that abounded with them. Yet the resemblances between the two thinkers are often striking. In their theory of

is persistently misused. The nature of any being, says Maistre, is only the sum of the qualities attributed to it by the Creator, and the nature of man is to be a 'cognitive, religious and social animal', so that what he is is determined by all that he does *as* a rational entity. As Burke profoundly remarks, 'Art is man's nature'.

On the other hand it is no less true that men 'naturally' have an insatiable craving for power and possession. Infinite in their desires and always discontented with what they have, they love only what they have not.[29] All are born despots and there is none who does not abuse power if he can get it. Thankfully the Author of nature has himself set bounds to this abuse: he has willed that it destroy itself once it goes beyond its natural limits. Thus in any general assessment of human nature both sides of it must be kept in view. They are contradictory, of course, but they co-exist, and therein lies the paradox. The mind of man is not at one with itself; it is as though he has two souls.[30] Certainly he is both moral and corrupt, just in his understanding but perverse in his will. He has therefore to be *governed*, if the social and anti-social elements within him are not to render society at once necessary and impossible.[31] The continued existence and welfare of the social order depend upon the submission of man's pride — the ultimate source of moral evil — to the laws of God, of which the good in human nature is a reflexion.

But how is moral evil to be explained? The Christian religion supplies the answer in its doctrine of the fall and original sin. As a dogma this is a mystery, but it also has a 'natural' aspect that is understandable even by our limited intelligence.[32] Leave aside, says Maistre, the theological question of *imputation* and consider only the commonly accepted principle 'that every being with the power of propagating itself can produce only a being similar to itself' — a rule without exception and holding good of the moral realm no-less than of the physical. If a being is corrupted its descendents will no longer

sovereignty they were wholly at odds, but they come much closer to one another in their practical conclusions. Maistre would undoubtedly have agreed with Rousseau on the impossibility that a representative assembly can sufficiently embody and articulate the general will, with the result that popular sovereignty cannot be realized in large states. Both men were also convinced that what truly matters — more so than the actual source of sovereignty — is the unity and intensity of the life which the community achieves. They alike believed that this quality is attained by some divine inner illumination or instinct. Both again were aware of the division in human nature between the actual and the ideal: a division, however, which can and must be overcome if man is to realize his social destiny — to reach a point, as it were, 'outside' history. Moreover, for Maistre as for Rousseau this ideal state of man was exemplified in some original or primitive condition: in Rousseau's mind it was the state of 'nature' enjoyed by the 'noble savage', in Maistre's a supposed antediluvian 'Golden Age'; and both employed the notion — it was indeed its real purpose — as a basis for a critique of existing society. The fact is that the two philosophers shared the same fundamental aim, namely to harmonize man's nature by resolving the conflict between his uncontrolled passion, pride and self-will and his natural aptitude for society. This they thought was to be accomplished by the subordination of the individual to the state under which alone would his true good be reached.

[29] *Étude sur la Souveraineté*, II, c. ii.　　[30] *Éclaircissement sur les sacrifices* (1821), c. i.
[31] *Du Pape*, II, c. ix.　　[32] *Les Soirées de Saint-Pétersbourg*, 2me entretien.

resemble it in its original state but will reproduce the condition to which it has since been reduced. A mere physical sickness is not indeed transmissible, 'but that which vitiates the humours becomes an *original malady* capable of tainting the whole race'. And the same applies, Maistre thinks, to moral maladies. 'Some belong to the ordinary state of human imperfection, but there are certain transgressions or certain consequences of transgression which can degrade man absolutely.' At root the phenomenon of moral malady can be presented as follows: The essence of all intelligence is to know and to love. The truly intelligent being knows by nature everything he should know, as likewise no intelligent being can by nature love the bad: were it not so God would have created man evil, an impossible supposition. That man is subject to ignorance and evil can, then, only result from some accidental degradation consequent upon a crime. But that he *is* subject to evil is a fact beyond dispute: by what is good in him he is almost angelic, but by the evil he can descend to the brute. 'An incredible combination of two different and incomparable powers, a monstrous centaur, he feels that he is the outcome of some unknown crime, some detestable mixture that has corrupted him even in his deepest nature.'

Only when man's disposition is rightly understood can his history be properly interpreted. If he is a sinner it is because he possesses free will; he is under no mechanical necessity of acting in one way or another, nor is he constrained by any declared ordinance of God. A coerced will is a contradiction in terms, for the will can be moved and led only by sympathy, which cannot detract from liberty. The burden that weighs upon our unfortunate human nature is its dual capability, its capacity for moral alternatives; and the reason for this is partly because we have been created in the divine image, partly because we have been invested with a power of conscious decision denied to an animal. Fundamentally however it is because the moral order and indeed the whole meaning of moral action depend on a real volition. An enforced action cannot be a moral one, and God in permitting such freedom conferred on mankind a status superior to the rest of creation. For when man is in harmony with his Maker he is sublime and his own action becomes creative. But as his dignity lies in his liberty to choose the good so equally does the choice of evil defile him. For the truth is that the human will can contradict the Creator's.

A created will cancels out, not perhaps the *exertion*, but the result of divine action... God desires things that do not in fact come to pass because man himself does not desire them.[33]

When man separates himself from God and acts on his own he does not thereby cease to be powerful, since power is the privilege of his nature; but his acts are negative and lead only to destruction.[34] Thus for better or worse

[33] *ibid.*, 5me entretien.   [34] *Essai sur le Principe générateur des constitutions politiques*, xlv.

he is a free agent. But Maistre is no deist, and secondary causation does not mean for him that the physical order is not ultimately under divine control, nor does human decision in the political sphere mean that God himself cannot or does not intervene. Without accepting the possibility of direct divine intervention neither the creation nor the continuance of governments is explicable. Providence operates through a multiplicity of wills working to the same end, so revealing the fact that they are simply instruments; but supremely does it operate 'in the wonderful mechanism that makes use of all the circumstances we call accidental, indeed of our follies and our crimes, to maintain and even, at times, to establish order'.[35] Here again is paradox, — something like Hegel's *List der Vernunft*. God is the universal moving force, yet each and every entity is moved according to its particular nature, for 'man having been created free he is freely led'. History is the complex outcome of this interaction, this web and woof, of divine and human willing; though how precisely God controls, how exactly his providential purpose is realized, is a mystery we cannot fathom.

So explicitly theological a view of the historical process causes Maistre no embarrassment: it is not more question-begging, he thinks, than the 'philosophical' notion of an intrinsic harmony of human wills issuing in an automatic progress.

Undoubtedly man is free; he can make mistakes, but not enough of them to derange general plans. We are all bound to the throne of God by a flexible chain which reconciles the self-propulsion of free agents with divine supremacy.

Especially is this true of human society. 'How can we deny that the body politic has also its law, its soul, its form-giving force, and believe that everything is dependent on the whim of human ignorance?' There is a 'directing spirit' in each state which animates it as the soul animates the body.[36] Thus back we come again to contemporary events.

There are no means of preventing a revolution, and no success can attend those who wish to impede it. But never is purpose more apparent, never is it more palpable, than when divine replaces human action and works alone. That is what we see at this moment.

Untalented and ignorant leaders have ably driven what they call 'the revolutionary chariot'; yet at the same time they were subject to a power more far-sighted than themselves. Even so, the Revolution was not a wholly inevitable occurrence: it could have been avoided if men within the limits of their freedom had heeded the voice of God. For God 'speaks' in history in the sense that historical events provide the media through which he makes known his will for men; and if men ignore it the consequences, though in the resulting circumstances unavoidable, are implicitly of their own choosing.

[35] *Les Soirées de Saint-Pétersbourg*, 3 me entretien.   [36] *ibid.*

The idea of historical retribution is of course a biblical one, yet rather surprisingly Maistre has very little to say about the Bible as a source of revelation. Still more surprisingly, perhaps, he does not discuss in detail how the authority of either the church or the papacy is exercised over the secular world. That authority, he believed, most certainly existed and *Du Pape*, as we have seen, was written expressly to assert it. Yet the ecclesiastical *magisterium* as such is not what Maistre wishes to stress. His deeper concern is with the role of *tradition*, to which he would add the promptings of an uncorrupted conscience and the insights of men of outstanding genius. By tradition he understands society's fundamental beliefs as inherited from the past; no very original view, on the face of it, since at that time, in England and in Germany as well as in France, the defence of received ideas and institutions against the innovating doctrines of ideological theorists was gaining an army of recruits. Usually, however, the plea was the pragmatic one that survival was self-justifying and what was well-tried ought in prudence to be retained. Maistre was attempting more than this: tradition for him was not simply useful but a matter of principle, as itself a divine revelation, and he cites in this connexion the maxim *quod semper, quod ubique, quod ab omnibus creditum est* as the test of truth. For in spite of the degradation into which man has fallen he has not lost all memory of his original endowment of divine knowledge. Man 'may well have covered over and (so to speak) encrusted the truth with the errors he has heaped upon it, but these errors are local and universal truth will show itself'.[37] There are profound intuitions which the human race has maintained over long centuries. For example, no nation in the past doubted that there is expiatory virtue in the shedding of blood, an idea, so Maistre holds, which neither reason nor folly could have invented and still less got accepted. 'It is rooted in the furthest depths of human nature, and on this point the whole of history does not disclose a single dissenting voice.'[38] The same is true of the basic idea of sovereignty, which is as ancient as society itself.[39] Certainties like these are not the creation of individuals but the common possession of humanity and as such derive from God.

Reason when left to its own resources has in fact only a very limited utility in the life of men. It is completely incapable 'not only of creating but also of conserving any religious or political association'.[40] Instead it is a cause of dispute and disunity: what man needs is beliefs, not problems.

[37] *ibid.*, 5me entretien.
[38] *Éclaircissement sur les sacrifices*, c. i.
[39] *Étude sur la Souveraineté*, i, c. iii.
[40] In the *Soirées*, however, Maistre takes a more moderate view. 'J'accorde', he says, 'à la raison tout ce que je lui dois. L'homme ne l'a reçue que pour s'en servir, et nous avons assez bien prouvé, je pense, qu'elle n'est pas embarrassée par les difficultés qu'on lui oppose contre la Providence. Toutefois, ne comptons pas exclusivement sur cette lumière trop sujette à se trouver éclipsé par ces ténèbres du cœur' (3me entretien). What Maistre totally mistrusts is

His cradle should be surrounded by dogmas; and when his reason awakes all his opinions should be given him . . . Nothing is more vital to him than *prejudices*.[41]

Prejudices, that is to say, are not ideas which are false but simply opinions which have been adopted without examination; and as such are precisely what man needs. So far from being obstacles to progress, 'they are the real ground of man's happiness and the palladium of empires'. To religion, morality and government alike they are essential, whereas the so-called philosophers have only encouraged a systematic doubt that is utterly unconstructive and inimical to life. Indeed the destructive pride of reason is the most telling evidence of man's fall. By contrast his inherited, unreasoned sense of right and truth testifies a primitive state of wisdom and happiness, a remote Golden Age of which we may know little positively but whose vestiges in the human consciousness prove it to have been one of perfection compared to modern decadence. History and myth, the poets and the philosophers, Asia and Europe speak on this, Maistre thinks, with one voice. 'Such complete agreement of reason, revelation and all human traditions constitutes an argument that cannot be contradicted.'[42]

With tradition goes also language. No tongue could have been the invention of a single man, who obviously could not have compelled obedience, nor yet by several, who would have been unable to understand each other. Hence speech must have been created by God, and from this original the different languages have evolved. Each of these has its own particular genius or inherent character which excludes all idea of arbitrary formation or studied agreement.[43] But the point Maistre especially wishes to make is that every language taken separately mirrors the 'spiritual realities' present at its birth, and the more ancient it is the more discernible these realities are.[44] The further we go back into the ages, supposedly of ignorance and barbarism, in which mankind's various tongues had their beginnings the more do we appreciate the essential logic and profundity of insight that went to the making of verbal expression. Unfortunately the creative vitality which belonged to those far-off times disappears as one approaches the ages of civilization

'reasoning', which usually serves only to cloud the truth of man's *innate* ideas. Hence his opposition to Locke. 'Comment l'homme recevra-t-il une verité nouvelle, s'il ne porte pas en lui-même une verité antérieure par laquelle il jugera l'autre? . . . Dès que vous séparez la raison de la foi, la révélation, ne pouvant plus être prouvée, ne prouve plus rien' (*Examen de la philosophie de Bacon*, II, c. i).

[41] *Étude sur la Souveraineté*, I, c. x.

[42] *Soirées de Saint-Petersbourg*, 2me entretien. Maistre's idea of an antediluvian Golden Age is incongruous with the biblical doctrine of the fall. What he stresses is man's loss of knowledge as a result of tasting the forbidden fruit, so that the root of sin is ignorance rather than pride.

[43] A very similar view is propounded by Bonald. See below, pp. 43ff. Edgar Hocédez (*Histoire de la Théologie au xixe siècle*, i, 1948, p. 105) describes Maistre as the 'precursor' of traditionalism, Bonald as its 'father' and Lamennais as its 'herald'. But A. de Margerie (*Le comte Joseph de Maistre*, 1882) refuses to class Maistre as a traditionalist at all; as likewise M. Ferraz (see p. 53n. below).

[44] *Soirées*, 2me entretien.

and science. The notion fostered by men like Condillac that language can be improved by 'philosophy' is thus wholly false. Rationalism is uncreative and in general only etiolates and deadens.

Another source of primary knowledge is in the instinctive reactions of a right-thinking man.

The upright man is very commonly informed by an inner sentiment of the falsity or truth of certain propositions before examining them, often without having made the studies necessary to be in a position to examine them with full knowledge of the case.[45]

This state of mind is attained only by 'rectitude of heart and habitual purity of intention', which are capable of hidden effects extending far beyond what is commonly imagined; even, possibly, into the field of the natural sciences. In matters of theoretical philosophy, morality and natural theology it is 'well-nigh infallible'. Further this 'secret instinct', these deep-seated intimations of truth, are not a privilege reserved for the few; all men have them so long as they do not forfeit them to the sophistries of a misconceived 'reason'.

Finally — and here Maistre the romantic stands with Fichte and Hegel — enlightenment is brought to mankind by the great individual, the genius. 'Genius', he says, 'is a grace.' The true man of genius acts 'by movement or by impulsion'. It is not, as Bacon supposed, mere method that leads to new knowledge but personal inspiration and insight. The great artist possesses them, and the great scientist. Bacon conceived of 'method' as something impersonal, yet Kepler, Galileo and Descartes were his contemporaries and Copernicus his predecessor. Science like art is the achievement of gifted individuals and is necessarily 'connected with the moral condition of man'.[46] And what is true of the scientist and the artist is still more so of a great national leader. 'It is always from a single man that each nation takes its dominant trait and its distinctive character.'[47]

Endowed with an extraordinary penetration, or more probably with an infallible instinct (for often personal genius does not realize what it is accomplishing — which is what above all distinguishes it from intelligence), he divines those hidden powers and qualities which mould a nation's character, the means of bringing them to life, putting them into action, and making the greatest possible use of them.

Such a man of destiny, Maistre tells us, is never seen writing or debating; his mode of acting springs from inspiration, and when he does take up a pen 'it is not to argue but to command'.[48]

A people's fate, then, lies in the purpose of God, who affords them the guidance they need in their traditions, in the dictates of conscience and in heroic leadership. Yet this Maistrean philosophy is by no means a bare authoritarianism, a Hobbesean worship of the mere power of government. A

[45] ibid., 1er entretien.
[46] ibid., 5me entretien.
[47] Étude sur la Souveraineté, I, c. vii.
[48] ibid.

nation is an organic growth, and political sovereignty, as still more the institutions in which this is embodied and exercised, exists only to promote
and serve that life. No doubt it can mistake its own interests and misconceive its destiny, as France had done in the Revolution. But every nation has
a soul and a vocation which it must discover and to which it must be true. The
experience may be painful, since error always brings retribution. But it is thus
that the lessons of history are learned.

Reflexions like these, however, lead on to the still deeper problems raised
by the meaning and origin of evil. For if Providence is a reality what part can
evil have in its dispensations? Is it reconcilable with the will and character
of a beneficent deity? These are among the questions to which Maistre
addresses himself in the *Soireés de Saint-Petersbourg*.[49] They have taxed the
human mind in every age, but above all at moments of great social crisis. The
Revolution had posed them in an acute form: why had such suffering been
permitted if God, as religion teaches, is good and the world is under his
control? The sort of answer supplied by the eighteenth century thinkers
does not satisfy Maistre. If men suffer it is not fortuitously but as a deserved
punishment. 'All pain is punishment, and every punishment . . . is inflicted by
love as much as by justice.' It is not God but man who is unjust. In any case
it is in general untrue that in this world crime prospers and virtue suffers. On
the contrary, good and evil are a lottery in which each of us without distinction can draw a winning or a losing ticket. Thus the question should be
changed to: 'Why in the temporal world are the just not exempt from the evil
which can affect the guilty; and why are the wicked not deprived of the
benefits which the just can enjoy?'[50] This Maistre sees as a different issue
and one that involves basic principles. If a good man meets his death in war
or through disease it is not an injustice but a misfortune, and to injustice
all men, good or bad, are subject. A general law, if it is not unjust to all, cannot
be unjust to an individual. The just law is not that which takes effect *on*
everyone but that which is made *for* everyone. The effect on a given individual is no more than an accident.

The just man suffers, therefore simply because he is human; but why, we
may ask, should mankind suffer at all? Maistre's reply rests on what he believes to be a truth beyond doubt — that God himself cannot be the author of
evil *as such*; and he quotes St Thomas Aquinas' statement that if God does
bring about evil it is the evil which punishes, not that which defiles.[51] The

---

[49] Begun in 1809, the *Soirées* take the form of a series of conversations between Maistre
himself (the Count) and two companions, a Chevalier and a Senator. But in fact the three
voices are all Maistre's own. As R. Triomphe observes: 'La critique ne s'est-elle guère
trompée en reconnaissant dans ce trio de complice les tendances divergents de Maistre lui-
même' (*Joseph de Maistre*, p. 360). G. Guyau suggests that the three personalities represent the
author at three different periods of his life. The *Soirées* was never finished, although a sketch
of the concluding portion was included in *Lettres et opuscules inédits* (ed. R. de Maistre), 1851.).

[50] *Soirées*, ler entretien.   [51] *Summa theol.*, P. I., qu. 49, art. iii.

latter springs from man's freedom, as something which he wills and chooses. Even of God as the author of retributive evil it must be said that he causes it only indirectly, in that physical evil itself would not exist if rational creatures had not made it necessary by abuse of their liberty. Thus there is a natural link between moral evil and physical. Yet why is it that often crimes go un-punished and virtues unrecompensed. In Maistre's judgment the anomaly is merely apparent and can be explained. If, for example, the terrace on which he and his companions are sitting were about to collapse ought one really to expect divine intervention to prevent it, simply because three worthy men might otherwise be injured? Were miracles of this sort to occur, supposedly to protect the innocent and expose the vicious to their deserts, should not they do so daily and from moment to moment? In that case, though, what would become of the laws of nature? The result would be the return of chaos, a thing infinitely more terrible than any occasional accident. Besides, were it true that virtue could count on reward and vice on punishment what would be-come of morality? Right conduct would then be a mere matter of self-interest. The principle to be recognized, therefore, is simply that 'the greatest amount of happiness, even temporal, belongs not to the virtuous *man* but to virtue'. Otherwise there would be neither vice nor virtue, merit nor demerit, and hence no moral order. But because rewards and punishments are not auto-matic it does not follow, says Maistre, that good things and evil are distributed among men indiscriminately. On the whole the just are rewarded and the wicked suffer. To maintain the moral order it is sufficient that much the greater share of temporal happiness be allowed to virtue and a proportionate share of unhappiness fall to vice; as also that the individual himself can never be sure of anything — which in fact is the case.

The image of God which thus emerges is certainly a formidable one. Men live under the cloud of an angry power, a power that can be appeased, it seems, only by sacrifices. Not that the idea of God is born only of fear, for men address him as Father as well as Lord and Master; but since God is righteous and man guilty expiation of sin is always required.

Primitive men, from whom the whole of humanity has received its fundamental opinions, believed themselves culpable. All social institutions have been founded on this dogma, so that men of every age have continually admitted original and uni-versal degradation and said, like us, if less explicitly, *Our mothers conceived us in sin*. Whence the institution of blood sacrifices.[52]

For if man is guilty through his flesh, his physical life, of which to the ancients blood was the very principle, then appropriately the curse fell on his blood. But this, again, means that the innocent have sometimes to pay for the guilty, even if it has come to be allowed that a less precious life may be offered and accepted in place of another. Thus innocent suffering plays its part in the divine

---

[52] *Éclaircissement sur les sacrifices*, c. i.

government of the world, as expiation for human wrongdoing. A Voltaire
may bewail the deaths of children, 'crushed and bloody on their mothers'
breasts', and demand to know what crime or sin they could have committed.
The appalling logic of the only acceptable answer has, Maistre replies, to be
grasped without flinching. 'If we allow truth to submit to "difficulties" philosophy is at an end.'[53] An unapproachable mystery it may well be, but it is foolish
to use the incomprehensible as an argument against things that we can
comprehend.

In this context Maistre turns to the particular issue of war. It is a subject,
he is only too conscious, that inevitably gives rise to the profoundest moral
questioning. The thinkers of the Enlightenment mocked it as a grotesque
absurdity, although Kant and the abbé de Saint-Pierre discussed in all
seriousness the possibility of abolishing it. Later Hegel and Victor Cousin
were actually to expatiate on its civilizing role. Maistre's view, which has
something in common with Pascal's, inclines to neither side, seeing it instead
as a special aspect of the problem of evil and hence as a fact of life the real
nature of which must be appreciated. War, in other words, is providential,
the most powerful of all the instruments of divine wrath, — divine 'in the
mysterious glory that surrounds it, and in the not less inexplicable attraction
that impels us towards it'. Though the work of the soldier is terrible it is a consequence of 'a great law of the spiritual world' and none should be astonished

that all the nations of the earth are at one in seeing in this scourge something still
more peculiarly divine than in others. You can well believe that there is a good and
deep-seated reason for the title LORD OF HOSTS being found on every page of the
Holy Scriptures. Guilty, and unhappy because we are guilty, we ourselves make necessary all physical evils, but war above all.[54]

A common but mistaken impulse is for men to blame their rulers for it,
whereas strife is in fact inherent in nature itself. 'There is not an instant of
time when some living creature is not devoured by another.' It is a law from
which mankind assuredly is not exempt; for if it is in human nature to do
wrong it is in God's to punish it: a hard conclusion, but one which the conditions of man's existence will necessitate until the divine lesson is at last
learned.

The Creed of Reaction

The doctrines of the generation immediately preceding the Revolution were
not the only target of Maistre's polemic; in addition to the *philosophes* and
deists the older English thinkers, Locke and Hume, came under his lash. The
former had proved his philosophical incompetence by his attack on the
theory of innate ideas. He had begun indeed by stating that all our ideas have

[53] *Soirées*, 4me entretien.   [54] *ibid.*, 8me entretien.

their source either in the senses or else in reflexion, understood as the knowledge which the mind acquires of its own operations. 'Then, torturing the
truth, he confesses that general ideas come neither from the senses nor from
reflexion but are actually created — or, in his absurd phrase, "invented" — by
the human mind.' Inasmuch however as Locke himself expressly excludes reflexion it follows that the humand mind 'invents' general ideas *without* reflexion, that is, without any knowledge or examination of its intrinsic processes.
Yet clearly every idea not originating either in the mind's interaction with
external objects or in its own self-consideration must of necessity derive from
the mind's own substance. Thus, Maistre triumphantly concludes, there are
bound to be ideas which are *innate*, as anterior to all experience: a conclusion vital of course to his own system of doctrine. Had Locke, he urges, shown
more insight, diligence or good faith he would have said that an idea is 'innate for every man who possesses it', since if the idea was not pre-existent
the senses would never have given birth to it. But what, he asks, was to be
expected of one who held that the voice of conscience is no proof of innate
principles *merely* because its demands differ from person to person? And
with Locke Maistre couples also Hume, 'perhaps the most dangerous and the
most culpable of those fatal writers who will not cease to damn the last
century in the eyes of posterity' and who, using 'the most talent with the
most composure to produce the most evil', could even declare, regardless of
morality and religion, that 'truth comes before everything else'.

Nevertheless it is for Bacon that Maistre reserves his deepest scorn. Besides
attacking him in the *Soirées* he devoted a whole volume to a point-by-point
examination of his thought. But his antagonism is further sharpened by the
adulation which the English philosopher received from the eighteenth-
century French pundits. The Baconian conception of a 'new instrument' of
scientific method is dismissed at once as wholly unnecessary; in fact his
namesake and predecessor of an earlier century knew more of science than
did he. 'Bacon was a barometer who announced good weather, and because
he announced it people believed that he had made it.'[55] But his chief offence
in Maistre's sight was in having so fastened attention on the physical sciences
as to divert it from other branches of knowledge. 'He rejected all metaphysics, all psychology, all natural and positive theology, and locked them
up in the Church, forbidding them to come out.' His dismissal of the question
of final causes as harmful to true science — a gross but 'infections' error — even
imperilled belief in God himself. By contrast a man like Linnaeus did not fail
to admire the wisdom of God as manifested in creation, the marks of which
he traced in even the least of nature's works; and that he did so in no way
detracted from his stature as a scientist.[56] Newton himself, venerated as he
was by the mechanistic philosophers who claimed to be his disciples, left his

[55] *Soirées*, 5me entretien.   [56] *Examen de la philosophie de Bacon*, ii, c. vi.

readers to determine whether the agent which produces gravity is physical or spiritual.

To liberal thinkers of an after-age Joseph de Maistre has appeared as a strange and even grotesque figure, hostile to virtually everything which for them constitutes the very elements of an acceptable social science. His total repudiation of the revolutionary ideal seems incomprehensible, except as the futile gesture of a man deliberately closing his eyes to the direction in which history is moving. Today, however, this summary verdict, if not quite to be reversed, may be seen to omit something of truth. Maistre was no blind obscurantist; he valued ideas and recognized their potency. But he believed that false doctrines inevitably have evil consequences, and false social and political ideals are likely in their cumulative effect to spell disaster to a whole generation. What he was tireless in denouncing was the abuse of 'reason', an abuse for which in his mind the age d'Alembert had declared to be the 'century of philosophy' was singularly blameworthy. His own teachings developed therefore into a sustained assault on rationalism in any shape or form. Against it he appealed to authority, to tradition, to the concrete facts of man's on-going experience, to human nature itself, on the grounds that the so-called Enlightenment had denied all of them in the name of abstract theory based on individual reasoning. Here of course he took too sweeping a view. The eighteenth century was not an age of rationalism pure and simple; some of its most outstanding and influential thinkers were well aware of the limitations of the reason: not only Locke and Hume and Kant, but even the arch-sceptic Voltaire had been forced to admit a confinement of the intelligence as real in its way as that of the body.

The interest of Maistre's thought lies not in its negations – the expression for the most part of misunderstanding and prejudice – but in the strength of his positive insights. Thus he rejects a merely *a priori* approach to social problems, his attitude to which is empirical and even pragmatist. If the nature of society is to be rightly understood it must be seen in historical perspective, for man in his concrete social existence is not the consistently rational being which a superficial optimism likes to imagine. Human development has always been subject to the fortuitous, the imponderable and the uncontrollable. Geography and climate, custom and psychology have been major causes of the deep differences among men in their social groupings, and in any case no logic exists which could have predicted the actual course of events themselves.

What Maistre desiderates is a *politique expérimentale*, meaning thereby a politics grounded in the experience of history, which informs us that no single type of government is unreservedly good. Indeed the question of what is the 'best' government has as many admissible answers as there are 'possible combinations in the relative and absolute positions of nations'. Political institutions can evolve successfully, that is, only under the conditions imposed by their historical situation. To speak of 'true' or 'false' in this area of human existence is to misapply terms; the only veridical criterion is what is beneficent or harmful.

From this position of conservative historicism Maistre's doctrine of authority follows naturally. Abstract social theories are the product not of governments or communities but of self-opinionated individuals, and society is far too complex a thing to be refashioned in accordance with the speculative notions of private persons, who in challenging its accepted beliefs serve only to undermine its stability. Against the threat of anarchy authority, spiritual as well as temporal, is alone effective. If this is irrationalism, so be it; Maistre is undismayed. 'The human reason', he declares, 'is manifestly incapable of guiding men; for few can reason well, and none well on every subject.'[57]

Ballanche described Maistre as a 'prophet of the past',[58] a label that has stuck to him ever since; and indeed the kind of theocracy he envisaged would have put time in reverse and carried Europe back again to the days of Innocent III. But his arguments can impress even the reader of today by their sheer audacity and Voltairean insolence. Is he not, in fact, among the harbingers of twentieth-century authoritarianism, a fascist before fascism? The charge has certainly been made,[59] and much can be adduced to support it, in his doctrines of blood-sacrifice and war, of the mystique of power, of the virtues of corporateness and the sins of individualism. His views have moreover the sharp-edged consistency of the modern political ideologue. He may appeal to history to endorse them, but his interpretations of the historical are prefabricated and he sees for the most part only what he wishes to see. Hence his conclusions, one senses, are no more than an explication of the prejudices with which he started and which he deliberately declines to submit to examination.

On the other hand it may be urged that although he devoted so much thought to political problems it was not fundamentally by these that his imagination was gripped. His deepest concern, paradoxically enough, was with the individual and the individual's relation to the state as the instrument of God. In other words, Maistre is so far a genuinely religious thinker; almost in the biblical meaning of the term is he a prophet, forthtelling to men that the power exercised over them by legitimate rulers — not necessarily monarchical — is holy, and that to disobey or even question it is impious. Man's sole good lies in the providence of God, a good which it is the mission and duty of authority to realize. But if this is the true gist of what Maistre was saying a sceptical and egalitarian age will find it barely intelligible. Even his preoccupation with Catholicism seems to have its roots less in theology than

[57] *Soirées*, 2me entretien.
[58] L'homme des doctrines anciennes, le prophète du passé' (*Essai de Palingénésie sociale*, 1827. *Œuvres*, 1830, iii, p. 259).
[59] As, for example, by Sir Isaiah Berlin. See *The Hedgehog and the Fox* (1953), p. 49.

in an obsession with questions of authority and sovereignty. Indeed he may well strike the modern reader as not merely more Catholic than Christian, but in some respects more Hebraic than Catholic. The spirit of the New Testament, the motif of divine love, is noticeably absent from these pages. When he writes of the church it is the quasi-political *imperium* rather than the fellowship of love that is the focus of his thoughts and the object of his admiration. In any case he sees Catholicism as something timeless and immobile only because he chooses not to look beneath the surface. Thus even as a religious thinker Maistre's concerns are scarcely those of a man of faith: he was less interested in Catholic dogma as a revelation of saving truth than in its applicability to man's social necessity.[60] He attempted, in fine, what the eighteenth-century authors whom he so bitterly assails had themselves sought to do, namely to discover for human society a permanent principle of moral unity. If therefore his venture has to compensate in dogmatism for what it lacks in realism in this too he is far from being unique.

[60] As Morley truly says: 'Throughout his book on the Pope, De Maistre talks of Christianity exclusively as a statesman and a publicist would talk about it; not theologically or spiritually, but politically and socially' (*Critical Miscellanies*, ii, p. 314). There is not a little in Maistre which recalls the attitudes of Charles Maurras and the Action Française a century later, and Auguste Comte too was indirectly his disciple. But Faguet is wrong in describing him as utterly irreligious at heart and his teaching as 'a slightly cleaned up paganism' (*Politiques et moralistes*, p. 25).

3

TRADITIONALISM AND CHANGE

Bonald's philosophy of language

Joseph de Maistre was by no means alone in his resistance to what he regarded as the subversive effects of individualistic rationalism or in his insistent call for a return to the beliefs and values of the past as the only basis for a stable society. With his name must in this respect be coupled that of his almost exact contemporary, Louis de Bonald, with whom the doctrine known as traditionalism is especially associated, as also those of Ballanche and Buchez, much younger men both of them — themselves indeed separated from one another in age by a space of twenty years — but markedly influenced in their outlook by the two older thinkers. In the present chapter we shall consider the three together as representatives of differing types of a philosophy of history that seeks to understand man's nature and prospects largely in terms of the social experience of the past. All of them adhered in one way or another to the view that (in Bonald's words) 'Man exists only for society, and society shapes him only for itself.'

A close comparison between the first-named and Maistre, his senior merely by a year, would seem obvious. Both were reactionaries, tireless in opposing the ideas and ideals of the century to which by birth they belonged and ardent in their desire to witness the restoration of the old order. To both the union of throne and altar was a matter of principle. Both trusted in the power and permanence of that universal reason which they saw as the property of the human race itself, by virtue of its divine origin. Both moreover were aristocrats who had personally suffered through the Revolution. 'Is it possible', wrote Maistre to Bonald (a little too flatteringly), 'that Nature should have amused herself by drawing two chords so absolutely alike as your mind and mine?' And again, 'I have never thought anything that you had not previously written, nor written anything that you had not previously thought.'[1] Nevertheless, when the broad likenesses have been duly noted the area of

[1] Bonald was not unaware of the flattery. He noted in the margin: 'L'assertion, si flatteuse pour moi, souffre cependant, de part et d'autre, quelques exceptions.' See Faguet, *Politiques et moralistes*, p. 691. Faguet comments: 'Il n'y a peut-être pas deux esprits concluant dans le même sens en pensant si différemment. Leurs natures intellectuelles sont opposées ... l'un est un merveilleux sophiste, et l'autre un scolastique obstiné, intrépide et imposant.'

difference between the two authors remains undiminished. Joseph de Maistre possessed much the greater gifts, as thinker and as writer. He also was the more learned man, a genuine if unprofessional scholar. Bonald, on the other hand, has been described as 'the last of the scholastics' — a system-builder. Of the Savoyard's brilliance he had little and his voluminous works are the product of a mind essentially unimaginative.[2] Louis-Gabriel-Ambroise, vicomte de Bonald, was born at Monna, near Milhau in the Auvergne, in 1754. Educated by the Oratorians at Juilly, he served for a short while as an officer in the royal guard before marrying and settling down in his native town, of which for a few years he was *maire*. He also took his seat in the assembly of the Auvergne and in time became its president. His opposition to the civil constitution of the clergy led, however, to his resignation followed by his emigration and enrolment in Condé's army. Shortly afterwards we find him living at Heidelberg with two of his children, helping them with their education but otherwise engaged in the preparation of a full-scale treatise on political theory. This, in three volumes, was published at Constance in 1796 under the title *Théorie du Pouvoir politique et religieuse dans la société civile, démontrée par raisonnement et par l'histoire* — contemporaneously, that is, with Maistre's *Considérations sur la France*. Staunchly royalist and reactionary in its standpoint, most of the copies of it which reached France were destroyed by order of the Directory. Undeterred, the author himself returned thither a year later, although he prudently kept out of public view and devoted his time to writing. The fruits of this literary effort were an *Essai analytique sur les lois naturelles de l'ordre social*, which came out in 1800 under the pseudonym of 'Saint-Séverin', a pamphlet on divorce (1801), and the work for which (apart from his political activities) he is chiefly remembered, *La Législation primitive considérée dans les derniers temps par les seules lumières de la raison*,[3] which at once singled him out as the leading publicist of the *émigré* cause. The First Consul too became interested, much approving his bold assertion of authoritarian principles, and sought to enlist him in the state service. The outcome was that Bonald became a counsellor of the Université, although not until 1810. (A further request, to supervise the education of Louis Bonaparte's eldest son, he refused.) But with the Restoration he immediately entered politics and from the start figured as a leading spokesman of the party of reaction. As deputy for Aveyron he was a member of the notorious *Chambre Introuvable*, doing all he could to secure political expression for antilibertarian ideas and to advance the temporal interests

[2] His style of writing is at once pompous and obsequious. His letters, it has been said, 'reveal the courteous pedant who goes through life like a footman at a court function' (H. J. Laski, *Authority in the Modern State*, 1919, p. 163).

[3] 3 vols., 1802. 2nd ed., 1817. The book is prefaced by a 'preliminary discourse', partly sociological and political, partly philosophical in scope, which, together with the first five chapters of Book I, contains the essentials of Bonald's doctrine. The second edition is identical with the first, except for the fourth part.

of the church. In 1813 he was nominated a peer of France and entered the upper house, where he conducted a campaign against the freedom of the press and personally assumed the congenial role of president of the censorship commission. His product as a writer during this period consisted of two collections of essays entitled *Mélanges littéraires, politiques et philosophiques*, published in 1819, and his two-volume *Recherches philosophiques sur les premiers objets de nos connaissances morales*, of 1818–21. He also collaborated with Chateaubriand in the *Conservateur* (1818–20), despite their open differences on policy, and with Lamennais and others in the *Défenseur*, after the former journal had ceased to appear.[4] The July revolution of 1830, however, brought Bonald's political career to an abrupt end, leaving him to spend the remaining ten years of his life in retirement at Monna. He died in 1840, at the ripe age of eighty-six. His last published work was a *Démonstration philosophique du principe constitutif de la société*, largely a re-hash of the ideas and opinions expounded thirty-six years earlier in the *Traité du pouvoir*.[5]

Bonald undoubtedly thought of himself as a philosopher as well as a politician. At any rate his principles offered an appropriate rationale for his practice. But for all his metaphysical and theological interests his real purpose was social. His aim was the re-organization of post-Revolutionary France as an authoritarian and clericalist state. He believed without question in the power of the written word to shape the society of the future: books, he maintained, are the things that have made revolutions. He set himself in everything he wrote to overthrow the work of the eighteenth century and to bring its successor to an acknowledgment of the divine right of monarchy and the duty of obedience to the Catholic church. Like Maistre he saw the thinkers and publicists of pre-Revolutionary France as the architects of political and social ruin. Nevertheless Maistre's passionate contempt is lacking: Bonald's condemnation is studiously unemotional. It is not his reader's feelings that he seeks to provoke: *Les grandes et légitimes affections viennent de la raison*. Calculated argument he regards as his proper weapon, and his entire doctrine – political, religious, even domestic – is derived deductively from what he holds to be fundamental truth. But the result is a theory of society more remarkable for its consistency than for its realism. 'He assumed an abstract man and confounded him with men.'[6]

Though claiming to write as a philosopher Bonald holds philosophy itself,

[4] In his *Réflexions sur l'intérêt général de l'Europe* he not only demanded for France the security of her natural frontiers but for the Holy See a formal recognition of independence.
[5] For an account of Bonald's life and work generally see H. Moulinié, *De Bonald: La vie, la carrière politique, la doctrine* (1916).
[6] Laski, *Authority*, p. 165. But Laski's judgments on Bonald are not unprejudiced. Victor Giraud, writing from a very different point of view, speaks of his 'perfect probity of thought', adding, 'sous les abstractions qu'il entasse, se cachent et se dérobent une information et une expérience plus large et plus précise qu'à première vue on ne pourrait croire' (*De Chateaubriand à Brunetière*, 1939, p. 28)

considered as a purely rational discipline, in low esteem. Unlike Maistre he also shows little knowledge of its past, which he dismisses as merely a barren record of conflicting errors.[7] Even Kant he declines to take seriously. Yet his own views are put forward with all the gravity befitting a body of important teachings, the consideration that they too may be no more than an expression of personal opinion evidently not occurring to him. On the contrary, he claims to be building not simply upon individual reasoning but on external and publicly observable facts. Thus his starting-point is not speculative thought but language and the traditions which it conveys. Speech was mankind's primitive endowment: in the beginning was the *word*. And the word, he claims, was the gift of God, 'who is everywhere named, everywhere known, and in consequence existing'.[8] At any rate from the arguments set out in his *Législation primitive* and *Recherches philosophiques* language is demonstrably not of man's inventing, since without verbal expression thought is impotent. 'An expression without thought is a mere sound, but a thought without expression is nothing at all.' Words are the condition of thought, as sight is of vision and hearing of audition. Of the priority of language therefore Bonald is certain; where he shows himself less so is in determining its exact origin. Sometimes he seems to be saying that man was created *with* the power of speech; sometimes — and perhaps more usually — that *after* creation God intervened specifically and miraculously to instruct him in speech and to impart, along with it, the ideas necessary for its preservation and development; though the latter notion is more consonant with Bonald's traditionalism in general, which portrays man as essentially incapable of determining his own good and wholly in need of the revealed teachings that have been handed down through the generations. Humanity, that is, has at all times needed instructing and directing by authority. Apart from society and its institutions the individual can do nothing, and when he does think on his own account it is at the cost of the social good, with which his own is entirely identifiable, a belief akin, oddly enough, to the 'sensationalism' of Condillac and his disciples, who also held the view that the individual has nothing and that all he possesses comes to him from the social environment, which is fully adequate to account for his condition at any given time.

Ideas, then, for Bonald, depend upon language. He distinguishes however

[7] 'Philosophie moderne', he exclaims, 'nom de réprobation et d'injure; car, en morale, toute doctrine moderne, et qui n'est pas aussi ancienne que l'homme, est un erreur.' See Pierre Moreau, *Le Romantisme* (1932), p. 54. Bonald's one exception to this summary condemnation is Leibnitz, a 'Nordic Plato', he calls him. His own knowledge of the history of philosophy was largely drawn from Degérando's *Histoire comparée des systèmes de philosophie*, published in 1804. cf. J.-R. Derré, *Lamennais, ses amis et le mouvement des idées à l'époque romantique (1824–1834)* (1962). On Degérando's book see E. Boutroux, *Études d'histoire de la philosophie* (1897), p. 418.

[8] *Recherches philosophiques*, c. x. cf. *Législation primitive*, i, cc. iii and iv.

between general truths, or truths pertaining to the moral and social order, and the particular truths or facts of the physical. To acquire the latter words obviously are not necessary, since even animals recognize physical objects when they see them. Mere things, that is to say, are intelligible signs in themselves, imprinting a clear image on the mind. But with general truths this is not so; they do not derive from sense and we cannot *picture* them, so that it is through the medium of language alone that we acquire them.

Just as man cannot think of material objects without having within him the image which is the expression or representation of those objects, so also he cannot think of objects that are non-material and do not relate directly to any of his senses without having within himself and *mentally* the words which are the expression or representation of his thoughts and which become discourse when imparted to the hearing of others.[9]

Thus the impossibility of inventing language, Bonald thinks, is demonstrated *a priori*: 'La parole a été nécessaire pour penser même à l'invention du langage'. Without language mankind must have remained in the condition of the animals. And even if it had been invented how is it, Bonald wonders, that the inventor himself — a person surely of the most singular genius — should have remained utterly unknown to history? Hence the only conclusion open to us is that man 'was in possession of words as soon as of thoughts, and of thoughts as soon as of words, and that these thoughts, emanating from the supreme intelligence along with the words, would not have been other than thoughts of order, truth and reason, so constituting the whole body of knowledge requisite to man and society'.[10]

It would be pointless to dwell on the implausibility of this curious theory. Speech we have no reason to regard as anything but a natural growth, the origin and early development of which lie far beyond the historical memory, so that even the most ancient of surviving tongues, judged by the prehistoric time-scale, represent only a late stage of advance. Nor need we consider Bonald's equally ill-founded notions on the origin of writing, for it too he supposes to have been divinely revealed. Nevertheless these ideas, so far from being merely peripheral to his doctrine, are displayed as its basis. Civilization has been built up not on man's inventive reason but on the sole foundation of a primitive tradition. Not only the beliefs of Christendom but those of 'natural religion', so-called, have likewise been specifically revealed. And the same goes for morality; it too would have been beyond the discovery of mere intelligence.

Man knows nought concerning morals which he has not learned through his ears and eyes, that is, by the spoken and written word.

Conscience of itself can tell us nothing, since it has no natural perception

[9] *Recherches philosophiques*, c. xi.   [10] *ibid.*, c. i.

of moral values whatever. 'Let us leave aside that expression, "Natural laws graven within the heart"', says Bonald. Men think of them so only because none can recall the moment when the idea of them was first imparted to the mind. In all the higher matters of human concern our proper attitude is that of *faith*, and we should believe nothing that men have not always believed. The truths that make up the human heritage may be said to constitute a natural presumption.[11] Further, although in particular societies this original tradition may have been forgotten or perverted, God has supplemented the oral form of it with a written, which fixes it and renders it permanent.[12] There are, Bonald contends, repeated indications, at first in ancient Jewish society, as later in the Christian, that this written revelation, Holy Scripture, furnishes 'the general law of which all peoples disclose in their local laws at least an imperfect knowledge'.[13]

Man and Society

Having thus identified the one source of truth, Bonald proceeds to detail its practical consequences for man and society. And at once we are presented with a new principle as dogmatic as and no more demonstrable than his first. It is the triad of cause, means and effect, exemplified (he claims) throughout the entire area of man's social relations by the three distinct and easily cognizable factors of power, minister and subject.[14] Every society, domestic, political or religious, attains its perfection in the degree to which these essential components are manifested.

Take domestic society first. It consists of three elements, father, mother, child. The father as 'cause' of the family embodies the power which produces and preserves his child, and he exercises it by the 'ministry' of the mother, the child himself, as it seems, being no more than the effect of his action and the 'subject' of his will. Power in the family is therefore unitary; division is incompatible with its nature. It also is perpetual, for in respect of his parents a child is always a minor. Finally, it is independent and absolute, since if its independence were at all qualified it would cease to be power. Indeed where political society is non-existent or enfeebled the head of the family has the power of life and death over its members. Ministry belongs to the mother insofar as she receives from the father a measure of his own power of production and preservation, which she in turn transmits to the child. The one she obeys, the other she commands, although in her own nature she has something of both the man

---

[11] *Recherches philosophiques*, c. x.
[12] 'La nécessité de l'écriture qui fixe et étend la parole est évidente, puisque nulles autres sociétés au monde n'ont retenu toute la loi orale que celles qui ont connu la loi écrite' (*Législation primitive*, ii, c. ii).
[13] *ibid.*, ii, c. i.
[14] *ibid.*, i, c. vi. 'Le pouvoir est au ministre ce que le ministère est au sujet.'

(reason) and the child (temperament). As for the latter, subject as he is to the will of both father and mother, he has no function beyond obedience. Nor, as a child, has he responsibility; responsibility rather has regard to him. He himself *is* a responsibility and among the burdens which in all societies have to be carried by the stronger for the benefit of the weaker.[15]

The organization of the family is reproduced in that of the state. Here too, quite distinctly, there exists sovereign power — unitary, perpetual, independent and absolute — together with a ministry — in the shape of the nobility — which assists that power by both its counsels and services, two differing functions originally combined in the same persons although later separated into a *noblesse de robe* and a *noblesse de l'épée*. And over against these are the governed themselves, mere subjects, who being without political responsibility can exercise power only within the sphere of their own families. The form of political society can be either monarchical or polyarchical, in the way that domestic society can be either monogamous or polygamous, although monarchy itself is of three kinds, royal, despotic and elective, of which the first — as traditionally in France — is the most perfect.[16] For under a monarchy of this type the three social elements of sovereign power, minister and subject are homogeneous, the hereditary principle being common to them all. Power is independent without being tyrannical, since it rests with king and council, the military role is mainly the nobility's, and the world of industry and commerce is properly that of the third estate. (The clergy, Bonald thinks, constitute an order of their own.) Such at least is the theory. Despotic and elective monarchies, on the other hand, are those in which two of the three elements co-exist without homogeneity. In Turkey, for example, power is hereditary, but its agents are not so, whereas in Poland the monarch's agents (the nobility) are hereditary, while the power itself is not. The result is that whereas in Turkey the power is excessive in Poland it is insufficient, which explains why one of these states is dying and the other dead.

The opposite of monarchy is democracy, the sovereignty of the people, a system in which the three components or 'persons' of the social order merge into one and in which 'there is no heredity, no fixity, but a perpetual

---

[15] *Démonstration philosophique du principe constitutif de la société*, cc. i—iii and v.

[16] Princes, Bonald believes in all sincerity, are the ministers of God, and as such their interests coincide with those of the people committed to their charge. The king is both the symbol and the instrument of the nation's unity, since if society is one it can have but a single head. His absolutism thus is necessary for his function. See *Théorie du Pouvoir*, i, Bk I, c. ix. Division of power is fatal — as Louis XVI discovered when he summoned the States-General. On the other hand absolute power is not to be confused with arbitrary power. Absolute power is exercised for the public benefit whereas mere arbitrary power — such as Napoleon's — is not. Nevertheless a king's errors could not in Bonald's view justify his deposition (*ibid*). cf. *Législation primitive*, ii, c. iv. In a legitimate monarchy the ministerial body affords a sufficient check on the arbitrary or irresponsible use of power. See *Principe constitutif de la société*, c. x. In any case the actual laws which the monarch imposes are not simply a matter of personal inspiration but are the product of rational inquiry and a knowledge of already existing institutions. cf. *Essai analytique sur les lois naturelles de l'ordre social*, p. 65.

mobility'.[17] Subjects aspire, that is, not only to ministry but to the exercise of sovereign rule. Indeed they are no longer merely subjects but call themselves 'citizens'. Thus democracy is essentially the régime of the 'little man', an alliance of the mediocre comparable to an association in commerce rather than to a government in any true sense of the word. For government by the people means that power is in fact exercised by those — always the vast majority — least capable of using it wisely or effectively. Fortunately it cannot last, for democratic systems, in pandering to the ambitions of the unscrupulous or irresponsible, are the breeding-grounds of both civil strife and foreign wars, in either of which they perish.

The third alternative, aristocracy, retains at all events two of the three social elements and has something of the stability of monarchy. But it is really an 'acephalous' monarchy, its nominal head being no more than the executant of the decisions of the oligarchy by whom it is appointed.

Has, then, constitutional monarchy anything to be said for it? Very little, in Bonald's opinion, for Montesquieu was wrong, he thinks, in supposing that power can be shared. A king subsisting on a civil list has lost his independence, and his power so far from being absolute is rarely if ever exercised, since the actual decisions of government rest with his ministers. Moreover an elected régime, subject as it is to the incessant criticisms of a free press, can never carry out a bold policy and has to confine itself to petty adjustments.[18] A further risk incurred under systems of this type is demagogy, by which a nation can be incited to war despite the fact that the growth of the industrial and commercial classes will simultaneously have weakened its martial spirit.

When Bonald turns from the political order to the religious it is of course Catholicism that he has in mind as beyond question the most satisfactory of all religions.[19] In the Catholic church power is universal, being that of God himself, 'maître universelle des intelligences'. The subject too is universal, since it comprehends the totality of men; while the minister or mediator, the God-Man (Christ), is homogeneous with both power and subject. In founding his Church Christ provided it with a visible seat or centre of power in the person of his representative on earth, the pope, who is charged with the responsibility of teaching all nations. The Christian society therefore is a truly royal monarchy, in which power, minister and subject maintain a

[17] *Principe constitutif de la société*, c. xv.

[18] 'Avec des mots on pervertira la raison des peuples' (*De la liberté de la presse*, p. 3). The press in Bonald's view merely represents editorial opinion; its censorship is a necessity for good government (*ibid.*, p. 29).

[19] Christianity may not yet be perfect, but it has no serious rival. Comparing it with other religions, 'j'ai cru', says Bonald, 'que la vérité était dans le chrétienté, qu'elle y avait toujours été, et que les désordres locaux et passagers qui avaient pu s'y manifester, prouvaient seulement que la vérité n'avait pas été toujours et partout complètement développée; car tout ce que les hommes peuvent espérer de mieux dans la recherche de la vérité, est de découvrir des vérités fécondes et non des vérités complètes' (*Principe constitutif de la société*, Préface).

clear distinction of status and function. But just as political society has its deviations from the norm so has the religious. The Reformation of the sixteenth century, in trying to improve the state of Christendom, succeeded only in causing confusion and schism. Calvinism, by admitting the subject to a share in both power and ministry, is the religious counterpart of democracy.[20] Indeed, as history shows, it was itself a prime factor in the rise of democracy. Again however, as between Catholicism, with its proper dictinction of three 'persons' in the religious sphere, and Calvinism which recognizes but one, there is the *tertium quid* of Lutheranism (wherewith Bonald presumably classes Anglicanism), which as the political equivalent of aristocracy or oligarchy allows of two. Ministerially, that is, it has preserved a measure of hierarchy to become a sort of 'acephalous' Catholicism. As a rule it is associated with 'mixed' types of government in which aristocracy predominates, as in England, Denmark and Sweden. Whence the conclusion should be drawn that a genuine monarchy has every reason to uphold the Catholic religion as its natural counterpart alike in principle and organization.[21]

Bonald's idea of the unity of the political and the ecclesiastical societies is, in fact, the focal point of his entire system. No society can exist without religion. 'Wherever', he says, 'the knowledge, worship and service of the God-Man are lacking, there is forgetfulness of God and oppression of man. The whole science of society, the whole history of man, all religion, all politics are in this.'[22] And again, even more explicitly:

What we really mean by religion is a religious society, and the political order no more than the religious can tolerate a belief, a principle of conduct, deeds or actions that derive their right to exist only from the individual conscience.

But if the creed of throne and altar is once more to be accepted by a nation long indoctrinated by a false philosophy a proper scheme of education becomes imperative. The children of today will be the adults of tomorrow and

---

[20] Bonald denies to Protestantism the true character of a church, if what is meant by the word is 'une société des chrétiens réunis par la même foi, par les mêmes principes religieux et les mêmes moyens de salut; ce n'est plus qu'une masse d'hommes dont ceux des classes les plus civilisées et les plus instruites ont cessé d'avoir pour la plupart aucune liaison avec Luther, Calvin, etc.' (*ibid.*, c. xv).

[21] Because in its essence Protestantism is the gateway to anarchy Bonald regards the Edict of Nantes as a fundamental mistake, only belatedly rectified by its revocation in 1689.

[22] Bonald is even prepared to verify religious doctrine in terms of its social utility. 'Existence et unité de Dieu, spiritualité et l'immortalité de l'âme, ces dogmes sont vrais parce qu'ils sont utiles à la conservation de la société civile; car s'il pouvait y avoir quelque dogme utile à la conservation de la société qui ne fut pas vrai, la société manquerait de quelque moyen de conservation, donc elle ne pourrait se conserver. Or la société est un être nécessaire, en supposant l'existence de l'homme, puisqu'elle dérive nécessairement de la nature de l'homme: donc la société se conserve nécessairement; donc il ne lui manque aucun moyen de conservation: donc le dogme de l'existence de Dieu et de l'unité de Dieu ... sont nécessairement vrais. Tout ce qui est nécessaire est une vérité: donc toutes les vérités sont utiles aux hommes ou à la société; donc tout ce qui est dangereux pour l'homme et pour la société est une erreur' (*Théorie du Pouvoir*, i, c. v).

must be brought to a right understanding of their place and responsibilities in society. Education, though, may be either domestic or social, according to the individual's age and the career he is to pursue. For private life the end in view will be less the training of intellect than of character; although for a public career both are requisite. On the other hand a purely vocational training is insufficient, since one who serves the public cause should be a subject fully capable of choosing the particular form which his service will take. Bonald's scheme provides for a sufficient number of residential colleges to cover the whole of France. Parents who could afford to pay for their children's education would be expected to do so, otherwise it would be at public expense. (Jewish families, we note, would not enjoy these benefits). Further, as the main aim of education is to imbue the nation's youth with an identical spirit all would receive the same kind of education — basically classical — imparted by a uniform teaching body constituted as a religious order. Apparently there would be no free choice of curriculum for fear of its dissolvent effects on society.[23]

Bonald's whole social philosophy thus emerges as a rationale of totalitarianism. The interests of the individual are completely subordinated to those of the state, which in turn is seen as the church in its national and political aspect. Jews, not being Christians, would have no place in society, or at least no rights. But what of other minorities, Christian though not Catholic, such as the Protestant community? Bonald's reply is simply that their position is anomalous, good Frenchmen though they are. Education, again, is a privilege to be denied to the masses, for whom, as largely a peasantry, the ability to read is unnecessary. That such a society would assume an increasingly backward place among nations with more liberal standards and educationally more progressive seems not to have troubled Bonald. His sole desire was to preserve the past, unchanged and unchanging.

It would be of no avail to attempt to discuss Bonald's doctrines in detail. His philosophy can now be assessed only as a whole, and in its historical context. Implacable in his opposition to the spirit of the eighteenth century, his real concern, like Maistre's, is to uphold the authority of tradition. Both men are ideologists of reaction. But the differences between them are quite as important as the similarities. The former was a traditionalist in a way that the latter was not. Maistre does not belittle man's reason; on the contrary, civilization, he holds, is its splendid product. Culture and the institutions of society express the intrinsic capabilities of human nature and participate in its creative life. But for Bonald there appears to be no organic connexion between the two; in its root-principle the civilized order is external to man, a useful tool not really of his making with which he achieves no natural self-fulfilment. Maistre, vehement opponent of change as he was, does not de-

[23] *ibid.*, iii, c. liv.

humanize humanity after this manner. His view of man allows room for inspiration and spontaneity, whereas Bonald's in effect leaves him with no more 'nature', self-reflective and creative, than does that of Condillac and the 'mechanists'.[24] The fact is that Bonald's central and predominant interest was in politics, for which his philosophy was little more than a prop. To this end his 'theology' of language as expounded in the *Théorie du Pouvoir* is fundamental, his metaphysical ideas being but outworks. Together they make up a system of a kind, but Bonald for all his scholasticism was not a philosopher by either temper or interest. His was the character of a social doctrinaire viewing all things, religion included, from the politico-social angle. Yet it is at this point that the two thinkers disclose their common aim. Both are convinced of the necessary unity of society's dual aspects, the civil and the religious: without a shared standard of belief, without a universally acknowledged moral authority, the elements that compose the body politic will cease to cohere and disintegration will result. Such a standard and authority only the Catholic church can supply. Maistre, however, was an ultramontane, Bonald was not; he did not believe in the papal infallibility and his own position was Gallican.[25] But Bonald's theory of society is consistently theocratic. If all truth is ultimately referable to a divine act of disclosure then those who are qualified to determine what is or is not true must presumably be the clergy. The author of the *Théorie du Pouvoir* may not have said so expressly, but the inference was there to be drawn.

Ballanche's Palingenesis

It was not only self-declared reactionaries like Maistre and Bonald who prized the values of tradition. Among the more avid readers of *Considérations sur la France* at the time of its publication was a young *lyonnais*, Pierre-Simon Ballanche (1776–1847) by name, who was himself to anticipate the aesthetic traditionalism of Chateaubriand in a volume entitled *Le Sentiment considéré dans ses rapports avec la littérature et les arts* which made its appearance in

[24] M. Ferraz questions whether Maistre, as compared with Bonald, is rightly to be described as a traditionalist at all. See *Histoire de la Philosophie en France au xixe siècle*, ii (1880), p. 161.

[25] The pope, he held, is not the monarch of the religious society but simply its constable. The supreme ecclesiastical authority is a general council 'et le monarque n'en a et n'en peut avoir aucune'. Yet Bonald was prompt in coming to Maistre's defence against his critics: 'On aurait, ce me semble, dû considérer que les opinions qu'on a reprochées à l'auteur étrangère, plutôt nationales que personelles, et qui sont celles de toute l'Europe catholique, la France exceptée, n'ont jamais été condamnées par l'Église; qu'on est hors de France, et même en France, libre de les adopter, libre de les combattre; ... on aurait reconnu que M le comte de Maistre a présenté la papauté, comme centre et premier moyen de toute civilisation du monde et de toute perfection morale de la société, sous les points de vue les plus magnifiques, les plus nouveaux et les plus vrais' (*Œuvres complètes*, ed. 1859, iii, p. 541). Moulinié, *De Bonald*, believes that Bonald's own views on the papacy underwent some change.

1801. Introspective and almost neurotically sensitive by nature, he had been able as the son of a bookseller to indulge a compulsive appetite for reading, his favourite authors being Virgil, Fénelon, Rousseau and Bernardin de Saint-Pierre. What he had witnessed with his own eyes of the events of the Revolution enacted in his native city had appalled him and the experience coloured his imagination for life. Most of his writings date from the period of the Restoration, however, and this first literary venture of his was excluded from the collected edition of his works, although its intrinsic interest should not be overlooked. Faguet describes it as 'un Génie du Christianisme enfantin', and it would seem in fact, since he actually quotes from it *verbatim*, that its author had had access to Chateaubriand's manuscript, possibly through the agency of Fontanes, whose wife was herself a *lyonnaise*, whilst it is likely that Chateaubriand in turn made use of *Le Sentiment* in preparing the final draft of his own book. In any case there are marked resemblances between the two works, for Ballanche's also is an apology for the religious sentiment as a source of aesthetic inspiration. Christianity, 'to which we owe benefits so many and so great is', he urged, 'still the fertilizing principle of all our successes in literature and the arts'. But the spirit of the younger writer's book differs nonetheless. In *Le Sentiment* there is a mystical or theosophical strain entirely absent from *Le Génie*.[26] Chateaubriand uses images, Ballanche symbols, and these he discovers everywhere, in both the past — classical antiquity especially — and the present. In his *Essai sur les institutions sociales dans leurs rapports avec les idées nouvelles* of 1818 he declares characteristically that 'everything is a veil to be lifted'.

The problem which above all others fascinated Ballanche — engrossed him, one might say — is the justification of human history. The Revolution had posed it in a way that touched his feelings and conscience at the roots, as it had Maistre's. What, then, was the answer? Does history make moral sense, and if so how? The restoration of the Bourbons seemed to offer at least a clue, on the principle that although change is inevitable there must also be continuity. Equality and liberty would be the watchwords of the future, but they would have to be affixed to the institutions of the past. Ballanche's views are worked out in detail in the *Essai*, which ranges over the territory of both philosophy of history and politics and which he himself describes as 'a treaty of alliance between the past and the future'. To challenge the basic forms of social existence, as the revolutionaries had done, will always, he points out, be disastrous.

Social doctrines cannot be stripped entirely naked. The statue of Isis was covered

---

[26]Was he influenced to any degree by the Lyons mystical group of Saint-Martin and his friends, as Maistre had been? It cannot be claimed for certain that this was so, but as Giraud notes, 'l'atmosphère morale de la vieille cité en cette fin de siècle n'a pu que renforcer ses dispositions natives à un certain illuminisme' (*De Chateaubriand à Brunetière*, p. 38). See C. Huit, *La Vie et les œuvres de Ballanche* (1904).

with a triple veil: the first was raised by the neophytes, the second by the priests, but the third was sacred for all.[27]

Movement all the same is necessary for life, as well for the spirit as the body; but the course to be followed is predetermined by what has gone before. The future is thus in a sense fated.[28] The Revolution of 1789 had erred on the side of destructive innovation, but the Restoration would be guilty of an error no less grave in striving to recover what had now finally disappeared. A new society was in the making which would fashion institutions of its own in accordance with its aspirations. Furthermore, as a romanticist Ballanche realizes that with new institutions will go new literary forms, civilization being a coherent whole. A return to the splendours of the seventeenth century was no longer possible and the cult of the classical ideal was therefore delusive. Bossuet, it could be said, was more 'dated' than the writers of antiquity.[29]

A basic reason, Ballanche thinks, for the current confusion of opinion on political, religious and literary matters arises from differences about the origin of language and what it involved. For some it is a divine gift, for others merely a human contrivance, and both are wrong in their dogmatism. The traditionalists or 'archaeophiles', as he calls them, have some truth on their side: they are right in regarding man as essentially a social animal, society being as necessary to him as the air he breathes, and for social intercourse language is the indispensable equipment. The 'neophiles' too are right in supposing that thought, having at last freed itself from the leading-strings of speech, can now be regarded as emancipated.[30] No doubt in the sphere of religious belief such emancipation cannot be entirely realized, Christianity being absolute in its revelation of truth and therefore not open to change or modification. Yet in other areas of life, where man's knowledge is only partial and relative, thought must have freedom to enlarge and improve itself.[31]

Ballanche's social doctrine is naively idealistic, but in many of its insights it is strikingly ahead of its time. He believes in constitutionalism, as also that the society of the future will be motivated by pure altruism and that war will be abolished through a universal humanitarianism. Remarkably for his day he objects to the death-penalty as justified by no social right or need and as demoralizing to society itself. The literature of the new social order will have its characteristic type, he suggests, in the parliamentary speech. Literary criticism will continue, but will be concerned much less with forms than with substance, since literature itself will be valued primarily as an expression of the social consciousness. Historiography — and here he shows considerable prescience — has before it a great future, but in the form of a science

---

[27] *Essai sur les institutions sociales*, p. 18.

[28] 'Nos destinées futures ont donc cela de *fatal*, qu'elles sont, en quelque sorte, la conséquence nécessaire de nos destinées passées' (*ibid.*, p. 50).

[29] *ibid.*, c. iv. [30] *ibid.*, p. 350. [31] *ibid.*, c. xi.

resting on exact knowledge of the requisite data. Archaeology too, and especially that of the ancient eastern civilizations, is an area of investigation ripe for proper development.

The work, however, which, although unfinished, gave Ballanche's imagination full rein was his *Palingénésie sociale*.[32] Here his theme is nothing less than the whole destiny of mankind viewed in the light of a vaguely Platonist and rather fanciful metaphysic. The eternal Ideas are first introduced, to be followed by a grand Miltonian spectacle of the creation. Then, to give meaning to the process of nature, man appears, although his inordinate ambition encompasses his fall. But the Creator is merciful and affords him the means of making good; thus man has it in him to advance in the course of his history to ever greater moral and spiritual heights. The author deals next with the question of immortality, and here again we are shown the prospect of an always possible spiritual progress and self-fulfilment open to the soul which exerts itself.

On leaving this life [we read] we do not enter upon a definitive state. Every creature has to achieve his end, and inasmuch as a human destiny has something to accomplish — to bring about progress, that is to say — nothing is for him completed. Perfection is in the accomplishing, as with all the works of the Creator ... That is why it is impossible that this life should be the end of all things; why also it is impossible that soon after this life man should not discover a further state of liberty wherein he may continue to gravitate towards a perfection relative to the good he has already attained.[33]

Ballanche even envisages the ultimate dissolution of individual personality, which as we know it is dependent on memory, although he is no wise modifies his belief that beatitude hereafter involves effort of will and implies merit.[34] What as a Catholic he understands by eternal punishment he does not disclose, but the apparent drift of his doctrine is towards a universalism which is clearly not orthodox. Yet although he allows that the Catholic religion cannot itself change, our understanding of it, in his opinion, does and must do so. 'The veil falls away, the seals of the sacred books are broken, a new spirit bursts from the letter of the old texts and things take on a different aspect in the light of a new day.'

The dominant theme in Ballanche's social *palingenesis* is therefore that of a continuous spiritual meliorism, both here and in the world to come, on the basis of a primal divine revelation. Maistre and Bonald shake hands, so to speak, with Condorcet. The starting-point is the fall, but he believes that man is presented by both nature and history with a series of challenges in

---

[32] Publication began in 1827, but only three sections appeared: *Prolégomènes, Orphée* and *La Ville des expiations*. The last of these was re-issued in an edition by A. Rastoul in 1926. The *Œuvres complètes* were reprinted in 1973 (six volumes).

[33] *Palingénésie sociale*, p. 131.

[34] The soul, says Ballanche, is like a chrysalis, but 'il faut qu'elle doit s'élever de région en région, jusqu'au séjour de l'immutabilité et de la gloire éternelle' (*ibid.*, p. 139).

meeting which he has the power to raise himself to ever new levels of moral achievement. Each fresh and successful encounter becomes, as it were, the initiation to a new life. The leadership in this effort lies with certain supremely gifted individuals. A great man, in Ballanche's estimation, is he who can most fully embody and express the spirit of his age and place. In this regard he acquires such an intuitive and prophetic character as to make of him the instrument of Providence. (And not only the great man but the great woman also; the woman, that is, with the psychic or prophetic gift, like the sybils in antiquity or Joan of Arc.) But the vital thing is that he should *maintain* this concentratedly representative function; the moment he begins to lose it his role is over.[35] Nevertheless the course of history as a whole is basically one of advance towards freedom; thus the plebeians of one epoch become the patricians of the next. Progress also demands its martyrs as well — individuals who in opening up new eras have to sacrifice their own lives, as did Joan of Arc or — surprisingly to the modern reader — Louis XVI, who in Ballanche's eyes was the victim of his own far-sighted generosity to his people.

But above all it is Christianity which has been the main motive-force in history towards the realization of liberty and equality among men, for in uniting mankind in the worship of the one universal God it has in principle abolished all distinctions of race and caste. From religious liberty, that is, civil liberty follows as a natural consequence.[36] Indeed Christianity implies democracy. Hence Ballanche's outright condemnation not only of slavery and the slave trade but the racialism that would defend them, while for the underprivileged everywhere he shows profound sympathy. Not that he necessarily favours political democracy, the weaknesses of which, he, like Tocqueville, perceives clearly enough; but they who have the responsibility of ruling must express the mind of the people over whom they exercise it. As soon as a governing class ceases to do this its days are numbered.

Ballanche was a man of intuitive imagination, but as a thinker he lacked discipline and method and may be classed as a philosopher only in a broad sense. Not only was there too much of the *illuminé* about him, he was deficient in critical capacity, over-ready to accept tradition at its face value, a fact which, for all his liberalism, brings him more or less into line with Maistre, Bonald and Lamennais. Yet although today largely forgotten, he was not without influence, especially upon the school of Saint-Simon, as Sainte-Beuve was among the first to note.[37] If his ideas were wanting in both precision and system he undoubtedly had vision, and in an age of reaction was awake to the real direction events were taking. This it is which, with

[35] *ibid.*, pp. 139, 283.
[36] 'Il y'a donc un droit public tout entier qui a été frappé de mort par le christianisme et qu'on ne peut ressusciter sans abolir le christianisme lui-même' (*ibid.*, p. 61).
[37] On the Saint-Simonians see Appendix I, p. 288 below.

his feminine gentleness of temperament, distinguishes him from his contemporaries among Catholic social theorists. 'I would readily say to M de
Maistre and his followers', he once remarked, '"You are the Jews of the old
law, and we are the Christians of the law of grace".'

Buchez and the Science of History

If Ballanche's social theorizing has an *illuministe* and even apocalyptic
quality, Philippe-Joseph-Benjamin Buchez, his junior by twenty years, can
be regarded as the herald of the Catholic socialist movement.[38] A political
philosopher and for a short while, as president of the Constituent Assembly
of 1848, a practical politician, he was born in the *département* of Ardennes
in 1796, of a family which strongly supported the Revolution. His early education seems to have been perfunctory, and under Napoleon he served as a
customs official, but with the return of the Bourbons he resigned from government employment and took up the study of medicine, in due course qualify-
ing as a physician. But his deeper interest was politics; he helped to found the
French branch of the Carbonari in 1820 and became involved in an attempted
military *coup*, an escapade which might have cost him his life. He then joined
the Saint-Simonians although, political radical that he was, he had no sympathy with the anti-Catholic ideas that usually accompanied radicalism and
were to be seen in a somewhat bizarre form in the teachings of the *quondam*
abbé Enfantin. On the contrary what Buchez hoped for — though himself
not yet a professing Catholic — was a reconciliation between Catholicism and
the Revolution, which he extolled as 'the final and most advanced product
of modern civilization'. It was only a matter of time therefore before he broke
with Saint-Simonianism, and when eventually he did so, soon after Saint-
Simon's death in 1825, he applied himself to the working-out of a social
doctrine of his own, mainly in the columns of the *Européen*.[39] Early in the
eighteen-thirties he turned to Catholicism, although he never became a
practising churchmen. 'I found there', he afterwards wrote, 'not only the
proof but the precise indication of the most fruitful scientific ideas, and,
among others, of the doctrine of progress which explains so much. I admired
and I believed as I did when a little child.'[40] But there were aspects of ecclesiastical life and policy of which he remained critical: Gregory XVI's encyclical *Mirari vos*, for example, drew from him angry comment on the 'perjury' of

[38] On the origins and early development of French 'social' Catholicism see J.-B. Duroselle,
Les Débuts du catholicisme social en France 1822—1870 (1951), and on Buchez's own career as
a Christian socialist A. Cuvillier, *P.-J.-B. Buchez et les origines du socialisme chrétien* (1948).
[39] From 1831 to 1832 and again from 1835 to 1838 he was sole editor. With the help of
P.-C. Roux-Lavergne he also edited a vast *Histoire parlementaire de la Révolution française*,
the original of which extended to forty volumes (the second, of 1846, was reduced to six). It
was from this that Thomas Carlyle quarried much of the material for his own history of the
French Revolution.
[40] Duroselle, *Les Débuts*, pp. 82f.

a pope who had 'let himself be tied to the back of the chariot of civilization in order to retard its progress'. His own belief was, as he declared, that the 'great social crisis' of the time could not 'be solved till the day when the revolutionaries are Catholics and the Catholics revolutionaries'.[41] He himself worked tirelessly for the socialist cause until Louis Napoleon's *coup d'état* forced him into retirement. When he died in 1865 he was already a forgotten figure.

For all his activism Buchez may fairly be described as a political philosopher. The first of his two chief works in the speculative field, *Introduction à la Science de l'histoire*, published in 1833, opens with an account of the distresses from which contemporary society seemed to him to be suffering, the rest of the book being offered as a prescription for their remedy. Governments, he contends, pursue limited and selfish aims in disregard of the welfare of their subjects. Instead of uniting the people they divide them and society falls into two antagonistic classes: 'One is in possession of all the instruments of labour — land, factories, houses, capital; the other has nothing, it works for the former.'[42] Further, in the unbelieving world of the day the latter had even lost any expectation of justice hereafter. What therefore is needed is both the realization of justice on earth and the restoration of the Christian hope of heaven, two supreme ends which in Buchez's mind should be conjoined. The first thing to understand is that man is essentially social, that he cannot live apart from society; but what constitutes society is community of purpose, and the meaning of this can be learned only from the study of actual societies in all their variety. Thus may history become a science, viewed, that is, as a pattern of inter-relating events and consequences on the basis of which the future is predictable. As much indeed is already obvious from the way statesmen commonly appeal to the past for guidance; but what needs to be realized is that given exact knowledge of the controlling principles of social development precognition of the future state of society becomes a clear possibility. The reason for this, says Buchez, is that man although in part free is in part also determined, and what is determined can be calculated. Even freedom is not arbitrary since men invariably act from recognizable motives. Hence if human behaviour can be intelligibly analysed it can likewise be foreseen and the necessary provisions made for dealing with it.

A science of history rests, Buchez argues, on two fundamental concepts neither of which was seriously entertained in antiquity — humanity and progress. The historical force that created or elicited them was Christianity, though the modern world takes both for granted. The Christian religion sees mankind as children of the one heavenly Father, a spiritual insight first systematically stated by St Augustine, while the further idea of social perfectibility was introduced by Vincent of Lerins.[43] But it is the latter concept which

[41] *ibid.*, p. 97.
[42] Cuvillier, *P.-J.-B. Buchez.*, p. 38.
[43] *Introduction à la Science de l'histoire*, i, cc. 2 and 3.

especially interests Buchez; for progress, he believes, is a natural thing, springing from the very nature of man — essentially conative — and the conditions under which he exists. Man has it in him in fact to remake not only himself but his social and physical environments as well, each of which he is capable of subduing and shaping to his needs and requirements. The course of his terrestrial life therefore is a process of gradual but continuous betterment, the outcome of which amounts virtually to a new creation. That this is true of man's physical existence Buchez holds to be perfectly feasible: the body can be developed so as to acquire new and heritable capacities; but it is true also of society and the world of nature. What the individual in isolation may achieve is as a rule slender enough, but collectively men have the resources to change their living conditions to a perhaps unlimited degree. Actually the forms which such changes assume are what constitute civilization, a transmissible asset: as physique can be improved through heredity so cultures are enriched by succeeding generations. Nor is progress confined to the human sphere; geology affords evident proof that animal species have developed gradually from simple to highly complex forms, of which man himself is the supreme example. Finally, however, progress is to be observed in the order of divine revelation, with the four successive stages of man's religious enlightenment, since in addition to those usually listed by theologians — the Adamic, the Mosaic and the Christian — Buchez would include another covering the beliefs of ancient Egypt and India, for which he entertained a special respect. To these divine disclosures man owes the order of his historic social development through family, tribe and nation to the Catholic concept of humanity as a whole.

All this the author of the *Science de l'histoire* describes with a fine generalizing air, even if the evidence is either distorted, false or simply absent. Moreover, like others of his contemporaries in France, he appears to estimate the value of Christianity mainly in terms of its social significance, claiming that 'la civilisation moderne est sortie toute entière de l'Évangile'. For the gospel, he insists, relates to this world and not merely to the next. Christ came to increase the sum of human happiness, so that the church's message of salvation must extend to mankind's temporal welfare. Christianity is, in a word, the hope of the poor, and the historical focus of its authority, the Roman papacy, is or ought to be the providential instrument for intimidating the powerful and exalting the humble and meek. Buchez's view of the church may be said to follow Saint-Simonian lines: the cohesion of society lies in the organized pursuit of a common end by its different classes or 'estates' — the clerical, the military and the industrial (employers and workers) — each contributing its particular service. He also would concede to the clergy not only the religious care of souls but the lead in education and the cultural direction of society generally, in a manner somewhat reminiscent of Coleridge's notion of the 'clerisy'.

Criticism of Buchez's views is easy enough. His idea of elevating (or reducing) history to the level of an exact science, attractive though it is from a certain aspect, is inadequately thought out and fails to take account of the immense complexity of historical phenomena with their countless imponderables. The same applies to his belief in the continuity of progress: the principle itself may lodge in the mind as a guiding conviction, but to state the conditions of such progress in anything approaching exact terms is still not possible. Buchez's faith remained therefore merely doctrinaire. Indeed he further elaborated it in an ambitious *Traité complet de Philosophie au point de vue du catholicisme et du progrès*, published in the same year (1840) as Lamennais's *Esquisse d'une Philosophie* but seven years after Bautain's *Philosophie du Christianisme*, to which it is rather too obviously indebted. But Buchez had little personal equipment for the task he set himself beyond his native intelligence: apart from some elementary manuals his reading in philosophy was minimal. Yet a closely-reasoned intellectual scheme was perhaps not really to his purpose. What he wanted was an ideology, a plausible theory to justify a preconceived policy; although it is only fair to point out that he was not alone in this: Lamennais's objectives were likewise overridingly practical, as were Saint-Simon's and Auguste Comte's. Social reconstruction, at least as a more or less romanticized ideal, was much in the air of France during the bourgeois torpor of the July monarchy. Buchez shared the current vision of a unified system of socially useful knowledge in which philosophy would have the co-ordinating role. That philosophers had not yet succeeded in assuming this was because they so far had failed to grasp the significance of the immense progress being made in the natural sciences or to catch up with the social needs of the time. The service which philosophy could best render the coming generation would thus be to provide it with certain common principles and standards as the basis of a common social purpose.[44] The only question was where these standards and principles were to be found: Buchez, like other Catholics of his day, naturally turned to Catholicism itself, which enjoyed the obvious practical advantage of an actual social embodiment of vast extent and long experience. The trouble was that, from the philosopher's standpoint, the Catholic church, or at all events its central authorities, appeared in no frame of mind to supply them. The condemnation of *L'Avenir* was an inauspicious event. Yet the belief of Catholics who in one way or another espoused liberal aims was such that they could continue to face the future with no small measure of assurance, despite setbacks and disappointments.

[44] cf. *Traité complet de Philosophie*, i, p. viii. On the whole subject of romantic progressivism in France at this period see D.G. Charlton, *Secular Religions in France 1815—1870* (1963).

4

LAMENNAIS AND LIBERAL CATHOLICISM: (I) A NEW APOLOGETIC

Early Writings: the Church

When we turn to Félicité de Lamennais, traditionalist and liberal, ultramontane and deist, royalist and revolutionary, it is to be confronted by one of the outstanding religious personalities of the era; a man in whom his friend, the composer Franz Liszt, saw, as he put it, *le christianisme du xixe siècle*. A devout priest who in the end was to break with the church entirely, he remains, like Kierkegaard and perhaps Newman, enigmatic. A passionate individualist whose life was spent in controversy, a fervent believer whose papalism was an embarrassment to the pope himself, Lamennais's reputation at the last was that of an apostate who had betrayed his church, his priesthood and his faith. Of a deeply introverted, not to say melancholic, disposition, always longing for the remote and tranquil countryside of his native Brittany, his energies were nonetheless completely dedicated to the public mission which he never doubted it was his duty to fulfil, no matter what opposition he might have to encounter.[1] Yet when he abandoned Catholicism he still did not receive the full confidence of those among whom his new opinions naturally ranged him, and his role in the National Assembly of 1848 — in which he found himself little at ease — was undistinguished. When he died a few years later it was in the shabby obscurity he seemed to wish for. Such was the man to whom the sovereign pontiff had once offered an apartment in the Vatican palace and for whom, so rumour had it, he actually intended a cardinal's hat.[2]

Lamennais's biographers are at one in their assessment of his strangely tormented character, in which so many conflicting impulses and aims had their focus.[3] Of the force of intellect which he brought to bear on all he under-

---

[1] cf. E. Forgues, *Correspondance entre Lamennais et le baron de Vitrolles* (1886), p. 55.

[2] Of the several studies of Lamennais that have appeared in recent years the following are of special note: A. R. Vidler, *Prophecy and Papacy: a Study of Lamennais, the Church and the Revolution* (1954); A. Gambaro, *Sulle orme del Lamennais in Italia* (1958); Derré, *Lamennais, ses amis et le mouvement des idées à l'époque romantique (1824—1834)* (1962); R. Colapietra, *La chiesa tra Lamennais e Metternich* (1963); A. Simon, *Rencontres mennaisiennes en Belgique* (1963); W. G. Roe, *Lamennais and England: the Reception of Lamennais's ideas in England in the Nineteenth Century* (1966); I. Le Guillou, *L'Évolution de la pensée religieuse de Félicité de Lamennais* (1966).

[3] See in particular V. Giraud, *La Vie tragique de Lamennais* (1933) and R. Vallery-Radot, *Lamennais ou le prêtre malgré lui* (1931).

took there can be no question and in the movement of his mind there is an un-deniable logic, even to the final overthrow of convictions once ardently held. But Lamennais's is also a symbolic personality. He was the mirror of his age, in which old and new, tradition and innovation, conservative instinct and romantic aspiration met in turbid confusion. 'He stood', it has been said of him, 'at the parting between two worlds. He strove to arrest the onset of forces he was at the last driven to recognise as irresistible. It is the dramatic quality of his challenge to those whom he had so splendidly led which gives him in the nineteenth century a place at once exceptional and important.'[4]

Hughes-Félicité-Robert de Lamennais was born 19 June 1782 at St Malo, in the same rue des Juifs in which Chateaubriand had first seen the light of day thirteen years earlier. His father, the head of a firm of merchants and shipowners, belonged to a family ennobled by Louis XIV and was com-fortably circumstanced until the Revolution shattered his fortunes.[5] Félicité, the fourth son, was brought up by his uncle Robert des Saudrais and by his own elder brother Jean, who in 1804 became a priest and whose equable and confident temperament presented a complete contrast to that of his more brilliant sibling.[6] Féli (as he was commonly called) had from an early age read widely and when still barely in his adolescence was captivated by Rousseau.[7] But his education was not at all systematic — he was in fact largely an autodidact — nor does the knowledge he so rapidly acquired appear to have been very profound, although he learned foreign languages with ease. Much of his time was spent in the rural solitude of a small family property at La Chênaie near Dinan, a place he loved and thought of as home throughout his life, but no good training-ground for that world of men and affairs in which writers like Maistre and Bonald moved with assurance. His native interest in theological and moral questions was eagerly cultivated for him by his brother and in this field of study he showed a keen aptitude, although he seems not to have made his first communion until the age of twenty-two. In 1816 he himself took priest's orders, without ever having attended a seminary. The decision was a difficult one and ran contrary to his own incli-nation.[8]

Lamennais's first published work appeared anonymously in June 1809

[4] Laski, *Authority in the Modern State*, p. 190.

[5] See C. Maréchal, *La Famille de La Mennais sous l'ancien régime et la Révolution* (1913).

[6] cf. C. Sainte-Foi, *Souvenirs de Jeunesse 1828–1835* (ed. C. Latreille, 1911), p. 70; 'L'abbé Jean était ... un homme tout pratique, peu exercé dans les matières qui faisaient le sujet habituel des méditations de son frère, et pour qui les plus hautes spéculations ne valaient pas une bonne œuvre. Il s'entendait mieux à faire le bien qu'à en définir la nature.'

[7] But too much should not be made (with Maréchal, *La Jeunesse de La Mennais*, 1913) of Rousseau's influence on Lamennais's mature thinking. cf. Vidler, *Prophecy and Papacy*, p. 42 note.

[8] A friend of his, abbé Teysseyrre, wrote to him on 27 February 1816: 'Vous allez à l'ordina-tion comme une victime au sacrifice.' But he made the mistake of taking Lamennais's state of mind at the time as in some way a mark of divine favour. See A. Blaize, *Œuvres inédites de F. Lamennais* (1866), i, p. 259.

under the title *Réflexions sur l'état de l'Église en France pendant le xviiie siècle, et sur sa situation actuelle,* the first edition of which was seized by the police, probably because of its ultramontane tendencies, even though these were not pronounced.[9] His next undertaking, *Tradition de l'Église sur l'institution des évêques,* publication of which was delayed until the late summer of 1814, was like its predecessor the fruit of collaboration with Jean de La Mennais, but whereas Lamennais included the former in his *Œuvres complètes* the latter was deliberately omitted, a fact suggesting that he regarded the work as more Jean's than his. Nonetheless *Tradition* may fairly be listed in the Mennaisian canon since in style and standpoint it is quite clearly Félicité's.

Réflexions sur l'état de l'Église en France comprises two parts of unequal length, the first and longer being an historical survey of the church's trials and struggles since its beginnings, a story that reaches its climax in the eighteenth century, the second, in which the author's real purpose emerges, listing a number of practical reforms. Most of the characteristic Mennaisian ideas already find expression: the necessity of authority as the basis of certitude in religion; the place of theology in the hierarchy of the sciences; the implications of religion for politics; the condemnation of religious 'indifference'; the freedom of the church; the need of an educated clergy; and the establishment of episcopal synods, parochial missions and Christian schools for the poor.[10] The manner of writing is also unmistakably Lamennais's — imaginative, ironic, aphoristic, abrasive. Strangely perhaps there is no mention of Chateaubriand,[11] but the influence of Bonald, whose name is repeatedly invoked, is manifest. The Reformation is treated as the prime source of Christendom's contemporary ills:

The Reformers of the sixteenth century undermined simultaneously the foundations of religious order and of social order. They set up the principle of anarchy in the church and in the state, by attributing sovereignty to the people and the right of private judgement in matters of belief to each individual. Thus the final outcome of their aims has been the most complete destruction of religion and the most fearful disruption of society.[12]

[9] cf. Vidler, *Prophecy and Papacy,* pp. 51f. Actually his *Guide spirituel ou le Miroir des âmes religieuses,* a translation of an ascetic and mystical treatise by a sixteenth century monk, Louis de Blois, had come out earlier in the same year.

[10] C. Boutard, *Lamennais: sa vie et ses doctrines* (1905—1913), i, p. 55, remarks: 'La plupart des idées exposées dans la seconde partie des *Réflexions* sont devenues aujourd'hui des lieux communs. Elles étaient, quand elles furent exprimées, neuves et originales, car bien peu d'hommes avaient alors l'intelligence des besoins des temps nouveaux.'

[11] Years later Lamennais spoke of the *Génie* as 'un ouvrage d'un ordre supérieur et plein d'intérêt', but at this date his appreciation was evidently more qualified. See F. Duine, *La Mennais: sa vie, ses idées, ses ouvrages* (1922), p. 30.

[12] *Œuvres complètes,* vi, p. 6. Lamennais's knowledge of Protestantism remained superficial and his judgment of it prejudiced. 'Ce ne sera rien non plus qui ressemble au protestantisme', he wrote in *Affaires de Rome* (p. 338), 'système bâtard, inconséquent, étroit, qui, sous une apparence trompeuse de liberté, se résout pour les nations dans le despotisme brutal de la force et pour les individus dans l'egoïsme.' One of the chief reasons for Lamennais's dislike of

The Revolution is seen as the direct result of the corruption of public opinion by 'philosophy', to which conventional Catholic apologetic made only a very inadequate reply — 'too deficient in literary appeal and those adornments which an austere reason may despise, but which nevertheless it ought to allow and even require itself to employ in order to render the truth more attractive to ailing souls'.[13] It was a deficiency, in fact, which Lamennais himself was in due course to attempt to repair.

Whereas this work was scarcely more than a pamphlet, *Tradition de l'Église* had all the appearance of a substantial piece of scholarship.[14] The question whether the canonical institution of bishops did or did not require the formal authorization of the pope had occupied Jean de La Mennais for many years and he had come to the conclusion that history leaves no doubt as to the pope's exclusive rights in the matter. His materials he now passed on to his brother, whose task it was to present it in an effective literary shape.[15] The book opens with a short historical survey of the ancient patriarchates, which are depicted as having been instituted by authority of St Peter himself, their own privileges depending thereafter on that of the apostolic see. The authors contend that the doctrine of both the Eastern and the Western churches is in this regard the same and that no objection to the papal prerogatives can be sustained on the basis of the sixth canon of the Council of Nicæa.[16] Metropolitans, in consequence, possess no other authority than that conferred on them by the Holy See. Thus the ultramontane position is plainly vindicated. However the distinction between the temporal and spiritual spheres is not to be obscured; in the former the pope has no authority, direct or indirect, over duly constituted rulers.

In the political as in the religious society, the Church teaches us to reverence a power which comes from God, and which commands in the name of God —

a power whose responsibility is solely to 'the all-powerful Being whom it represents and who established it'. The two authorities, which under the natural and divine law have an equal right to obedience, pertain to two different orders. 'Let them remain sincerely united, *without seeking to invade one another's jurisdiction.*'[17]

This last sentence should be noted, since the words we have italicized state a principle which Lamennais was never to relinquish. But on the historical foundations of ultramontanism he is much more vulnerable to

England was its Protestantism. He was bitterly critical of Anglicanism. cf. Roe, *Lamennais and England*, pp. 67f.

[13] *Œuvres complètes*, vi, pp. 50f.

[14] On its composition see Maréchal, *La Famille de La Mennais.*, cc. v, vi and viii.

[15] He had also to take account of the strongly Gallican arguments of Tabaraud's *Essai historique et critique sur l'institution canonique des évêques*, published in 1811.

[16] A. D. 325. The sixth canon deals with the privileges traditionally belonging to certain sees.

[17] *Tradition de l'Église*, ii, p. cxv.

criticism. He frankly declares, following Bonald, that the facts of history are 'an obscure labyrinth in which the greatest scholars soon get lost' unless illuminated and guided by a pre-constituted theory, or what Bonald calls a *fil directeur*, resting on a just consideration of 'the nature of things'.[18] Such a principle, Lamennais claims, provides the key for all difficulties and is 'the best commentary on the monuments of the past'. 'Put these great maxims at the head of history and everything becomes clear, everything falls into place; the facts, hitherto scattered and unconnected, arrange themselves around this common centre in an order as simple as it is magnificent.'[19]

Simple and magnificent indeed was Lamennais's view of the place and pre-rogatives of the Holy See, as subsequent events were to demonstrate. But the timing of this particular book was unfortunate, since with the fall of Bona-parte and the return of Pius VII to Rome the issue with which it dealt ceased to be pressing. Moreover the Bourbon restoration seemed rather to revive the old Gallican sentiments than to foster the new, ultramontane ones. *Tradi-tion* thus caused no sensation whatever, much to its author's disappointment. Only a few copies were sold and sales did not begin to boom until the appear-ance of the *Essai sur l'indifférence* three years later.[20]

The decision to accept ordination was taken largely under the influence of a fellow-Breton, abbé Guy Carron, whom he met in London.[21] But to the last he had doubts about his vocation, being under no illusion as to the burden of responsibility he would be assuming, not least towards himself. Whether Lamennais ought to have been ordained is a question on which opinions may reasonably differ. Henri Bremond thought him a priest 'to the marrow of his bones'.[22]

On Indifferentism in Religion.

But the time was ripe for Catholicism, after the long twilight of eighteenth-century scepticism and the darkness of the Revolutionary era, to show itself in a new and appealing light, a light not merely aesthetic, as in *Le Génie du Christianisme*, or sociological, as in Bonald's *Législation primitive*, but one that reflected both the growing mood of romantic traditionalism and the demand for a religious philosophy capable of meeting rationalist arguments on a wider front than the old-style apologetics had done.[23] Of the need of such a philosophy Lamennais himself was very conscious. 'Evidence' theology,

[18] cf. Maréchal, *La Famille de La Mennais*, pp. 393–9.

[19] *Tradition de l'Église*, ii, pp. 93f.

[20] cf. Blaize, *Œuvres inédites*, ii, p. 181.

[21] Lamennais visited England in 1815 and for a time was employed as a schoolteacher in Kensington. See Roe, *Lamennais and England*, c. iii.

[22] *Pour le romantisme* (1923). cf. Vallery-Radot, *Lamennais ou le prêtre* and P. Harispe, *Lamennais: drame de sa vie sacerdotale* (1924).

[23] cf. Hocédez, *Histoire de la Théologie au xixe siècle*, i, pp. 20f.

relying on the supposedly conclusive testimony of prophecy and miracle, seemed to him, as to Coleridge in England, totally inadequate. 'Proofs', of this kind made simply no impression on *incroyants*.

Indeed [he wrote to Maistre] I know several people who used to be Christian but have become unbelievers through reading apologies for religion ... They ought to realize at Rome that their traditional method, according to which everything is proved by facts and authorities, is no doubt admirable in itself, and one neither can nor need abandon it, but it is insufficient, because it is no longer understood. Since reason has proclaimed itself sovereign one must go straight at it, seize it on its throne and force it, on pain of death, to prostrate itself before the reason of God.[24]

Taking the initiative himself, therefore, he brought out in 1817 the first volume of his *Essai sur l'indifférence en matière de religion*, the success of which was instantaneous and far exceeding anything he had dared hope for. Although the early printings were anonymous the author's identity was not for long a secret and his name was on all lips. Within two months the first edition was sold out. Abbé Frayssinous, a theologian of the old school, declared that the book would waken the dead.[25] Young Catholic intellectuals were wild in its praise.[26] 'C'est magnifique', exclaimed Lamartine, 'pensé comme M de Maistre, écrit comme Rousseau, fort, vrai, élevé, pittoresque, concluant, neuf, enfin tout'.[27] Chateaubriand, Bonald and Maistre all welcomed it generously. According to Sainte-Beuve Lamennais was everywhere hailed as a new Bossuet.[28] Before long the French government itself was eager to enlist his support.[29]

What, then, were the reasons for this literary triumph? To begin with the work was opportune: the public was in the mood to receive it. But the enterprise was also fully equal to the opportunity. The writer's arguments were bold and impassioned, giving no quarter to what he saw fit to denounce. Here at last, it was felt, was a priest with the literary style of a master — vivid and imaginative and unencumbered by philosophical technicalities. Clearly Lamennais had taken the measure of the readership he sought to attract and win over. Indeed he himself could enter into their state of mind, and had done so.[30] He spoke, that is to say, for his own generation, both recognizing their doubts and sensing their latent faith. Having trodden the path of their

[24] *Lettres et opuscules du comte Joseph de Maistre* (1869), pp. 120f.
[25] cf. A. Roussel, *Lamennais d'après des documents inédits* (1893), i, p. 127.
[26] In comparison with *Le Génie du Christianisme* the *Essai* displayed intellectual muscle. 'Après Chateaubriand, il [Lamennais] croyait qu'il restait à montrer que le christianisme est capable, non seulement d'exciter des émotions esthétiques, mais de satisfaire les besoins de la pensée (A. Feugère, *Lamennais avant l'Essai sur l'indifférence d'après des documents inédits 1782–1817*, 1906, p. 187).
[27] In a letter of 8 August 1818. See Maréchal, *Lamennais et Lamartine* (1907), p. 60, quoted Vidler, *Prophecy and Papacy*, pp. 71f.
[28] cf. Duine, *La Mennais: sa vie*, pp. 60f.
[29] cf. Blaize, *Œuvres inédites*, i, p. 285.
[30] cf. Maréchal, *La Jeunesse de La Mennais*, p. 635.

own error he could the better lead them to the truth he was confident that he himself had found. 'He attacked the modern spirit', it has been said, 'at the roots, forcing it to go back beyond the sixteenth century. Never for many a year had Catholicism assumed an attitude so aggressive and disdainful. It was the eye-to-eye struggle of outright faith against modern thought.'[31]

The aim of the *Essai*, or at any rate of this initial instalment of it — for it was no more than an introduction to the system Lamennais had in mind and other volumes were to follow — was to impress upon public opinion the urgency and even the inevitability of the religious question, on the grounds not merely of church—state relations but of personal belief. A return to their ancestral faith would be to the greater good of the whole French people. Hence the book's title; but the 'indifference' which it opposes is not what is commonly meant by the term — personal carelessness or disregard of religion — but one of principle, namely the intellectual objection that truth or certainty in religious matters is in the nature of the case unattainable and therefore that no discrimination in favour of any one religion is justifiable. What, in a word, the author was opposing was an attitude of *tolerance* in a realm in which certainty is not only possible but necessary. Human conduct, understood to include the order of society itself, depends, he insists, upon right belief.

Everything proceeds from doctrines: morals, literature, constitutions, laws, the prosperity of states and their calamities, civilization, barbarism, and those terrible crises which destroy whole peoples or renew them.[32]

It is in fact the social implications of religion, more than individual morality, with which Lamennais is predominantly concerned.[33] Appeal to the individual reason, sanctioned by the Reformation and upheld by the *philosophes* as the sole criterion of truth, had had a wholly disintegrating effect. Its consequence was a libertinism of the intellect, by which the divine reason had been ousted and the human sacrilegiously installed in its place.[33] Every man

[31] P. Janet, *La Philosophie de Lamennais* (1890), p. 9. But Janet finds in the book an expression as much of its author's own unresolved inner conflicts as of conscious purpose to refute the delusive philosophies of his day. 'Un tel livre devait secouer les âmes plus que d'éléver les esprits.'

[32] *Essai sur l'indifférence* (ed. Garnier), i, p. 30.

[33] That this essentially is his viewpoint is emphasized in the preface to the second volume of the *Essai*, published three years later, where he writes: 'Il n'y a de paix pour les peuples que lorsqu'ils sont "certain" d'obéir à l'ordre. La société n'est si agitée, si calamiteuse, que parce que tout est "incertain", religion, morale, lois, pouvoir; et "l'incertitude" vient de ce que les esprits ne reconnaissent plus d'autorité qui ait sur eux le droit de commandement. Le monde est la proie des opinions; chacun ne veut croire que soi, et dès lors n'obéir qu'à soi. Plus de dépendance, plus de devoirs, plus de liens. L'édifice social, réduit en poussière, ressemble au sable du desert ou rien ne croît, rien ne vit, et qui, emporté par les vents, ensevelit les voyageurs sous ses montagnes brûlantes. Rétablissez l'autorité: l'ordre entier renaît, la vérité se replace sur sa base immuable, l'anarchie des opinions cesse, l'homme entend l'homme, les intelligences unies par une même foi, viennent se ranger autour de leur centre, qui est Dieu, et se ranimer à la source de la lumière et de la vie' (ii, Préface, p. 48).

[34] *Ibid.*, i, p. 35.

had become his own law and anarchy erected into a social principle. The end of the process could only be society's self-annihilation. So let the facts be faced. 'Nous ne le disons point: Croyez; mais: Examinez.'[35]

Indifferentism in religion, as Lamennais sees it, is of three kinds. The first is the attitude of those who, although themselves atheists, profess to believe that religion is good for the common people; politically useful, that is, as a means of popular restraint. Something like this had been the opinion of the *philosophes* and Lamennais regards it with contempt, for whilst denying religion it hypocritically seeks to exploit it.[36] The second view is the deist and it too will not suffice, since in rejecting supernatural revelation it effectively promotes atheism.

Be good [it says], and that is enough; everything else is arbitrary. *Everything else* is merely worship, doctrine, the soul's immortality, future rewards and punishments, the existence of God — nothing but that![37]

The great exponent of this so-called natural religion is Rousseau, and he has proved himself a false prophet. Thirdly there is Protestantism. Protestants no doubt recognize the need of revelation but limit it to doctrines which they themselves select as fundamental and repudiate the rest. Yet 'when Jesus Christ sends his apostles to proclaim Christianity to the nations does he say to them: Teach men to distinguish carefully the basic dogmas from those that are not so?' Protestantism takes Scripture as its sole authority, but its interpretation of it is capricious. Moreover, not only has its outcome been the fragmentation of Christendom, but like deism it tends in the end to unbelief, thus contributing its quota to social anarchy.[38] All three positions rest on a single postulate, either stated or implied: that knowledge is reached by individual reasoning and action approved by the individual conscience. In its theoretical form this was Descartes' principle, in its practical Rousseau's. Those who accept it choose to submit all things to free inquiry; whence our present disruption, both intellectual and social.

The force of Lamennais's attack is undeniable; nothing like it had been seen since Bossuet. But what of the thing he defends? Has he anything new to say about Catholicism? That he was highly critical of the conventional apologetic we have noted. But although the novelty of his own approach did not become fully evident until the appearance of the *Essai*'s second volume in 1820 indications of a new method of apology were already present. Truth, he seemed to be saying, is conveyed only within the context of an age-old tradition. (Here of course Bonald had helped him, with his theory of lan-

[35] p. 28.
[36] pp. 35—8.
[37] p. 126. 'C'est un fait remarquable, qu'il n'exista dans aucun temps de peuple déiste' (p. 112).
[38] Lamennais takes Pierre Jurieu (1637—1713), an object of Bossuet's polemic, as a signal example of Protestant error.

guage as in origin a supernatural endowment.[39]) But what in fact he had conceived was a system of Catholic philosophy such as in his view the times called for, a system to which the 1817 volume was no more than a general introduction, and the originality of his own thinking was in no way diminished by his readiness to make use of others' ideas, which under his pen quickly assumed fresh vitality and interest.[40] This philosophy is grounded in a theory of knowledge, or more precisely, of *certitude*. As we have seen, Lamennais did not regard truth as the acquisition merely of the reasoning faculty. Hence a rational critique of reason would for him have been pointless, serving only to encourage the notion that reason itself can lay down the limits beyond which knowledge is impossible — the argument to which religious indifferentism always resorts. What Lamennais seeks to demonstrate is, first, that if a true religion exists it is 'of an infinite importance for man, for society, for God himself'; next, that such a religion actually does exist and that by virtue of its truth it is unique, offering mankind the sole means of salvation; and finally, that all men can easily distinguish it from religions which are false. This last claim, though, raises some difficult questions and in defending it Lamennais has to extend his undertaking over two more volumes — a projected fifth was never accomplished.[41]

Discursive reasoning then, he is saying, cannot lead to truth. Certitude, or the assurance of possessing the truth, depends on authority, and the true religion 'is incontestably that which rests on the greatest visible authority'. Why mere reason cannot yield such certitude is to Lamennais clear: it offers only three ways to truth, those of 'sense', 'sentiment' and 'reasoning', and all of them are inadequate. In exposing the defects of sense he falls back on the familiar sceptical arguments without adding anything to them or recognizing their vulnerability to criticism. Sometimes indeed his questions are no more than rhetorical: 'What is it', he asks, 'to feel? Who knows? Am I even certain that I feel?' Sentiment or intuition he finds no more reliable. 'Feelings' of truth or falsehood, of right and wrong, vary widely with time and circumstances. They are inherently subjective and therefore cannot finally be trusted. (The measure of agreement that actually exists among men on truth and goodness or their opposites he apparently ignores.) As to reasoning — self-sufficient rationalism, that is — its sophistries are manifest.

[39] Lamennais had a high opinion of Bonald as a thinker and had said of him: 'Déjà un homme de génie a pénétré avec succès dans cette nouvelle route ouverte au défenseurs du christianisme; et ses ouvrages immortels, que la postérité appréciera, feront un jour revolution dans la philosophie comme dans la politique' (*Réflexions sur l'état de l'Église en France, Œuvres complètes*, vi, p. 78. Cf. Maréchal, *La Famille de La Mennais*, p. 235, as also W. Ward, *William George Ward and the Catholic Revival*, ed. 1912, p. 93). On Lamennais's differences from Bonald see, on the other hand, J. Poisson, *Le Romantisme social de Lamennais* (1932). Bonald's ideas, however, were by no means necessarily approved in traditionalist Catholic circles.

[40] cf. E. Spuller, *Lamennais: étude d'Histoire politique et religieuse* (1892), p. 40.

[41] The third and fourth volumes appeared in 1823, but their impact on public opinion was much reduced.

What truth has reasoning left intact? What, by its aid, cannot be denied, or what affirmed? It serves and it betrays all causes alike. It gives or refuses sovereignty to all causes alike.

It is the road only to universal doubt and social anarchy. In sum, the fact has to be faced 'that our senses, our intuitions and our reason deceive us often and that within ourselves we have no means of knowing when we are mistaken nor any infallible rule by which we may know what is true. Nay, we cannot in strictness affirm anything at all, not even our own existence. Nothing is proven, because the proofs themselves would need other proofs, and so on *ad infinitum*'.[42]

The Doctrine of the Sensus Communis

But man cannot live without certitude. He must believe before he can prove and sometimes in total default of proof. Faith, in other words, precedes reason. But faith itself rests on authority:

In order to avoid the scepticism to which the belief of the isolated individual leads one should not look to oneself for the certitude of a primary truth but start from a fact, namely, that insurmountable faith which is intrinsic to our nature, and admit as true that which all men invincibly believe. Authority, or the general reason, or what all men are agreed upon, is the rule for governing the judgements of the individual man.[43]

We learn in infancy to obey those whose ideas and decisions we can trust; why then should we not continue to do so in later life? Man's true guides are custom, tradition, education, the collective judgments he receives, spontaneously and continuously, from the society of which he is a member.

Here, then, is Lamennais's doctrine of the *sensus communis* or the general reason. Each one of us has a natural tendency to admit as true 'that which all men invincibly believe', and when confronted by complete scepticism, which is sterile and destructive, it is mere elementary prudence so to do.

Take away faith, and everything dies. Faith is the soul of society, the basis of human life. If the labourer tills and sows the earth, if the mariner crosses the ocean, it is because they believe. And it is only by virtue of a like belief that we share in transmitted knowledge, that we make use of language or even of food.

The practice of the arts and crafts, and men's methods of teaching both rest on the same basis. Science itself appears first as an 'obscure sort of dogma' which we afterwards come more or less to understand because we previously accepted it without such understanding and on faith.

Were faith for an instant to fail society would come to a sudden halt — no more government, or law, or business, no more trade, or property, or justice. For all these

---

[42] *Essai sur l'indifférence* (1821), pp. 179f.
[43] *Défense de l'Essai sur l'indifférence* (1821), pp. 179f.

subsist only by authority and under the shelter of the confidence man has in his own word, a confidence so natural, a faith so powerful that nothing can wholly stifle it. Even he who refuses to believe in God despite the testimony of the human race has no hesitation in sending one of his own kind to death on that of a couple of men.[44]

The quest for certitude is the quest for an inerrant, infallible reason, and infallibility belongs to men in general, not to individuals. It is incapable indeed of proof in any absolute sense, but if absence of proof is equivalent to doubt then to be consistent we should have to doubt everything.[45] The sound maxim is that 'what all men believe to be true is true'.[46] *La philosophie* merely perverts this general reason, isolating one man from another and acting as a dissolvent of social order.[47]

The primary truth to be learned from the *sensus communis* is that of the existence of God. All men, by their very humanity, unite in testifying it. It is the first principle and ultimate explanation of everything that is and thus the one true ground of our knowledge. For when God's existence is affirmed on the authority of universal reason the individual acquires a foundation for all the ideas which he previously found himself obliged to accept without being able to explain. The form of the belief has differed from age to age and from one people to another, but the vital truth has persisted, having been revealed by God himself to mankind's first parent, along with all the other religious and moral truths attaching to it, in his original gift of language, and the human race has adhered to it ever since. Thus the general reason carries the weight of a supernatural authority. Human opinions may in many

---

[44] *Essai sur l'indifférence*, ii, pp. 234–7.

[45] *Ibid.*, pp. 171f. In his fear of the perils of scepticism Lamennais recalls Pascal, his debt to whom he freely admitted. 'L'ouvrage de Pascal', he wrote to his brother Jean before the *Essai's* publication, 'doit se retrouver presque en entier dans le mien, et n'en fera pas loin de la moitié.' See Blaize, *Œuvres inédites*, i, p. 279. cf. Janet, *la Philosophie*, pp. 30f.

[46] cf. *Défense de l'Essai*, Préface, p. xv: 'En un mot, nous soutenons qu'en toutes choses et toujours, ce qui est conforme au sens commun est vrai, ce qui lui est opposé est faux; que la raison individuelle, le sens particulier peut errer, mais que la raison générale, le sens commun est à l'abri de l'erreur; et l'on ne saurait supposer le contraire, sans faire violence au langage même, ou à la raison humaine, dont le langage est l'expression.' Lamennais accepts Bonald's theory of the anteriority of language to thought, but his main concern is to repudiate both 'innate ideas' and 'private reasoning' in favour of the inherited truth belonging to society as such.

[47] An obvious objection to Lamennais's argument would seem to be the fact that what once were everywhere accepted as truths beyond question — for example, the pre-Copernican astronomy — have since been disproved by a science built up on individual discovery. However, the traditionalist answer to this is that in earlier ages men judged soundly within the limits of their knowledge, and that in any case science itself depends on an act of faith in that its first principles are not demonstrable and its hypotheses are always subject to change. Scientific progress, accordingly, is not strictly the achievement of individual reason; its necessary starting-point is the common understanding. Lamennais's distrust of individualism may in part at least have stemmed from his own experience. He realized the dangers, where the individual is left to himself, both of a reason prone to error and an introspective self-absorption. cf. *Essai sur l'indifférence*, ii, pp. 17–21. At the same time his very negative view of the results of philosophy owed much to Degérando's *Histoire comparée des systèmes de philosophie relativement aux principes des connaissances humaines*, published in 1804.

matters err, but this in no way infringes the rule of truth, since it bears a sanction higher even than that of society itself. The adherence of the individual is therefore required, but in giving it he finds that experience entirely justifies him. The whole drift of the argument means that Lamennais substitutes fideism for logical reasoning at every level of thought. As he wrote to his life-long friend, Baroness Cottu: 'Faith is the act of the will which submits, often without conviction and sometimes even against conviction, to what an exterior and more exalted reason declares to be true. This also is why faith is always possible, mediating a grace that is never refused, and why too it is meritorious. Whoever wishes to believe, believes; for this will is faith itself.'[48]

Not only does the *sensus communis* afford assurance of divine existence, it also conveys a knowledge of the true religion, definable as the body of right relations subsisting between God and man, creature and Creator. These relations are necessary, being grounded in the nature of things, and apart from them man has no hope of salvation. A false religion is one that misrepresents both God and man. But how is true religion to be recognized? Not, as experience proves, by an act of individual judgment likely to yield only 'natural religion' or Protestant heresy: it is to authority and authority alone that one must turn for the answer. For authority, however, to be effective it has first to be visible. Before the coming of Christ it resided in the human race as a whole, in the unanimous witness of the different peoples – 'Whatever had been believed always, everywhere and by all.' But after Christ it has had its focus in the Catholic church, 'inheritor of all the primitive traditions . . . and of all the truths known from ancient times, of which its doctrine is but the development, and which, going thus back to the world's origin, offers us on its own authority all others combined'.[49] The Christian religion may therefore be said to have existed in one form or another since the beginning of the human race and to have shown those characters of antiquity, perpetuity and universality which are the mark of truth. For true religion teaches and has always taught the existence of one only God, the difference between good and evil, the spirituality and immortality of the soul, the penalties and rewards of a future life and all other truths of the same order. Such are the common patrimony of mankind and the Catholic church is their exponent and guardian.[50]

Outside the Catholic church, then, Lamennais finds no authority or even religion, properly speaking. Protestantism and other heresies are merely

[48] Comte d'Haussonville, *Le Prêtre et l'ami: lettres inédits de Lamennais à la Baronne Cottu 1818–1854* (1910), p. 207. 'Chercher la certitude', he wrote in the Avertissement to the fourth edition of the *Essai*, 'c'est chercher une raison infaillible; et son infaillibilité doit être crue, ou admise sans preuves.' See also c. i, where he speaks of the mistake which 'dogmatists' make 'en voulant donner pour base à leurs connaissances une vérité prouvée, au lieu d'une vérité *invinciblement crue* sans prouver'. cf. also a hitherto unpublished letter to Bonald quoted by Le Guillou, *L'Évolution de la pensée religieuse de Félicité de Lamennais*, pp. 38–40.
[49] *Essai sur l'indifférence*, iii, pp. 29ff.   [50] *ibid.*, pp. 32f.

branches severed from the Catholic tree and fail to meet the criteria of truth, whilst Judaism has no distinctive features, doctrinal or ethical, other than those that exist among good men anywhere. As for paganism, with its endless diversities and inconsistencies, Lamennais refuses to classify it as a religion at all, although at the same time it is not a mere tissue of errors since it embodies at least some beliefs of permanent validity in which it anticipates Christianity. Under the false cover of polytheism or ancestor- and hero-worship it reveals man's natural aspiration towards the infinite and a latent sense of the one true God. Its impulse is good though its object is unworthy. Thus the ancient religions of India and China can be cited as basically monotheistic, and although the Persian cult is confessedly dualistic here too the dualism disappears in the remote figure of the Eternal, 'Zerouane-Akerene'. Other Christian doctrines – immortality, the moral law, the fall, the incarnation itself – can similarly be seen to have their anticipations or counterparts elsewhere. All these phenomena, Lamennais contends, witness to the antiquity, continuity and universality of the general reason enshrined in Catholicism. Every religion therefore has its measure of truth, but the Christian believer can rightly claim to *know* what the religionist before Christ only groped after with a faith or insight more or less dim.

These arguments are developed at length in the third and fourth volumes of the *Essai* and presented an overall defence of Christianity very different from that of the familiar seminary manuals.[51] The truth of Catholicism, it was to be concluded, is effectively demonstrated not by exclusive appeal to its miraculous credentials – a consideration that has no force against contemporary scepticism – but from its perpetuation in their most impressive form of those beliefs which the human race has found to be necessary to an ordered social life.

Certain features of this doctrine, however, at once call for comment. In the first place, it appears to obscure the distinctiveness of a special divine revelation. Not only *some* truths but all truth is communicated by God. If, as Lamennais claims, Christianity 'has ever been and ever will be as universal as society itself, in that it comprises all of man's duties and consequently the principles of his life', then, as the deists were wont to argue, it is 'as old as the creation' and its basic doctrines were known from the first, in any case long before they were committed to the scriptures of the Old and New Testaments. Secondly, the primary vehicle of divine revelation thus becomes oral tradition, as expressing the *sensus communis* of the race. The Christian

---

[51] Lamennais was not perhaps entirely original. Bishop Huet of Avranches had already used it, as too had F. Creuzer in his *Symbolik und Mythologie der alten Völker* (1810–1812), in which he advanced the view that religious myths are really symbols of theological doctrines or moral principles, finding in the latter their proper intellectual interpretation. See Derré, *Lamennais, ses amis*, pp. 45–54.

religion rests in part at least on the wisdom of pagan antiquity. It follows therefore that Christianity cannot be criticized on rational grounds at all, since its teachings embody the only form of reason to which appeal can legitimately be made. Lamennais allows that Christian doctrine marks a progressive stage in man's thinking, but not to the extent of implying that beliefs vital to human society were not already held from the beginning. Clearly this was a new style of Christian philosophy commencing not with the formal dogmas of faith but with the principles to which all men are supposed to have adhered throughout history. For apologetic purposes — given the intellectual climate of the times — this approach was undoubtedly telling, but its effect was also to minimize the responsibility of the individual reason and conscience and even to reduce the Christian creed itself to a position where it merges with the 'natural' wisdom of the human race. Perceptive readers could thus already have detected in the Catholic *Essai* a tendency of thought which was to have its outcome in the deistical *Esquisse* years later.[52]

The final volumes of the *Essai*, in pursuing the question of the marks by which true religion is to be identified, devote a good deal of space to the citing of historical examples. Not all are very apt, but Lamennais's aim is to try to explain why, given a primal revelation of the truth, error and corruption should have been so widespread. The decline of religion into idolatry he sees as the result of the fall. This it was which necessitated a second revelation, the Mosaic, providing, in the shape of a system of positive law, a clearer statement of the principles inherent in the first. The third and final revelation, in the advent of the God-Man, has gone farther than either of its predecessors in declaring what is needed for man's *perfection*, but all three

---

[52]Maréchal is among those who have urged the consistency of Lamennais's earlier views with those at which he eventually arrived. The *Essai*, he contends, has been seriously misunderstood by admirers and opponents alike, and he denies that Lamennais's teaching was traditionalist in the Bonaldian sense. On the contrary, he maintains that Lamennais was really a Christian rationalist in the line of St Thomas and Descartes, working out his philosophy on the basis of faith. The author of the *Essai* no doubt rejects the famous *Cogito* as the ultimate ground of certitude in favour of the general reason, but according to Maréchal this does not mean that men's rational faculties are unable to develop existing knowledge or make new discoveries in both the scientific and the moral spheres. He also holds that Lamennais's essential rationalism is proved by the *Esquisse d'une Philosophie*, in which, with the dropping of the Catholic faith, only the rationalism is left intact. One is justified, he submits, in assuming in respect of Lamennais's thinking the sort of continuity one would naturally and rightly expect in a philosopher of his standing. See Maréchal's Introduction to his edition of *Essai d'un système de Philosophie catholique* (1830—1831) (1906), *La Mennais: la dispute de l'Essai sur l'indifférence* (1925: the author's doctoral thesis), and two articles in the *Revue philosophique* for, respectively, October 1947 ('La Mennais, Descartes and St Thomas') and July 1949 ('La vraie doctrine philosophique de La Mennais: le retour à la raison'). Maréchal overstates his case: he dismisses the anti-Cartesianism of the *Essai sur l'indifférence* rather easily and allows insufficient weight to the unquestionable affinity between Lamennais's ideas and those of Maistre and Bonald — an affinity which Lamennais himself freely admitted ('Ma doctrine qui est au fond la vôtre', he told Bonald: see Le Guillou, *L'Evolution de la pensée*, p. 38). But there is truth in his argument.

constitute a continuous tradition whose last phase is a fulfilment of all that has gone before.

When Jesus Christ appeared on earth he did not bring with him a faith different from that which God had imparted to the first man and of which the knowledge was perpetuated in the tradition that belongs to all peoples. 'He came not to destroy but to fulfil', and the evangelical law is but the development or, as Saint Irenaeus puts it, the extension or dilation, of the one universal law revealed from the beginning.[53]

The strength of the church's testimony is that it is capable of appealing to all men as the abiding truth.[54] It is for this reason, Lamennais claims, that a mere apathetic indifference to the teachings of religion is inexcusable. Somewhat incongruously, however, he rounds off his work with a resumé of the familiar arguments from prophecy and miracle, presented in the usual textbook manner. Why he does so can only be surmised. Perhaps it was to assist readers unable to follow his bolder and more abstruse reasoning; perhaps also to allay the fears and suspicions of conventional minds, especially those in positions of authority.[55]

The acclaim with which the *Essai*'s first volume was received was not repeated for its successors. The second in particular gave rise to vehement controversy, in face of which the author saw fit to produce his *Défense*, although it turned out to be less an explanation of his position than its re-affirmation in still plainer terms, with his attack on Descartes if anything sharpened. Not a few even among his admirers were disturbed at the direction his views seemed to be taking.[56] Some of this criticism may well have had a personal motive — Lamennais had a gift for making enemies as well as friends; but the new apologetic certainly seemed to many to be too radical a departure from the established teaching. His denigration of the individual reason appeared not only dangerous but inconsistent, since only by the exercise of it could the authority of the general reason be recognized in the first place.

To this last objection Lamennais's reply was simply that the role of the individual reason is confined to acknowledging the authority to which it thereafter must submit.[57] The error, he insisted, is in taking the individual reason to be itself the gound of certitude. The force of the argument clearly is in the way it goes beyond either Maistre or Bonald as well as the eighteenth-

[53] *Essai sur l'indifférence*, iii, p. 251. See also pp. 266f. and ii, p. 283.
[54] *ibid.*, iv, pp. 136f.
[55] cf. P. Dudon, *Lamennais et le Saint-Siège 1820—1834 d'après des documents inédits et les archives du Vatican* (1911), pp. 12f.
[56] Thus abbé de Trévern, afterwards bishop of Strasbourg, wrote to a friend: 'Notre admirable Lamennais s'est cruellement fourvoyé dans son second volume. Nous en sommes tous désolés', whilst Frayessinous, who had been so impressed by the *Essai*'s first instalment, considered the theology of the second as no more than 'mediocre', man of genius though he believed Lamennais to be. See Duine, *La Mennais: sa vie.*, pp. 86f.
[57] *Essai sur l'indifférence*, iv, p. 249.

century apologists in engaging modern scepticism at its source, questioning, that is, the very principle of free inquiry open to all. Nonetheless so brusque a rejection of Cartesianism was bound to meet with resistance.[58] To the theologians of Saint-Sulpice, for example, who (as we may presume) knew nothing of Hume and little enough of Kant, the novelty of such a procedure was baffling: Lamennais was invoking scepticism in order to refute scepticism. The fact that he was trying to show how science and philosophy also involve assumptions based on authority they did not appreciate and perhaps could not have understood.[59]

Yet the more adventurous spirits were undeterred by Lamennais's equivocal methods. His party, it has been said,

was composed, first and foremost, of the younger generation of Catholics which in 1823 was considerable in numbers. Whether they were priests or laymen, the younger members of this party were looking in their religious studies for more movement and life, above all for a new spirit. They were indignant that the French clergy seemed to be only muttering in their sleep and repeating the centuries-old arguments and formularies of the ancient apologetic. So they were enraptured by a doctrine that opened up new horizons for their minds. Eager and enthusiastic, they had no other ambition than to range the whole of France, and then Europe, behind the banner of *la raison traditionelle*, and they would doubtless have succeeded, if all that had been needed for that had been activity, ardour, and talent.[60]

Evident signs of approval came from the Vatican itself with the granting of an *imprimatur* for an Italian translation of the fourth — somewhat modified — edition of his *Defense* — a fact the more impressive in that certain of Lamennais's critics had tried to get the *imprimatur* refused, with the result that the book had been subjected to close theological scrutiny. Lamennais's own reactions to this mingled praise and censure were characteristic: at one moment he was jubilant, at another downcast. Ever keenly sensitive to criticism, he contemplated, in moods of depression, retirement to his native countryside and the complete abandonment of further public activity. Yet his sense of mission meanwhile increased rather than lessened and he

[58] As, for instance, in *Observations critiques adressées à M. l'abbé de La Mennais* (1823) by abbé Flottes, professor at the Royal College of Montpellier, and G. Baston's *Antidote contre les erreurs et la réfutation de l'Essai sur l'indifférence* (1823), which rejects the whole traditionalist notion of a primitive revelation of truth. The Jesuits, it may be noted, were especially hostile. cf. J. Burnichon, *La Compagnie de Jésus en France: histoire d'un siècle* (1914–1916), ii, p. 22. A systematic refutation of the philosophy of the *sensus communis* was prepared by Père Jean Rozaven, S. J. — a fellow Breton — in 1826, but not published until 1831, when it took the form of an examination of Gerbet's book *Des doctrines philosophiques sur la Certitude*. See below, p. 79.

[59] cf. Duine, *La Mennais: sa vie*, pp. 86ff.

[60] M. Dechamps, 'Souvenirs universitaires', in *Mémoirs de l'Académie des sciences, inscriptions, et belles-lettres de Toulouse* (1893), p. 35 (quoted Vidler, *Prophecy and Papacy*, pp. 89f.). Duine observes: 'Les antagonistes semblaient n'être que des vieux et des impuissants, universitaires, gallicans, sulpiciens, irrités d'être bousculés hors de la routine classique, tandis que les jeunes, et ceux dont les yeux cherchent avidement tout aurore de salut, trouvaient quelque chose de chaud et de lumineux, de simple et de décisif, dans le système de sens commun' (*La Mennais: sa vie*, pp. 89f.).

decided to leave matters to the judgment of Rome, in which he had implicit trust. In 1824 he made his first journey thither and, as is well known, was welcomed by the Vatican officials as a distinguished visitor. Received in audience by Leo XII with undisguised warmth of feeling, it even came to be said that the pope had chosen him as a cardinal *in petto*, though the truth of this is questionable since no real evidence for it exists.[61] But that Lamennais had every reason to think himself *persona grata* at Rome is undeniable. The change which only a few years were to bring about he could not have foreseen.

The Mennaisian School

Partly by the originality of his teaching, partly by the force of his personality, Lamennais soon gathered around him a band of disciples amounting indeed to a school. Its *milieux* were the rue de Vaugirard in Paris; Juilly, within easy reach of the capital, where his Congregation of St Peter took possession of the old Oratorian college; Malestroit, where a former conventual building was used to house members of the Congregation under training for the priesthood; but above all Lamennais's Breton retreat of La Chênaie.[62] Thither were drawn many of the most ardent and intelligent of the younger generation of French churchmen, both clerical and lay: Lacordaire, Montalembert, Gerbet, Salinis, Coux, Guéranger, Combalot and numerous others. Even such 'fringe' believers as Sainte-Beuve and Maurice de Guérin were to be counted in the Mennaisian circle.[63] It had its own organ, moreover in *Le Mémorial catholique*, founded in 1824 by Salinis and Gerbet. Lamennais's influence as thinker, writer and priest was all-pervasive, but by no means constraining.' We pursue in our studies', wrote one of his followers, 'our natural taste and bent; we all have only one end in view; the science of God, the Catholic science; but we are making for it by different routes, thus fulfilling the great law of diversity in unity.'[64] All the same, Lamennais demanded not merely sympathizers and admirers but dedicated adherents, embracing his own ideas and aims regardless of the doubts and criticisms these were beginning to arouse among both ecclesiastics and politicians. How these ideas and aims were to develop still remained to be seen. The *Essai* itself was no more than an

[61] The story is repeated by Cardinal Wiseman in *Recollections of the Four Last Popes* (1858), pp. 335ff. But cf. Dudon, *La Mennais et le Saint-Siège*, p. 30.

[62] For a delightful account of life at La Chênaie penned by Lamennais's friend, Hippolyte de la Morvonnais, himself a Breton, see E. Fleury, *Hippolyte de la Morvonnais: sa vie, ses œuvres, ses idées* (1911), pp. 118–35.

[63] On Sainte-Beuve's relations with Lamennais see C. Maréchal, *La Clef de 'Volupte'* (1905), as also Sainte-Beuve himself, in *Les grands Écrivains français: xixe siècle: Philosophes et assayistes.* (ed. M. Allem, 1930), ii, pp. 321, 323. Other friends and sympathizers included Lamartine, Alfred de Vigny and Victor Hugo.

[64] On the range of studies pursued by the Mennaisian group see Harispe, *Lamennais: drame de sa vie*, p. 10.

introduction; the Mennaisian philosophy as a whole and the programme of action dependent on it were as yet only in process of formation. The Master himself however was emerging more and more plainly as the apostle of a new, 'liberal' Catholicism oriented towards Rome as the centre of a re-vivified Christendom.

Of Lamennais's immediate circle during these years (1824–1831) none was better equipped intellectually than a young Burgundian, abbé Philippe-Olympe Gerbet (1798–1864), a trained theologian with a considerable knowledge of the early church Fathers.[65] He also had a clear, precise mind and his own exposition of the *sensus communis* – he played Melanchthon, one might say, to Lamennais's Luther – is in some respects superior to Lamennais's own. In 1826, having spent twelve months with Lamennais at La Chênaie, he published his first work, *Des doctrines philosophiques de la Certitude dans leurs rapports avec les fondements de la théologie*. An investigation of the meaning of religious faith, its debt to Lamennais's *Essai* is obvious. Of the idea of faith as commonly presented in the theological text-books Gerbet is strongly critical. The whole Aristotelian-scholastic and Cartesian notion of it as basically the product of individual reasoning applied to supernatural truths he deems to be mistaken, a thorough misconception of what faith really is and how it arises. Revelation certainly is rational inasmuch as it is an expression of the divine word itself, but belief in it does not depend upon a series of rational judgments concerning specific 'evidences', since it is the fallibility of these same judgments which is in question. The difficulty of believing is to overcome initial doubt, not in accepting authority once certitude has been reached. Descartes's fundamental error was to suppose that the individual can deliver himself from doubt by purely rational means. This one can do only by identifying oneself with the general reason, as it finds utterance in tradition. Satisfaction of the sceptical intellect may not be immediately possible, but an act of volition is. To submit to the authority of the church as the guardian of tradition is open to any man. Were the individual reason capable of achieving certitude apart from faith acceptance of revelation would then stem merely from a natural conviction of truth, a view Gerbet sees as incompatible with the church's positive teaching that faith is free and therefore meritorious. One must actively *will* the truth, that is, as well as acknowledge it. To try to make reason the ground of faith is to reverse the proper order of things. The actuality is plain: a man born into a Christian society accepts its beliefs without preliminary demonstration of their truth; by willingly yielding to authority he acquires a faith that is both free and certain. Were he to refuse such authority along with all that it represents – in the end the common beliefs of the entire human race – he could not save himself from out and out scepticism.

[65] He afterwards became bishop of Perpignan. See H. Bremond, *Gerbet* (1907), which expresses a high opinion of Gerbet's talents as both thinker and writer.

The principle of faith in the truths contained in the Gospel is simply the principle of faith in every truth whatsoever, and, from the first article of the creed to the last, there is no point at which the order of faith can be halted.[66]

Thus what Gerbet is concerned to stress is the essentially *moral* character of faith. The church teaches that grace is its precondition, but a right will is also necessary, and with it a due recognition of the limitations of individual reason. Faith is not a merely natural act, an assent of the mind to what is either self-evident or to be inferred from admitted premises. Rather is it a virtue and the parent of virtues. Faith can and should employ reason to seek understanding; but it is not founded upon reason.[67]

Gerbet follows Lamennais in maintaining that because faith is necessary to the moral and social life of man there must have existed from the beginning a visible authority teaching infallible truth. It is precisely here, in his opinion, that Protestantism, with its attachment to Scripture as the sole source of revelation, proves its inadequacy. The Mosaic covenant, for example, was made with a particular people at a particular point in history, but what guidance had the rest of mankind either before its delivery or beyond its bounds? For the gentiles there must have been in all ages a heritage of faith preserved in the continuity of family life, in which the truths of the gospel were at least implicit and of which the church, like the synagogue that preceded it, has become the authoritative custodian and expositor. Moreover the Catholic has no need to appeal to private reason in support of the church's authority as the Protestant does in testifying to Scripture; he already believes in the principle of authority itself as sustained and endorsed by the continuous experience of the human race. Thus the Catholic is less troubled by doubt since he does not invoke the means by which it finds entry. During the previous century Catholic teaching had mistaken the real basis of faith in substituting verification by evidence for the immemorial witness of collective tradition; and Gerbet cites the much-respected Mgr Frayssinous as an example. By confronting rationalism with rationalism Catholic philosophy had undermined its own defence against scepticism. Lamennais, Gerbet claims, has rendered the church the service of exposing the weakness of its conventional apologetic by returning to the sounder methods of the Fathers.[68]

Attractive though this whole argument might appear to some readers, theologians of the old school disliked it and a vigorous reply was soon forthcoming from a Jesuit well-versed in the scholastic method, Père Rozaven

---

[66] *Des doctrines philosophiques de la Certitude*, p. 69.

[67] See Appended Note to this chapter.

[68] Further expositions of Mennaisianism were provided by abbés Rohrbacher (*Catéchisme du sens commun*, 1825) and Doney (*Nouveaux éléments de Philosophie d'après la méthode d'observation et la règle du sens commun*, 1830). On the publications of the Mennaisian school generally see Mignon, 'La réaction contre le cartésianisme dans le clergé de France au début du xixe siècle', in *Annales de Philosophie chrétienne*, 1900, pp. 405ff.

(1772–1851), who for personal reasons had been reluctant to engage in controversy with Lamennais himself.[69] Rozaven emphatically denies that the philosophy of the *sensus communis* is in line with Catholic teaching and he sets out to answer Gerbet point by point. Not only, he contends, are terms like 'fallible' and 'infallible' given a novel and unsatisfactory meaning, but the very notion of the 'general reason' lacks any precise connotation. Does it, for instance, signify men's individual reasons taken collectively, or is it something over and above this? Are 'infallibility' and 'certitude' synonymous? Or is certitude equivalent only to faith? Again, is faith in the traditionalists' sense to be identified with divine or supernatural faith? On all these matters the new philosophy is, he thinks, far from clear. The last point, however, is the most disturbing, for Mennaisianism would appear to obliterate the distinction between ordinary human credence and that divine or 'saving' faith which is the express gift of God. It would seem to imply indeed that all religious belief is on the level of 'natural' religion.[70] No real place, that is, is left for a specific revelation *sui generis*. The objection is perhaps not quite fair to Lamennais, who in the *Essai* had himself anticipated it. As he sees it there is both a 'natural' — though ultimately divine — faith represented by our basic presuppositions, intellectual and moral, and a 'supernatural' faith in the more strictly theological sense. 'There is no question here', he says, 'of the faith which is a supernatural grace in the order of salvation. We understand by the word a belief not determined by any rational proof.'[71] Yet it can hardly be claimed that he defines where the essential difference lies or wherein exactly 'divine' faith contrasts with a merely 'human' faith that is itself of divine origin. Rozaven's criticism certainly calls for answer.[72]

By 1832 the disapproval of Mennaisianism thus voiced assumed something like official weight with the drawing-up of the so-called Censure of Toulouse. Its full title as published was: *Censure de Cinquante-six propositions extraites de divers écrits de M. de la Mennais et ses disciples par plusieurs Évêques de France, et lettre des mêmes Évêques au souverain pontife Grégoire XVI; le tout précédé d'une préface où l'on donne une notice historique de cette censure, et suivi des*

[69] See p. 77 above, note 58.
[70] *Examen d'un ouvrage intitulé Des doctrines philosophiques sur la Certitude*, pp. 167f.
[71] *Essai sur l'indifférence*, iv, p. 248. Compare this with his statement in a letter of August 1821, in which he categorically affirms: 'Il n'est question dans mon ouvrage de la foi *divine*: évidemment je ne pouvais en parler aux incrédules, parmi lesquels il en est qui n'admettent pas même l'existence de Dieu. D'ailleurs, on dit tous les jours en français: *j'ai foi dans vos paroles, dans votre jugement, etc.*' (Cited Blaize, *Œuvres inédites*, i, p. 402). But if it is idle to speak to non-believers about *one* kind of divine faith how can they be expected to recognize any other, no less divine in fact though less specific?
[72] He himself, as he records, failed in a conversation with Lamennais in 1824 to secure any definite explanation from him. 'Je trouvai que dans la discussion il ne tenait ferme nulle part; et que dès que je l'arrêtais sur quelque principe, il m'abondonnait pour passer à autre chose.' See Dudon, *Études*, 1908, pp. 617f.

pièces justificatives.[73] Its promoter was Mgr d'Astros, archbishop of Toulouse, although its actual preparation was largely the work of members of the teaching staff at Saint-Sulpice, and within a few weeks it had secured the support of some fifty bishops out of the total of seventy-three composing the French episcopate at that time.[74] This document was sent to Rome in the expectation that the Vatican would take determinate action. Gregory XVI, however, is reported to have evinced no great enthusiasm for it and nothing was done. Condemnation of traditionalism thus was deferred.

We may conclude this chapter with a reference to a work of Lamennais's the original manuscript of which did not come to light until the present century, his *Essai d'un système de Philosophie catholique*. As we already have said, he regarded his *Essai sur l'indifférence* as little more than the introduction to a new system of philosophy; his gradually formed plan was to develop its argument in such a way as to set forth the basic and constitutive principles of the whole social order. In the earlier treatise his purpose had been to challenge the prevailing idea of the capacities of the human reason; now he would correct any imbalance by showing that 'the Catholic faith, which is said either to stifle reason or to reduce it to a purely passive state, in fact stimulates and fertilizes it, whilst at the same time guiding its activity'.[75] To this end he began the systematic work on which he was to continue to labour down to the time of his breach with the church some ten years later, after which it developed into what was eventually published in 1840 under the simple title of *Esquisse d'une Philosophie*.[76] However by 1831 it had already reached a provisionally complete form as a series of lectures delivered by him to the Congregation of St Peter at Juilly. But the text of these subsequently disappeared and although Maréchal ventured a reconstruction of it from notes taken down by some of Lamennais's hearers he considered the original

[73]Toulouse, 1835. See Dudon, *Lamennais et le Saint-Siège*, pp. 167–71, 243–63. An analysis of the contents of the Censure is given in *Dictionnaire de Théologie catholique*, viii, coll. 2510–13.

[74]Among Lamennais's critics at Saint-Sulpice mention may be made here of Père Boyer, whose *Examen de la doctrine de M. de Lamennais* came out in 1834. He defends the Cartesian-style scholasticism generally taught in the seminaries and set out once again in Frayssinous' 1825 lectures, which had been attacked in the *Mémorial catholique*. Boyer holds that a method which was good enough for Bossuet is sound and that the Christian philosopher has nothing to fear from taking universal doubt as his starting-point. The Mennaisian theory of certitude, on the other hand, remained open to the objections which earlier criticisms – Flottes's, for example – had urged against it. Finally he protested against the sort of propaganda with which the new philosophy had become increasingly associated, the effect of which was unsettling and even subversive. But Boyer's book, although welcomed by a broad section of the clergy trained in the old ways, was too backward-looking to make much of an impression and in any case its author lacked the talent to clothe conventional attitudes with a new appeal.

[75]The words quoted are from a letter of Lamennais's to Victor Cousin dated 30 June 1825. See Feugère, *Lamennais avant l'Essai*, pp. 302f.

[76]Although comprising three volumes as then published, it was still incomplete according to its author's design. In fact three more were projected.

to have been lost. By good fortune it was discovered in the university library at Rennes and published by Ives Le Hir in 1954.[77]

In these lectures, according to Sainte-Beuve, who had himself heard them in part, Lamennais attempted 'to embrace by a wholly rational method the entire order of knowledge on the basis of the most simple concept of Being'. Admittedly the new *Essai* is much more than a resumed effort to establish the grounds of certitude, presenting rather the outlines of a metaphysical system having its starting-point in ontology and comprising a cosmology, a rational psychology and an aesthetic. But beyond the metaphysic itself Lamennais envisages a 'modern' social philosophy grounded in the principles of Catholic dogma. (For was not the very idea of God as essentially triune, he asked, a 'social' one?[78]) Of particular interest is the section he devotes to psychology, in which a more schematic attempt is made to work out a theory of knowledge. He begins with some reflexions on the epistemology of Kant, which he criticizes as both too abstract and too individualistic and in any case fatally severed from its roots in the divine reason. But he commends Kant for having rejected the extreme empiricism of Condillac and Hume and for recognizing instead the mind's own systematizing activity, even though the categories themselves have only a limiting or even negative function.[79]

Lamennais also reconsiders the nature of faith. Acceptance of the general reason continues to be seen as the only effective safeguard against scepticism, but greater emphasis now falls on the volitional element. Belief involves not only understanding but the *will*, and so far is free: one may believe or disbelieve, or temporally suspend belief, which would be impossible if the force of logic or of evidence were in this area constraining. Every individual therefore has a responsibility in *choosing* to embrace the truth which the general reason teaches. But although the *Essai d'un système de Philosophie catholique* is in a number of respects an advance upon the earlier work its theological traditionalism is in all essentials the same. Under the form in which Lamennais finally cast his thought the entire doctrine was of course to come in for drastic overhaul. No longer was a philosophy to be built on revelation but on reason, and on reason moreover as exercised by the individual, in personal inquiry and speculation and on the basis of an intuitive knowledge after a manner reminiscent of Schelling. This development, however, was to be the outcome of the disillusioning experience of the intervening years. For with the new decade Lamennais's career took on an

[77] For Maréchal's reconstructed version see his *Essai d'un système de Philosophie catholique* (1830—1831) *par F. de La Mennais* (1906).

[78] 'Le Père, le Fils, l'Esprit sont les trois principes effectifs et nécessaires de tout ce qui est' (*Essai d'un système de Philosophie catholique*, ed. Le Hir, p. 31).

[79] Lamennais's knowledge of Kant was presumably second-hand, perhaps through Victor Cousin, since he could not read German and no French translation of the *Kritik der reinen Vernunft* was available at that date. See L. Ahrens, *Lamennais und Deutschland* (1930), pp. 70ff.

increasingly public character as his interests became focused more and more upon the church's mission and the problem of its relation to the state. Thus apologetics gave way to politics, a process swiftly culminating in the Vatican's repudiation of the movement of which Lamennais unquestionably was the leader, and with it the reversal of his hopes of an alliance between the papacy and democracy and the consequent disintegration of his own faith as a Catholic. These events, or more properly the ideas which set them in train, must form the main topic of the ensuing pages.

Appended Note: The Order of Faith and the Order of Conception

A cardinal point in the Mennaisian philosophy is its distinction between the order of faith and the order of conception. This is stated briefly but with great clarity in a paper which Lamennais included as an appendix to his book *Des progrès de la Révolution et de la guerre contre l'Église* (1829), entitled 'Sommaire d'un système de connaissances humaines', which formed part of the programme of studies at Malestroit, although the actual drafting was the work of Gerbet (see E.-D. Forgues, *Lamennais: Correspondance* (1863) ii, p. 21). It is a distinction necessary if the intellect is to retain its freedom, since on the assumption that the primary truths of life were revealed to mankind at the beginning and are therefore beyond either proof or question, what function, it may be asked, remains for the reason itself to perform except to contemplate the ever-receding past? By the order of faith Lamennais means 'all that is certified by the general reason' and accordingly is not open to proof. But at the same time it is, he recognizes, in the nature of man to try to give a conceptual form to beliefs; on other words, to pass from simple faith to understanding, 'as far as the limits of his mind will allow' ('Sommaire', p. 303). Thus faith and knowledge are united by a 'natural and indissoluble bond'. There is no conception without faith and no faith without at least the first steps in the way of conception. It is the application of conception to the affirmations of faith that results in dogma and theological metaphysics. Thus the two orders are seen to correspond to two needs inherent in human nature: that, on the one hand, of a common body of teachings for the sake of the unity of society, and, on the other, that of the individual mind to develop its own particular resources (*ibid.*, p. 309). The problem facing the Catholic philosopher is to secure a balance between them: in effect, that is to say, between liberty and authority, multiplicity and unity. Plainly no man is free to erect his personal ideas and beliefs into a law for the whole of mankind. Speculation has always to be controlled by reference to faith, which is its basis and rule, and the philosopher has no right to isolate himself from tradition or contradict the *sensus communis*, of which the truth of God's existence is the first and determinative principle. Nevertheless reason does have its rights and what is static must be reconciled with what is mobile – an axiom which Lamennais readily concedes in the sphere of religion, wherein theological systems have a subordinate but relatively independent role. The dogmas of faith, he agrees, are facts, *data*, and convey an 'absolute certitude'. 'Mais les explications des dogmes qui ne reposent que sur le raisonnement, sont toujours plus ou moins incertaines. Aussi varient-elles à l'infini, même chez les catholiques. Qui n'a entendu parler des systèmes des théologiens? Voilà la science, une mer de doutes, de conjectures, d'incertitudes, quelquefois de contradictions, une source intarissable de disputes. Et sur quoi dispute-t-on? Sur le dogme; on dispute, non du fait, qui est certain par le témoignage ou la tradition; mais sur l'explication du fait, éternellement incertain comme le raison qui l'explique' (from a statement quoted by Le Guillou, *L'Évolution*, pp. 93ff.).

LAMENNAIS AND LIBERAL CATHOLICISM:
(II) CATHOLICISM AND DEMOCRACY

The Temporal and the Spiritual

'Lamennais's sovereign idea or ideal', it has been said, 'was the social regeneration of France, and indeed of Europe, through the renaissance of Catholicism.'[1] At no time was he the pure theologian or philosopher whose pursuits draw him away from active concern for the needs and distresses of his age. On the contrary, the sense of mission grew on him, gaining strength from a disposition naturally passionate and impulsive. He himself made ready use of the expression 'Catholic action' and from the outset regarded his philosophy as the ideological preface to a scheme of reform in both church and society. The grounds of certitude, that is, had first to be established: enough social and political havoc had already been wrought through the anarchy of reason; but a philosophical inquiry would be merely academic did it not point to a reconstitution of the social order on the basis of established truth. During the years 1825 to 1830 the ideal had by degrees come to be articulated in terms of a social strategy relying neither upon the reactionary monarchism of the 'ultras' nor upon the republican liberalism of their opponents. For Lamennais, despite his earlier association with the politics of the *Drapeau Blanc* and his insistence on the place of authority in society, had no wish to see the *ancién regime* re-instated or the church used as an instrument of government power. But neither, on the other hand, could he identify himself with a conception of liberty which would end, as previous events had shown, only in destructive licence. What he wanted, increasingly, was both order *and* liberty, a stable society *and* a church free to fulfil its spiritual calling. Authority and liberty, he was convinced, could co-exist,[2] but only in a society genuinely Catholic. The church, however, would have to eschew the spurious liberties associated in France with the Gallican tradition to which the royalist party was still indissolubly wedded.

---

[1] Vidler, *Prophecy and Papacy*, p. 101. 'He is thoroughly political in his views and feelings' was J. H. Newman's opinion (*British Critic*, October 1837, p. 276. Cited Roe, *Lamennais and England*, p. 110).

[2] 'Plus le droit, le pouvoir et la loi sont parfaits, c'est à dire plus l'ordre est complet, plus la liberté est grande; car la liberté consiste dans l'exclusion des bornes arbitraires mises à la volonté; et quand elle n'est borné que par des volontés obligatoires ou légitimes, l'homme alors jouit du plus haut degré de liberté possible' (*Essai sur l'indifférence*, ii, p. 165. cf. i, pp. 326ff.).

Thus if Lamennais himself remained a royalist it was with a notable difference.

The direction his opinions were taking found expression in a book published by him in 1825 and 1826, *De la Religion considérée dans ses rapports avec l'ordre politique et civil.*[3] The first part, in the nature of a pamphlet or tract, offers a picture in the gloomiest colours of what the author sees as the actual situation. The second, more of a treatise, has greater detachment and presents a clear-cut argument. Thus the two parts in a sense balance one another. But the tone of the first is consistently negative. France, says Lamennais, is not a Christian country. Its law at any rate is 'atheistic' inasmuch as it articulates a democratic polity under which the popular, not the divine, will is sovereign.

The king is a venerable memento of the past, like the inscription of an ancient temple which has been placed on the façade of an entirely different building.[4]

The Restoration was no more than a pretence: James II of England had sounder ideas, even if he lacked the capacity to make them effective. No longer did power belong to the monarch but only to a ministry dependent on parliament, which in turn derived its own authority from the people. Hence under the existing constitution the French government could act in a way completely at variance with the divine law, 'the primal source and necessary basis of all human laws'.[5] Moreover a democracy is essentially unteachable: it is contemptuous of authority and flatters the mediocre, who through a 'free' press manipulate the mass opinion whose favour they seek. Despite the Napoleonic Concordat, which still obtains,[6] the French monarchy bears no real resemblance at all to that of the ancient kingdom of France.[7] Not that a democracy is bound to attack the church, but its whole tendency is to neutralize the church's own authority and reduce its position to that of a docile organ of state. The setting up of a 'national' church in France could only mean the virtual abolition of her inherited Christianity.

The whole argument looks paradoxical when one remembers that the Restoration government has been consistently indicted for its reactionary clericalism.[8] But the logic of it is clear. Lamennais's use of the word 'athe-

---

[3] The first instalment came out in May 1825, the second in the February the following year.

[4] *Œuvres complètes*, vii, p. 17.

[5] *ibid.*, p. 240.

[6] An attempt to replace it by a new Concordat in 1817 failed.

[7] 'Ce qui ne ressemble à rien de ce qui fut; et l'idée contraire est la source d'une multitude d'erreurs qui, à force d'être répétés, passent enfin pour des vérités établies' (*Œuvres complètes*, p. 76).

[8] cf. Dudon, *Lamennais et le Saint-Siège*, p. 33; but also Derré, *Lamennais, ses amis*, pp. 367f. ('Si la violence de certaines pages a pu sembler a bon droit anachronistique et outrancière, la rigueur du raisonnement permet de dégager une pensée fortement liée, dont l'intransigeance même n'est sans grandeur.').

istic' to describe the state is question-begging and no doubt was intended to be provocative. What he meant was 'neutralist' or 'secular'; he did not imply that the king or his ministers or even the majority of the French people were actually *incroyants*. But in his view the constitution, in adopting a neutral attitude, was in effect anti-Christian and anti-Catholic, as was shown plainly enough by its policy on education.[9] His principle was that 'whosoever is not for us is against us'. A laicist society could not be described as Christian.

In the remainder of his book Lamennais takes a more positive although still controversial line. The question to be answered is, under what conditions would the existence of Catholicism really become possible in the modern world? The Gallican doctrine, he is utterly convinced, will not suffice. Christian theology teaches that power has been divinely conferred on governments as well as upon the church, but as is obvious the former repeatedly overstep the bounds of their own authority to usurp that of the latter. Indeed Lamennais provides a list of specific instances of how the French government itself attempts this. It will not, for example, permit the establishment of ecclesiastical courts with the right of final appeal to Rome, or the holding of national or provincial synods. Independent church schools are still prohibited and even seminary teaching suffers bureaucratic interference. Worse, communication between the bishops and the pope himself is restricted.[10] In what conceivable sense, Lamennais asks, can these unjust and hampering controls be called 'liberties'? Rather has the church become the creature of the state, a mere political tool; which is why it is fast losing its hold on the French people. The much-vaunted Gallican Articles amount to two essential propositions: that the temporal sovereignty is by divine institution independent of the spiritual and that a general council is superior to the pope; and neither of them is admissible since both are destructive of the unity which in Lamennais's view is the primary condition of social well-being. Acceptance of them entails that man-made law can have equal status with the laws of God.

What, then, is the true relation of the temporal to the spiritual? Lamennais's own answer is quite clear: they are alike of divine origin but each rightly exercises the sovereignty appropriate to its sphere alone. In principle however — and history witnesses to its truth — the temporal is ultimately subordinate to the spiritual, as is the body to the soul. On matters where right is disputed the final decision must rest therefore with the spiritual authority. For when politics loses touch with religion it becomes mere force directed by interest.[11] The temporal power is constituted by God for the good of human society and in promoting that good is answerable to him. And he who in the last resort interprets the divine law for men is the pope, the unique sovereign to whom all monarchs are as subjects.

[9]*Œuvres complètes*, vii, pp. 62—8.   [10]*ibid.*, p. 97. cf. also pp. 269—91.   [11]*ibid.*, p. 116.

Basically, as Lamennais understands it, the pope's authority is 'directive and ordinative', but he has the right to use spiritual sanctions against transgressors. In extreme cases he can absolve subjects from their oath of allegiance, and in any event the people have a duty to resist open defiance of God's law since in so doing they act in his name. Hence the spiritual power is to be seen as the 'supreme defender of justice and of the rights of humanity', and as a check on the arbitrary exercise of temporal power.[12] Tyranny can have no moral justification whatever, though if the Gallican doctrine were accepted with its full implication despotism would admit of no reproof because the decisions of temporal rulers would be absolute. As for the relationship of the pope to a general council, the Gallican theory would mean that sovereignty in the church is collective, with the result that what is essentially a spiritual monarchy would be transformed into an aristocratic republic like that of ancient Rome or mediaeval Venice.[13] In other words, the episcopate as a whole would become the centre of unity, though even this would subsist only during a council's actual sessions. Further, the summoning of such a council devolves upon the prince, which in effect is to subordinate the spiritual to the temporal, 'to enslave to the kings of the earth the bride of the King of heaven'.[14] Such conclusions Lamennais thinks inescapable once the decrees of 1682 are accepted.

To weaken the church's allegiance to Rome is thus to destroy its corporate character and subject it to the will or indeed the caprice of secular governments. In this matter there can be only one principle that is truly Catholic: *Point de pape, point de l'Église.* Nay more: *Point de l'Église, point de christianisme*, for Christianity itself depends on the Catholic church. Nor is the chain of inference complete even then, since without Christianity there can be no religion, at all events for a people which has once been Christian. And without religion, as reason and experience alike teach, there can in the end be no society. To the objection that in countries which have rejected Catholicism society nevertheless survives it is enough to reply that it does so only on the basis of a residual Christianity which cannot last indefinitely. Pre-Christian societies were able to exist on the primordial religion which, as part of the *sensus communis*, was handed down through the family from generation to generation.[15] But nothing of the sort will compensate for the disappearance of the Catholic church, the inevitable outcome of which would be barbarism. To attack the papacy by circumscribing its authority would therefore be a crime against society itself; and Gallicanism is guilty of it. To save society, or attain to the proper stature of a civilized humanity, mankind must embrace the ultramontane principle. What the state needs is not a nation-centred church subserving its immediate wants — a church, that is, devoid of any real spiritual authority —

12 *ibid.*, p. 255.   13 *ibid.*, pp. 201, 231.
14 *ibid.*, p. 228.   15 *ibid.*, p. 293.

but one which, in embodying a universal ideal of truth and morality, enables it to fulfill its own authentic destiny.[16]

Lamennais rounds off his book with a statement of the options facing his own country. There exist, he says, only two forces in society: a force of conservation of which Christianity is the strength, and a force of destruction penetrating everything, — traditional beliefs, institutions, power itself. Yet a renewal of genuine order is not be expected immediately. The outlook of a people cannot be changed in a few years, and until there is a change of outlook a rebirth of Christianity is impossible. Violence will not bring it about, but only conviction, for its foundation is faith, not the sword.[17]

What Lamennais seemed to be envisaging was to all intents a papal theocracy. But this did not mean that he wished to see freedom suppressed. On the contrary, he had always been opposed to tyranny and it was clear from his earlier writings that he had come to regard the papacy as the one safeguard against it. Thus liberalism and ultramontanism were to make common cause; society needed their alliance: 'On tremble devant le libéralisme: eh bien, catholicisez-le, et la Société renaîtra.'[18] Royalism with him had never been a very deep attachment and its inveterate association with Gallicanism now alienated him. 'From distrust of princes and governments, perhaps also from a vague sense of latent rivalry between the two powers, even when they seemed to be most intimately connected, the protagonist of ultramontanism, to the great surprise of his admirers, had brusquely turned in the direction of liberalism.'[19] To those however who had been at all closely acquainted with his mind the gesture was less brusque than might appear, and it was facilitated moreover by the example of the Catholic liberals of Belgium, who greatly impressed him.[20] Thus his next work, *Des progrès de la Révolution et de la guerre contre l'Eglise*, prompted by the royal ordinances of 1828 relating to ecclesiastical secondary schools, then mainly under Jesuit control, gave clear signs of the road his thoughts were taking. He displays his concern in the preface. We demand for the Catholic church, he says, the liberty promised by the *Charte* to all religions, the liberty enjoyed by Protestants and Jews, and the followers, if any there be in France, of Mahomet and Buddha; we demand freedom of conscience, freedom of the press, freedom of education. For these precisely are the

[16]'Quoiqu'en puissent penser ceux dont la science n'a su jusqu'à présent que détruire, la vie de la société n'est pas de l'ordre matériel. Jamais l'état ne fut fondé pour satisfaire aux besoins physiques. L'accroissement des richesses, le progrès des jouissances ne créent entre les hommes aucun liens réels, et un bazar n'est point une cité,' (*ibid.*, p. 241).

[17]*ibid.*, pp. 298f.

[18]Forgues, *Correspondance*, ii, p. 106.

[19]A. Leroy-Beaulieu, *Les Catholiques libéraux* (1885), p. 80.

[20]On the Belgian movement see H. Haag, *Les Origines du catholicisme libéral en Belgique, 1789–1839* (1950).

freedoms called for by the Belgian liberals, 'oppressed by a persecuting government'. In the needed new social order such requirements will have to be satisfied; a return to Christianity may have to be gradual, but only under conditions of freedom will the people be persuaded once more to embrace their ancient faith. A merely reactionary royalism like that supporting the restored Bourbons has become obsolete and another revolution is on the way. Between the alternatives of despotism and anarchy a new Christian order offers the sole hope and to create it Catholic and liberal must unite. For what both seek is a society resting not on sheer force but on morality and the law of God. The immediate challenge to Christians therefore is to dissociate themselves from the current political antagonisms and look to the future from a more elevated standpoint. This does not signify repudiation of political responsibility, but a fresh and searching attempt to comprehend the political and religious aspects of life in their mutual bearing.

Lamennais was not concerned, however, only with the social problem. The church as he saw it had a particular responsibility to forward the gospel in a way that could meet the intellectual and moral requirements of the age. He again complained of the manner in which theology was taught in the seminaries — 'only a degenerate and paltry scholasticism' was his description of it — affording students no idea of the scope of religion or of its interest and relevance to the human mind. 'It was not so conceived by St Thomas who, in his immortal works, made it the centre of all the knowledge of his time.' The old routines of study would no longer suffice; everything had changed: institutions, laws, customs, all were different from what the older generation had known. Of what use was zeal without knowledge of the kind of society in which it was to be exercised? Even so the issue was larger than that simply of the training of the clergy: it involved nothing less than the church's whole attitude to contemporary culture. 'During the last thirty years immense undertakings have been set in motion and are being carried on by scholars in all lands. It is time that Catholic science began to gather in the rich harvest that has been prepared for it.' The church ought to extend the bounds of her own scholarship, especially as regards antiquity, a study from which her knowledge of the Bible and early Christianity would immediately benefit. But what above all was needed was 'a regeneration of the moral sciences'. Thus the church 'even in what relates purely to knowledge, has a magnificent role to fulfil. To her it belongs to bring order out of chaos and for a second time to separate the light from the darkness'.[21]

Des progrès sold well, but it provoked a good deal of hostile criticism. The Jesuits did not conceal their displeasure. To the political Right it

[21] *Œuvres complètes*, ix, pp. 192—5.

reeked of revolution. To the bishops its offence was its lauding of the ultra-montane idea. The archbishop of Paris, de Quélen, warned the faithful against its 'subversive' doctrines. The rumour circulated that even the French government, through its ambassador in Rome — at the time Chateau-briand — tried to get the book placed on the Index.[22] But the campaign on behalf of a new-style Catholicism was only just beginning. Furthermore, with the revolution of July 1830 and the abdication of Charles X the political situation in France underwent a complete change. The time was ripe, in the eyes of Lamennais's friends and followers, for a new daily newspaper, identified with views not only Catholic but liberal. The *Avenir*, the first number of which appeared in October 1830, was the outcome.[23]

'God and Liberty'

The prospectus of the *Avenir* was drawn up by Gerbet.[24] There were now, it declared, two liberalisms, an old and a new. The former, as 'the inheritor of the destructive doctrines of the philosophy of the eighteenth century, and in particular of its hatred of Christianity, ... exhales intolerance and oppression', whereas the latter, 'which is growing and which will end by supplanting the other, confines itself, in regard to religion, to demanding the separation of church and state', a separation desired by all enlightened Catholics as necessary for the liberty of the church itself. Hence the journal's motto: *Dieu et la liberté*. Its broad aim, in Lamennais's words, was 'to unite upon the basis of freedom men of all shades of opinion who adhere to order'.[25]

Lamennais did not himself assume the editorship, or at least not at first, but his influence was reflected in every issue and he himself contributed many of the most important articles.[26] Of special note are those on the particular doctrines to be propagated by the newspaper,[27] on the pope,[28] on the future of society,[29] and on the nature of Catholicism in the coming

[22]Though see Dudon, *Lamennais et le Saint-Siège*, pp. 130—6.
[23]The actual suggestion seems to have been made by a certain Harel du Tancrel, whose name is listed among those of the editorial staff but of whom little is otherwise known. See F. Mourret, *Le Movement catholique en France de 1830 à 1850* (1917), pp. 75f., and Duine, *Lamennais: sa vie*, p. 138.
[24]See A. Trannoy, *Le Romantisme politique de Montalembert avant 1843* (1942), p. 138.
[25]Forgues, *Correspondance* , ii, p. 173.
[26]From 1830 to 1831 he was living mainly at Juilly. As he wrote to a friend in January 1831: 'Je suis tout à fait en dehors de la partie administrative, et je ne puis même habituelle-ment m'occuper de la rédaction, vu mon éloignement de Paris' (Forgues, ii, p. 194). However, in the issue of 5 May 1831 the *Avenir* itself said of its *comité de rédaction* that 'M de La Mennais le préside et n'a point cessé un seul instant de la présider' (*Articles de l'Avenir*, 1831—1832, iv, p. 190).
[27]7 December 1830 (*Œuvres complètes*, x, pp. 196—205).
[28]22 December 1830 (*ibid.*, pp. 206—11).
[29]28 June 1831 (*ibid.*, pp. 315—27).

age.[30] Together they present the aims of the liberal movement clearly
and forcefully. Thus in the article of 28 June 1831 Lamennais writes that
Catholicism, so far from having cause to fear the coming changes, should
see itself rather as the agent of change as of something necessary to its
own proper development; that the church will be saved only by insisting
on its boldest and seemingly most exorbitant claims; and that it is only
upon a Catholicism so understood that a new social order can be founded.
The July revolution was, he pointed out, significant of the profound social
changes that were taking place in France.

Society as a whole is aware that a new order must take the place of the old and
that the world is moving forward to a new destiny. To suppose that the movement which impels it can be arrested is to wish to bring time to a stop. Every
attempt of the kind has produced only violence.[31]

Liberty is what all men now long for, and if society is to be re-created it will
have to be under conditions of freedom. The future lies with democracy.

Of all the elements that can enter into the constitution of a State, the democratic
is the only one to survive in France. Hence it follows that she has the choice
between two governments, that of the sword and that of opinion.[32]

Plainly then there would have to be an alliance between Catholicism and
the forces of liberty. Each needs the other; the church cannot realize its
mission without liberty, nor liberty be secured without the church. The
latter proposition, in the eyes of genuine liberals, is easy to substantiate,
but the dependence of the church itself upon liberty is a truth more difficult to bring home to Catholics, and especially to the hierarchy or even
the pope himself. To do this effectively is the task to which liberal Catholics
must therefore dedicate themselves. As the result, in the main, of the
Protestant Reformation of the sixteenth century the advance of Catholicism
has been impeded by two causes: the widening division between faith and
secular knowledge and the condition of servitude to the temporal power
into which the church has gradually sunk.[33] The re-uniting of faith and
knowledge can be achieved only by free discussion: coercion is impossible.
But the truth is all-powerful.

We firmly believe that the progress of modern enlightenment will one day bring
not only the French but all Europe into Catholic unity, which eventually and by
successive advances will draw to itself the rest of the human race and will constitute
it, through an identical faith, into an identical spiritual society.[34]

As for the other cause of weakness, liberty alone will deliver the church
from it. The existing relations between church and state — 'an inevitable

[30] 30 June 1830 (*ibid.*, pp. 338—50).   [31] *Avenir*, 1 July 1831 (*ibid.*, p. 351).
[32] *Avenir*, 27 January 1831 (*ibid.*, p. 238).   [33] *ibid.*, p. 330.   [34] *ibid.*, pp. 150f.

mixture of the two powers, the spiritual and the temporal' — is simply an
anachronistic survival from a condition of society which no longer obtains.
For too long have these distinct if complementary realms been confounded.
'The king in the State, like the father within the family, exercises as a
matter of fact ... direct authority over the thought and consciences of
his subjects', and as this authority belongs essentially to the church 'it
follows that the *royal paternity* is ultimately subordinate to the spiritual power
of the church, must be altogether dependent upon and instituted by that
power'.[35] The time has come, therefore, to make a clear demarcation
between the two realms: to render to God the things that are God's and
to Caesar no more than his due — in Lamennais's view not overmuch.

It is plain [he says] that government will not, in the society of the future, exercise
any spiritual power whatever, and that the entire people will, in this sphere, obey
only the Church and its Head, and these they will obey freely ... Liberty of thought
and conscience will, through the unity of faith, constitute the reign of Christ, not
only as high priest but as king, since his vicar will in fact be the only spiritual
power, under temporal conditions, actually existing and recognized. Outside this
what then remains? An administrative order essentially and wholly independent
of the Church. What authority indeed has the Church over the property affairs
of the family, the commune, the province, as well as over all that relates to
them? None. Her sole power is to regulate morals by precept and beliefs by revealed
dogma.[36]

So not only was the church to be freed from state control, the latter would
in turn be free of control or undue influence by the church. Politics and
religion, citizenship and church loyalty would no more be confounded.

In the article summarizing the *Avenir*'s viewpoint Lamennais itemizes the
liberal Catholic demands under six heads. First, liberty of conscience and
religion: no form of belief is to be either privileged or penalized.[37] Hence
the inevitability of complete separation of church and state, a separation,
incidentally, written into the *Charte* as something which both alike should
wish.[38] Without it Catholics themselves will be lacking in freedom. If it
entails the suppression of the ecclesiastical budget (i.e. the state payment
of the clergy) it means also that in the spiritual sphere the clergy will be
entirely independent (e.g. as to the nomination of bishops), the individual
priest remaining subject like any other citizen to the laws of the land, and
to the same degree. Concordats should be abolished.[39] Second, freedom in
education: this is a natural right apart from which there can be no true
religious liberty or freedom of opinion. In any case it too has been stipulated
in the *Charte*. Laws and regulations like the objectionable 1828 ordinances

[35] *ibid.*, pp. 332f.   [36] *ibid.*, pp. 335ff.
[37] cf. *Articles de l'Avenir*, i, pp. 205—12.
[38] See also 'De la séparation de l'Église et de l'État', *ibid.*, i, pp. 23—30.
[39] cf. *ibid.*, ii, pp. 43—7.

should therefore be repealed. Third, freedom of the press: a liberty covered by freedom of speech, the printed word being only an extension of the spoken. 'Let us have faith in the truth.' Fourth, liberty of association, which again is a natural right. The existence of associations is an embodiment and safeguard of individual freedom; to inhibit such a right is to open the way to tyranny. Fifth, universal suffrage: the vote ought not to be the privilege of the affluent. Lastly, administration should be decentralized; its over-centralization in France is 'a deplorable and shameful relic of the imperial despotism'.

These liberties, Lamennais told his readers, would have to be fought for. The means were available. 'Let us organize ourselves legally; let us form a great confederation embracing the whole of France, a vast mutual assurance society wherein each finds the guarantee of his safety and his rights.'[40] 'Should we be but menaced the way of redress is open to us. And if redress is not forthcoming, let us remember that we are a democracy, indeed a republic, that the people are sovereign and that as a consequence it belongs to the people to make and unmake kings.' In face of repression resistance becomes the most sacred of duties.

It was to advance these aims that at the end of 1830 Lamennais founded his *Agence générale pour la défense de la liberté religieuse.* More specifically, its objects were (i) to secure legal redress for encroachments upon the proper liberty of the church's ministers; (ii) to protect all educational institutions against arbitrary government interference with the liberty provided for by the *Charte*; (iii) to maintain the right of all citizens to associate for any legitimate religious, philanthropic or cultural purpose; and (iv) to establish itself as a link between all local associations set up for the defence of religious freedom. Moreover the final number of the *Avenir* called for 'an Act of union proposed to all who, despite the murder of Poland, the dismemberment of Belgium, and the conduct of governments that style themselves liberal, still hope for the freedom of the world and desire to work for it'. The issue, as Lamennais now saw it, was nothing less than that of establishing among the peoples themselves, to the fullest possible degree, 'a great concerted effort to defend, along with religious liberty, all those high and noble franchises which are the common patrimony of all free people'. And that the pope would put himself at the head of this new crusade Lamennais could not doubt. Indeed on the death of Pius VIII, he went so far as to indicate to his successor, whoever he might be, the glorious mission that was now reserved for him. Never, he proclaimed, since the time when the world's deliverance was accomplished was there a more splendid opportunity; an entirely new era in Christianity was opening. The task of the supreme pontiff would be to restore 'the broken balance of

---

[40] *Œuvres complètes,* x, p. 170.

human nature and of its indestructible laws in making once more effective the intimate union of faith and knowledge, of might and right, of power and liberty'. In announcing the suspension of the *Avenir* in view of the opposition of both the government and the hierarchy — it had run for little more than twelve months — Lamennais explained that 'if we retire for a moment it is not from weariness, still less from despondency; it is that we may go, as once upon a time the warriors of Israel went, *to consult the Lord in Shiloh* . . . We leave the field of battle for a moment, in order to fulfil another duty which is equally pressing'.[41]

His words are indicative of the mood of exalted confidence in which, in company with his friends Lacordaire and Montalembert — three 'pilgrims of God and of liberty' — he set out for Rome to plead the liberal Catholic cause before the pope himself. The little party reached the Eternal City on 30 December 1831, after a journey of over a month, 'assez pénible'.[42] But the hoped-for audience with the new pontiff, Gregory XVI, was not immediately granted. When at last it took place, on 13 March 1832, it proved a sadly disappointing occasion, being merely brief and formal, although Lamennais himself affected to be satisfied.[43] He remained in Rome until 10 July — Lacordaire, more quickly disillusioned, had already departed — when he and Montalembert left for Munich, and it was at Munich some weeks later that he was finally apprised of the pope's mind when a copy of the encyclical *Mirari vos* (15 August 1831) was placed in his hands. The letter's contents were for the most part generalities, but its drift was plain enough. The *Avenir* itself was not mentioned, nor was Lamennais named, but the newspaper's doctrines were censured by implication and the pope's judgment was evidently final. The supreme pontiff saw no need for radical reform in the church, nor for its separation from the state, nor for any alliance with liberalism. The encouragement Lamennais and his adherents had given to revolutionary movements was condemned. Even the demand for freedom of the press and of opinion was dismissed as 'imprudent and immoderate'. To Lamennais it came as a bitter blow: 'the condemnation of liberty and the abandonment of Polish nationality', were his words. But he added: 'God has spoken: all that remains for me to say is: *Fiat voluntas tua!* and to serve these two causes by my prayers, since

---

[41] The fact however was that the paper had lost subscribers. According to Montalembert they had 'never amounted to three thousand', and they may well have been considerably fewer. But the attitude of the hierarchy is apparent from a letter of a French bishop to his clergy when he urged them: 'N'oublions jamais l'objet principal de notre ministère: respectons et observons les lois; prenons peu de part aux évènements journaliers qui agitent le monde . . . occupons-nous peu de l'avenir de cette vie, mais pensons souvent, pensons beaucoup à l'avenir de l'autre, à cet avenir qui seul il est important, puisque seul il est éternel' (quoted Vidler, *Prophecy and Papacy*, p. 191).

[42] See Blaize, *Œuvres inédites*, ii, p. 89. Also Forgues, *Correspondance*, ii, p. 232.

[43] The fullest account of the event is that contained in Montalembert's journal. See P. Lecanuet, *Montalembert* (1910–1912), ii, p. 286.

he forbids me by the voice of his vicar on earth to serve them with my pen.'[44] As a Catholic, therefore, he submitted. The provisional suspension of the *Avenir* was confirmed and the *Agence générale* dissolved. Even so, in a private brief to the archbishop of Toulouse dated 8 May 1833, the pope questioned the sincerity of his act, although later, in a personal letter to him, Lamennais once more declared his resolution 'for the future, in my writings and in my actions, to have nothing to do with matters affecting the church' and his submission to 'all decisions that have emanated or that shall emanate from the apostolic see, on the doctrine of faith and morals, as well as any laws of discipline promulgated by its sovereign authority'.[45]

In the autumn he resumed work on his philosophical treatise; meanwhile however he had written the famous *Paroles d'un Croyant*, the publication of which was deferred until the end of April 1834.[46] Its appearance created an even greater sensation than did the first volume of the *Essai*.[47] It has been described as a lyrical version of the *Communist Manifesto*.[48] Certainly it is a most extraordinary utterance, a modern apocalypse in the spirit and style of *Daniel* or *Revelation*, a romantic vision, Christianly inspired, of a juster world than anything that could remotely have been glimpsed on the horizons of contemporary history. In the words of a modern commentator:

Like the prophets of the Old Testament Lamennais believed that he had received a mission from heaven; and in order to strike the tyrants and to cast their insults and blasphemies in their teeth, he shows them in terrifying visions their shame and their ruin; to the men who are victims of an atrocious tyranny he unveils the peaceful horizons of the Promised Land and the splendours of the New Jerusalem.[49]

In manner, as Bautain remarked, it was of a studied naivety, but into it Lamennais had poured all his deepest feelings for the freedom of mankind.[50] 'As you know', he wrote to the archbishop of Paris, 'I am convinced that as nothing can henceforth arrest the advance of political and civil liberty one must try to combine with it order, right and justice unless one wishes society to be rent from top to bottom. That is the goal I have set myself.'[51]

[44] Lecanuet, *Montalembert*, i, p. 325.
[45] See *Affaires de Rome*, pp. 158ff.
[46] The manuscript was finished by June 1833, since Montalembert had read it on the occasion of a visit to La Chênaie at that time. Later the young nobleman besought Lamennais not to publish what he thought could only cause an 'immense scandal'. cf. G. Goyau and P. de Lallemand, *Lettres de Montalembert à La Mennais* (1932), pp. 196ff. Lamennais's name was not printed on the title-page but, rather curiously, on the back cover of the book. cf. Vidler, *Prophecy and Papacy*, p. 244.
[47] 'Ce fut le plus grand succès de librairie de l'époque' Y. Le Hir, *Les 'Paroles d'un Croyant' de Lamennais: texte publié sur le manuscrit autographe*, 1949, p. v.
[48] Laski, *Authority in the Modern State*, p. 255.
[49] Y. Le Hir, *Lamennais écrivain* (1948), p. 329.
[50] Bautain however judged that 'la *machinerie* de l'imagination tient lieu de pensée solide'. See P. Vulliaud, *Les Paroles d'un Croyant de Lamennais* (1928), p. 123.
[51] See *Affaires de Rome*, p. 172.

The *Paroles*, for all its mysticism — not to say mystification — had two very deliberate aims in view: to protest against oppression wherever, despite the approaching triumph of liberty, it still existed, and to urge the need of Christianizing the new democratic order which the future was bound to bring about. But it was the first of these that struck Lamennais's readers most forcibly. To the less sympathetic among them — Bautain, like Newman, thought the author's whole outlook dominated by politics — it was calculated to inflame revolutionary sentiments. Cardinal Lambruschini, papal nuncio in Paris from 1827 to 1831, reported to Rome that 'whoever should call the *Paroles* a new apocalypse, inspired by Satan in order to stir up new scandals in the church and occasion fresh troubles for the world, would be pronouncing an exact judgment.'[52]

Les Paroles d'un Croyant was condemned by Gregory XVI in the encyclical *Singulari nos*, dated 24 June 1834 — to Lamennais's own considerable surprise, inasmuch as he did not himself regard it as containing anything censurable on theological grounds, although he realized it could hardly be welcome to the Vatican and that diplomatic pressure might be brought to bear to secure its condemnation.[53] But with what he had had to say now off his chest Lamennais retired to his beloved La Chênaie in a fairly tranquil frame of mind. He had previously felt himself compromised by his unqualified submission in December 1833, and the publication of *Les Paroles*, as Sainte-Beuve noted, had now dispelled all doubt as to his true position, not least in his own eyes.[54] Yet in a letter to one of his followers, Comte de Coux, written only about a month before the appearance of the second encyclical, Lamennais declared his intention to remain submissive in the church, albeit free outside it. For the church, he was convinced, would undergo 'a necessary transformation', even though no one as yet could say exactly what it would be or how it would be carried through. Meantime 'one should stay united to the existing institution, adhering sincerely to all that is good and true in it, and separated as sincerely from all that is evil and false'.[55]

---

[52] cf. Dudon, *La Mennais et le Saint-Siège*, p. 325. Lamennais was described as 'Robespierre in a surplice'. For other such phrases applied to him or his book see Boutard, *Lamennais: sa vie*, iii, pp. 38f. Also Vulliaud, *Les Paroles*.

[53] The encyclical had called it a 'book ... small in size but immense in its perversity' (*libellum ... mole quidem exiguum, pravitate tamen ingentem*) and had also alluded, somewhat darkly, to a 'fallacious system of philosophy, recently invented', by which presumably was meant the doctrine of the *sensus communis*. Metternich in correspondence with the Austrian ambassador at Rome referred to Lamennais as 'this atrocious man' and regretted in the present instance that the burning of heretics and their works had been abandoned! See Boutard, *Lamennais: sa vie*, iii, p. 76.

[54] *Nouveaux lundis*, i (1891), pp. 39—41.

[55] Quoted C. Perin, *Le Modernisme dans l'Église d'après des lettres inédites de La Mennais* (1881), p. 12; though as to the date cf. Le Hir, *Les Paroles d'un Croyant de Lamennais*, p. 4.

The Last Phase

Lamennais was never formally excommunicated and it is impossible to say precisely when he came to regard himself as having left the church. He spoke of himself quite definitely as a Catholic in the autumn of 1834[56] and it would seem that he was still attending mass as late as 1836. But the further development of his thought in a liberal democratic direction and away from religious orthodoxy is evident from his published works of this period: namely, the long preface, 'Du catholicisme dans ses rapports avec la société', to *Troisièmes mélanges* — a collection of articles chiefly from the *Avenir* — early in 1835; *Affaires de Rome*, published in November 1836 — probably his best-written book; and *Le Livre du peuple*, dating from 1838. In these, and especially the last-named, we have the unmistakable beginnings of the third and final phase of Lamennais's intellectual and moral development. According to Duine indeed it is the first of them which 'can perhaps be considered the public and definitive act whereby Lamennais separated himself from Catholicism'.[57] At any rate the writer is here taking stock of his opinions. The doctrine of the *sensus communis* still seems to him to be true, but also insufficiently clear. He regrets the impetuosity of the *Avenir* campaign and is no longer very satisfied with his attempt to delimit the civil and ecclesiastical in the way he had done. Finally, broadening the issue, he points out that the problem is only a single aspect of the whole vast question of the relations of humanity in general with the spiritual authority as the Catholic church conceives it. In *Affaires de Rome* he muses on the papacy and its future. The state of Catholicism in Europe is far from flourishing; but it might have been revived under wise and clear-sighted leadership from Rome, had Rome not failed it. Instead the Vatican had chosen the secular course of reaction and repression; and Lamennais sees in this the inscrutable working of Providence. *Le Livre du peuple*, a short treatise on ethics, continues the theme of the preceding volume. It voices an unhesitating belief in the progress of the human race under the guidance of religion, but the religion here envisaged is neither Catholicism, which has set its face against progressive movements, nor Protestantism, of which Lamennais remains as contemptuous as ever. What in fact his Christianity now amounted to is not at all certain. The Christian *idea* inspired him still as the great impelling force toward future social good, as a summing-up of all human duty and moral idealism. Nevertheless it is not to be confounded with any of its historic forms, which have been of only partial and transient value. Collectively, however, the benefits which these have conferred upon

---

[56] In a letter to Ballanche, dated 6 October 1834, he writes: 'Je suis catholique et je veux l'être sans que cela m'oblige à adopter [la ligne] suivie par les hommes de la hiérarchie ni en général leurs opinions en ce qui ne touche pas la foi.' See Feugere, *Lamennais avant l'Essai*, p. 364.   [57] *Pages choisies de Lamennais*, p. 13.

mankind are, he thinks, undeniable. The Christianity of history has imbued
the peoples of the modern world with a spirit of justice and kindness unknown to antiquity, and where it has not maintained the integrity of its
own standards the cause is to be found in the uncontrolled passions of
men. So far from despairing of it there is every reason to go on believing
in it once the materialistic garb in which it now appears has been shed.

It may be said, as we have suggested, that Lamennais was now at last
perceiving the real drift of his doctrine of the 'sens commun' and that his
new position was in fact more consistent with it than was the orthodox
Catholicism he had hitherto been defending. The religion of 'tradition', he
was coming to see, was not to be identified simply with Christianity or with
any other type of positive religion; rather was it the basis or essence of
them all when stripped of their local and temporary forms. In other words,
it was the residual belief or body of principles which every religion may
be held to incorporate in one way or another and which enables it to provide,
under its own special conditions, the requisite means to social order and
harmony. Thus what was gradually taking shape in Lamennais's mind was
no longer the traditionalist theory elaborated in the *Essai* but a rationally
conceived natural religion.

The systematic treatise on philosophy which he had for years been
planning, or at least the first part of it, made its appearance in 1840, with
the three volumes already mentioned, dealing with God, man and the
universe.[58] It had no great public impact and sales were meagre.[59] The
truth doubtless was that Lamennais the Catholic turned deist was a less
interesting figure than the turbulent priest-revolutionary. Yet the *Esquisse
d'une Philosophie* may be said to be the crown of his career as a writer and,
although the success of the *Essai sur l'indifférence* was not repeated, it is
in a number of respects a better work, being more detached and more
closely reasoned.[60] In any general account of Lamennais's thought therefore it must be given a place. It may seem odd that a treatise designed on
so ample a scale should have been described by its author merely as a
'sketch': it represents an attempt at a philosophical synthesis as ambitious
as any which nineteenth-century France produced. That it not infrequently
betrays the shifts in Lamennais's own viewpoint over the years is no more
than could be expected.

Its aim, then, is to set forth a comprehensive metaphysic covering the

[58] A fourth, on science, was added in 1846.

[59] In 1847 Lamennais told his Swiss Protestant friend, David Richard: 'Je voudrais finir
L'Esquisse, s'il était possible. Ce n'est que le public m'encourage beaucoup. Les frais
d'impression du 4e volume ne sont pas encore couverts et ne le seront peut-être jamais. Le
silence des journaux en est en partie la cause' (A. Roussel and A. Ingold, *Lamennais et
David Richard*, 1909, p. 103).

[60] On the *Esquisse* as compared with the *Essai* see Janet, *La Philosophie*, p. 101.

whole realm of human knowledge.[61] That philosophy, Lamennais now says, may often shake traditional ideas has simply to be recognized; once the spirit of inquiry is unloosed it cannot be arbitrarily stopped in its course. All the same one has the right to demand that the diverse conclusions reached by individual reasoning be controlled by the unchanging principles of the universal reason.[62] His original criterion of certitude is thus maintained; his method, however, is not epistemological or psychological but ontological, as with the mediaeval scholastic philosophers.[63] The concept of being is seen as fundamental: but for the *fact* of it nothing would exist, and apart from the *concept* of it knowledge would have no starting-point. And being in its ultimacy, as one, infinite, eternal and therefore *necessary*, is what men call God — *He who is*. From this basic truth all other truths respecting the universe and man duly follow.

Every philosophy, in its inception and in its latest developments, proceeds from the fundamental idea of God. Whatever it contains of truth is always proportionate to the degree in which it knows him, just as its character is determined by the manner after which it conceives him. For it never does anything other than to apply to contingent beings its anterior ideas about the necessary Being. That is why it is of sovereign importance to clarify and deepen, so far as our very limited and feeble reason can do, this great concept of God, from which all others are but deductions more or less remote, more or less near.[64]

The idea of God is the root of all our interpretations of reality, whether consciously so or not. For the theist the prime cause is a personal Creator; for the atheist it is creation itself: the finite, the relative and the contingent are as it were 'absolutized', the artifact is confounded with the artificer. In

---

[61] In introducing it Lamennais is modesty itself. See *Esquisse d'une Philosophie*, i, Introduction, and in particular what he says on p. XXV.

[62] It is plain that Lamennais is still far from abandoning the concept of the *sensus communis*; indeed his view of it may be said to have matured. Thus he writes: 'L'humanité conserve et transmet aux générations successives toutes les connaissances indispensables à l'homme, toutes les vérités constitutives de l'intelligence, dont chacun porte en soi le germe impérissable et qui représentent la raison commune; elle conserve encore et transmet la connaissance des faits observés, des faits permanents de l'univers et des faits historiques. L'ensemble de ces connaissances s'appelle *tradition*; et l'on ne saurait se faire une plus juste idée de la tradition, qu'en la considérant comme la memoire du genre humain, au moyen de laquelle il acquiert et possède sans interruption le sentiment de son identité: car il est un, aussi bien que chaque homme, quoique d'une manière différente, et même son progrès parfaite vers laquelle il gravite suivant une loi universelle des êtres' (*Esquisse*, i, pp. 15f.).

[63] Lamennais had always been deeply interested in the great metaphysical systems of the past, Platonism and the philosophies of Malebranche and Leibniz especially. Contemporary influences included Rosmini and Schelling. Schelling he met in Munich, and he may have made Rosmini's acquaintance when in Rome. cf. Janet, *La Philosophie*, pp. 108f.

[64] *Esquisse*, i, p. 51. In a letter of 1841 to Mazzini he wrote: 'Tout l'avenir de l'humanité dépend de sa conception future de Dieu et jusqu'à ce qu'elle se soit formée, le monde, privé de direction, continuera de flotter au hasard, incapable de se fixer, incapable de sortir de la confusion présente.' See Blaize, *Œuvres inédites*, ii, p. 172.

other words, the atheist does not so much deny God as replace him by an
alternative concept. Others again, while allowing that God exists, cannot
admit to any positive knowledge of him. For them he is simply the great
Unknown. Yet they too invest phenomena with some underlying energy
or energies that are primal and eternal. God, that is to say, is acknowledged
under a different guise. Even with dualism the antagonism of the two
opposing principles is itself ulterior to both and in a sense constitutes a
final unity.

Is therefore that ultimate unity which all philosophies thus assume
merely indeterminate and impersonal, or is it personal and the summation
of all perfections? Is it potentiality constantly in process of realization, or
pure actuality, possessing all the fullness of being? Lamennais's own belief
is not in doubt: ultimate reality is wholly determinate and essentially
personal, and is to be thought of under the threefold aspect of power,
intelligence and love. It, or rather he, is power inasmuch as existence implies the energy whereby it is perpetually actualized; intelligence, as possessing a perfection the lack of which would contradict his infinity; love,
because love is the *nexus* between self-realizing power and the intelligence
by which that power is totally informed. 'Considered in his substance the
infinite Being is an absolute unity, so that each of his properties contains
that substance in its entirety.' At the same time these properties, whilst
embodying the whole, are also distinct.

Thus what Lamennais describes is in essence the Trinity of Christian
dogma, virtually in Augustinian terms. The primordial divine power is
symbolized by the Father; the knowledge by which divinity knows itself,
by the Son, or the Word which the Father eternally utters; the love which
it feels for itself, by the Holy Spirit. The first is the principle whereby all
created things subsist, the second that of all intelligence, the third that
of all unity and life.[65]

Lamennais next considers the doctrine of creation. Over the centuries,
he says, it has been conceived in a diversity of ways. It may be thought of
as an emanation from the infinite Being — a view that amounts to pantheism — or as constituted out of pre-existing matter, an idea implying that
God is not infinite.[66] A third concept is that of *creatio ex nihilo*; but the
objection to this, at least in its familiar form, is that besides denoting an
addition to the self-sufficient being of God it postulates what is intrinsically
impossible.[67] The doctrine Lamennais himself prefers states that 'in the

[65] 'Si l'Être se réalise perpétuellement par le Père, s'il se connaît par le Fils, il se sent
ou jouit de lui-même par l'Esprit, qui, en terminant Dieu, consomme intérieurement sa
félicité souveraine.' See *Esquisse*, i, pp. 55f. Janet (*La Philosophie*, p. 111) is probably right
in supposing that this section of the work dates from the author's Catholic days. Mazzini
found too much Christian theology in Lamennais's philosophy.
[66] *Esquisse*, i, p. 101f.
[67] This idea, Lamennais thinks, 'fait intervenir dans la notion de la création un terme qui

creative act all creation, as such, passes from non-being into being'. The Word, or immanent Reason, has within itself the archetypes of all particular existences. 'To create is to produce or realize externally that which formerly had its existence only within the divine mind.' In creating God gives being by drawing it, so to speak, out of himself, 'for clearly no part of being can exist which did not have its source in the infinite Being'. But the act of creation is free, not a determinate necessity of the divine nature itself. It represents as it were a sacrifice on God's part, inasmuch as in bringing other beings into existence he imposes a degree of limitation on his own substance. 'Here', Lamennais says, 'we touch the mystery of creation, and it would be absurd to pretend to be able to penetrate it, since we know that substance, for all finite beings, is radically incomprehensible.'[68] Matter itself is the limiting principle, but at the same time there is no such thing as pure matter, the very idea of which would be self-contradictory ('The existence of anything which limits implies that of the thing which is limited'). Lamennais rounds off his theory with the notion of cosmic progress. All creatures are capable of developing indefinitely, for not only have they their roots in the divine substance, which is inexhaustible, but it is their destiny to accord to it, under the conditions of finitude, an ever larger manifestation. As for the universe itself, just as its continuance in being implies an inherent dynamic or energy so its order and vitality imply an intelligent and life-giving principle. These, in Lamennais's eyes, represent within the order of creation the same attributes of power, intelligence and love which constitute the divine Being. In the universe itself we distinguish the inorganic, the organic and the intelligent.

These different classes of beings, intimately connected with each other, also presuppose one another as the parts of the whole, and under this aspect the universe is but a vast organism to which we give the name of nature, because in sum it is composed of all the diverse natures harmoniously united.

So the hierarchy of created being with its differing degrees points us to the divine. But the actual *process* of the universe has been one of immensely slow development from a primal state of chaos, a truth on which both ancient cosmogonies and modern science are in agreement. Out of a few original forms of great simplicity, that is, a vast number of others of very varying complexity have gradually been evolved. Nevertheless the orderly course of this process has not been without its mishaps. The presence of evil, physical and moral, is everywhere in evidence and cries out for explanation. Following Augustine Lamennais sees it as lying not in any essential defect in the balance or harmony of things but in the sheer fact of limitation or

exclut toute réalité quelconque, ce qui fournit des armes dangereuses pour combattre la création même par l'impossibilité évidente que la puissance, même infinité, s'éxerce sur ce qui n'est pas et ne peut être' (*ibid.*, pp. 102f.).
[68] *ibid.*, i, p. 106.

finitude, a negative not a positive condition.[69] To the objection that in this case God himself must finally be responsible for it Lamennais replies that God indeed is responsible for what from the standpoint of finite intelligences will be *seen* as evil; but finite intelligence does not and cannot view it in respect of the *whole*. 'Seeming disorder is but order itself established and maintained by the eternal laws which control the development of God's handiwork.'[70] In other words, the cause of what to us is evil is that necessary conditioning and limitation apart from which there could be no creation at all. To complain that there is evil in the world is to complain of existence itself. Here the influence of Leibniz is apparent, except that instead of saying that this *is* the best of all possible worlds Lamennais would rather claim that it is on the way to becoming so. For he believes progress to be continuous and that new heights of attainment always lie ahead. Suffering therefore must be accepted as no more than incidental to the process.[71]

The doctrine of original sin Lamennais rejects: the *Genesis* story is only a symbol of what occurs in individual experience. Every man, that is, is born innocent, but innocence is not a perfection because reason and conscience are not yet awake. As soon however as these begin to emerge man is on the way to acquiring the knowledge of good and evil and the liberty — along of course with the possibility of moral failure — which goes with it. Under no other conditions could our humanity be conceived. Moreover the notion of an hereditary transmission of sin is self-contradictory so long as the *moral* significance of sin depends on volition and personal responsibility.[72] What man should have in mind is not a lost virtue but those possibilities of rational and ethical advance which are always open to him and by means of which the quantity of evil can be steadily reduced, although from the nature of things never entirely eliminated. In the meantime the persistence of evil is itself the spur to progress.

Lamennais's discussion of human achievement in science and industry, art and society need not detain us, although what he says on art in particular is still worth reading. Taken as a whole the *Esquisse d'une Philosophie* is remarkable for the boldness with which it attempts to synthetize all knowledge on the basis of a theistic metaphysic. Its essential weakness is in its author's continued use of the idea of the *sensus communis* as the real criterion of truth; a criterion furthermore which he himself quietly drops whenever it suits his purpose. For the fact is that the so-called general reason

[69] 'Consideré en soi, dans sa notion la plus générale, le mal n'a rien de positif, il n'est qu'un moindre être' (*ibid.*, ii, p. 18).

[70] *ibid.*, pp. 20f.

[71] Suffering, Lamennais contends, is 'un bien, un immense bien; elle est un développement inappréciable de l'être, développement limité néanmoins en dépendence de certains conditions qu' implique son essence même' (*ibid.*, p. 23. cf. pp. 27, 40).

[72] *ibid.*, pp. 58f.

affords of itself no guarantee that the knowledge which it supposedly embodies is well-founded and not a perpetuation of error arising from ignorance. In the *Essai sur l'indifférence* Lamennais's position was at least consistent in that he accepted the traditional system of Catholic dogma in its entirety, but in the *Esquisse*, and especially in its later chapters, he picks and chooses, disregarding tradition when it suits him to do so in favour of that same individual reasoning in which hitherto he had discovered only the germ of all evil, intellectual and social. Thus he retains the Christian concept of God as fundamentally necessary to human society but jettisons that of original sin and its consequences because in conflict with his personal belief in social perfectibility. It is of significance also that in neither work is the doctrine of Christ's redemption given any prominence: the author's real concern always lay elsewhere.[73]

The *Esquisse* was hailed by some of Lamennais's later admirers — Béranger, Vitrolles and Hauréau, for example — as a major event in the history of modern philosophy, but among the less sympathetic it met with severe censure. One of the keenest of his former disciples, Rohrbacher, denounced it as the work of an apostate who today repudiates what he yesterday extolled and proclaims as an original discovery what he has merely imbided from others: 'Dans cet état de ruine, son exposé ne travaille qu'à se ruiner toujours davantage.' In the main, though, reviewers were cool rather than hostile. Jules Simon in the *Revue des Deux Mondes* characterized the book as an attempt to create a system of doctrines 'whereof no prestige of style can disguise the radical inadequacy'. This time, unhappily, Lamennais had not so much disturbed his readers as failed to interest them.

After the revolution of 1848 he turned to active politics, founding *Le Peuple Constituant* (February to July) in order to lend his support to the newly-created republic. On 23 April he was elected to the Constituent Assembly as a deputy for the Seine and a year later to the Legislative, where he sat on the extreme Left. He also continued his political journalism as editor of *La Réforme*. But with the *coup d'état* of 2 December 1851 he retired into private life and devoted himself to his translation of Dante, the Introduction to which — in the event unfinished — became to all intents an anti-papal diatribe. He died on 27 February 1854, a recluse. To the end he declined the ministrations of the church and was buried, without religious ceremony, in a common grave at Père Lachaise, in accordance with his own wishes.

Lamennais's influence on nineteenth century thought — bearing in mind the fame he achieved during his lifetime — is not altogether easy to assess. In the field of Christian apologetics he at first made an immense impact,

[73] Fr George Tyrrell's summary of Lamennais's views — 'What all religions agree in, he holds to be true' — is not unjust. See *The Faith of the Millions*, 1st series (1901), pp. 139f.

exposing the inadequacy of the old methods and substituting for them a new and, in the circumstances of his times, considerably more attractive type of religious philosophy. Much-needed improvements in the programme of clerical studies may likewise be attributed to him. But if romanticist traditionalism reached its apogee in the first volume of the *Essai sur l'indif-férence* it thereafter declined, and following sharp criticism from more than one quarter was listed in Pius IX's *syllabus errorum* of 1864 and formally condemned six years later at the Vatican Council. The fideistic and onto-logistic note in Lamennais's doctrine, however, was to re-echo in French Catholic philosophy for some time to come before its eventual silencing by the Thomistic revival of the eighteen-seventies. Whether the modernism which made its appearance towards the close of the century owed much directly to him or indeed to liberal Catholicism generally is doubtful, the later movement being, rather, a spontaneous intellectual response to the predicament of faith in a world that had changed greatly since Lamennais's day.[74] What on the other hand does not admit of question is the impetus he gave to ultramontanism, if not indeed to the form in which it eventually triumphed.[75] It is equally certain that the traditionary Gallicanism of the French clergy was greatly shaken by the attacks he made on it. In fact the paradox of Lamennais is his combination of ultramontanism with liberal-ism — a paradox resolved for him personally only when Gregory XVI made plain to the world that the papacy, although gratified by so fervent an assertion of its authority and claims, could not endorse it at the price of swallowing the liberal and democratic theories that accompanied it. Never-theless the period of the *Avenir* venture, although ending as it did in the anti-ecclesiastical apocalypticism of *Les Paroles d'un Croyant*, left a lasting mark on French Catholicism: thenceforward the church had to take up the challenge of democracy in a spirit no longer merely negative, even if final reconciliation with the republic was to remain a still distant goal. Lamennais's deep sense of commitment to the 'people' and his anguished call for social justice make him, moreover, a pioneer of the social Catholicism of men like La Morvonnais, Armand de Melun and Léon Harmel, except of course that politically he was far more radical than were they.

On the stage of secular politics his influence has been varyingly estimated. Some have seen in him the forerunner of the Christian Democratic politics of the present century.[76] Such a view need not be contradicted, but should not be exaggerated: Lamennais was not a constructive political thinker, still less a practical politican. He was a visionary revolutionary, the

---

[74] cf. A. R. Vidler, *The Modernist Movement in the Roman Church* (1934), p. 51.

[75] See Appendix II, p. 290 below.

[76] cf. M. P. Fogarty, *Christian Democracy in Western Europe, 1820–1953* (1957), pp. 155f., as also R. Havard de la Montagne, *Histoire de la Démocratie chrétienne de Lamennais à Georges Bidault* (1948).

prophet of a coming era of social emancipation and renewal, when the masses would at last be freed from the oppression of centuries. Others therefore have been able to discern his figure even behind Marxist communism.[77] But this again is to read too much into the attitude of one who, for all his support of the *Comité démocratique socialiste*, was in no real sense a socialist doctrinaire. Today it is neither for his Christian philosophy nor his revolutionary idealism that he is best remembered. What retains posterity's interest is the man himself, with his strangely divided personality and the indefinable quality of genius which pervades all that he attempted, rendering his very failures impressive by their pathos.

Lacordaire and Montalembert

Of all Lamennais's associates and followers Henri-Dominique Lacordaire and Charles de Montalembert stand out most prominently. They it was who had accompanied him on the ill-starred pilgrimage to Rome in 1832. Trained for the law, the former (1802—1861) had not always been a believer by rational conviction. 'I have an extremely religious soul', he once wrote, 'and a very unbelieving mind', adding, 'but as it is in the nature of the mind to allow itself to be subjugated by the soul, it is probable that some day I shall be a Christian.' At the time he was twenty, and the next two years brought about his intellectual conversion. He continued nevertheless in his liberal political views, having, as he confessed, 'not been able to hide all that separated me in this respect from the clergy and Catholics of my time. I felt myself alone in these convictions, or at least I met no mind that shared them.'[78] When however he met Lamennais, who in his eyes 'exerted more influence and possessed more authority over the younger clergy than did the bishops and cardinals', he at once threw himself into the liberal movement. Yet although an effective contributor to the *Avenir* his personal relations with Lamennais were never very intimate. He perceived more quickly than did his over-sanguine leader the implications of the pope's aloofness, and when at length the blow fell which shattered Lamennais's hopes his own doubts about the Mennaisian doctrine had already begun to grow. The appearance of *Les Paroles d'un Croyant* only confirmed his misgivings. He even went so far, in an article in the *Univers* of 2 May 1834, as to announce that the Mennaisian school had ceased to exist and that each of its members, 'faithful to what his heart demanded of him in regard to the past', now recognized no other guide than the church.[79] However this

[77] So Laski, *Authority in the Modern State*, p. 255. G. D. H. Cole (*Socialist Thought, the Forerunners 1789—1850*, 1953, pp. 189—200) maintains that Lamennais 'influenced Marx a good deal more than Marx himself realised' and calls attention in this regard to the former's essay, *De l'esclavage moderne*.

[78] Comte d'Haussonville, *Lacordaire* (1910), p. 22.

[79] *Œuvres complètes*, vii, pp. 33f.

might in fact have been — and the judgment was precipitate — his own position was made plain in *Considérations sur le systeme philosophique de M. de La Mennais*, published in May 1834, in which he sought to refute the new philosophy and to argue the superiority of traditional methods.[80]

Lacordaire agrees that individual reasoning in religious and moral matters, as Bonald had earlier insisted, offers no reliable road to faith and that philosophical systems produced in this way, brilliant though they may appear, contribute little or nothing to the spiritual education of humanity or the promotion of Catholic truth. At the same time Catholic tradition, founded on divine revelation, has certainly not taught the infallibility of the general reason or regarded it as the criterion of supernatural knowledge. In any event the notion itself is vague and incapable of precise definition, and all the more dangerous on that account.[81] For it confuses not only theology with metaphysics but also the specific revelation in Christ, upon which the Christian religion rests, with that primitive and general form of revelation imparted to man at the beginning; although Lacordaire admits that the early Fathers were prompt to see anticipations of Christian truth in pagan philosophy. Indeed he has now come to think the doctrine of the *sensus communis* 'le plus vaste protestantisme qui ait encore paru'. Lamennais's most conspicuous fault, however, was in having failed to stress the unique authority of Christ himself and of the community which lives by his divine spirit. It is not the human race as such but the Catholic church that is the repository of the infallible tradition of belief, a tradition going back ultimately, through the synagogue, to the Old Testament patriarchs. Lamennais was right in the first volume of his *Essai* to demonstrate the need for authority in religion, but the collective reason of sinful mankind cannot itself provide that authority. It is precisely because the human race does *not* possess it that an infallible Church is necessary and has been established by Christ for the purpose.

Lacordaire himself distinguishes four different sources of knowledge: the principles of logic, which in themselves are purely abstract and give no information about existence; empirically ascertained facts, as in science, the area of which is nevertheless limited; society as the teacher of moral principles and the basic tenets of natural religion; and finally the Catholic church,

---

[80] B. Chocarne, *Le R. P. H.-D. Lacordaire, sa vie intime et religieuse* (5th ed., 1879), endeavoured to minimize Lacordaire's involvement in the liberal movement generally. But see H. Bremond, *Gerbet*, especially pp. 15f.

[81] See e.g. *Œuvres complètes*, vii, pp. 129f. and 138f. 'La grande erreur de M. de La Mennais', Lacordaire wrote, ' . . . a été de vouloir fonder une école philosophique, et d'espérer que cette école serait le lien des esprits, la base de la religion, le salut de la société. Il n'y a pas eu depuis Jesus-Christ une erreur plus décevante que celle-là. Jusqu'alors . . . la philosophie n'avait été dans l'Église qu'une *préparation à la foi* par la démonstration des vérités religieuses accessibles à la raison, et qu'une *confirmation* de la foi par l'explication vraisemblable des vérités inaccessibles à la raison. Jamais la philosophie n'était allée plus loin dans l'Église' (*ibid.*, p. 107).

as the teacher of revealed religion and its related ethic. His own role as a priest, he had become convinced, was to be that of a preacher, proclaiming Catholic truth in its integrity to an audience consisting (as he hoped) mainly of unbelievers or deists. The outcome of this resolve was the famous series of lecture-sermons — the *genre* was one that he made peculiarly his own — which he gave from time to time in the cathedral of Notre Dame de Paris, with the somewhat hesitant approval of Mgr de Quélen. The first series, on the Church, was delivered in 1835 and created a profound impression on its hearers, whose interest had already been quickened by both his *Avenir* articles and a previous course of his at the Collège Stanislas.[82] It marked, in fact, a new era in French Catholic preaching and a decided break with the Gallican tradition as maintained by Frayssinous and his like. Subsequent courses dealt with church teaching in general, its nature and sources (1836), the effect of Catholic doctrine on the mind (1843), on the soul (1844), and on society (1845) respectively, and the doctrines of Christ (1846), man's relation to God (1849), and the fall and redemption (1850—1851) — in all seventy-five addresses composing a thoroughly comprehensive programme of instruction.[83] Lacordaire believed that the best way to catch the attention of the *jeunes incrédules* was to relate the church's teachings, and especially those regarding its own nature and claims, to the needs and aspirations of contemporary society. Thus in effect his message was a continuation of that of the first part of the *Essai sur l'indifférence*, in appealing to the secular world to return to the authority of Catholic order, *la société des hommes avec Dieu*. Man, he declared, is 'a being who has to be taught',[84] and for that very reason is always exposed to deception. The church exists basically therefore as an authority teaching the truth. Like all other authorities it disposes of power, though its own power consists not in force but in the dual persuasion of reason and charity. Its right to teach, which it does infallibly, derives from its possession, by virtue of its divine origin, of the highest rational certitude along with the highest moral authority. Within the church the pope is the head of the hierarchy, exercising an historic spiritual supremacy sustained by an incorruptible divine revelation. To the question why, if the church is necessary to human welfare, its appearance in history was so long delayed, the answer is that before Christ God had already provided for mankind's salvation through tradition and conscience.[85] In

---

[82]See T. Foisset, *Vie du R.P. Lacordaire* (2nd and revised ed., 1873), i. c. vii.

[83]A similar course given at Toulouse in 1854 dealt with the moral and spiritual life. The *Conférences de Notre Dame* were published in four volumes, 1844—1852. The Toulouse series appeared in a single volume in 1857. See J.-D. Folghera, *L'Apologétique de Lacordaire* (1911).

[84]*Conférences de Notre Dame*, i, p. 17.

[85]'Notre premier père apprit de Dieu même quelle était (sa) fin, d'où il venait et où il devait tendre; il pénétra d'un regard, en entendant Dieu parler, tous les secrets et tous les ressorts de sa destinée; sa lumière extérieure, vivifiée et rassurée par cette lumière extér-

the matter of its relations with the temporal power its own responsibility is the propagation of supernatural truth and virtue, which it can do only under those conditions of freedom to which both divine and natural right entitle it. When the church is at liberty to pursue its intrinsic mission the truth of Christianity will be demonstrated in the benefits it confers upon society.

But Lacordaire's addresses aroused criticism as well as enthusiasm. His method of procedure was itself novel, beginning, as it did, not with God but with the church, and many of the older clergy openly disapproved. He neglected the traditional authorities — the schoolmen, Bellarmine, Suarez — and his ultramontanism was uncongenial. What at first was not appreciated was that the speaker was seeking to provide not mere conventional textbook 'instruction' but a presentation of the faith as a genuinely rational option to all, especially among the young, who felt it to lack relevance or meaning. He wanted, as he put it, 'to have his feet on the ground of living reality'.[86] To this end he drew, as occasion demanded, upon philosophy, psychology, history and social theory with the intention of offering not so much a systematic treatise in apologetics as a personal *confessio fidei* in which he could explore intellectual and moral problems in terms of current debate. His concern was to avoid technicalities and abstract argument in order to dwell on those aspects of belief to which his hearers could most easily respond. It was the sense thus conveyed of the preacher's own involvement in the issues raised — aided by his singular skill as an orator — which kept his audience alert and receptive.

Montalembert's connexion with Lamennais began at about the same time as did Lacordaire's, but in spite of differences of viewpoint — in particular his own staunch monarchism and belief in aristocracy as contrasted with Lamennais's republican liberalism — there was a greater degree of affinity between Lamennais and the young nobleman than between the former and Lacordaire, and their friendship soon ripened. The Comte de Montalembert (1810–1870), a fervent Catholic, shared to the full Lamennais's ideal of a free church as the focus and instrument of a nation-wide religious revival. He collaborated enthusiastically in the *Avenir* venture, which he did much to finance, besides supporting the less radical *Correspondant* as well. He also joined the *Agence générale pour la défense de la liberté religieuse* and became one of its directors. It was as a member of this organization that, along with Charles de Coux, he opened a 'free school' in Paris on 10 May 1831 in defiance of the authorities, an act which ended in his trial by

ieure, se repose dans la paix combinée de l'évidence et de la foi. La fleuve de la tradition avait jailli de Dieu dans la conscience de l'humanité' (*ibid.*, pp. 83f.). Lacordaire here shows himself still to be attached to traditionalist ideas.

[86] As he wrote to Foisset in April 1834 concerning his College Stanislas lecture-course: 'J'expose la *doctrine catholique* en suivant son cours naturel dans l'histoire; je la prends comme existante, comme un edifice digne d'être étudié' (*Lettres du R.P. H.-D. Lacordaire à Theophile Foisset*, 1886, i, p. 256).

the upper house of parliament which he had himself just entered on succeeding to his father's peerage. His speech in his own defence turned out indeed
to be a memorable event. The publication of *Mirari vos*, however, inevitably
created tension between Montalembert's loyalties as a churchman and as
the friend and disciple of Lamennais, and by 1833 this became acute.
Lacordaire's abrupt change of heart especially grieved him. In May 1833
he produced his translation of Mickiewicz's *Le livre des Pèlerins polonais*,[87]
token enough that he still stood firmly in the liberal camp, but at the same
time he did his best to restrain Lamennais from precipitate action, both
personally, while staying with him at La Chênaie, and subsequently by letter
from Germany, whither he went in August that year. But his efforts to dis-
suade him from publishing *Les Paroles* were unavailing, and when *Singulari
nos* appeared he urged him to submit, as he did himself in a letter of 8
December 1834 to Cardinal Pacca.

From 1834 to 1836 Montalembert kept out of the public eye, residing
mainly in Germany where he renewed his acquaintance with Schelling,
Baader and Görres, and also came to know Ignaz von Döllinger. But in
1837, after his marriage, he entered political life, although he did not abandon
his studies, and certainly not his struggle on behalf of the liberal Catholic
cause, as he now conceived it. He still adhered to the motto, *Dieu et la liberté*,
and the fight was now concentrated on the educational issue.[88] In this he
was strongly supported by the ultramontane Louis Veuillot in the *Univers*,
as too by the *Correspondant*, which had lately been revived. He even succeeded
in winning some measure of episcopal approval. Nevertheless the opposition
remained formidable. In face of it his aim was to unite militant Catholic
opinion in a political party, the *Comité directeur pour la défense de la liberté
religieuse*, which had for device the legend 'Dieu et mon droit'. Its organ was
to be the *Univers*, but it had also the support of the *Correspondant*. Its
headquarters were of course in Paris, but diocesan committees were set up
in the provinces. The result was that in the elections of 1846 one hundred
and forty deputies were returned to parliament with the avowed intent
of securing complete freedom for religious education.

Montalembert's main literary achievement was his famous *Les moines*

[87] Montalembert did little of the actual translating, since his knowledge of Polish was
slight. See P. de Lallemand, *Montalembert et ses amis dans le romantisme 1830—1840* (1927),
p. 321. But he contributed a foreword to it that left no doubt where his sympathies lay.
Lamennais was influenced by the book when writing his *Paroles d'un Croyant*. cf. E. Forgues
(ed.). *Lettres de Lamennais à Montalembert* (1898), p. 133. The Gallican journal, *L'Ami de la
Religion*, described it as 'un éloge continuel de la révolte et une philippique contre les
souverains' 14 September 1833, p. 307).

[88] The ultimate outcome of the campaign was the passing of the *Loi Falloux* of 1850,
establishing freedom of secondary and higher education subject to state inspection. Thus
the monopoly of the *Université* was broken. But not all Catholics were satisfied. Extremists
like Veuillot denounced it as a miserable compromise. See C. S. Phillips, *The Church
in France 1848—1907* (1936), pp. 35—40.

d'Occident depuis Saint Benoît jusqu'à Saint Bernard. About 1835, after the appearance of his *Histoire de Sainte Elizabeth,* he conceived the idea of a life of Saint Bernard with the ulterior motive of publicizing the religious orders. To present his subject in full historical context he felt obliged, though, to carry his survey back to St Benedict himself. Thus the study of the great Cistercian, published in 1847, became the nucleus of a much more ambitious work, which by 1867 had extended to five volumes. It reads now as rather the *plaidoyer* of a rhetorician than a critical history, since its obvious purpose is to edify.[89] Yet although many dismissed it for its credulousness — and its use of mediaeval legends is lavish — there were not a few among his Catholic readers who detected a rationalistic bias.

Montalembert lived long enough to hear of the summoning of the Vatican Council in 1869. 'He received the news', says Lecanuet, 'with astonishment and rejoicing. But as soon as the real purpose of the Council became suspected [he] changed his tone.' Montalembert's sympathies had always been ultramontane, but he disliked despotism, and not least when it wore an ecclesiastical garb. A definition of papal infallibility, whether or not one held it as a personal belief, would, he feared, only heighten a risk which the policies of Pius IX — 'the Louis XIV of the papacy', as he dubbed him — had already done over-much to induce. Hitherto, as in the matter of the 1864 *Syllabus,* he had differed from that stalwart opponent of infallibilism, Dupanloup, bishop of Orleans. Now they joined in a common protest, although Montalembert himself had no illusions about the outcome. He did not however live to see the doctrine promulgated to which he was so opposed.[90] No profound thinker, but an ardent and generous spirit and man of honour, he had given liberally of his personal energies and his substance in the causes of both the church and freedom.

[89] Another of Montalembert's causes was the appreciation of Gothic architecture. This likewise was connected with his religious convictions — 'cet art est à mes yeux catholique avant tout'; the Renaissance and neo-classical styles he considered secular and pagan. Gothic art was 'la manifestation la plus imposante de l'Église dont je suis l'enfant, la création la plus brillante de la foi que m'ont léguée mes pères' (*Œuvres complètes,* vi, p. 8). He believed that in order to be faithful to his mission the artist, like the priest, ought to be simple, 'l'homme de Dieu et du peuple' (*ibid.,* p. 26). Montalembert, like Mme de Staël, counselled his fellow-countrymen to look to Germany, where the spirit of the middle ages was still much stronger than it was in France, as 'la patrie de l'art régénéré, la seconde Italie de l'Europe moderne'. His enthusiasm for things Teutonic grew indeed with knowledge. In July 1834 he wrote to Lamennais from Munich: 'Je me suis donc décidé à me livrer exclusivement à l'étude du passé, où mon cœur, mon imagination et ma foi trouvent encore des aliments; et nulle part le moyen âge n'est exploité, étudié, dévoilé comme en Allemagne; j'y trouve chaque jour de nouvelles ressources, de nouvaux trésors tirés depuis peu de l'oubli; en un mot, j'ai ici ce qui me manquerait complètement à Paris: *les livres et les hommes,* qui s'expliquent et s'éclaircissent mutuellement.' See G. Goyau and P. de Lallemand (edd.), *Lettres de Montalembert à Lamennais* (1932), p. 181.

[90] It is said that when a friend asked of him what he would do were the doctrine to be defined by the Council in union with the pope, he replied calmly, 'Eh bien, tout simplement je croirai'. See C. Butler, *The Vatican Council 1869—1870* (ed. Christopher Butler, 1962), p. 253.

6

THE FIDEISM OF LOUIS BAUTAIN

Bonnetty and Annales de Philosophie Chrétienne

The defection of Lamennais and a change of heart in some of his best-known disciples did not mean that traditionalism ceased to have a voice among Catholic intellectuals. For many years afterwards — in fact down to the very eve of Leo's XIII call to the Catholic world for a renewed study of St Thomas Aquinas[1] — the traditionalist theory was stoutly maintained by a layman, Augustin Bonnetty (1798–1879), in the periodical, *Annales de Philosophie chrétienne*, which he himself founded in 1830 and of which he remained editor until his death. A Provençal by birth, Bonnetty had at first thought of the priesthood, but decided that as a layman he would enjoy a greater independence of mind. Lamennais's *Essai sur l'indifférence* had impressed him profoundly, so much so that his whole life-effort was to be devoted to justifying and developing what seemed to him to be the only satisfactory religious philosophy: that, namely, which sees in Christianity the one universal belief whose basic tenets no age or civilization has really lacked. In his first editorial, 'De la Religion dans ses rapports avec la science', he reminded his readers that faith ought always to be a stimulus to understanding and showed no diffidence in describing himself as a 'conciliateur entre la science de Dieu et celle du siècle'.[2] But despite the review's title its contents were at first of more interest to the historian than to the philosopher. Proof of the doctrine of the *sensus communis*, Bonnetty held, could be derived from a systematic study of man's remoter past. His own contributions covered a wide range of subjects, including geology, palaeontology and prehistoric archaeology, which last, he believed, would provide ample confirmation of the historicity of *Genesis*. More apologist, in fact, than dispassionate inquirer, he met the differing theories of the geologists with the rejoinder that 'it does not matter to us which system one adopts provided it accords with that of Moses'.[3] Influenced to some extent by Eckstein, he was in general agreement with the interpretation of ancient religions set out in Creuzer's *Symbolik*.

New advances in philosophy and philology also won his attention, particularly in the field of oriental languages, he himself being a member of the Paris

[1] See below, p. 181.
[2] *Annales de Philosophie chrétienne*, i, p. 13.   [3] *Annales*, iv, p, 346n.

Asiatic Society. He greatly admired the Egyptologist Champollion, considering the decipherment of the Egyptian hieroglyphics as 'perhaps the most serious and important event of our epoch'. He had an interested eye, too, for the antiquities of the Americas, the nature of which, in his opinion, demonstrated how right were Maistre and Bonald to have seen in modern savages the descendents of civilizations that had long since fallen into decay. He was always on the look out for scraps of folklore, from whatever quarter, which could be taken as authenticating the biblical history.[4] But his presiding concern was with the philosophy of history.

One begins to understand [he wrote] how all religion as a whole rests on tradition: on history, that is to say, not upon reasoning. One has also to recognize that if for some time past Christianity and the beneficent influence of the Church upon the destinies of peoples have come to be better appreciated, this is attributable to historical discoveries, and above all to progress in that area of historical science which bears the name of Philosophy of History.[5]

One of Bonnetty's collaborators, Sylvestre Foisset, superior of the seminary of Dijon, expressed the firmest belief in the educational value of historical study, and not least in theology. 'History', he declared, 'is the essential and primitive element in education ... Catholics, let us study history; today our strength lies there, as too our glory.'[6] For the proper understanding of dogma a knowledge of its historical evolution is indispensable.

Why then do we not make history the basis of theological teaching? ... It is on the gradual development of Christian dogma, revealing itself from day to day in councils and tradition, that we would wish theological instruction to be concentrated.[7]

For apologetic purposes he also advised the study of modern anti-Christian or anti-Catholic writers such as Benjamin Constant or Saint-Simon.[8]

In the realm of pure philosophy Bonnetty saw to it that the *Annales* kept up a steady critique of scholastic Cartesianism, and although in 1855 a ruling of authority obliged him to modify his strictures the review continued to proclaim its faith in the capacity of Catholic thinking, in accord with liberalism in politics and romanticism in letters, to adjust itself to the needs of the contemporary world.[9] Bonnetty himself consistently stressed the necessity of

[4] e.g. *ibid.*, p. 59. Bonnetty had great faith in the ability of archaeologists to prove the truth of the patriarchal stories. Resemblances among ancient national traditions he welcomed as evidence of mankind's universal kinship (cf. *ibid.*, ii, p. 210). (The article is entitled: 'Des déluges. Synchronisme des annales indiennes et chinoises avec la Genèse relativement à l'existence et à l'époque du déluge universel.')

[5] *ibid.*, xi, p. 401.

[6] *ibid.*, iii, pp. 29f.

[7] *ibid.*, iv, pp. 143f.

[8] *ibid.*, p. 139.

[9] *Annales de Philosophie chrétienne* continued publication down to 1913 (see below, p. 248), and in its last years was a forum of Modernist opinion. Under the editorship of abbé Charles Denis it became, in A. L. Lilley's words, 'almost the official organ of theological liberalism in the Church of France' (*Modernism: a Record and Review*, 1908, p. 27).

4

giving an 'honourable place' to the humane sciences in the curriculum of ecclesiastical studies 'in order', as he put it, 'to be able to follow the sometimes vagrant course of world civilization'.[10]

We should note that traditionalism as a philosophy was not by any means confined to France, even though its best-known and most influential exponents were French. Germany was least responsive to it, Belgium perhaps the most. But it had its representatives in Poland, with Felix Koslowski and Valerian Sernatowski, and in Spain — in an extreme form — with Donoso Cortès, Marquès de Valdegamas. These writers are not our concern, but its Italian advocate, the Theatine (formerly Jesuit) Gioacchino Ventura di Raulica (1792—1861) is of interest here, both for his association with Lamennais, whose condemnation he tried to prevent (in spite of his own criticisms of the *Avenir* policy), and for his sojourn (for political reasons) in France, where he acquired a considerable reputation as a preacher.[11] In a course of addresses delivered at the Madeleine in Paris in 1851, published under the title *La raison philosophique et la raison catholique*, he outlined his personal position. Philosophies, he held, fall into two main groups: the speculative, which aspire to the discovery of new truths solely by the exercise of reason, and the demonstrative, which see their task as simply the justification of truths known from tradition. The first comprises the various types of rationalism, ancient and modern, whose unreliability is evident from the way in which they contradict one another. The second is the truly Catholic philosophy, represented by the Fathers of the early church and by the mediaeval scholastics. For although reason may be capable of valid conceptions at the phenomenal level it does not yield certitude in spiritual matters and cannot attain to the knowledge of God even when it comprehends the need for such knowledge. Hence the necessity of divine revelation, the content of which is handed down from generation to generation in the form of *tradition*. But this does not imply that in the realm of religion reason can only be silent; for although it could not have discovered truths of this order by itself it can elucidate and verify them. Faith, that is to say, is and must be antecedent to reason.

Ventura's preaching aroused some controversy, among his critics being Victor de Bonald, the philosopher-statesman's son. In reply Ventura brought out a further work in which he sought to render more precise account of his own ideas in relation to Bonaldianism.[12] Bonald he judged right in denying

[10]Bonnetty's literary energies were not confined to the pages of the *Annales*. In 1836 he took over direction of the *Université catholique*, which Gerbet and Salinis had founded. Here he concerned himself especially with clerical training and its deliverance from what he regarded as the dead hand of scholasticism.

[11]See A. Cristofoli, *Il pensiero religioso di P. Gioacchino Ventura* (1927); also pp. 176—9 below.

[12]'L'esprit humain, en connaissant les choses spirituelles par la révélation, peut s'en rendre compte, les discuter, les développer, les démontrer, les appliquer. Mais il ne les invente pas, il ne les découvre par la raison; seulement, il les connaît, mais par la révélation, en sorte que

to man any capacity actually to invent language but wrong in assigning to
tradition a knowledge which reason itself was quite capable of discovering.
On the other hand Ventura seems to have laid himself open to the charge
of 'Mennaisianism' for having failed, like the author of the *Essai sur
l'indifférence*, to draw any proper distinction between natural and supernatural faith, thus in effect identifying theology with philosophy.[13] To this
his answer was that as in the ordinary concerns of life there is a natural 'faith'
which in fact precedes reason so, in regard to supernatural truth, there are
'preambles' which it is the function of reason to justify.

'A French Newman'

A rather different approach to the problem of religious belief was that of
Louis Bautain, another strong opponent of rationalism of any kind. Bautain
sees faith as an independent and self-justifying principle in a way markedly
reminiscent of Newman.[14] Moreover, as with Newman, temperament and
personal experience go far towards explaining the nature and standpoint
of his religious philosophy. Not indeed that he possessed the complex and
nuanced qualities of mind which distinguish his great English contemporary;
nor does he disclose the same grace and persuasiveness as a writer. Compared too with Lamennais his light shines more dimly: he had neither
Lamennais's powers of leadership nor his imaginative brilliance. Yet as a
thinker he was by no means the inferior of either. Certainly he never succeeded in making anything like the same impression on public opinion in
France as did Lamennais, and for the most part he has been neglected by
Catholic historians.[15] Yet his influence on the religious thought of his
century was extensive and even had its repercussions in Modernism.[16]
Bautain also resembled Newman (though not Lamennais) in his marked
deference to authority and at all stages of his career he was ready to modify
the public expression of his opinions when they gave offence, a fact which
sometimes makes exact interpretation of them difficult.[17]

vouloir atteindre la connaissance des vérités immatérielles sans révélation d'aucune espèce,
même naturelle et sociale, est aussi insensé que vouloir obtenir la vision des choses physiques
sans lumière' (*La raison philosophique*, ii, Préface, pp. xlviiif.).

[13] *De la vraie et de la fausse Philosophie* (1852). Ventura's case against rationalism was restated in *La Tradition et les semi-pélagiens de la philosophie* (1856).

[14] See R. M. Horton, *The Philosophy of the Abbé Bautain* (1926), p. 297. Horton's book remains
the best assessment of Bautain's teaching yet published.

[15] See, e.g. the sketchy and biased article in the *Dictionnaire de Théologie catholique*, li, coll.
481–4. cf. Hocédez, *Histoire de la Théologie*, ii, p. 74 ('La philosophie de Bautain est tombée dans
l'oubli').

[16] Horton goes so far as to describe Bautain as 'a Modernist before the Modernists' and as 'one
of the grandparents of Modernism'. This is an overstatement. It all depends on what is to be
uderstood by Modernism, a very complex phenomenon.

[17] As with Newman, Bautain's work is more occasional than systematic. The reader often has

Louis-Eugène-Marie Bautain was born in Paris in February 1796 and brought up as a faithful Catholic. He entered the École Normale in 1813, where he was a pupil of Victor Cousin and a fellow-student of Jouffroy and Damiron, with both of whom he formed close friendships. Here the attractions of philosophy, as represented by Cousin's eclecticism, completely seduced him. The result was that his not very sophisticated religious beliefs suffered eclipse. Indeed the cultivation of the intellect became for him itself a kind of religious devotion. But Cousin's teaching also had in it a strong admixture of Platonism, an influence which his young disciple was to imbibe with lasting effect.[18] On graduating, at the age of twenty, Bautain was appointed to a teaching post at the Collège Royale at Strasbourg, where – as it is said – his success was instant.[19] Cousin naturally was delighted and invited him on a tour of Germany to meet some of that country's leading philosophers, including the great Hegel, who is reported to have been much struck by the young Frenchman's abilities. He also met Fichte and Jacobi, to both of whom his own thinking was in some respects indebted. His outlook at this time was, like his master's, eclectic. The untrammelled human will, he considered, is fundamental and might accomplish anything. 'Pure liberty', the eager young lecturer would say, 'is the goal of human life.' And to its attainment reason of course was the only guide.

Then suddenly a change occurred, totally ending what Horton calls 'the Promethean phrase' in Bautain's development. In March 1819 he had a breakdown in mental health which left him (as in the instance of J. S. Mill) in a state of acute depression and nervous exhaustion. Quite unable to work, he seems even to have contemplated suicide. His recovery sprang largely from his friendship with a middle-aged spinster not only pious but unusually erudite, Mlle Louise Humann, niece of the archbishop of Mayence, Mgr Colmar. He first met her at Baden, but the acquaintance was renewed at Strasbourg, where she herself had lately come to reside, and it quickly ripened. She it was in fact who may be said to have brought about his reconversion to Catholicism.[20] In Bautain's own words, 'it was a treasure I had discovered . . . I had never met any woman or any person who talked [on German philosophy] more pertinently and more clearly'.

to guess at the pattern of thought that underlies the published statement. cf. Foucher, *La Philosophie catholique en France au xixe siècle*, pp. 70f.

[18] A work of Bautain's published posthumously in 1868, *Les choses de l'autre monde: journal d'un philosophe recueilli et publié par l'abbé Bautain*, is recognized as being in large measure autobiographical. See E. De Regny, *L'abbé Bautain: sa vie et ses œuvres* (1884), a book which Horton rightly regards as indispensable for the study of Bautain: it is so still. Cousin's once-famous book, *Le Vrai, le Beau, et le Bien*, although not published until 1836, was based on a lecture-course of 1818.

[19] cf. Regny, *L'abbé Bautain*, p. 11.

[20] Her place in Bautain's life was in some ways comparable with that of Mme Swetchine in Lacordaire's. See Mme Fliche, *Une Françoise d'Alsace: Mlle Louise Humann*, (2nd ed., 1921).

I acquired the conviction ... that Christian doctrine is philosophy's crown, or if you will, her last word ... How I had been led to this conviction, in truth, I could not tell in detail. But at any rate I had arrived there, ... led by the luminous and affectionate words of my good angel, who without ever imposing anything upon me, ... simply answered my needs as fast as they made themselves manifest ... Never was a man's liberty more fully respected, and never, too, was it more fully conquered.[21]

One influence in particular for which Mlle Humann was responsible was that of Franz von Baader of Munich (1765—1841), whose own type of thought, vitalistic and mystical, represented something quite different from what German philosophy had hitherto stood for in Bautain's mind.[22] He also undertook a renewed study of Kant, whose teaching on the incapacity of reason in the metaphysical realm he now saw in a new light. For he had himself been brought almost tragically to the realization that abstract philosophizing is unable to grapple with the problems of life at its deeper levels. He resumed his practice as a Catholic at Einsiedeln in Switzerland, where he made his confession nearly two years after his first meeting with his 'good angel'.

Restored to health at last, Bautain re-commenced his lectures in 1821 with a course on metaphysics. But he now was an altered man. The rationalism which he previously had espoused with such happy confidence he completely repudiated. His personal experience had taught him no longer to place his trust in the natural capacities of man, and quite certainly not in reason as the current philosophy seemed to understand it. In this regard Kantianism reinforced his own judgment. Henceforward not only speculative idealism but the traditional scholasticism would have to be ruled out. The mystery of existence was to be fathomed, if at all, by some more penetrating faculty. In fact, from the standpoint of abstract reason, Bautain's position was virtually one of complete scepticism; which for an academic teacher of philosophy in the prevailing atmosphere of eclecticism was altogether anomalous. The authorities were offended and for a time suspended him from duty.[23] He took the opportunity of his new-found leisure therefore to prepare himself for the priesthood, though the bishop of Strasbourg, de Trévern, spared him the usual course of seminary training on the convenient grounds that he was already sufficiently well qualified. Accordingly he was ordained at the end of 1828.

Already Bautain had become the centre of a 'school' comprising Protestants as well as Catholics and even a number of Jews, three of whom — Théodore Ratisbonne, Isidore Goschler and Jules Lewel — were won over to

[21] Regny, L'abbé Bautain, 53f., 60f.
[22] See below, pp. 128f.
[23] Bautain's new frame of mind caused no slackening of his activity, and to his existing degrees in letters, law and theology he now added (encouraged by Mlle Humann) others in medicine and experimental science.

Christianity.[24] To these years belong also his earliest published writings: *Variétés philosophiques* (1823), *Propositions générales sur la vie* (1826) — a study in genetic psychology — and *La morale de l'Évangile comparée à la morale des philosophes* (1827).[25] But it was his essay *De l'enseignement de la Philosophie en France au xixe siècle* which first caught the attention of the general public and before long brought him an acclaim rivalling that of Lacordaire, whose star at this time was well in the ascendant.

Preliminary, however, to an attempt at more detailed study of Bautain's thought, whether as adumbrated in the latter work or as fully articulated in his *Philosophie du Christianisme*, it is worth while to note some revealing remarks of his in a letter to the rector of the Collège Royale at the time of his suspension. Dated 1 July 1822, this letter provides us with a brief sketch of his whole religious philosophy as subsequently worked out.[26] In it Bautain categorically states that his teaching, although apparently novel in form, 'is simply *Platonism* purified by the light of Christianity'. The seeming novelty stems from the fact of its having to be adapted to the needs of his audiences, including as these did many Protestants and Kantians. For Kant, he thinks, is to be praised for having 'brought back many minds from gross material-ism', if not to revelation and faith, at least 'to the conviction that reason can know nothing above the world of the senses, and to the despair of ever lifting themselves by its aid to the higher world'. Further, Kant's antinomies clearly prove that the human reason 'can demonstrate the *pro* and *con* with equal success so far as ultimate questions are concerned'; whence, philosophically speaking, the grounds for 'indifferentism in things metaphysical and divine'. Thus when one faces a combination of Kant's negative criticism with the Protestant tendency to *rationalize* religious dogmas one begins to appreciate the difficulty of addressing the sort of audience he himself was used to on the subject of metaphysics. To pursue the argument in a merely abstract way would be fruitless. For of what use is learning if it does not make men *better*? Their need is for practical truth, as this is contained in the Christian gospel.

I therefore [he continues] announced Plato as my chosen master; and I expounded his teaching, as far as I could, in terms of the pure forms of mathematics. I made the light of the Gospel dominate the spirit and form of my discourse, and without my speaking positively of the fundamental dogmas of Christianity they became evident through the facts of nature and its laws.

All attempt to *prove* the basic truths of Christianity on purely rational prin-

[24] Among those of Bautain's disciples who afterwards themselves attained to prominence were Henri de Bonnechose, subsequently a cardinal, and Alphonse Gratry, who unlike others remained loyal to his master's original teachings. Another follower was Eugène de Regny, to whose book on Bautain reference has here been made.

[25] For a complete list of Bautain's publications see Regny, *L'abbé Bautain*, Appendix D.

[26] It is among the Bautain papers preserved at Strasbourg. Others are at Juilly. See Horton, *The Philosophy*, pp. 73ff.

ciples is to misconceive their very nature and deny faith its real character.
'God, I told my hearers, cannot be demonstrated by reason': by the methods
that is, of either equation, deduction or induction. 'God is the Universal, the
Infinite, the Absolute. Can reason then conceive Him and embrace Him?'
And in phrases that Newman might have used Bautain goes on to declare:

I do not think that a passionate or wretched man can be calmed or consoled by
arguments. Syllogisms have no power against the soul's distress or the heart's
agitations. Something loftier and deeper is needed: namely, faith in God, the feeling
of His activity within us and His providence over us, surrender to the higher Will —
none of them things that reasoning will ever yield.

It is possible to believe in God whilst ignoring or rejecting the familiar arguments for theism. 'There is not a rational proof of the existence of God to
which an equally cogent disproof cannot be opposed.' (Again, Newman
comes to mind.) Indeed the God of philosophy is not the God of religious faith.
Divine things cannot be judged in terms of reason, being beyond its range
and sphere.

When we speak of God, the question is not to prove that it is impossible he should
not exist; the problem is to make men feel that he does exist.

And this is to be achieved, if at all, only by self-mortification, faith and insight.
The reality of God is a datum apart from which no metaphysics is possible;
a reality, moreover, which needs to be *sensed*, registered subjectively in an
affective reaction. The real proof of God is that which he himself renders
'by his action upon our hearts, and by the mediating action of Nature upon
us'. Reasoning follows upon such experience, but is not its precondition.
Bautain ends with a reference to the effect of his teaching on his audience:

I showed them [he says] the divine activity working upon men from the moment
of their birth, seeking to penetrate their hearts . . . I had the joy of seeing my words
take effect, and the seed take root in the soil which had been apportioned to me.
Doubts were dissipated, and a secret and simple faith scattered the clouds of reason.

Bautain's fideism never received more forthright expression. Such views,
when afterwards stated publicly, were to land him in trouble with his bishop;
but at present Mgr de Trévern thought so well of him as to give him charge
of the *petit séminaire* at Strasbourg, a responsibility which the still inex-
perienced priest, aided by some of his friends, undertook with enthusiasm,
especially as it involved a complete reorganization of the curriculum. At
the same time he retained his place in the faculty of letters at the university,
despite the political changes brought about by the events of July 1830. Rather
surprisingly he continued to enjoy the encouragement and support of Victor
Cousin.

A Critique of Contemporary Philosophy

Bautain's *De l'enseignement de la Philosophie en France au xixe siècle* came out in 1833.[27] A mere brochure of ninety-one pages, it was no more than a pointer to the contents of the lecture-courses which his friends had been pressing him to publish; its primary aim was negative and polemical. For with the then existing state of philosophical teaching in France he was profoundly dissatisfied. *La philosophie, voilà notre dernière ressource!* he had exclaimed; but it was now manifest that by *philosophie* he meant none of its current forms. These he distinguishes under five different heads, criticizing each in turn and as far as possible in terms one of another. First there is the 'sensualism' of Condillac and the ideologists, powerfully influential at the close of the preceding century but now in decline. Its fatal weakness being its atomistic psychology, it ends by reducing man to a bloodless abstraction or a mere mechanism in which 'the will, the *foyer* of life' has no place.[28] The Scottish philosophy, introduced into France by Royer-Collard of the Sorbonne, is next considered. Clearly its empiricism has much to be said for it, since it at least bases its arguments on concrete facts; while unlike Condillacian materialism it allows room for the soul and morality, if only as 'primitive facts' or 'first principles' whose existence has to be assumed. All the same, its methods produce no adequate results: too many assumptions are involved and on ultimate questions it is altogether silent, thus in effect abdicating philosophy's proper role. 'One should not give the name of *science* to descriptions which at bottom explain nothing.' Mere 'monographs on the faculties, no more consistently related than the treatises of our Physics courses or the chapters of our Physiology text-books, do not yield the science of man'.[29] In any case the inherent defects of the Scottish philosophy were finally exposed by Kant.

Turning to the eclecticism in which he had himself been nurtured, Bautain grants that it tries to understand man in respect of the human race as a whole and not simply the individual; but instead of any genuine doctrine of its own its substitutes only the history of philosophy, with no criteria for making any meaningful choice between one school and another. By identifying itself with all doctrines at once it merely 'perverts the mind'.

Having dealt with what may be called the 'secular' positions, Bautain now concentrates his fire on targets nearer to hand, namely scholasticism and the new philosophy of 'common consent'. The first he sees as really little more than a moribund tradition. In place of a living doctrine it offers only a sterile methodology, the spirit of the original having been exorcized by Cartesian rationalism. Descartes's aim had been to free reason from faith, so as to allow it — supposedly — to reach metaphysical truth solely by its

---

[27] In a subsequent edition it was included in the author's *Psychologie expérimentale*, which appeared in 1839.
[28] *Psychologie expérimentale*, p. xix.
[29] ibid., p. xxv. cf. *Philosophie du Christianisme*, ii, pp. 33ff.

own light. The immediate result was of course deism; but the church's own teaching was also profoundly affected by it. For faith was now made to rest on syllogisms, while the philosophy taught in the seminaries had degenerated into a pointless formalism, a kind of intellectual gymnastics. The *philosophie de Lyon*, still indeed enjoying much episcopal patronage, was the final outcome of this sorry process.[30]

But does the Mennaisian doctrine present an acceptable alternative, as its upholders claim? Bautain thinks not; on the contrary, he launches a vigorous attack on it. He objects, in the first place, that it has no authentic 'principle of knowledge', in that between man and the world of experienced fact, which it is the task of reason to comprehend, this philosophy interposes only human *authority*. The general testimony — if such it is — can lead us to *believe*, but it cannot make us *see*, there being no knowledge without evidence. By invoking tradition as an infallible law from which there is no appeal 'it attacks the most noble prerogative of man, his liberty, by which he has the power to grant or refuse his assent to that which is set before him'.[31] Plainly, then, this so-called philosophy is not really a philosophy at all, since it concedes no autonomy to reason. Nor is it properly Catholic; for God himself is the only truly infallible authority: the 'general testimony', founded upon mankind's own history, represents no more than human judgment. All it can presume to establish is that in the main the majority is right.[32] It is even ineffective as apologetic. It gains little sympathy among the young, 'who desire *evidence* and not authority, who desire to see the truth for themselves and not to receive it on the testimony of another'. 'They have not considered it possible to philosophize by proxy, nor do they judge that common sense absolves a man from the need of knowledge, or that men collectively had been entrusted with the job or thinking for each.' Mennaisianism appealed chiefly to the ecclesiastical schools; beyond them its influence was slight.[33]

Yet Bautain also admits to a large measure of agreement with Maistre, Bonald and Ballanche. Is he then, in spite of his criticisms of Lamennais, to be counted among the traditionalists after all? For light on this question note should be taken of a lengthy statement of his ('Sur le sens commun') to the *Revue Européenne*.[34] In it he re-affirms his opposition to the basic principle of the *sensus communis* as providing no adequate foundation for either metaphysics or religious faith. But he concedes that Lamennais's apologetic has been successful against both rationalism and contemporary idealism: the

[30] The classic statement of the 'Lyons philosophy' is Valla's *Institutiones philosophicae, auctoritate D. D. Archiepiscopi Lugdunensis*, published in 1792.

[31] *Psychologie expérimentale*, pp. lviif.

[32] *ibid.*, p. lx.

[33] *ibid.*, pp. lxif.

[34] vi (1833), pp. 637–73. The *Revue européenne* was founded in 1831 as an offshoot of the *Correspondant*, in which Mennaisian ideas were consistently publicized.

speculative reason alone will not discover ultimate truth. Again Bonald was right in insisting that language is necessary to thought, for reason 'cannot develop spontaneously and as it were by its own effort'. 'Neither man in general, nor a people, nor an individual, has ever had this initiative in his development.' The normal thing is for a man to receive what he knows from society at large. But traditionalism as expounded by Lamennais makes the fatal mistake of trying to see in common consent the sole criterion of truth. For of itself the collective reason has no surer access to the highest truths than has individual reasoning. Knowledge of these comes by the word of God alone, which constitutes a specific revelation to be received by faith.[35] And the repository of this revelation is not the *sensus communis* of mankind but Scripture and the Church, following the Synagogue. The Mennaisian doctrine has misled a whole generation and is certainly not the philosophy for which Europe is still waiting.[36] What is wanted is a true science of man — his nature as a moral being, his laws and his destiny; a science of man, that is, in his relation to the absolute and the eternal. This the natural sciences, necessary as they are for their purposes, cannot supply. At the same time such a philosophy must rely on *evidence* as its criterion of truth, for whatever the abuses of rationalism may have been no philosophy can rest merely on authority.

Bautain's own position in regard to the traditionalists is then very largely to agree with them in what they deny but to criticize them in what they affirm. Their rejection of a narrow and doctrinaire intellectualism is fully to be endorsed, but the substitution for this of an external authoritarianism is equally unacceptable. Authority has its rightful place as a guide, unquestionably. The child has its parents' authority; the disciple his master's; the 'outer man and the truths which bear upon his self-preservation', that of society.[37] So too with the authority of the church: it is necessary for pedagogical purposes, for without authoritative teaching there can be no knowledge of the gospel. But the instruction received, from whatever source, is always to be verified in experience, and in the end faith will give place to sight.

De l'enseignement de la Philosophie en France met with a good deal of criticism. The Lamennais school were understandably displeased, but apart from one rather scurrilous anonymous publication they did not openly attack it. Not so, however, with the seminary theologians. A widely-read Catholic journal, the *Ami de la Religion*, at once took up a hostile stand, trouncing the author for what it considered his slip-shod thinking. Moreover among his strongest

---

[35] cf. *Philosophie du Christianisme*, i, p. 175: 'Il faut qu'une parole supérieure vienne lui (man) annoncer les principes, lui dire que Dieu est, qu'il est créateur, et il faut qu'elle croie cette parole, sous peine de rester païenne et ignorante.'

[36] The phrase 'L'Europe attend une philosophie' Bautain took from Bonald, whose *Recherches philosophiques* had particularly impressed him. cf. *Philosophie du Christianisme*, i, p. 328.

[37] *Revue européenne*, vi, p. 650.

opponents were two members of the Strasbourg *grand séminaire*, abbés Liebermann and Raess.[38] Both were scholastics of the most rigid type who considered Bautain's anti-rationalism as virtually a heresy. In this indeed they could rely on a fair amount of support from the Strasbourg clergy generally, among whom the Bautain group were not especially popular. The upshot was intervention by the bishop of Strasbourg who, himself worried at the direction Bautain's teaching appeared to be taking, drew up six questions to which he demanded specific answers. These Bautain supplied, readily and fully. But the bishop was still not satisfied and issued an *Avertissement* to the clergy of the diocese warning them of the dangerous tendency of the doctrines now being promulgated in their midst and listing six 'orthodox' counter-propositions, copies of his statement being sent to Rome and to the entire French episcopate. Shortly afterwards Bautain and his associates were dismissed from their posts at the *petit séminaire* and inhibited from preaching.[39]

By this time the dispute had become something of a public *cause célèbre*. With Strasbourg divided into two mutually opposed theological camps the newspapers took the matter up and pamphleteers got hurriedly to work. In France itself, the home of rationalism, Bautain's views were on the whole received coolly, but in Germany J. A. Möhler at Tübingen came out firmly on his behalf.[40] At Bonn, on the other hand, where Georg Hermes wielded

---

[38] B.-F.-L. Liebermann of Mayence, author of *Institutiones theologicae*, a much-esteemed but utterly unoriginal textbook, had strong ultramontane leanings. He had been Jesuit-trained. His pupil, Andreas Raess, a man of some ability, was appointed superior of the *grand séminaire* in 1831. cf. Hocédèz, *Histoire*, ii, pp. 320, 323.

[39] cf. J. Burnichon, *La Compagnie de Jésus*, ii, p. 428. Burnichon describes the six propositions as of 'doubtful orthodoxy'. adding: 'C'était un curieux conflit que celui qui mettait aux prises l'évêque, dépassant la mesure dans la défense des droits de la raison, et l'universitaire exagérant ceux de la foi.' The propositions in question were:

i. Le raisonnement peut prouver avec certitude l'existence de Dieu. La foi, don du ciel, est postérieure à la révélation; elle ne peut donc pas être alléguée vis-à-vis d'un athée en preuve de l'existence de Dieu.

ii. La révélation mosaïque se prouve avec certitude par la tradition orale et écrite de la synagogue et du christianisme.

iii. La preuve de la révélation chrétienne tirée des miracles de Jésus Christ, sensible et frappante pour les témoins oculaires, n'a point perdu sa force et son éclat vis-à-vis des générations subséquentes. Nous trouvons cette preuve dans la tradition orale et écrite de tous les chrétiens. C'est par cette double tradition que nous devons la montrer à ceux qui la rejettent, ou qui, sans l'admettre encore, la désirent.

iv. On n'a pas les droit d'attendre d'un incrédule qu'il admette la résurrection de notre divin Sauveur, avant de lui en avoir administré des preuves certaines, et ces preuves sont déduites de la même tradition par le raisonnement.

v. L'usage de la raison précède la foi, et y conduit l'homme par la révélation de la grâce.

vi. La raison peut prouver avec certitude l'authenticité de la révélation faite aux Juifs par Moïse et aux chrétiens par Jésus Christ.

The documents in this affair, preserved in the episcopal archives at Strasbourg, were published in summary in the *Ami du Clergé*, liv (1937), pp. 622–4.

[40] The university gave signal proof of this by awarding Bautain an honorary degree in theology.

influence, he was opposed.[41] In the midst of the controversy Bautain published what was to be his most important work, *La Philosophie du Christianisme*.[42] Although not amounting — despite its bulk — to a fully articulated metaphysical system, the book develops its author's previously stated ideas in both scope and detail and must be considered as among the most impressive attempts at a Catholic apologetic which the century has to offer, in no wise inferior to Newman's *Grammar of Assent*, published thirty-five years later. But before taking a closer look at it and the mode of thought which it represents — and it has shown itself capable of more than one interpretation — we may note the outcome of the Strasbourg dispute. The bishop, as already stated, sent a copy of his *Avertissement* to Rome, but the Vatican, concerned at that moment with the case of Hermes' allegedly heterodox *rationalism*, delayed to act in the matter of Bautain's imputed *fideism*. For where precisely, in the heat of current controversy between rationalists and anti-rationalists, was the line of a safe judgment to be drawn? Temporarily at least Rome was not prepared to commit itself. In France however attempts were made at mediation and Bautain himself was anxious to counter a possible charge of heresy by signing an agreed statement, more particularly as a committee of theologians appointed by the bishop to look into his teachings had reported on them not unfavourably. Then at Lacordaire's suggestion Bautain and one of his followers, Bonnechose, travelled to Rome to present their case to the pope personally. They were received with courtesy, but as with Lammenais before them the hoped-for answer was delayed, the task of examining the Strasbourg doctrine having been entrusted to the eminent Roman theologian Perrone, who evidently was in no haste to finish his work. In any event Bautain and his companion had pledged themselves to accept the verdict whatever it might be. Meanwhile Mgr de Trévern, weary by now with the whole business, appointed a coadjutor to settle the matter once for all as far as the diocese was concerned. Unfortunately for Bautain the man named for this office was his long-standing critic, Raess, whose opinion, as was to be expected, left Bautain no quarter. The latter therefore, having already pre-empted himself with his promised submission to an authoritative judgment, had no option but to recant his errors. On 8 September 1840 he signed a second formulary, more or less identical in substance with the original six propositions presented to him seven years

[41] See E. Baudin, 'La philosophie de Louis Bautain', in *Revue des Sciences religieuses*, i (1922), p. 22.
[42] Two volumes, 1835. The book is in the form of a series of letters, collected and edited by H. de Bonnechose, written by Bautain to individuals among his friends and followers, namely Adolphe Carl, Ratisbonne, Goschler and Lewel. The case for Christianity is argued as against the Jewish position, with Carl as go-between. How far Mlle Humann assisted in its production is not clear, although her authorship has been claimed for certain of the letters. cf. *Louise Humann, par une arrière-petite-nièce* (1937).

previously.[43] His action in so doing, however, was in effect a repudiation of his principle that faith is ultimately verified not by external evidences or rational argumentation but in personal experience. Nor, even so, was this his final submission. On 26 April 1844 he brought himself to sign yet a third such document.

From 1840 onwards Bautain's career gradually ceased to arouse public interest. The thirties had been his great decade. Also by now his patroness was dead and his circle of followers, after taking over the college of Juilly in the hope of carrying their educational schemes further, had broken up. Eventually men like Ratisbonne and Bonnechose dissociated themselves from him completely. Still more regrettable was his own apparent loss of confidence in his most characteristic ideas. His deference to authority verged on the obsequious and when faced with censure he could readily persuade himself that he really had fallen into error. He continued to lecture, to write voluminously and to publish, but his later works are guarded in expression and in content seldom rise above the conventional.[44] For the space of ten years (1853—63) he taught moral philosophy at the Sorbonne, his colleagues there including Maret and Gratry, but although his courses were well attended the days when he could fire the imagination of the most varied audiences were past. Inspiration had been stifled by official intolerance. Bautain died in 1867.

A Rationale of Faith

But to return to *La Philosophie du Christianisme*. When it made its appearance in 1833 the French intellectual scene was already a good deal changed from what it had been when Lamennais published his famous *Essai*. Eighteenth-century attitudes, typified by Condillacian sensualism, had become a thing of the past. Romanticism now dominated the literary stage. In its theoretic and speculative form it came as a frontal attack on everything associated with academicism and philosophic intellectualism. The mood of the younger men under the July monarchy was affirmative and enthusiastic, not cool and sceptical. They were deeply conscious of a *besoin de croire* and longed for the appearance of some new creed capable of embracing all their manifold

---

[43]The two most important changes in the 1840 text were the substitution for the original propositions v and vi of the two following:

1. 'Sur ces questions la raison précède la foi et doit nous y conduire.'

2. 'Quelque faible et obscure que soit devenue la raison par le pérché originel, il lui reste assez de clarté et de force pour nous y guider avec certitude à l'existence de Dieu, à la révélation faite aux juifs par Moïse, et aux chrétiens par notre adorable Homme-Dieu.'

[44]Bautain's later publications include the first two parts of his projected *Philosophie*: the *Psychologie expérimentale*, re-issued in 1850 as *L'Esprit humain et ses facultés*, and the *Philosophie morale* of 1842, re-issued in 1866 under the title *Manuel de Philosophie morale*. In *Les choses de l'autre monde* and *La Religion et la liberté considérées dans leurs rapports*, consisting of addresses which he gave in Notre Dame de Paris in 1848, Bautain's earlier voice is still to be heard.

spiritual hopes and insights no matter how paradoxical. The common sentiment now was for the totality of things, an aspiration increasingly nurtured
on the obscure but potent doctrines of German idealism. What they were
seeking was not only a new aesthetic involving a fresh conception of nature
but a new *art de vivre*, in fact a new religion. A question, however, which
occurred to not a few was whether after all the old religion, revivified and
reinvigorated, might possibly be able to supply it. Thus from the standpoint
of the Christian philosopher the problem was not only to combat a doctrinaire atheism but to channel the new urge to believe into courses wider and
freer than the dry and unimaginative school-doctrine which was all that
the ecclesiastical establishment seemed capable of offering. To the Strasbourg
group the latter, as we have seen, had become the target of unsparing criticism; but what had they — since they repudiated Mennaisianism — to put in its
place? Polemic was not enough; the younger generation was looking for
positive guidance, for the satisfaction of an awakened spiritual longing. To
meet just this need was the purpose of Louis Bautain in the ambitious work
which he now gave to the public. And in this respect, it should be remembered, he was the first to act. The *Essai sur l'indifférence* had created a furore
in its time, but its author's more systematic treatise was still in process of
composition and when at last it did appear in 1840 it was no longer the product of a Catholic. Buchez's less weighty enterprise, itself plainly indebted
to Bautain's work, belonged to the same year as Lamennais's.

La Philosophie du Christianisme was designed as apologetic in, so to speak,
a new key, a specific example of how Christian faith might be presented
to the intellectual mood of a fast-changing age. The appeal predominantly
is to the 'heart' (in Pascalian language) — to the imagination, that is, and the
will. Persuasion of the reason has its place but is not a first priority. The true
and convincing verification is a practical one, the pragmatic *Taste and see!*

'It will not be your reason, or all the reasons put together', says the Master, 'that
will give you the certitude of the intrinsic truth of the divine Word. Only itself can
testify to the truth; and to this end you must . . . receive it, and you must taste it, even
as one can judge of a fruit only by eating it.'[45]

But to appreciate the force of Bautain's argument one has to consider his
philosophical position more generally, as this emerges not only in the
Philosophie du Christianisme but elsewhere in his writings.[46]

[45] *Philosophie du Christianisme*, i, p. 309. There is a pronounced strain of pragmatism all
through Bautain's thinking. It is for him a primary test of religion that it should 'work'. On the
other hand he neither says nor implies that the meaning of truth in this or any other sphere
is merely equivalent to its practical effect. The will has a leading role, but the independent
demands of the intelligence must also be met. Nevertheless what constitutes for him the
'irrefutable proof' of God's existence is not any argument drawn from inferior nature or the laws
of reason but from man's own felt *need* of God. Here he is with Coleridge and Newman.
[46] The *Philosophie du Christianisme* does not itself offer a complete system of philosophy, and for
some idea of what such a system might have been had Bautain succeeded in producing it there

For in abandoning the familiar rationalism, which as a disciple of Cousin he had taken more or less for granted, Bautain by no means turned his back on philosophy as such. He does not say that 'faith' is all or that in religion the demands of reason can be ignored. In the order of *experience* faith does come first, and is bound to do so. But faith is under obligation to seek understanding and to render a just account of its own certitudes.

An authentic Christian philosophy must, then, avoid two manifest errors, one of which — Bautain is insistent — is an arid intellectualism. The God of metaphysics, he repeats, is not the God of the Bible and the Christian life.

Do you realize [he asks his Jewish friends] that between a true Israelite and a deist there is the same difference as between a civilized man and a child growing up in savagery? The God of the deist is force, nature, fate, destiny: He is a general Cause, assumed to exist because the reason demands such for the effects which it perceives, ... a gross image, ... or else a rational entity, an abstraction, an idol of the mind. And that is what you would substitute for the God of Israel and of Moses, the living God who created man in His image, animated him with His Spirit, and preserved him with His Providence.[47]

But if scholasticism and deism are blind turnings for the Christian philosopher German idealism is certainly not less so. For the danger here is pantheism, which destroys the biblical conception of God completely, admitting in its stead a new and more insidious rationalism: insidious because of its fundamental subjectivism and moral solipsism. We formerly, says Bautain, were offered, as the science of man and nature, 'experiments, particular observations, deceptions, words'. But:

Today there is first laid down the Idea, the principle which each bears within himself. The Idea contains everything; all that remains to be done is to open it out and draw from it its consequences, which everyone deduces, as a matter of fact, in a way to suit himself, so that our scientific systems took very much like poetic creations ... Hence great confusion in doctrine, though supposedly one; any amount of obscurity regarded as profundity; and an immense vagueness miscalled universality.[48]

is notable evidence in an unpublished early manuscript (1823/24) in the possession of the Congrégation des Dames de Saint-Louis at Juilly entitled 'Philosophie, théologique et métaphysique' (*Fonds Bautain* v, 10). In this he dwells on the need for philosophy to take due account of the empirical knowledge afforded by the natural sciences, whilst at the same time renewing its spirit by contact with theology. By 'theology', however, it is clear that Bautain does not mean a self-consistent body of dogmas or doctrine so much as a *théologie expérimentale* — a 'practical' theology of the living experience that lies behind the formulated system. He even speaks of freeing the 'fundamental dogmas' of Christianity 'of all scholastic subtlety, of every historical addition, of everything that the speculative reason, depending always and necessarily on the senses, on times, places and circumstances, has added to it'. It is the experience itself, he urges, that must be offered to simple faith, 'the condition *sine qua non* of all knowledge'. Philosophy's own task, as he conceives it, is that of synthetizing or unifying knowledge by the light of this basic experience. Strictly speaking it is the science of man himself, as distinct from that of nature or of God. It has to be said, however, that Bautain's view of reality as an organic whole in which one part provides an exact analogue of another leads him to some fanciful conclusions.

[47] *Philosophie du Christianisme*, i, pp. 209f.   [48] *ibid.*, pp. 161f.

As for the subjectivism:

Behold these proud philosophers who wish to write with all the dignity of high morality, the triumph of independence! They talk incessantly about the Absolute, yet they know only phenomena ... Enclosed as they are in the narrow sphere of their own understanding they cannot escape the law of contradiction which prevails there ... They think themselves heroes of virtue, of disinterestedness, of magnanimity; yet they do not see that the *Ego*, as the sole principle of their actions, is also their fate, that Egoism is a vicious circle in which they are caught.[49]

The terminology of absolute idealism varies from one thinker to another, from a Fichte to a Schelling and from a Schelling to a Hegel; but underlying all these systems are certain shared concepts which religiously speaking add up to pantheism, with its confounding of God and the universe. Whatever the emotional attractions of the pantheistic *Weltanschauung* ethically it is disastrous and Christian philosophy can have nothing to do with it.

But how is a genuinely Christian metaphysic to be defined, when rationalism and idealism have alike been eliminated? On what lines, if any, can the intellectual justification of faith proceed? Bautain's answer reveals his essential Platonism, clad though it is in a romanticist garb. Speculative reason, as the ground of certitude, has demonstrated its bankruptcy; Kant himself had shown its impotence in the metaphysical realm. But the Kantian argument only leaves us in a state of agnosticism.[50] For the certitude which is founded on objective knowledge we have to go back to Plato with his doctrine of a transcendent Absolute in which we see 'all that the Greek genius can produce of grace and lofty nobility'. Ideas, pure essences, as Plato understands them, are not the creation of the human mind and so lie beyond the range of Kant's criticism. The world of the senses can be left to the empirical interpretations of science, the limitations of which Kant has made plain; but the *intelligible* world can be known only by revelation. Plato's own attitude no doubt has its shortcomings; he has 'more light than warmth and affection', and in his philosophy 'truth was rather contemplated and admired by the intelligence than received in the heart, tested and practised'.[51] Nevertheless his basic insight remains profoundly true; whereas with Aristotle Greek philosophy took a plunge into rationalism and sophistic, in which the spirit of his great master disappeared.[52]

[49] *ibid.*, i, pp. 63f.

[50] 'Ici je vous renvoie aux antinomies de Kant, où vous verrez les plus forts arguments pour ou contre l'existence de Dieu, opposés l'un à l'autre, s'équilibrant, se neutralisant ou s'effaçant, comme les termes positifs et négatifs dans une équation, et donnant pour résultats zéro, d'où Kant conclut que la métaphysique est impossible ... Cette décision est le coup le plus rude qui ait jamais été porté au rationalisme' (*ibid.*, ii, p. 75).

[51] 'La philosophie platonicienne, si brillante en théorie, s'est montré stérile et vulgaire dans la pratique de la vie' (*ibid.*, i, p. 360).

[52] cf. *ibid.*, i, p. 363. 'La doctrine d'Aristote ... isole l'homme du Ciel, le soustrait aux inspirations sublimes, obscurcit l'intelligence, rétrécit l'horizon intellectuel, empêche le génie de prendre l'essor, si elle ne le tue, et va fatalement aboutir au panthéisme systématique' (p. 362).

The theory of ideas, however, needs to be Christianized, after the manner of the early church Fathers. For the Alexandrians — Clement and Origen — and of course Augustine, Bautain reserves the highest praise. It was they who pointed to the source and explanation of the Platonic ideas in the one divine Being,[53] man's knowledge of the truth coming not by *anamnesis*, for which experience furnishes no evidence, but by revelation, apprehended by faith. Yet they also realized that faith needs the illumination of understanding, since the word of God, far from inhibiting human reason, brings to it the stimulus that enables it to reach its highest goal.

All the same Bautain's Platonism draws nourishment from contemporary sources as well, in particular Baader, as already remarked. Baader's teaching, which was in the current romanticist vein, has a decidedly theosophist bent, encouraged by his study of Eckhart, Boehme and Friedrich Christian Oetinger.[54] Reality he envisaged as a series of 'regions' one above the other, each deriving its 'life' from that immediately above it, the divine Life itself being the apex. A similar notion is found in Bautain's early *Propositions générales de la Vie*, a work of signal importance in the construction of his system.[55] 'Life', he there states, 'is the active and absolute principle of all that exists, a principle known only through its manifestation. Now the manifestation of life is movement, development, creation. It issues from a single centre — from that Being who is the source of all life, radiating it out of Himself.'[56] Its determinate forms make up existence, and its characteristic is spontaneity, though the spontaneity is dependent on the principle of its origin. The 'law' of life is a kind of pulsating movement, a going-and-coming, so to say, in which the reaction of the passive (or 'female') subject depends on the action of the active (or 'male') object. 'At the instant when the passive and active unite the life-giving ray or "virtue" of life reaches the *foyer* of the mother-form and triumphs over its concentration; the conception or intussusception of life takes place.'[57] Hence life is never a pure or unconditioned activity. It is given, received and in turn communicated under conditions of struggle which are at once limiting and creative. At the human level the life-process becomes the subject of knowledge, of self-reflexion. Man's intelligence is a divine gift, to be recognized by him as such.

[53] God, says Bautain, *is Being*. He is *He who is*; and the idea of Being is the fundamental idea, the *idée-mère* of the human understanding, without which it would be incapable of conceiving any existence. Thus it is only the fool who can say: God (Being) is not — for a man believes in spite of his negation. See *Revue européenne*, vi, pp. 646f.

[54] On Baader's theosophism see E. Susini, *Franz von Baader et le romantisme mystique* (1942).

[55] Bautain, like Newman, is more concerned with the psychological aspect of the problem of belief than with the strictly philosophical one. For this reason his treatment of Kant is somewhat perfunctory, and it is only when he deals with the sort of questions involved in the actual experience of apprehending truth that he produces any really interesting analysis of his own.

[56] *Propositions générales*, ii, pp. 7ff.

[57] *ibid.* cf. *Psychologie expérimentale*, pp. 83ff.

Man who is soul, mind and body does not exist merely to live in his body, nor yet in body and mind and only for himself and his fellows. He must also live in his soul for the sake of the Being who is the primary source of life as a whole, and to whom in the end all life must be given back.[58]

But man's relationship to God, like all personal relations, is not to be conceived simply in terms of 'reason'. 'Every real relation presupposes two terms which are living and not mere creations of reason. They actually exist, and the reason is obliged to admit them as necessary data in order that a relationship may be possible.'[59]

Bautain's meaning becomes clearer when we examine his epistemology, or psychology. He distinguishes three 'faculties' or channels of knowledge: imagination, reason and *intelligence* (or intuition). The first relates directly to the world of sense-experience, whereas the second, identified with the power of judgment, is concerned partly with the senses and partly with the 'pure' intellect: its function is to produce notions or concepts, although this conceptualizing role also imposes its own limitations. 'It operates on the things of the spirit as anatomy does on the body: it dissects, divides, decomposes, and consequently it presupposes death, or effects it.'[60] In a word, its fault, inherent in its nature, is *abstraction*. What it cannot do is to convey an idea of the concrete reality, the organic wholeness of things.[61] Hence its powerlessness in regard to the spiritual order. That such an order exists it can tell us; *what* it is, however, it cannot do, since rational knowledge is basically empirical. If then there is to be — as in fact there is — a knowledge of spiritual reality as such — a knowledge of *ideas*, as Bautain puts it, making use of Platonic categories — it is because man possesses a higher faculty of intuition, or capacity for spiritual apprehension. Whereas, then, 'the action of the reason' is 'always complex, successive, fractional', proceeding from the known to the unknown and 'borrowing the aid of middle terms to unite extremes whose relation is not immediately seized', intuition, by contrast, has the instant quality of *vision*. Indeed it is interior vision, as distinct from exterior.

In neither is there any reflexion, any admixture of thought. When I look at an object, I observe, I consider, but I do not think at all. And as soon as I think, I no longer observe the outward object, but its image in my understanding. It is the same with the contemplation of Truth, or an Idea: I see, I look, I admire, I am penetrated by the light of the thing and feel it deliciously, but I do not think; and if reflexion intervenes, contemplation ceases and enjoyment with it.[62]

---

[58] *Psychologie expérimentale*, p. 48.　　[59]*ibid.*, p. 83.　　[60]*ibid.*, p. 333.
[61]Bautain seems at times to take reason in the narrowest sense, as meaning mere deduction. cf. *Philosophie du Christianisme*, i, p. 170: 'La raison n'est point un principe, ni la puisance des principes, mais seulement la faculté de déduire ce qu'ils renferment.'
[62]*Psychologie expérimentale*, ii, p. 408. Bautain's distinction between *raison* and *intelligence* is in line with Coleridge's between Understanding and Reason. In making it both may well have been influenced by Kant (or possibly also by Jacobi); but for each alike the root of the distinction

Another characteristic of Bautain's philosophy is its voluntarism. Man is not made simply to know and admire but to *love*. Love is the condition of any really penetrating knowledge in the personal sphere; it 'alone unites intimately with the object'.[63] 'It is the sovereign Good; by love is man's intellectual perfection consummated.' The will is the profoundest thing in man, that which finally unites him with God, because the deepest level of his nature is his need of the infinite. The conditions of knowledge therefore are fundamentally moral: truth is to be desired as a *good*. Accordingly the will has its own power of apprehension: a man can become more enlightened by becoming better.

The role of faith as a willingness to make assumptions is now apparent.

Knowledge is born of belief and never precedes it: . . . nothing is more absurd, more contrary to the law of your mind, than the pretence to know, to judge and to reason before believing.

In default of actual knowledge and the certitude of self-evidence faith is necessary.[64] It is hardly then surprising that Bautain should have been charged by his contemporaries with 'fideism' in the sense of minimizing the rational element in belief and of endorsing (if it came to the point) a Tertullianic *credo quia absurdum est*. Unfortunately the label has stuck, although Bautain at no time advocated irrationalism or a 'crucifixion' of the intellect. He says emphatically that the priority of faith does not mean that knowledge of metaphysical realities based on reason is impossible, but only that faith is the beginning of a way that leads to 'self-evidence, knowledge, absolute certitude.[65] But there is another, more personal aspect of the matter which to Bautain is no less important: the *openness* of faith to truth. To believe, in the most general sense, he states, is simply 'to let in the truth and react freely towards it. It is in essence a vital act. To refuse to accept an impression, or, having accepted it, to refuse to ponder its implications, is to shut the door on knowledge'.[66] Such receptivity is the mark of the believing mind and without it understanding cannot follow: *credo ut intelligam*. Yet it would be a mistake to regard faith as merely the *condition* of knowledge: it is itself a mode of *perception*, an inchoate knowledge, something 'felt' rather than actually 'seen'. It might perhaps be described as a 'foretaste' of the truth. In other words, faith is the *root* of the idea, just as the idea is the principle of knowledge and knowledge the basis of doctrine.

But [he insists] let no man be deceived: faith, obscure as it is on account of its depth, is intelligent; it is an intelligence penetrated by the action of truth but not yet

---

lies in Platonism, as Bautain himself is fully aware. Thus he refers explicitly to Plotinus's contrast between the eye of the body and that of the mind (*Enneads*, i, 6) and St Augustine's between *intellegere* and *ratiocinari* (*de spiritu et anima*, i, 14. cf. *de Trinitate*, vii, *in fine*), as too to similar ideas in Anselm, Aquinas and Gerson.

[63] *ibid.*, p. 408.　　　　　　　　　　[64] *Philosophie du Christianisme*, i, pp. 296f.
[65] *ibid.*　　　　　　　　　　　　　　　　[66] *ibid.*, p. 293.

conscious of itself and of that which penetrates it. It is an unreflecting and hence less brilliant light.[67]

In the matter of religious faith specifically — as distinct, that is, from general belief — we can claim that it is more 'intelligent' than 'intelligence' itself, because it brings the soul into contact with the divine, of which the rational understanding has no more than an inkling (*pressentiment*). It is a deep-down apprehension of truths which the intellect does not clearly grasp. Thus faith alone can have any firm hold on the Christian doctrines of the incarnation and trinity.

In view of Bautain's voluntarism it is to be expected that he would stress the role of the will in believing, and he certainly does so. Reason, he points out, is implicated in both sides of the issue, and is therefore advocate more than judge. In fact reason *alone* never decides, 'although it is most often employed to proclaim and justify, like a clerk of the court drawing up the *arrêt* after the judge's sentence. In man the judge of last resort is the *will*, placed between two contending worlds and destined to give itself to the one or the other . . . in order to perform an act of liberty'.[68] As Bautain phrases it in an early pamphlet, *Variétés philosophiques*:

It is not from reason, properly speaking, but from *the centre of the human being*, from that which is profoundest, most mysterious in man, that judgments come.[69]

Thus although volition is central to the act of faith its operation is not arbitrary and there is no element of mere wilfulness. Faith is not blind, nor a sheer leap in the dark. On the contrary, it reflects a deeper level of intelligence than that of the self-conscious intellect. Hence although there is no faith without a certain adhesion of the will the latter is not the master of faith. 'It can neither create it for itself nor stimulate the sentiments which accompany it, any more than it can root it out or destroy it.' To sum up, faith is not simply a judgment of reason nor simply a movement of the will, as still less a mere sentiment or feeling. It involves all three and should be conceived as a reaction of the 'whole man', expressive of the entire personality. Thus although faith is the beginning of knowledge it also is the beginning of worship and love.

If the claim that faith always *precedes* reason amounts to fideism Bautain plainly is a fideist, his whole philosophy being designed to show that it does. The priority of faith to reason he considers evident, that is, however one chooses to look at it. From the standpoint of logic faith supplies reason with its principles or axioms, reason taking them on trust, as it were. Again, psychologically, the stage of reflective elaboration or ordered knowledge depends on a primary condition of more or less vague apprehension: one 'feels' or 'senses' the truth of a given position previous to elucidating and

[67] *Psychologie expérimentale*, ii, pp. 376f.
[68] *ibid.*, i, p, 217.   [69] p. 41 (italics ours).

demonstrating it. Genetically and historically, as is obvious, the age of reason is a later development, in the race as in the child. Above all, metaphysically the superiority of faith arises from the fact that whereas (as Kant argues) reason is limited to the phenomenal world, faith gives access to ultimate reality. Yet Bautain repeatedly urged that it was not his intention to denigrate reason. As he explained to his bishop:

We have never meant to exclude reason from the consideration of metaphysical and moral truths; we have never wished to banish it either from philosophy or from theology. Those who have cast reproach against us have gratuitously ascribed to us an absurdity which is not of our making. It is perfectly evident that wherever man makes use of his powers of thought and of speech, the reason is exercised and applied. Now how does one study philosophy or theology without thinking or speaking?[70]

Faith, in any real meaning of the word, is open only to a rational being; but reason works on what faith provides. Instances may possibly be found of unbelievers having been led to faith by metaphysical arguments, but they must be regarded as highly exceptional. Certainly 'among true Christians one believes from the first'.

Intuitionist though he is Bautain is far from wishing to commit religious belief to the realm of pure subjectivism. Faith exists in an *objective* sense as the historical deposit, so to say, of the experience of men of genius participating in the spirit of God — prophets, poets, apostles. 'The life of heaven has been communicated to humanity from the beginning', and this communication is maintained and renewed across the centuries.[71] Such cumulative experience becomes a tradition which provides the individual with an objective norm. In Bautain's view a main argument in favour of a primitive revelation derives from the principle of 'recapitulation', according to which the knowledge of truth in the race parallels that of the child; as a child has to be taught by others, so the man who grows up outside society and in ignorance of its traditions cannot develop as a person. The existence of an authority to conserve the truth and impart it to individuals is therefore an obvious necessity, for although the individual can 'see' the truth when presented to him his faith cannot of itself create it. He owes in fact three things to society absolutely: language, which kindles the intelligence, tradition, which comprises universal truths and the inheritance of factual knowledge, and a certain soundness of judgment which comes of intercourse with men. To that extent individual experience, in form as in substance, is itself a social creation.

The principle which justifies the authority of society as a whole is also that which justifies the authority of the church. For the church is the channel through which truths otherwise inaccessible to mankind are communicated;

---

[70]From an unpublished document entitled 'Simple exposé de la question entre Mgr l'Évêque de Strasbourg et plusieurs prêtres de son diocèse', *Fonds Bautain*, H, 8 *verso* (quoted Horton, *The philosophy*, p. 174). [71]*Psychologie expérimentale*, ii, p. 406.

except that whereas the authority of human society, great though it is, is
fallible, the church as the custodian and guarantor of divine revelation is
infallible. But Bautain's method of proving the authenticity of revelation
is characteristic. The usual appeal to prophecy, miracle and historical
testimony he considers inconclusive. Like Coleridge, he believes rather in
the intrinsic power of scripture and church teaching to germinate faith. It
is certainly not a matter of proving mere *facts*. Reason may very well admit
the facts, but if they are to be accepted as revelation faith is needed. It is useless to try 'to prove by reason alone to a man of reason without faith that
a book written by the hand of man is a divine authority for all men'. To the
question whether the miracles of Jesus are not still sufficiently cogent for
this purpose Bautain's reply is that they will never lose their force in the
eyes of *believers*, but apologetic is not addressed to believers. 'We are concerned with learned pagans, with unbelievers, with deists. How shall one
prove the divinity of Jesus Christ and His Gospel *logically* and by the sole
authority of reason to men such as these?' To them, as Hume demonstrates,
it is miracles themselves which are in doubt. The traditional apologist
uses miracle to prove the gospel and the gospel to prove miracle; but that
the apostles were 'neither deceivers nor deceived' is not something which
for apologetic purposes can be taken as axiomatic, and to regard them as
inerrant witnesses is in effect to assume another miracle. It is idle indeed
to appeal to the bare fact even of Christ's own resurrection. 'What leads men
to believe in Jesus Christ, Saviour of mankind, is humility of heart as opposed
to the exaltation of the mind and the pretensions of a reason which thinks
itself all-sufficient.'[72]

On the issue of miracles as such Bautain is notably clear-sighted. It is,
he points out, impossible to distinguish true miracles from purely natural
occurences.

When human science shall have explained to us what nature is; when it shall have
marked the point to which its forces and its laws extend, we may judge whether
the extraordinary facts which we designate by the name of miracles are repugnant
to the general order and out of line with the common laws, or whether they are
not perhaps more striking manifestations or more energetic developments of them.[73]

But he indignantly denies his critics' accusation that he himself evidently
does not believe in miracles. His argument, he says, is simply that in the
existing state of human knowledge a given event cannot be definitely *identified* as a breach or suspension of a law of nature. Moreover there is a sense
in which all nature is a miracle.

Bautain's view of Christianity in general tends to be historicist; at least
the historical perspective is essential to his apologetic method. Eclecticism

---

[72]This argument is adopted by Bautain in his answer to the bishop of Strasbourg's *Avertissement*. cf. Horton, *The philosophy*, pp. 228ff.
[73]*La morale de l'Évangile comparée à la morale des philosophes* (1827), p. 68.

as a philosophical doctrine he rejected, as we have seen, early in his career, but he does not repudiate it when it comes to understanding Christianity, which he thinks is itself eclectic.

> The word of Jesus Christ is sown as a seed in the world; it takes root there, develops, blossoms and bears fruit in a marvellous fashion in the midst of pagan civilization and all the philosophical knowledge of the time.

It was in this variegated and cosmopolitan environment that the church was founded, and in the course of her early development she accepted anything that was not in contradiction of her principles and gathered in whatever could be reconciled with the gospel truth. Thus did elements of Platonism, Aristotelianism and Stoicism all come to be assimilated. Yet the eclecticism of Christianity as seen in history does not mean that it has no proper character of its own or that certain widely credited accounts of it are not in fact inordinate growths and perversions. The chief danger, as always in Bautain's opinion, is a false intellectualism, a bequest from Hellenism of which the Bible knows nothing. Old Testament religion is intuitive, not self-reflective; it does not argue God's existence, but simply proclaims his mighty acts. What philosophy it has therefore takes the form of a philosophy of history. To ultimate questions no rational answer is even envisaged, only a practical response. Hence as between the Hellenic mind and the Hebraic there is a deep cleavage. Only here and there, as in the Pythagoreanism taken up by Plato, does Hellenism ever disclose a truly religious character.

But of course the villain of the piece is Aristotle, for whom reality reduces itself to definitions and syllogisms; and unhappily it is Aristotle whom the church has virtually canonized. In primitive Christianity it was enough to quote the scriptures and point to actual events as fulfilling them. What the apostles proclaimed was the wisdom not of man but of God. In time however Christian faith had to be presented in more sophisticated terms; whence the adoption of Platonism, with no regrettable results. But Platonism eventually gave way to scholasticism, with its 'unprecedented infatuation for the Stagirite philosopher';[74] although even then not without some resistance, as in the disputes between the *doctores biblici* and the *doctores sententiarii*.[75] But whatever the charge against scholasticism may be — and it is a heavy one — the mediaeval synthesis of faith and reason meant that philosophy and theology remained united. With the Cartesian revolution this unity was broken. 'Whenever reason, fulfilled by practice, had perceived that she was

---

[74] *Philosophie du Christianisme*, ii, pp. 10f.

[75] Students of the Oxford movement will remember that a similar attack on scholasticism was also being mounted at about this time by Renn Dickson Hampden, whose Bampton lectures on *The Scholastic Philosophy considered in its Relation to Christian Theology* were delivered in 1834. In these he denounced 'that speculative and logical Christianity, which survives among us to this day, and which has been in all ages the principal obstacle, as I conceive, to the union and peace of the Church of Christ' (p. 52), and spoke of it as 'the chief cause of infidelity among speculative men' (p. 56).

mistress of the discussion, she tried to set herself up in the place of that authority.'[76] The inevitable consequence was the antagonism between relig- ious faith and science which has become a feature of the modern world. In fact only one philosopher since Descartes evokes Bautain's unqualified praise: Malebranche, who by means of a higher spiritual light saw all things 'in God'. 'Those who ridiculed this great man in the following century had no inkling of what he meant. They were incapable of understanding the sublime guidance of one who was a Christian philosopher.'[77] Kant's great critique had at any rate demonstrated that metaphysical truth is not open to speculative reason; and thanks to Kantism the task of the Christian thinker, so far from being abolished, is actually clarified. Let him forget Aristotle, therefore, and address himself to the ideas and outlook of the modern world, not by way of scientific rationalism – a wrong turning, all too confidently sanctioned by Anglo-Saxon philosophers – but by reversion to an essential Platonism. The temper of the age is a receptive one; men desire to believe as well as reason. 'Appeal, then, to faith', Bautain concludes, 'in a spirit of faith and she will answer you; for faith now is everywhere awake and looks only for a stimulating ray of light to warm and vivify our hearts.'[78]

In spite of the richness and variety of its content and its obvious affinity with the spirit of the times, Bautain's philosophy soon lost its interest for the educated public. The attitude of the clerical world was unsympathetic or dubious, the authorities indeed being openly hostile. Nor did Bautain him- self keep up the courage of his earlier convictions, for his later writings reveal not only more caution but noticeably less optimism concerning the intellectual trend of the age, with its growing positivism and materialism. Thus his work slipped gradually into oblivion. But it should not be con- cluded from this that its influence was thereby extinguished. Such was far from being the case, in that Bautain's type of thinking was to persist among Catholic intellectuals in France until the end of the century and beyond, where it can be traced in Blondel's philosophy of action and the modernism and religious pragmatism of Laberthonnière and Le Roy. Its more proximate effects, however, are to be seen in writings of Alphonse Gratry, who could well be described as Bautain's heir, and these we shall consider in due course. Meantime other developments must engage our attention, namely the voluntarism of Maine de Biran and his successors and the ontologism of the school of Louvain and its counterpart in France. The two chapters which follow will be devoted to each in turn.

[76] *Philosophie du Christianisme*, ii, p. 14.
[77] *Psychologie expérimentale*, i, p. 104.
[78] *Philosophie du Christianisme*, i, p. xii (Bonnechose's preface).

7

VOLUNTARISM: MAINE DE BIRAN
AND OTHERS

'Volo ergo sum'

So far our study of the movement of Catholic thought in nineteenth-century France has concentrated on those aspects of it which may be looked on as typical of the period. They are expressions, that is to say, either of the ultra-conservative politics of the Restoration, or of the alliance of liberalism with ultramontanism, or again of romanticist intuitionism and fideism. What unites them is their opposition to rationalism: as against the force of individual reasoning, which had been the criterion of the preceding epoch, they appealed, in quest of certitude, either to immemorial tradition, divine revelation and the absolute authority of the ecclesiastical institution, or to the impulses and intimations of the heart. But this opposition, as we have seen, was not directed only at the world of the *philosophes* and the revolutionary idealism to which 'philosophy' was judged to have given birth. Its object also included the kind of theological rationalism — mediaeval or Cartesian — associated with the church's seminaries, the *philosophie de Lyon* and the Paris *conférences* of Mgr Frayssinous. Nevertheless it would be a mistake to deduce from this that no serious effort was being made to counter the materialism of the age of Condorcet and Condillac with some sort of 'spiritual' philosophy aimed at coordinating faith with reason. During the first half of the century this enterprise had three notable exemplars, all laymen and all too original in their thinking to be set aside as mere custodians of tradition. They are Maine de Biran, Bordas-Demoulin and Jules Lequier. Since at least two of them are still relatively little known to English-speaking students of nineteenth-century thought it is worth while to consider their work in a measure of detail.

In his later years Maine de Biran described his system as a 'Christian philosophy', yet he began his career as a *philosophe* under the influence of such authors as Buffon, Rousseau and Condillac himself. The human mind, he then held, was simply an element in nature, to be studied as such. But reflexion rendered him more and more critical of 'sensationalist' assumptions until his final position might be characterized as an almost mystical 'personalism' according to which 'nothing takes place in the senses or the imagination which has not been willed by the self, or suggested or inspired by the ruling force into which this self is absorbed'[1] From the stress he places on the role of the will he has been aptly called the father of French voluntarism.[2]

Maine de Baran[3] was born at Bergerac in 1766, the son of a physician of good family. His life was spent not as an academic philosopher but in the public service, first under the Directorate, as administrator of the *département* of the Dordogne, later as sub-prefect of Bergerac (1806—1812), and finally, from 1818 until his death in 1824, as deputy for the same municipality. His days however passed uneventfully, even during the Revolution, for when not in Paris he lived on his country estate at Grateloup, near Bergerac. His earliest intellectual associations were with the so-called *idéologues*, in particular Destutt de Tracy and Cabanis, and he was a frequent visitor at the *salon* of Mme Helvétius at Auteuil. He subsequently became a close friend of the physicist, André-Marie Ampère, with whom he corresponded extensively. But he received no formal philosophical education and may fairly be said to have 'discovered' philosophy for himself simply by reflexion upon the facts and conditions of his own mind, subject as this was to stress and impulse. All his life he was acutely and even painfully self-aware, physically and mentally. Highly strung and introspective, he found the sheer business of living a perpetual effort and burden, and his intensely personal *Journal intime* is full of complaints not only about the manifold distractions by which he was beset but his own inescapable 'faiblesse de l'esprit'.[4] In addition, he was extremely fastidious about his work, with the result that although he wrote much very little of it appeared in print during his lifetime.[5] He in fact published only one full-length treatise, *L'influence de l'Habitude sur le faculté de*

[1] E. Naville, *Œuvres inédites de Maine de Biran* (1859), iii, p. 419.

[2] On Biran generally see V. Delbos, *Maine de Biran et son Œuvre philosophique* (1931); A. de La Valette Monbrun, *Maine de Biran, essai biographique et psychologique* (1914); H. Gouhier, *Les Conversions de Maine de Biran* (1947); P. P. Hallie, *Maine de Biran: Reformer of Empiricism 1766—1824* (Cambridge, Mass., 1959); F. C. T. Moore, *The Psychology of Maine de Biran* (1970). Dr Moore, it may be mentioned, censures La Valette Monbrun's book as 'arbitrary, unscholarly, and unintelligent' (*The Psychology*, p. 190).

[3] His real name was Marie-Francois-Pierre Gonthier de Biran. The name of Maine, which he preferred to use and by which he is always known, was that of an estate belonging to his father.

[4] The *Journal* as a whole was first edited by A. de La Valette Monbrun (2 vols., 1927—31), later — and definitively — by H. Gouhier (3 vols., Neuchâtel, 1954—7).

[5] On Maine de Biran's method of working see Moore, *The Psychology*, p. 188. 'If an idea struck him', writes Dr Moore, 'he would jot it down in his journal, or would take the paper that came to hand, and elaborate the idea there. As he read, whether the works of others, or his own earlier writings, he would constantly criticize and correct, making marginal notes, or more elaborate commentaries on separate sheets. Moreover, among his manuscripts is to be found a great deal of preparatory work for his finished writings, and a great deal of later treatment of related themes. In addition, we find the drafts, sometimes fragmentary, sometimes well worked out, frequently gone over and corrected so radically as to make them almost unintelligible, of projected but uncompleted works.' Naville, in preparing his edition, had to cope with more than twelve thousand pages in manuscript of philosophical writing alone (*Notice historique et bibliographique sur les travaux de Maine de Biran*, pp. xxiv—xxviii).

penser, which appeared in 1802.[6] But public acclaim was really the last thing
Maine de Biran sought. His official duties constituted the primary charge on
his time and to these he dedicated himself assiduously. Otherwise his life was,
as he put it, one of 'complete solitude consecrated to psychological medita-
tion'.[7] 'To philosophize', he would say, 'is to reflect, to make use of the reason
in all things and everywhere, alike in the turmoil of the world as in the study.'
To reflect, calmly and with detachment, was the philosopher's vocation.

At first, like other good *idéologues*, he was content to explain mental states
in terms of physical causes. 'If,' he argued, 'we recognized that our troubled
state, our state of anxiety, is almost purely physical, we should look upon it
as an illness, and having tested that which can guarantee us or prevent us
from falling into it so often, we should put these measures into practice.'[8]
But from this position he soon moved away. To view man in a strictly phy-
sicalist perspective, as simply a part of nature, he now regarded as a profound
error. Philosophy's true starting-point was the proper understanding of the
self; and to understand the self one has to weigh the significance of *effort*.
The classical rationalists, Descartes and Leibniz, had begun with *a priori*
ideal concepts, Locke and the empiricists with sensation, considered in the
abstract; and both in their diverse ways had blundered. The true method will
start rather with the 'primitive fact' of the *moi*, the intuition of self-hood,
and proceed thereafter by the light of the *sens intime*, or method of internal
observation and experiment — a psychological enterprise of experimental
self-observation of a kind altogether different from that of the *idéologues*.
'It is much to be desired', says a note in the *Journal*, 'that a man skilled in
introspection should analyse the will as Condillac has analysed the understanding.' Physics advances from particular facts to general causes; in psychology one begins with a sense of effort comparable with muscular action.

In effect, as we perceive it and reproduce it at every instant, there is no external sense
of excitation, and yet the muscular organ is brought into play, the contraction
operates, the motion is reproduced without any other cause than this proper force,
which is felt or perceived immediately in its exercize and without there being a
sign to represent it to the imagination or to any sense foreign to its own.[9]

The mistakes of philosophers hitherto resulted from their having failed to
grasp the nature of this internal experience of effort in its stark originality.

[6] Reprinted by Victor Cousin in *Œuvres philosophiques de Maine de Biran*, i (1834). Cousin's
edition of the works, in four volumes, was published during the years 1834 to 1841, Naville's
(in collaboration with Marc Debrit), in three volumes in 1859. The fullest and most recent is
that of P. Tisserand and H. Gouhier, in fourteen volumes dating from 1920 to 1949.
[7] 'Lorsqu'on porte le calme au dedans de soi-même, on peut méditer et faire des expériences
réfléchies, même au milieu du monde, dont on ne partage pas l'agitation; mais lorsqu'on est
agité intérieurement, tout fait distraction et la plus profonde solitude ne saurait nous calmer'
(*Journal* ed. Gouhier, i, p. 152).
[8] Naville, *Maine de Biran, sa vie et ses pensées* (1857; 2nd ed. 1874), p. 123.
[9] Naville, *Œuvres inédites de Maine de Biran*, i, p. 211.

For effort lies at the root of all consciousness. Apart from it perception, memory, habituation, abstraction and judgment are unaccountable. Descartes had said, I think therefore I am; what he should have said is, *I will* therefore I am. For willing is more basic than thought.

Such was the position Maine de Biran had reached by the time he wrote his *Essai sur les fondements de la Psychologie* in 1812.[10] He was now convinced that if one feels or perceives oneself to be a free cause then in fact one is so.[11] That man is 'an acting force' had acquired for him all the value and infallible certainty of a first principle.

Here then was a new type of spiritualistic philosophy, grounded not in *la pensée* but in *le vouloir*, and it marked the first of what Henri Gouhier calls Maine de Biran's 'conversions'. But although it indicated a complete change of viewpoint he still believed in the experimental or 'experiential' method, except that 'experience' is now given a broader connotation as involving not merely the senses but the 'whole man' centred upon the inner, motivating self.

The doctrine which he had come to hold implied therefore a philosophy not of the idea or concept as such but of the *action* of thought itself as expressing the free and spontaneous *moi*, the living, willing, striving *person*, who is always distinguishable from that external 'nature' with which one communicates through the senses. Volition, effort of will, that is to say, is the basis of our thinking, of our rational ideas indeed, no less than of our visible activity.[12] But meanwhile Maine de Biran sought to preserve his links with empiricism by accounting for the existence of ideas not as innate or as *a priori* conditions of reasoning but as arising from the 'immediate apperception' of self-activity. This theory of knowledge, however, he subsequently modified, after a further reading of Leibniz, in rationalist direction.[13] In *Fragments relatifs aux fondements de la morale et de la religion* he is even more willing to recognize a psychological power or faculty of belief as the ground of our ideas of God as omnipotent Creator and of the immaterial human soul. For this reason he has been spoken of as 'the French Kant',[14] although it is very doubtful whether he

[10] That at least is the probable date. In the *Essai*, which in a number of respects is a key-work, Maine de Biran reiterates and enlarges upon the views put forward in two earlier treatises, *De la décomposition de la Pensée*, written in 1805, and *Mémoire sur les Rapports du physique et du moral de l'homme*, dating from 1811. The *Essai sur les fondements de la Psychologie* was not printed until 1932, when it appeared in the Tisserand edition.

[11] *Nouvelles considérations sur les rapports du physique et du moral de l'homme* (1820) ed. Cousin (1841), iv, p. 249.

[12] As he wrote to Ampère: 'Comme je pense qu'il n'y a pas une idée intellectuelle, pas une perception distincte ou aucune perception proprement dite qui ne soit originairement liée à une *action* de la volonté je ne peux m'empêcher de considérer le système intellectuel ou cognitif comme absolument fondé pour ainsi dire dans celui de la volonté et n'en différant que par l'expression' (*Correspondance*, ed. Tisserand, vii, p. 400).

[13] His short *Exposition de la doctrine philosophique de Leibniz* (1819; ed. Cousin, *Œuvres*, iv) was among the very few works published during his lifetime.

[14] By E. König, for one. L. S. Stebbing, *Pragmatism and French Voluntarism* (1914), quotes König's statement (*Philosophische Monatshefte*, xxv, p. 169) that: 'The same idea of spontaneity

himself had anything more than an indirect knowledge of Kant's works, and
in any case his affinities with Kant are not very deep. It would be truer to say
that Maine de Biran was by this time moving towards both a broadly conceived Platonism and the sort of eclecticism represented by his friend
Ampère, by Royer-Collard, and most characteristically of all by Victor Cousin.
His earlier, eighteenth-century influences had by now fallen away, while on
the other hand he was not at all attracted by the fashionable idealism, at once
rationalist and pantheist, from beyond the Rhine. What he increasingly felt
the need of was a straight-forward doctrine upon which to base moral and
social living. In this he was much nearer to his contemporary and Catholic
fellow-countrymen, Bonald and Lamennais.

Maine de Biran had thus reached the conclusion that discursive reason is
essentially a function of the personality *as a whole*: 'L'homme n'est intelligent
que sous la condition d'être une puissance active et libre.'[15] Accordingly any
idea of God which reduces him to a mere impersonal first cause or principle
is really no more than a disguised atheism. To be the object of obedience and
devotion he has to be thought of in personal terms. Idealist systems with
their governing concept of the absolute lead only to pantheism, whereas a
personalist philosophy is bound to tend in the direction of religion. It will
present the idea of spirit, that is to say, under the category of 'will' or 'action'
rather than of 'substance'. But the life of the spirit, Maine de Biran is now disposed to think, is not the outcome of human effort alone but is the realization
of a divine call, a state of grace which stands in much the same relation to the
soul as does the soul itself to the body. For the soul, besides its intrinsic power
of reason, has 'faculties and modes of operation which derive from a principle
much higher than itself, . . . intellectual intuitions, inspirations, supernatural
motions in which the soul, delivered from itself, is wholly subject to the
action of God'.[16]

How, then, did Maine de Biran react to the current traditionalist trend
in Catholic philosophy? As a strong supporter of the Restoration he might be
supposed to have been in sympathy also with the views of its intellectual
apologists, but although he made a careful study of Bonald's *Recherches philosophiques* he was far from agreeing with its conclusions. In a 'Defence of

by means of which Kant reformed empirical epistemology Biran introduced into the sensationalist psychology. What was there an epistemological hypothesis is shewn to us here as
psychological fact; the empirical activity of the psychological subject appears as the counterpart of the transcendental function of the understanding.' But Miss Stebbing thinks that he
would better have been styled 'the French Schopenhauer' (*Pragmatism*, pp. 21f.). We may agree
with her in her opinion that the comparison with Kant is more applicable to Renouvier (*ibid.*,
p. 92).
[15] cf. Naville, *Maine de Biran, sa vie et ses pensées*, p. 321: 'Il est essentiel, pour commencer
la philosophie, de remonter jusqu'à l'origine de la personnalité comme condition nécessaire de
toute intelligence.'
[16] Naville, *Œuvres inédites*, iii, p. 549.

Philosophy' written in 1817[17] he not only rejected Bonald's claim that philosophy had been discredited by the sheer contrariety of the opinions held by philosophers themselves but criticized his basic argument that any speculative use of reason had been obviated by the primal divine revelation of all essential truth. Against it he invoked Malebranche's distinction between truths preserved in scripture and the tradition of the church and those whose fundamental principles had been implanted in the hearts and minds of all men and are thus accessible to the reason and conscience of individuals. This indeed is to affirm that all truth is ultimately of God, but also that men's remembrance or comprehension of it may grow dim or be impaired and so have to be reawakened or clarified by teachers of insight and understanding. Of such there have been many from Socrates onwards and all have in one respect or another contributed to that great tradition of European thought rightly known as the *Philosophia perennis*, a tradition which has consistently emphasized the supreme truth of personality in God and in man. It is this philosophy, of which Leibniz is the most recent representative, that provides the natural and fitting counterpart to the doctrines of Christianity. Bonald, in depreciating the individual reason, denies to man the very capacity necessary for receiving divine revelation in the first place. In short, without reason there would have been no revelation, and insofar as, in order to meet this difficulty, Bonald allows to no man in his natural state at least some measure of rationality he contradicts his main contention that all truth had to be divinely published. His denial of the idea that man's reason is capable of criticizing or even justifying revelation implies that truth is really something quite extrinsic to his nature and can never be held by him as authentically his own. In any case the Bonaldian theory of language is self-refuting, since how could language ever have been understood apart from the *thought* needed to render linguistic signs themselves intelligible? The real motive behind Bonald's thinking, in Maine de Biran's view, is his rigid political conservatism, suspicious of all individual judgment as potentially subversive of social order. But this is sheer prejudice, and the best way to condemn a false philosophy is by appeal to a true one.

Maine de Biran, like Bonald and Lamennais, has nothing good to say of scholastic rationalism, which he sees only as an intellectual by-path overgrown with idle logomachies.[18] Where, however, he considered Bonald and others to have gone astray was in their denigration of Descartes, whom he personally looks back to as a true Christian philosopher, father of the

---

[17] See his *Examen critique des opinions de M. de Bonald*, ed. Tisserand, *Œuvres*, xii (Défense de la Philosophie') (1939). It is contained in vol. iii of the Naville edition.

[18] cf. *Fragments relatifs aux fondements de la morale et de la religion* (ed. Naville, iii, p. 102): 'Certainement ce n'était pas des vaines disputes du peripatétisme, de ses questions abstraites et oiseuses, si propres à détourner ou à dissiper l'homme intérieure, que la vraie philosophie pouvait le relever.'

modern science of man in his intellectual and moral being. The 'social metaphysics' with which the traditionalists sought to replace individual intelligence seems to him almost meaningless, as well as a denial of the ancient Christian view of reason as the light that lightens every man coming into the world. As for Lamennais's apologetic, he finds it superficial and confused, failing as it does to explain how men can adhere collectively to a truth they have no means of testing individually and in any case misunderstanding the nature of authority, which is to regulate actions and not to control thought.

Experience, Faith and Reason

Maine de Biran's later thinking is more than simply a restatement of theism. It is the outcome of a deepening religious conviction originating in what may not inaptly be described as a conversion-experience, dating from 1815. He had been brought up as a Catholic and had never explicitly repudiated Catholic belief. Yet it was not until he reached his fifties that a nominal creed developed into a personal faith. This may be attributed in part to the new climate of opinion, but also, more importantly, to certain temperamental difficulties of his own, resulting in a conflict of reason and emotion. What he desired above all was tranquillity of mind, certitude of truth and the sense of a moral goal in life. But he had become increasingly dissatisfied with himself, with his outlook and whole way of living. To these personal anxieties must be added the influence upon him of political events and circumstances. The state of the country caused him disquiet and he was pessimistic about the future. Further, although his friends included many sincere Catholics, both priests and laymen, he turned more and more for consolation to the writers of that great age of French spirituality, the seventeenth century. He was now firmly convinced that a merely abstract or 'intellectualist' philosophy is useless in face of the problems raised by the meaning and conduct of life and that there is in man a natural propensity for religion such as achieves its fulfilment in Christianity alone. Atheism with its demand for external proof of truths that can be verified only inwardly is sheer folly. Nor is pantheism, which excludes the two essential realities of God and the soul, any better; to embrace it is 'to kill religion and personality alike with a single blow'. Hence the necessity of conjoining reason and faith in an authentically Christian philosophy.

Maine de Biran's very concern with the current traditionalist apologetic and his eagerness to expose its weaknesses is itself evidence of his growing preoccupation with the religious question, a preoccupation manifest in his *Nouvelles considérations sur les rapports du physique et du moral* of 1820. What he envisages in this is neither traditionalism nor Cartesian rationalism but a religious philosophy grounded in an inward experience or *sens intime* which nevertheless expresses itself in the form of a positive creed. Metaphysics, that is, must come to terms with the Christian revelation in a way that will yield a new type of natural theology more in tune with man's actual spiritual needs. This means that it will provide its best service when it poses questions which it is itself unable to answer, thus pointing to a source of spiritual enlightenment above and beyond itself. True spiritual understanding is reached not through the abstract intellect but through love, a kind of super-addition to life in the 'natural' sense and suffusing it as a 'grace' from without.[19]

But for a more detailed exposition of Biran's views the reader should turn to the *Nouveaux essais d'Anthropologie ou de la science de l'homme intérieur* on which the author was still working at the time of his death and which was intended by him as a considered statement of his whole philosophical position.[20] His plan here is to portray the life of man under three distinct but closely related aspects. The first and lowest — he regards the second and third as superimposed rather than successive[21] — is the affective: at this level, the merely animal, life is simply a mass of vague impressions or affections independent of the will and thus outside the periphery of organized knowledge. It could be described as the *totum* of man's organic dispositions, and Biran's account of it anticipates Freud's theory of dreams. The properly human appears only at the next level, the perceptive and volitional, to which reference has already been made. Here the key-ideas are those of attention and effort: seeing presupposes looking, as does listening hearing. It is at this stage that the self performs the basic intellectual tasks of comparing, classifying, generalizing and combining the things on which it focuses its interest. With the third level, the spiritual, the synthetizing power of the self comes into full play. Man now is open to divine revelation, not in the sense of something arbitrarily 'given', heteronomous and abstract, to be accepted purely on the strength of the external 'evidences' that accompany it, but as an inward force, a second 'primitive fact' clearly distinct from but analogous to the first (the effort, that is, by which our human personality is initially formed and developed). Only this time it is a communication of the divine personality itself, re-creating and enhancing our own. For in and of itself man's mind can secure no lasting satisfaction, no unequivocal good.

But for the most explicit and indeed emotional expression of his religious convictions Maine de Biran resorted to his *Journal*. 'The religious and moral beliefs', he there confesses, 'which reason does not establish but which are for it a basis or necessary starting-point, present themselves to me as my only refuge. I find no true knowledge save precisely there where formerly, along

[19] cf. Naville, *Œuvres inédites*, ii, p. 541.

[20] It was published for the first time by Naville. In the Tisserand-Gouhier edition (1949) it forms part of it. xii (pp. 269–310). The work was left unfinished, much of it existing only in note form.

[21] 'Il n'y a pas de passage logique ou métaphysique de l'une à l'autre; on ne peut que constater leur existence et non l'expliquer' (P. Tisserand, *L'Anthropologie de Maine de Biran*, 1909, p. 291).

with the philosophers, I saw only dreams and chimaeras.' And Again:

Not finding within me nor outside of me, in the world of my ideas or in that of objects, anything that satisfies me, anything on which I could support myself, ... I have for some time been more inclined to seek in the absolute Being, an unchanging end, that point of complete fixity which has become the need of my mind and of my soul.

The date of these entries is 1818.[22] In the end Biran was to arrive at an overtly mystical philosophy according to which the soul, finally absorbed in contemplation of the divine, loses even the sense of selfhood and freedom and becomes as it were de-personalized. Probably his now rapidly failing health had not a little to do with his longing for 'deliverance' from the burden of existence, but its roots really lie deeper. The moral attitudes of Stoicism, which at one time he had so much admired,[23] his own experience had taught him to recognize as futile; man's passions and sufferings were too great.

Yet Biran realized well enough that the religious sentiment, which he believed all men to possess, can easily be stifled or may never be awakened. Moral self-discipline is needed: one has to detach oneself from the world and its ties if the life of the spirit is to be attained. Like the English Tractarians he insisted on moral seriousness as the preliminary to religious conversion. Not only was it necessary to shun the grosser sins; respectable worldliness has also to be overcome. No less importantly, however, one must learn to pray, for without prayer the inner life cannot develop or grace fructify.[24] Further, the believer has need also of the guidance and stay of a positive religious tradition, of the Catholic church and its faith and sacraments. Mere Rousseauism was of small value as a means of training the soul, which must be brought, through a sense of its own inadequacies, actively to acknowledge its need of God.

Maine de Biran's acceptance of Catholic doctrine seems to have been perfectly sincere. He did not take the deist view of Christianity as no more than a republication in figurative terms of the truths of natural religion; on the contrary there is abounding evidence that he believed Catholic Christianity to contain a unique divine revelation, of which the doctrines of the fall and its consequences and of redemption and grace are the essential and authoritative articulations. One might even say that his was a soul *naturaliter christiana*, his final position being the goal to which his steps, intellectually as well as spiritually, had all along been finding their way.[25] But Maine de

[22] ii, pp. 126f. cf. La Valette Monbrun, *Maine de Biran*, p. 466.
[23] cf. *Journal*, 23 June 1816: 'Il faut que la volonté préside à tout ce que nous sommes: voilà le stoicisme. Aucun autre système n'est aussi conforme à notre nature' (i, p. 151).
[24] cf. La Valette Monbrun, *Maine de Biran*, pp. 471f.
[25] So La Valette Monbrun (*Maine de Biran*, p. 458). Tisserand, on the other hand, thinks differently. Speaking of Maine de Biran's Catholicism he says: 'Il s'efforça de l'acquérir, sans y réussir jamais parfaitement' (*L'Anthropologie de Maine de Biran*, p. 231). Yet the evidence of the *Journal* reveals a disposition which is genuinely religious and not simply moralistic.

Biran's mind was on the whole of an eighteenth-century cast, individualistic and moralistic, and the influence of his early enthusiasm for Rousseau was never entirely effaced. Add to this his naturally introspective temperament and it is clear that his religious convictions were not strictly of the dogmatic and ecclesiastical kind favoured by the more ardent apostles of the contemporary Catholic renaissance. His resolve to identify himself with integral Catholic belief was unfeigned — Biran was a man who weighed his own motives carefully — but it doubtless called forth effort.[26]

The problem at bottom was the not unfamiliar one of how to reconcile an authoritatively prescribed faith with the philosopher's right and duty of free inquiry. For Maine de Biran, unlike Lamennais or, later, Bautain, was not a priest with a specific obligation of obedience to the church of whose creed he was an accredited teacher, nor did he in any way present himself in the role of an apologist. The solution of the difficulty, so far as concerns himself, lies in his statement that religion possesses the answers to the questions which philosophy raises. In other words, revelation is not a heteronomous order of truth in regard to which the believer is simply a passive recipient, but a vital element in the latter's own experience, as integral to it indeed as are the difficulties, the doubts and the sufferings to which it is the only adequate reply. Faith therefore is as natural to man as are the searchings of his reason, and as such has no need to wait upon the guarantees either of metaphysics or of historical 'evidences'.

Maine de Biran may be taken as the founder of French activism and personalism. He believed that the life of the soul is a unity in which the highest reaches are continuous with the lower and that any attempt to divide them necessarily gives a false account of man's entire nature and experience, since the higher is itself inexplicable apart from the lower. He thus initiated a line of Catholic philosophy extending through Bautain and Gratry to Ollé-Laprune, Blondel and Le Roy. No doubt from the strictly theological viewpoint his balance is unsatisfactory. Although he stresses the mediatorial role of the church relatively little emphasis falls on sin, the call to repentance or the means of supernatural sanctification, while on the other hand there is too much of a quietist concern for spiritual tranquility and of the idea of faith simply as individual self-fulfilment. His individualist piety and want of feeling for the social implications of religion mark him off, in fact as a man of an older generation. In this respect he certainly differs from both the traditionalists and Catholic 'socialists' of the Buchez stamp. Even his idea of the good life tends to conform to old-fashioned notions of 'civic' virtue. Yet

[26] Victor Delbos felt he could describe Maine de Biran as a Catholic only with certain reservations. 'Il est incontestable', he wrote, 'que Maine de Biran n'envisage dans le christianisme que ce qui répondait à sa nature et à ses besoins; il ne l'a considéré ni dans le sens de la réalité historique, ni dans la plénitude ou l'intégrité de sa signification doctrinale.' (*Maine de Biran et son œuvre philosophique*, p. 279).

writing as he did, at least in his later works, at a time when the tradionalist doctrine had caught the imagination of so many young Catholic intellectuals he inevitably challenges comparison with the author of the *Essai sur l'indif-férence*, and it may be claimed that he stands up to it well. As a pure philoso-pher he is Lamennais's superior; his reasoning is more rigorous and his analyses more thorough. For where Lamennais appears only as a brilliant propagandist Maine de Biran is a metaphysician *de race*. Not surprisingly French philosophical thinking was to bear the mark of his influence for a century to come.

Bordas-Demoulin

A somewhat singular figure, but a thinker worth noting as one who even now has not received the recognition due to him, is that of Jean-Baptiste Bordas, usually known by his adopted name of Bordas-Demoulin.[27] His sin-gularity lies as much, it has to be said, in his personal disposition —ready as he was to sacrifice any comfort, convenience or even necessity in his total dedication to the life of the mind —as in his religious philosophy, which was neither traditionalist, Thomist nor ultramontane, but that rather — if we must attempt to categorize him — of a Platonizing neo-Cartesian and reformist Catholic. Born of peasant parentage in the remote village of La Bertinie in the Dordogne in 1798, he was a native of the same region of France as Maine de Biran, though in no other way did he resemble the older man apart from their common gift for metaphysical thinking. Orphaned in infancy, he was brought up by an aunt on strictly religious lines, but at the age of fifteen he left home to attend the college at Bergerac, where he soon showed signs of intellectual ability and that avid enthusiasm for study which was to develop later into an uncompromising dedication. His talents clearly lay in the direction of mathematics and philosophy — Rousseau engrossed him and Condillac's *Grammaire générale* he knew almost by heart; yet he was also keenly interested in religious questions. In 1819 he betook himself to Paris, but although he tried to eke out a living by teaching he failed to get any lasting or adequately paid work and was eventually reduced to penury. For five or six years he barely maintained himself above the starvation level and was often without boots to his feet. Such however was his nature that he willingly spent on entrance to a public lecture the few *sous* which would have bought him a meal. Happily from this wretched condition he at last was rescued by the generosity of a friendly priest who lodged him in his own house and helped him with his literary work. But poverty had hardened a

---

[27] M. Ferraz (*Histoire de la Philosophie en France au xixe siècle: Traditionalisme et Ultra-montanisme*, p. 433) goes so far as to call him 'one of the profoundest and most misunderstood among Catholic philosophers of our epoch'.

temperamental pride into stubborness and he ended by quarrelling with his benefactor. Nor was he tactful with those who, like Victor Cousin, could have advantaged him. Yet despite Bordas's bitter recriminations Cousin's good nature and impartiality secured for his book on Descartes the distinction of *couronnement* by the Academy of Moral Sciences, followed by similar recognition of his *Éloge sur Pascal* from the Académie Française itself. But Bordas's opinions on political and ecclesiastical matters, democratic and strongly ultramontane and expressed with a vigour which he saw no need ever to mitigate, were plainly of a kind to win him influential opponents. Indeed in his intransigent dissatisfactions he recalls Tertullian.[28] But he did succeed in making at least one loyal friend and disciple in F. Huet, professor of philosophy at the university of Ghent, afterwards his literary executor and a staunch defender of his views.[29] In 1859 Bordas fell seriously ill and had to be moved to the Lariboisière hospital, where on 25 July he died, firm to the end in his religious faith. His body he left to the faculty of medicine at the Sorbonne.

Bordas's writings cover the two fields of his interest, philosophical speculation and the reform of the Catholic church. Of his philosophical works the chief are his Cartesian studies, *Le Cartésianisme ou la véritable rénovation des sciences*, of 1843, and a collection of articles which had appeared over the years in a variety of periodicals — chiefly the *Gazette des Écoles* — entitled *Mélanges philosophiques et religieux* and published in 1855. His writings on ecclesiastical affairs included *Les Pouvoirs constitutifs de l'Église* (1855), a penetrating inquiry into the institutional structure of Catholicism, and a volume of *Essais de Réforme catholique*, produced in collaboration with Huet in 1856.[30] For the literary presentation of his ideas Bordas had very little concern; his attention always was fixed on the clarification of their substance. His style accordingly has the merit of being direct and concise, even brusque, since his aim was simply to state what seemed to him the truth.

Bordas's goal as a Catholic and an intellectual was to discover a way of reconciliation between Catholicism and progress both cultural and social. But to achieve it the misleading by-paths of most contemporary doctrines — Condillacian empiricism, traditionalism, eclecticism, pantheistic idealism — had all to be avoided. The highroad of thought lay in Cartesianism, or more precisely a Cartesianism grounded in and corrected by the 'perennial' tradition of Platonism, which with its theory of *ideas* alone offered an authentic basis for a Christian metaphysic. Descartes, he believed, was right in perceiving that philosophy really begins when the thinker grasps the significance of his own thought. To have done that is to have established the truth of the

---

[28] cf. I. Foucher, *La Philosophie Catholique en France au xixe siècle*, p. 117.
[29] Huet's *Histoire de la vie et des ouvrages de Bordas* came out in 1861.
[30] His literary remains (*Œuvres posthumes*) were published by Huet in 1861.

two fundamental principles or primary realities, the soul and God, both of which thought itself requires. It was here that scholasticism failed. 'Far from opening the door to philosophy it had only succeeded in closing it, since it merely externalized thought and enclosed it in words.'[31] On the other hand Descartes himself had failed to analyse the nature and status of ideas with sufficient thoroughness, so that his own philosophy remained more or less inchoate. Bordas's ambition was to take up the Cartesian argument where its great originator had left it and carry it forward to its proper conclusion. As he saw it, to philosophize is to classify entities according to types, the differentiation of which yields 'ideas' like those of number and extension, beauty and justice, or, even more fundamentally, perfection, unity, indeed being itself. Ideas are in fact constitutive of the understanding; they are not entities distinct from us, but essentially what we ourselves are as rational beings. Platonism, in realizing this, brings us nearer the truth than even Descartes succeeded in doing; for ideas are not simply *acts* of the mind — perceptions, that is: they are the mind's own *essence*. Hence their existence is permanent, not intermittent. This means that they are our inalienable possession, existing in us as do we in them. It is not, as Malebranche held, that 'we see all things in God', nor, as Aristotle maintained, that our ideas are merely the constructs of experience. Rather is it that, as Plato teaches in the *Republic*, human ideas are themselves necessary, unchanging and eternal inasmuch as they are the counterparts and correlates of the divine ideas, in which indeed they participate.[32] The truth of human knowledge depends therefore on its correspondence with the pre-established order of divine truth, accessible to us through the medium of our own God-given reason. But if Carteso-Platonism is the true philosophy, all others, consequently, are in varying measure false.[33] Hence the history of philosophy will have to be rewritten; and this, in outline at any rate, Bordas himself undertakes to do, mainly in opposition to the similar enterprises of Degérando and Cousin. The various philosophical systems he groups according to their coincidence or otherwise with his own views. The first group he censures for having eliminated human ideas: in effect its members teach that all thought is really the thinking of God himself. Examples are afforded in antiquity by the Stoics and among the moderns by Spinoza, Schelling and Hegel, besides of course Malebranche.[34] The second group falls into the contrary error of eliminating the divine ideas:

[31] *Le Cartésianisme*, i, p. 5.
[32] cf. *Mélanges philosophiques et religieux*, p. 91.
[33] Thus: 'Aristote, Zénon de Cittium, Épicure, démembrent Platon; Arnaud, Malebranche, Locke démembrent Descartes. Leurs doctrines ne sont que des ruines de la véritable. Rien de plus naturelle, puisqu'ils forment une superficielle ou faible intelligence de la pensée, un écart d'elle-même, une décadence' (*Œuvres posthumes*, i, p. 16). cf. *Mélanges*, p. 108.
[34] For Malebranche, says Bordas, 'toutes nos idées se trouvent dans la substance efficace de la divinité qui, en nous affectant, nous en donne la perception, et notre volonté n'est que le mouvement que cette substance efficace nous imprime vers le bien'. cf. *Mélanges*, p. 148.

here Aristotle, Aquinas, Kant and Maine de Biran can all be cited. The third group, which succeeds in eliminating any genuine conception of ideas whatever, includes, in addition to the Epicureans of old, all modern empiricists and sensationalists from Bacon to Condillac. But Bordas thinks that conceptualists, who deal merely in abstractions, and the Scottish school of Reid and his disciples in France, whose perceptionism abandons ideas for the bare facts of experience, also come within this category. The latter in truth is not so much a false philosophy as the negation of philosophy, with total scepticism as the final outcome.[35]

Bordas's fourth group alone is acceptable to him, teaching as it does a spiritualism which builds on the principle that the ideas of God, being, unity, cause and so on, are actual possessions of the human mind, correspondent with its real nature, and do not either come from outside with the primal revelation of language, as Bonald supposes, or, as Cousin holds, exist simply as a function of some kind of impersonal 'reason'.[36] Those on the other hand who have maintained that the existence within us of the divine reason, so far from excluding the human faculty, rather presupposes it, belong to a line descending from Plato through St Augustine, Descartes, Bossuet and Leibniz. It was Plato who taught the doctrines of providence and a future life and established the moral sciences. The great Neo-Platonists, Plotinus and Augustine, reflected deeply on God's own being and on his relations with mankind; their achievement was the science of theology. Finally Descartes, on the necessary basis of the two concepts of God and the soul, opened the way to an authentic science of nature. Carteso-Platonism is therefore the only metaphysic consonant with true religion. Indeed between it and Christianity there is not so much affinity as identity. At least it could be said that one is the root of the other.[37]

Turning then to the realm of religious faith Bordas affirms his conviction that Christianity alone provides mankind with the knowledge of God as the principle and source of his being, and that apart from such knowledge one merely loses oneself in a wilderness of sensualism and materialism, to succumb in the end to the despotism of the secular state.[38] The revolutionary movement of the age must therefore be Christianized if it is not to destroy mankind spiritually. One thing however is certain; return to the condition of the *ancien régime* is impossible, morally as well as politically. The liberties which the events of 1789 had brought in their wake are man's of right, by virtue of his humanity itself, and the state no longer has any title to regard him as merely under its tutelage. On the contrary, it is the state's obligation

[35] *ibid.*, p. 8.
[36] 'N'est-il pas aussi impossible de percevoir le vrai avec une raison étrangère que de voir les couleurs, d'entendre les sons, de digérer les aliments avec les yeux, les oreilles et l'estomac d'autrui' (*Œuvres posthumes*, i, p. 30).
[37] *Mélanges*, p. 295.   [38] *ibid.*, pp. 316ff.

to respect and safeguard those liberties, liberty of conscience above all. Modern man has arrived at maturity and is now able to follow the guidance of his own reason whether in the knowledge of God or in promoting a just society on earth. A penetrating reading of history would reveal that the Revolution and indeed all modern progress is ultimately the work of divine providence. Science is as much the fruit of Christian inspiration as was the Gothic art of the middle ages. Freedom, in a word, is part of the spiritual heritage of Christendom, which has no more place for political oppression than for the materialism and worldliness from which such oppression springs. This truth, Bordas urges, is the basis of all Christian social doctrine. Unfortunately the church has not as a rule seen it so and in order to discipline mankind has allied herself with political despotisms. In attempting to extend her own authority by these means she has herself become materialistic and paganized. Descartes and the Revolution of 1789 — Bordas's Gallic pride must be taken for granted — had together brought men back to a realization of the character and implications of their true destiny on earth. 'Religious' Christianity, in short, is now making way for 'social' Christianity, although the process is still impeded by the church's own leaders who fail to understand the movement of their times. Their attitudes may have been appropriate to society under the conditions of the Fall, but are not so in the era of Redemption. Ecclesiastical authority had become as purblind as its Jewish forerunner in the days of the gospel.[39]

Bordas's criticisms are astonishingly outspoken. Not that he is hostile to the clergy as such: the church's organization is a necessity of its being and work, as proper to its ends as that of the state. What he deplores are the evils of institutionalism — the multifarious vested interests and the political and social backwardness which prevent the hierarchy in particular from appreciating the real conditions under which the gospel has now to be preached. 'For the generations to be converted to the Gospel in religion they have only to wait upon the conversion of the clergy to the Gospel in politics.' But if the overgrowth of the institutional element is to be counteracted the church will need to be more closely associated with the life of the nation generally. Unfortunately the laity themselves have no real independence of judgment, lay opinion having become largely clericalized and subjected to an exaggerated papalism that has now reached its apex in the theory of the pope's infallibility. This last notion is a dangerous error, since to equate infallibility with sovereignty, as does Maistre, is to reduce the supernatural order to the natural and in effect to impugn the divine character of the Catholic religion itself.[40] In any case an infallible papacy would be incompatible with the state's own authority, which for all Catholic citizens it would necessarily

[39] ibid., pp. 369ff.
[40] Les Pouvoirs constitutifs de l'Eglise, p. 322. cf. Mélanges, p. 418.

replace.[41] Ultramontanism is therefore in conflict with the just interests of society.[42] Even apart from the infallibility question the pope's claim to universal sovereignty has no practical justification. The papacy has never been able to prevent war and its incursions into temporal affairs have usually been unwarranted and frequently disastrous. As against papal autocracy the bishops have rights of their own. So too have ordinary priests as against bishops, while the laity similarly has its rights as against clerics in general. When, under the Constituent Assembly, the French Revolution introduced the principle of election to ecclesiastical office it did nothing contrary to the Christian and Catholic spirit. Exclusion of the laity from responsibility in church affairs has resulted only in the now familiar cleavage between clericalism and secularism. Indeed it would seem that 'the church has no ambition but to throw itself back into the middle ages, from whence it had been rescued by the seventeenth century and the Revolution'. For the good of society itself a rational balance must be re-established between the spiritual and the temporal.[43]

Jules Lequier

Before concluding the present chapter we may pause to consider another writer of unquestionable interest whose name has hitherto been no more prominent in the history of either philosophical or Catholic thought than that of the man we have just been discussing. He is Jules Lequier. It was Lequier's views which were largely instrumental in converting Charles Renouvier from an Hegelian-style idealism to the pronounced voluntarism characteristic of his mature philosophy. Lequier was a Breton, born at Quintin in 1814, the son of a doctor, and educated first at Saint-Brieuc and then at the Collège Stanislas in Paris. At the age of twenty he entered the École Polytechnique, where he quickly struck up the friendship with Renouvier which was to last for the rest of his life. More even than Bordas, he was a solitary by disposition, always preferring to think and work on his own. In 1848 he finally quitted Paris to settle in his native province, to which,

---

[41] Bossuet, says Bordas, had clearly foreseen this. 'Voila, dit le grand évêque de Meaux, les plaies affreuses qu'on a faites à l'Église et à la discipline, en attribuant au Saint-Siège cette enorme puissance de régler à son gré ou plutôt de bouleverser les affaires temporelles' (ibid., p. 415.).

[42] Bordas's friend and disciple Huet was if anything even more forthright in his condemnation of the ultramontane movement. Ultramontanism, he declared, 'hates only liberty and its martyrs; it eulogizes only despotism and its executioners. It has made the venerable centre of catholicity the odious citadel of absolutism in Europe, and the successor of the apostles the ally of the kings against the emancipation of Christian people' (R. Rezsohazy, Origines et formation du Catholicisme social en Belgique, 1842–1909, Louvain, 1948, p. 26). Quoted A. R. Vidler, A Century of Social Catholicism (1964), pp. 86f.

[43] Essais de Réforme catholique, p. 129.

like Lamennais, he was deeply attached.[44] It was not far from his home at
Plerin on the Breton sea coast that on 11 February 1862 he was found
drowned, probably from an act of suicide.[45] Morbidly sensitive and fastidious,
he spent his years and his energies in a perpetual struggle after an unattainable intellectual ideal.

Lequier's thinking was dominated by his profound belief in liberty. Is man
truly free? All other questions seemed to him ultimately to resolve themselves into this. His aim accordingly was to establish such a new methodology
as would lead to a reshaping of both philosophy and theology on the basis
of the concept of liberty as the 'primary truth' of all knowledge.[46] The grand
design, however, was far from carried to completion and what he actually
produced amounted to little more than plans and sketches. But of the ampli-
tude of the philosophical gift to which these meagre remains testify Renouvier had no doubt at all.[47] Indeed he was convinced that if his friend had
lived longer he would have achieved some of the best philosophical work in
the French tongue.[48]

As a Catholic with no inclination to question the dogmas of his faith
Lequier in his role as a *penseur* sought to construct a scheme of ideas on the
foundation of one central and all-embracing truth.[49] Like Bordas he saw
himself as a kind of 'second Descartes'; but no less was he a child of the
Romantic movement, a spiritual kinsman of Lamennais and Bautain. With
them he strove to create a philosophy that would provide at once a secure
basis for morality and a means of reconciling science with religion. But at
the same time he could not agree with either Lamennais's traditionalism
or Bautain's fideist tendency; nor again could he follow Bordas into Platonism.
He chose rather to pursue a route of his own, even though he never succeeded
in quite reaching the goal ahead.

If, then, the central problem for philosophy is that of freedom it must be
one that is vital to the whole issue between religion and science. But while
still at the École Polytechnique Lequier came under the influence of German
idealism, more particularly through the doctrines of Fichte, whose *Bestim-
mung des Menschen* had lately (1832) appeared in a French translation.[50]

[44] He shared to the full the traditional Breton melancholy. cf. J. Grenier, *La philosophie de
Jules Lequier* (1963), p. 13: 'Il s'est imprégné de cette mélancolie et de ce goût du rêve qui
caractérisent le pays celte et qui font que le romantisme y a une existence profonde, alors que
dans les pays vraiment façonnés par la culture latine, il n'a jamais été qu'une façade.'

[45] On the matter of Lequier's death see Grenier, *La philosophie*, where the facts are fully set out
(Appendix B, pp. 266–82).

[46] See *La Recherche d'une première vérité* (ed. Renouvier, 1865).

[47] Renouvier re-published some fragments of Lequier's work as an appendix to the second
(1875) edition of his own *Essais de Critique générale* (t. iii: *Traité de psychologie rationelle*).

[48] cf. *Esquisse d'une classification systématique des doctrines philosophiques* (1885) ii, pp. 381f.

[49] With this enterprise Renouvier had himself the closest sympathy, but he perhaps underestimated the weight of the orthodox Catholic content of Lequier's doctrine. This lack of balance
has been corrected by more recent commentators like Grenier and Jean Wahl (*Jules Lequier*,
Geneva, 1948).   [50] A new edition came out in 1836.

What especially impressed him was the way in which the German thinker had insisted upon the creative role of the *subject* in the whole process of knowing, an idea having its outcome in a concept of the Absolute as pure subject and thus as total freedom. Although allowing to moral action a wider scope than that of rational knowledge, Fichte had nonetheless seemed to demonstrate that science is itself an expression of subjective freedom. Another important element in the idealist system was the counter-principle of necessity, the recognition that the scientific account of reality assumes a universal determinism; although Fichte himself had sought to resolve the difficulty by arguing that the contingency of the subject is ultimate.

It was a Fichtean-type idealism, therefore, which Lequier adopted as the framework of the Christian philosophy he now planned to work out. Freedom, he believed, is the basic postulate of Christianity itself. The danger of idealism in its Hegelian form was the slide into a deterministic pantheism with which Christian teaching could not possibly come to terms. Moreover, Lequier was attracted by Fichte's sense of philosophy as *action*, and not simply passive contemplation. Philosophical enterprise, that is to say, is essentially a struggle for freedom, involving a sustained effort of will and a venture of personal faith. The very possibility of knowledge implies motivated choice and confidence in the resources of the self. The truth, in a word, has to be *conquered*, the conquest being one on which human destiny itself depends. But the vocation to freedom is also what Christianity offers. It too promises deliverance from the thrall of sheer necessity, whether external or internal.

Yet the influence of Fichte, potent though it was, did not alter the inherently Gallic bent of Lequier's thinking. As an heir of the Cartesian tradition he had an unshakable trust in reason. But like Maine de Biran he was certain that man has an immediate consciousness of freedom in the very exercise of will, and that it is this which provides the right starting-point for philosophical reconstruction. Reason *per se*, as Hegelianism shows, leads straight to determinism, and we cannot look to it for any *a priori* vindication of the liberty we feel to be our intrinsic possession. The fact of freedom, it might be said, is a 'pre-rational' truth, intuitively apprehended, rather than a proposition open to rational verification. We establish our self-hood by willing and opting, actions which are the effective basis of all knowledge. The way in which we cognize our freedom should however be properly understood; it is not so much that we have a direct consciousness of it as that we are aware of not being *merely* the creatures of necessity. Freedom, it follows, is not unconditioned and our options are neither total nor arbitrary. Actual willing is bound to be limited by the circumstances and hence is always to some extent predetermined, as the mind—body relationship, for instance, clearly proves. All the same, reason and responsibility do signify power of initiative, self-control and at least a relative degree of creativity in regard to the environment. Human freedom, in short, is a conditioned image of what in God is an absolute.

But it is incapable of exact conceptualization, being the condition on which the growth and formulation of ideas themselves depend. I am *because* I think, and I think *because* I am creatively free. Man looks for the truth because he has need of it, desires it and loves it, despite all preconceptions and obstacles. It is something to which he brings the whole energy of his mind as a rational being. Knowledge therefore is not a merely passive receiving or assimilation or 'intussusception'; on the contrary, it is creation. Were I subject purely to the law of necessity I could not *affirm* anything, for my affirmation would be meaningless. Without freedom there could be no knowledge, since nothing could be recognized to be the truth as distinct from falsehood. The entire edifice of scientic reason has been rendered possible only because deliberately motivated choice and discrimination is an existential fact. Individual self-realization, social development, civilization itself can be summed up in the maxim *Freedom freely willed*.

On this basis, then, Lequier proceeded from about 1840 onwards to work out his philosophical interpretation of Christianity.

This great truth of free-will [he wrote], which all philosophers, with one exception [i.e. Aristotle, in Lequier's view] have misunderstood, those who have claimed to uphold it as well as those who have attacked it, — this truth *Par excellence*, the root and fruit of all others, first in order and in importance, the alpha and omega (according to the way one looks at it) of human knowledge, is the property of the Catholic Church.[51]

Catholicism, because its dogmas presuppose this truth and its ethic extols and exemplifies it, offers the one authentic form of faith. For in Catholic teaching faith is in full union with reason. Indeed, as Lequier sees it, it is not a matter simply of agreement but of mutual compenetration. Nevertheless his Cartesianism is worn with a difference; it is not so much reason's assignable achievements that are significant — great though they are — as the effort of reasoning itself, the intelligent assertion of the will. It is through the act of will, he holds, by which we affirm our own existence, that God reveals himself. He wills in our willing, just as is it his reason which activates our thinking. For God, Lequier believes, is a living God whose will it is that man should be a participator in his own freedom and creativity.[52] But the existence of a God who is the very life of our life is not to be demonstrated by purely logical argument or by appeal to external 'evidences'. That he does exist is a free act

[51] Cited Grenier, *La philosophie*, p. 223.
[52] Sometimes there is in Lequier a distinctly Kierkegaardian ring: 'Sans doute, rien n'était difficile à Dieu: Dieu est la puissance même. Mais créer un être qui fut indépendant du lui, dans la rigueur du terme, un être réellement libre, une personne, quelle entreprise! Tout son art s'y emploie, et l'on ne sent quel tour de force achève le chef d'œuvre' (*La Recherche d'une première vérité*, ed. Dugas, 1924, p. 143). Lequier papers in the university of Rennes, ms 252, f. 20.

of faith on our part, springing from a recognition of our own limitations and what they imply. Logical argument has its uses only *within* the framework of religion, chiefly in externalizing under abstract terms what is known primarily and essentially as an inward and personal experience. Religion and philosophy, that is, are entirely different activities, having differing origins.

Let us not forget that philosophy and revelation are profoundly and absolutely distinct. Philosophy bears upon the truths which the mind conceives to be eternal; religion rests upon a contingent fact.[53]

Philosophical conceptions of God invariably tend to pantheism and the significance of contingent fact is difficult if not impossible for them to grasp. But the truth about God as Christianity understands it turns upon contingent fact and is presented under the revelational forms contained in the Bible and the doctrine of the Church.

For Lequier, then, as for Bautain the role of philosophy in religion is simply that of elucidating under intellectual categories the nature and implications of what is apprehended by the believer in the shape of authoritative dogma.

The fundamental truths which have their dwelling-place in our hearts and to which we have access by reason alone are simply those that Adam possessed. But the truths of Christianity are of another order; it was necessary for them to be revealed to mankind after the entry of evil into the world. All the same, the truths of revelation need to be in harmony with the truths furnished by reason, in such wise that metaphysical thought can throw light upon them, even as metaphysics in turn draws its confirmation from them.[54]

Lequier moreover distinguishes two levels of theological truth. The first contains what he regards as the 'natural' truths of reason, including not only divine existence and creation but the dogma of the trinity as well, which he treats in the speculative fashion reminiscent of some other thinkers of his time, themselves more or less influenced in this by St Augustine.[55] The doctrines of the fall, original sin, the incarnation and the redemption, which are to be received as mysteries, belong to the second, which Lequier takes as covering the entire history of salvation viewed as a series of events contingent alike upon man's misused freedom and upon God's merciful response to the condition resulting from it.[56] A Christian philosophy, he thinks, will attempt an interpretation of both levels in terms of its fundamental principle of liberty.

[53] Lequier papers, ms 255, f.18.
[54] *ibid.*, f. 101 (quoted Grenier, *La philosophie*, pp. 196f.).
[55] *ibid.*, ff. 25, 38—46. It would seem that Lequier here was especially influenced by Lamennais's *Esquisse d'une Philosophie*. Whether Lequier ever met Lamennais in person is questionable. Maréchal thinks that if he had it would most likely have been at one of Lamennais's lecture-courses at Juilly in 1830 or 1831. cf. Grenier, *La philosophie*, p. 205.
[56] Bordas-Demoulin, on the other hand, saw the fall as a truth of reason.

Regrettably Lequier never succeeded in deploying his ideas systematically, although his surviving manuscript notes make it clear that he envisaged a complete restatement of Catholic dogma in the spirit of the great mediaeval scholastics. Further, and as the proper consequence of this, he suggests an ethical restatement giving 'views on the future of the idea of free-will in the education and development of the individual, the constitution of the family, the organization of the state and the life of the church'. But in spite of Renouvier's endeavours, Lequier's work remained virtually unknown until well into the present century. Since Grenier's study, however, it has gained rather more attention, the existentialist tone of its thinking having been especially noted by Jean Wahl, who would himself class Lequier with Schelling and Kierkegaard among the precursors of modern Christian existentialism. It is hardly to be wondered then that Lequier's ideas should sometimes have strained the bounds of contemporary Catholic orthodoxy.[57] But through Renouvier his quiet influence was to contribute not a little to the voluntarism of the next generation of French thinkers. The Modernist, Edouard Le Roy, could fairly be said to reproduce Lequier's fundamental teaching.

[57] Grenier considers that Renouvier 'mutilated' his friend's thought by exaggerating its unorthodoxy (Grenier, *La Philosophie*, pp. 239—45).

8

ONTOLOGISM

The Louvain Philosophers

The philosophical doctrine which goes by the name of ontologism enjoyed a considerable vogue among Catholic thinkers during the middle decades of the nineteenth century as an alternative to the authoritarianism of the traditionalists. In France it carried with it the prestige of the Sorbonne, while in Belgium its adherents in the university of Louvain were numerous and important enough to form a distinctive school, recognized as such throughout Western Europe. It also had its representatives in Switzerland, where the Jesuit Père Rothenflue was already in the thirties expounding its characteristic ideas,[1] and even in the United States of America, where Fr Brownson held similar views. Its foremost teachers, however, were the Italian philosophers, Gioberti and Rosmini-Serbati, the latter of whom seems to have been the first to use the term itself, in order to distinguish his own doctrine from the 'psychologism' which in his opinion marred the usual presentations of the Cartesian metaphysic. But a philosophy having as its starting-point not the mere act of knowing (*'cogito ergo sum'*), but the concept of being *per se*, was by no means a new departure, since its ancestry is traceable back well beyond Descartes to the great Platonist—Augustinian tradition of the middle ages, of which Anselm and Bonaventura are the most shining examples.

The main inspiration of the nineteenth-century ontologists was the seventeenth-century French Oratorian Malebranche, whose *Recherche de la vérite*, first published in 1674, united Augustinianism with the teachings of Descartes in a kind of mystical rationalism. For Malebranche's doctrine centres upon the Reason which all men possess in common and by virtue of which they participate in the divine life itself. The realm of truth, he held, does not simply *depend* on God: it *is* God, directly accessible to the minds of his rational creatures. Sensation and imagination are produced in us not by objects but by the deity himself; they subserve our practical needs, but because the essence of matter is extension and its only real property motion, they tell us nothing about the nature of things as such. Knowledge of the external world must

[1] His *Institutiones philosophicae theoreticae*, lithographed in 1836, was published at Fribourg in 1842—3.

therefore be innate; for like Descartes Malebranche separates mind from matter, denying that matter of itself can possibly act upon mind. Indeed ideas are spiritual entities whose origin requires a power no less great than that needed for the creation of things material. Whatever we know, then, is known to us only because it already subsists in the mind of God, so that when we confront the world of experience we behold 'the rule, the order, the reason of God'.[2] To possess the truth is to share in the divine Logos himself, who is our spiritual 'homeland' and the real *locus* of the ideas that form the content of our thinking. God, we may say, is not, as in Neo-Platonism, simply the 'sun' of the intelligible world, the light by which all things are suffused; he is himself the direct object of mental vision, subject only to the extent to which he is willing to reveal himself. And that it is his will to reveal himself is evident from the very concept of the Infinite, which is prior to all idea of finite reality. For God does not derive his existence from his creatures but, on the contrary, is the one and only source of theirs. Thus what actually we come to know in apprehending the world is nothing other than God himself in his all-embracing truth.

This remarkable doctrine was given a new lease of life in the century following by the Savoyard cardinal, Gerdil (1718–1802), whose wide-ranging interests included mathematics and physics as well as theology and philosophy. A lesser Leibniz, he was thoroughly abreast of the learning of his day, rejoicing in its scientific advances while at the same time by no means unaware of the threat they offered to Christian faith. One of Gerdil's main works contains a vigorous attack on the philosophical teaching of John Locke.[3] He himself holds that in the act of knowing the mind is passive. We do not perceive the object of knowledge by means of some interior faculty or illuminative principle of our own, nor again do we arrive at it by reflexion on experience. To know is the result, rather, of the object's action upon ourselves, so that our ideas must have an origin independent of us. They exist, that is to say, *prior* to any attempt on our part to call them into mind, as they likewise also survive us. They are in fact part of being itself, and in receiving them we enter into intelligible union with being. Absolute being is identifiable with God, who is wholly beyond sense-experience. But Descartes was right, Gerdil believes, in interpreting the concept of the absolute or infinite positively. For if it were possible to reach such a concept *mediately* (i.e. through created beings) it would itself be no more than a form of the finite, a thing determinate and limited. Thus God can only be known to us *immediately;* and, as Malebranche teaches, all things are known to us *in him.* Sensation, as a mere impression on the feelings incapable of producing any authentic representation of being, is a condition resulting from God's

[2] *De la Recherche de la vérité* (ed. F. Bouillier, 1880), ii, p. 373.
[3] *La défense du Sentiment du P. Malebranche, sur la nature et l'origine des idées, contre l'examen de M. Locke* (Turin, 1748).

pre-established laws for the practical ends and purposes of life, and no more. Action is explicable as a movement of the will in response to our basic ideas of good, evil and obligation — ideas which themselves are also 'immediate', in the sense that they lack any assignable origin in personal need or social custom but spring from the direct union of our minds with the divine Logos himself. They thus constitute an order of perfection which has its eternal principles in him, so that to live morally is to seek to realize this order through a willing submission to its laws.

Such in outline was the type of philosophy whose mid-nineteenth-century revival is the subject now before us.[4] Its academic forum, as we have said, was the university of Louvain, although not at first. With the university's restoration in 1815 the trend was towards authoritarianism and the theories of Maistre, Bonald and Lamennais were eagerly taken up. But an interest in the problem of knowledge, as distinct from that merely of certitude, which had been concern of the traditionalists, gradually brought about a change of outlook. Thus the Louvain group came to recognize the need for some sort of *critique* of human reason if the conditions of knowledge are to be rightly assessed. But they were also aware of the perils — as it seemed to them — of idealist subjectivism, and for a while at least a few of them even inclined to a Lockean theory of representative ideas.

This revised and somewhat eclectic traditionalism was associated with the names principally of Gérard-Casimir Ubaghs (1800—1874) and Arnold Tits, but others of the school included N.-J. Laforêt, rector of the university, P. Claessens, N. Moeller and B. van Loo.[5] Ubaghs, its leading exponent, was professor of philosophy at Louvain from 1834 until his resignation following condemnation of his views at Rome.[6] In general they distinguished between 'notions' and 'ideas', the former acquired, the latter innate. Notions arise from the action of the mind on sense-experience, but because objects are essentially material and individual they have only a relative universality. By contrast, it is the property of ideas to be immediate, eternal and true absolutely. Hence they must be innate. Nevertheless ideas do not attain full articulation — Ubaghs characterizes them as 'anticipations' only — until elicited and developed by the social environment. Thus although innate, they do not amount, properly speaking, to knowledge *apart from* the cumulative experience embodied in tradition. Society provides the occasion of and stimulus to an intellectual process which renders actual what at first was only potential or embryonic. It cannot therefore be claimed that language

---

[4] Gerdil's *Istitutioni filosofici* was published for the first time in an edition by C. Vercellone in 1863.

[5] See J. Henry, 'Le traditionalisme et l'ontologisme à l'université de Louvain (1835—1865)', in *Annales de l'Institut supérieur de philosophie de Louvain*, v. (1924).

[6] See H. van Grunsven, *Gerard-Casimir Ubaghs* (1933) which is especially informative on Ubaghs' later career. The latter's ontologism is most fully set forth in his *Essai de l'Idéologie ontologique* of 1863.

precedes thought, for the power of thinking is intrinsic to every rational being; but at the same time it can hardly be regarded as simply a human invention. Moreover it is apparent that the first man, Adam, must have received his entire knowledge directly from God, through a unique revelation. At least such was Ubaghs' opinion, although Laforêt considered Adam's knowledge to have been a purely natural endowment. Others again held it to have been natural in respect of its object but supernatural (or 'extranatural') in the manner of its acquisition.

For the Louvain school the theory of innate ideas was of central importance. Society, it recognized, exercises a powerful influence, but it operates only on what the individual already possesses. How, though, are *notions* acquired? To this Ubaghs and his friends replied that our knowledge of external objects is always *mediate*: what the mind directly knows is only the mental representation of such objects. But the question then arises of the correspondence of these representations with the objects themselves which, *ex hypothesi*, lie beyond the mind's reach. Ubaghs maintained that the fact of this correspondence is from the nature of the case impossible to prove and has to be accepted on faith. But is such faith justifiable, and why? As opposed to either the fideist position adopted by Bautain and Huet, who believed it to be a divine gift — certitude, that is, being supernaturally guaranteed — or to that of Lamennais, who appealed to the no less divine authority of the common tradition, the Louvain philosophers see it as nothing other than the reason's inherent *self*-confidence. According to Ubaghs the ground of all certitude is man's native reason itself, his intelligence having been so constituted as to make him capable of knowing the truth. Radical scepticism is therefore precluded, since doubt of this capability would contradict man's instinctive trust in his own rationality and if persisted in could only result in self-negation. Thus it is that philosophy itself becomes a possible undertaking: reason and reality, we feel, have a mutual consistency. But it also substantiates faith, even when faith outstrips proof. For faith itself is but 'Reason' — to adapt a Wordworthian phrase — 'in her most exalted mood'.

By 1850 the Louvain school, without wholly abandoning the traditionalist doctrine, had moved over to the ontologist position. Certitude, they now held, lies in the immediate intuition of what is known. This conclusion they had in part reached from their study of the Scottish philosopher Reid, whose criticism of the 'intermediarist' standpoint had much impressed them, although in the main their inspiration came from that deep-rooted Platonist tradition in Catholic thought to which we have referred and which in France culminated in Malebranche. But there was also a more proximate influence in the person of Vincenzo Gioberti, who at the time was living in Brussels and whose *Introduzione allo studio della filosofia* had been published there in 1840.[7] It is clear that Ubaghs himself was considerably affected by Gioberti's

[7] A French translation came out in 1847.

views, as too were Laforêt and Claessens. In any case their former tradition-alism itself, with its own doctrine of innate ideas, rendered the transition to ontologism fairly easy. Ontologism could well, in fact, be judged as its logical outcome, for were not 'ideas', as distinguished from mere 'notions', possessed of those very attributes of necessity, universality and immutability which in the eyes of ontologists were the mark of their divine origin? On ontological principles our ideas of truth *are* the truth itself, if not in all its completeness then at least so far as it comes within the orbit of human intelligence. Indeed to know the truth is to know God, since, as St Augustine says, *Deus est veritas.*

These doctrines did not pass without criticism. In 1843 five propositions allegedly culled from them were referred to Rome by the papal nuncio. The upshot was an instruction from the Index that in all future editions of the works in which they had appeared the errors specified were to be corrected, nor were they to be repeated in any of the university's lecture-courses.[8] Ubaghs responded with a memorandum which although making a favour-able impression failed to secure a lifting of the censure. Exception had been taken in particular to the opinion that the metaphysical proofs of divine existence have only a secondary value, such validity as they have deriving from man's innate idea of God, the objectivity of which rests on 'natural faith'. But even apart from official disapproval the views of the Louvain school soon provoked controversy. In 1845 the *Journal historique de Liège* launched a campaign against the Louvain philosophy generally, which Ubaghs attempted to counter with an article in the *Revue catholique* examining 'the question of the origin of our knowledge from the point of view of orthodoxy'. He maintained that his and his colleagues' views were not new, and that their orthodoxy had never been seriously questioned, certainly had never met with episcopal condemnation. The debate, however, continued with some acrimony, Ubaghs and Laforêt tirelessly explaining and defending their position against repeated attacks. Three issues especially formed the core of dispute: the mind's native resources and the need for education, the origin of language, and the doctrine of a primal revelation. Neither side admitted loss of ground and the rival journals both claimed the advantage.

In 1858 the ontologists met with a decided set-back. A canon of Liège named Lupus brought out an immense work of over two thousand pages in which he submitted their doctrines to minute examination from a rigidly scholastic angle, concluding that they not only were useless as against secularist rationalism but contrary to scripture and the teachings of the Fathers. Unless checked 'ontologism' would throw open the door to heresy. Unhappily for Ubaghs and his friends Lupus' book, besides securing the approval of the Belgian episcopate, won praise from the influential Roman theologian Perrone, a fact which moved the Louvain professors to despatch

[8] *Acta S. Sedis*, iii (1867), pp. 206f.

a summary of their teachings to Rome in the hope of gaining a fairer judgment from the Congregation of the Index, should it be called upon to give one. A prompt reply from the prefect, Cardinal d'Andrea, was reassuring: their statement had contained only personal opinions and in any case nothing censurable. However a Belgian prelate, J.-B. Malou, known for his hostility to the Louvain school, wrote direct to Pius IX himself criticizing their views and even casting doubt on the sincerity of their recent explanation. He also accused them of having published an official document, namely d'Andrea's letter, without the pope's express leave. This unexpected intervention had the support moreover of the bishops of Liège and Ghent. The result was that in the summer of 1861 the pope referred the whole matter to both the Index and the Holy Office, whose judgment was communicated three years later (October 1864) in a letter to d'Andrea's successor, Cardinal Patrizzi. Pointing out that Ubaghs had disregarded the Vatican instruction of 1843, it charged the Belgian hierarchy to prevent any further dissemination of these opinions whether at Louvain or elsewhere. The luckless professor — who also was a priest — thus felt bound to submit, which he did in a letter forwarded to Rome by the archbishop of Malines, Cardinal Sterckx. In addition he promised to revise his published works. Even so the affair was not entirely settled. In an article in the *Revue catholique* (1862) Ubaghs had argued that the ontologist propositions censured by the Holy Office covered doctrines only of a pantheistic tendency and not those which he and his colleagues held. But this did not satisfy Rome, and in a letter to Cardinal Sterckx, dated March 1866, Patrizzi rejected Ubaghs' modifications as inadequate, insisting that his teachings be eliminated altogether from the university's philosophy courses. Once again Ubaghs complied, although some of his friends urged the difference between teaching a doctrine authoritatively and merely presenting it as a personal opinion. But the Holy Office demanded submission *minus* conditions and the Belgian bishops drew up a carefully-worded statement for the professors to sign. The signatures were forthcoming and the Vatican, by the hand of Patrizzi, intimated its satisfaction that agreement had at last been reached. Thus the philosophy of the whole Louvain school was repudiated as, if not formally heretical, at all events 'dangerous' (*absque periculo tradi non posse*).

Ontologism in France: Branchereau and Hugonin.

The revival of ontologism in Belgium had its counterpart in France, but its adherents there differed from the Louvain teachers in not composing a localized group or school. However, among the French as in the neighbouring country, the type of thought we are considering united a variety of elements — Platonist, Augustinian, Cartesian, romanticist — along with a thorough distaste for the spirit and methods of scholastic rationalism. The example of the great seventeenth-century theologians, Bossuet and Fénelon as well as Malebranche,[9] had never indeed been forgotten, and in spite of the flowing tide of the Mennaisian philosophy in the twenties and thirties there were many during the earlier decades of the nineteenth century who continued to uphold what they regarded as the great tradition, a tradition as truly Gallic as it was Christian. But the outstanding figures were those of abbés Branchereau and Hugonin, and it is with their names that the nineteenth-century French ontologist movement is usually associated.

Louis Branchereau, a native of La Vendée, was born in 1819. The intellectual abilities already apparent in his youth turned out to be those less of an original thinker than a particularly gifted teacher, although Victor Cousin entertained a high opinion of him. In the field of philosophy he published only one work, dating from the early years of his career when he was still at Saint-Sulpice.[10] *Praelectiones philosophicae* (1849), written partly in Latin partly in French, contained a three-year course in philosophy for seminary students. Intended merely as a serviceable text-book, it was remarkable in its day for the freshness of its standpoint as well as for its consistency and clarity, a combination of qualities which put it in advance of most contemporary works of the kind.

Branchereau, as a good Cartesian, begins with the significance of *thought*. One cannot think unless one thinks *something*; and since thought is the primal fact, whatever one actually thinks is bound to have some measure of reality. Now the objects of thought are of two categories, the necessary and the contingent, but how are they to be substantiated, especially the contingent — unless they *impose* themselves on the mind? Do they have any existence outside thought? More particularly, how is the problem raised by Kant's sceptical relativism to be met, a problem which some even have pronounced to be insoluble? Branchereau's reply is that the solution lies only in linking the succession of contingent truths to the divine absolute, after the manner of Malebranche, since all things are relative when viewed in the light of absolute being. The one way of surmounting the Kantian position lies in a return to Platonism, restated in terms of the intellect's 'vision in God'. The guarantee and safeguard of objectivity is therefore a Cartesian ontologism that has nevertheless learned how to correct Descartes' one-sided emphasis on 'independent' reason and to relate it to supernatural faith. Malebranche also of course had taken his stand on Descartes, but thinking as such was of less interest to him than the ideas that form its actual content. For ideas

[9] For Fénelon as for Malebranche the idea of the infinite is 'the infinite itself present to my mind', since by no finite idea can the infinite be represented. 'Il faut donc conclure invinciblement que c'est l'Être infiniment parfait qui se rend immédiatement présent à moi quand je le conçois, et qu'il est, lui-même l'idée que j'ai de lui.' Again: 'L'objet immédiat de mes connaissances universelles est Dieu même.'

[10] Branchereau died in 1913. On his life and work generally see A. Crosnier, *Louis Branchereau* (1915).

have a reality apart from the knower, since their ultimate ground is the mind of God himself. With this assurance metaphysics becomes a possible enterprise and mere subjectivism, Kantian or Cartesian, is avoided.

In 1862 Branchereau summed up his theory of knowledge in a series of propositions on which he sought the judgment of the Holy See.[11] They state his belief that in epistemology an essential distinction has to be drawn between the thinker and his thought — that the subject-object relation defines the nature of knowledge. Every effort of the mind to determine what is true or represents reality as intelligible implies it. But the object of knowledge is distinguishable as either absolute or relative. In the one case reality has both infinite and concrete perfection since it is nothing less than *being* itself, not merely abstract and generalized but existing in all its fullness and power. It is what we mean when we speak of God; for by definition absolute being must be conceived as existing necessarily. Thus in principle at least Descartes's ontological argument is vindicated. But in the other case, that of relative being, we are faced with the contingent, with possibility and actuality. As a possibility a relative entity corresponds to the eternal and necessary idea which constitutes its essence, whereas when actualized it enters the realm of contingency and transience. In other words, its essence or intelligible content, as necessary and eternal, has its being in God, or more precisely in the divine Logos as the *locus* of all possible reality. Thus each and every contingent being has its metaphysical essence or archetype in God himself.

It may be noted here that Rosmini, the leading nineteenth-century exponent of ontologism, maintained that the 'intelligible essence' of relative existants must be understood as a purely formal or ideal mode of being. But in Branchereau's view the genuinely Augustinian tradition is that our ideas, as grounded in God, participate in his reality. It is because thinking implies immediate contact of the human mind with the divine that absolute being can be conceived as the guarantee of the objective truth of our ideas. To argue thus, says Branchereau, is not to fall into pantheism because that immediate relationship with the divine which constitutes knowledge is a relationship with God's Reason or Word and *not* his inner and intrinsic being, which in its infinity and absoluteness lies of course beyond the reach of human understanding. The claim that thought brings us into direct contact with the divine is simply to assert the objectivity of knowledge.

When however we consider *relative* being, not indeed in its ideal essences but merely in terms of particular entities subject to the conditions of time and space and the flux of actual existence, we realize that they no longer derive their metaphysical status from the 'vision in God' but from the power of the divine creativity. *As* created they are known to us neither as they exist in God nor as they are in themselves, but only as they appear to us in sense-

[11] cf. *Annales de Philosophie chrétienne* (1867) pp. 265ff.

perception. But our trust in this rests on our conviction that God does not allow us to be deceived in so fundamental a matter. Thus the link between the theory of knowledge and the doctrine of being, *ontology*, is seen to be the idea of creation. For by an act of his free will and power God renders actual whatever in him is *possible*, conferring substantive existence upon it without entailing any division or diminution of his own being and perfection. Hence created existence, which has its being through his will *ex nihilo*, can be said to stand 'outside' God: in no sense can it be equated *with* God. Creation simply means that a mode or degree of being already *in* God is given a degree or mode of being external to him, which further means that it is now no longer part of the divine perfection but subsists in a state in which change and decay inevitably occur, its 'idea' alone persisting outside time. The specific objects of our knowledge are therefore, in relation to God, so exteriorized and individuated as to exclude all risk of pantheism. Such, in Branchereau's view, is the principle of a genuinely theistic ontologism, rooted at once in the teaching of St Augustine, that we necessarily think our thoughts *in Deo* and by the light of his reason, and in the biblical doctrine of creation, which at no point confounds the creature with its Creator.

Flavien-Abel-Antoine Hugonin, the best-known of nineteenth-century French ontologists, was born in 1823 at Thodure in Dauphiné and educated at Saint-Sulpice and at Archbishop Affre's then recent foundation for the higher education of the clergy, the École des Carmes, to the teaching staff of which he was subsequently himself appointed. In 1850 he was ordained priest. Four years later he took his doctorate in letters with a thesis on the theory of form and matter in the philosophy of St Thomas Aquinas, and also published a study of Hugh of St Victor.[12] From 1859 he held a lectureship at the Sorbonne until his nomination to the bishopric of Bayeux in 1866.[13] Canonical institution to his see was deferred, however, until he had satisfied the Vatican that he no longer maintained positions in his philosophical teaching coincident with the ontologist doctrines censured by the Holy Office in 1861. Although such assurance was forthcoming — given through the papal nuncio in October 1866, a fact notified to the public press at the time — his consecration did not take place until May 1868. At the Vatican Council two years later he supported Dupanloup's opposition to the infallibility definition and was critical of the Council's mode of procedure in other respects. But his episcopal duties did not interrupt his philosophical work and new publications appeared from time to time.[14] He died at Caen in 1898.

The views which Hugonin propounded during his earlier career received

---

[12] *Étude sur les œuvres de Hugues de Saint-Victor* (1854).

[13] cf. A. Lebleu, *Vingt-cinq ans de Sorbonne et de Collège de France* (1884), pp. 36–75.

[14] They included: *Philosophie de Droit social* (1885), *Études philosophiques* (1894), and *Dieu est-il connaissable?* (1895).

definitive statment in what was to remain his most important literary work, *Ontologie, ou étude des lois de la pensée*, which came out in 1856. On this his achievement as a thinker largely rests. To many readers it seemed to offer precisely that new style of Christian philosophy needed to vindicate the rights of reason against traditionalism as well as to defend theistic metaphysics against the growing popularity of Comtean positivism. At the same time its appeal to intuition made a welcome change from scholastic rationalism.

Hugonin opens his treatise with a carefully-phrased introduction in which he argues the scientific character of ontology as the true form of philosophical thinking. That as the theory of being *qua* being it affords the mind its primary certitude —since it insists on the fact of being as the ground and presupposition of every question relating to being —was a truth well understood not only by Malebranche but by the best thinkers of both the middle ages and antiquity. It alone can turn the edge of the Kantian criticism.[15] Its starting-point is, quite properly, the Cartesian *cogito*, or in other words the self-reflective activity of thought whereby it apprehends its own possession of the truth (i.e. being rendered *intelligible*). For to say 'I think therefore I am' means that thought establishes being *per se* and not merely the particular being of the thinking subject. Hence the primal truth — it is the basis and condition of every other — that thought itself implies a reality which is distinct from the thinking process. This conclusion is inescapable, whether we refer to perception — there must be *something* to be perceived — or to judgment, for in judging we do not *make* the truth but only recognize the existence of what already *is*, be it object or relationship. It is not, then, the nature of mind or reason itself which first requires attention, but the reality or being upon which the mind operates. Ontology is thus the *sine qua non* of all coherent thought at the philosophical level.

But how in more precise terms is the relation of thought to being to be explained? One thing, Hugonin maintains, must be accepted at the start: that relationship is not in any sense an *inference*; there is no hiatus between mind and its object. Being is communicated *in* thought: when we think we *ipso facto* participate in being. 'To perceive is so simple an act that it escapes all analysis.'[16] It is to penetrate the reality of things, to receive the truth into oneself.[17]

Being is the law of my judgement, as it is the law of my perceptions. I affirm being as I perceive it, and just as I cannot perceive nothing so neither can I affirm nothing. *Being is*: such is the ontological element that I seek.[18]

[15] It is evident from Hugonin's whole conception of philosophy as 'the science of thought, its laws and its principal objects viewed as such' that he has the challenge of Kant very much in sight.

[16] *Ontologie*, i, p. 30.   [17] *ibid.*, p. 33.   [18] *ibid.*, p. 53.

Our thinking would be meaningless did it not itself share in being. It does not have to discover being or establish it, for no sort of mediation is necessary. The mind knows spontaneously and immediately that being *is* and that it is the reason's instant possession.[19] But being can be thought of either as unlimited — pure being, that is, or being *per se* — or as limited — being particularized and defined. Unlimited being is at once the supremely intelligible and the supremely real, infinite and perfect: in a word, *God*. Limited being, on the other hand, is being as circumscribed by negation; we speak of it in terms of some particular aspect or degree or property. Moreover we distinguish essence from existence. Many, following the Aristotelian tradition, would claim that existence precedes essence: we first must know *whether* a thing is before we can ask *what* it is. But ontology puts essence before existence: the 'what-ness' of a thing, its intelligibility, is the primary question. Is it, we ask, something intrinsically possible and not self-contradictory, something which is genuinely amenable to thought? Existence is less easily defined; we could perhaps designate it as the state of being *more than merely possible*. Aristotelians conceive it as the union of matter and form. But whatever explanation we give of it, and none is likely to be wholly adequate, the distinction between existence and essence remains clear. Existence is individual and contingent, essence universal and necessary.

Being in itself has three determinate properties or attributes, namely unity, truth and goodness. Unity is intrinsic to being *per se* as an absolute. In the case of limited beings, however, it is only relative, although an individual entity is properly intelligible only if it is in some way itself a unity. Truth is being as apprehended in thought; and truth — or in theological language the divine Word — includes the manifold perfections of order and harmony, summed up in the concept of beauty. When the scholastic philosophy defines it as *adaequatio rei et intellectus* what basically is to be understood is that being, limited or unlimited, is always in fact the thought of a *supreme* intelligence. Truth as it pertains to particular existants stands in that essence which constitutes their particularity, an essence which has its potential or antecedent being in God. The good, finally, is being as loved and willed. It requires reality and truth as its precondition, but it is not to be thought of as merely a subjective 'value', a product of human desire or a quality attributable to human action. Goodness, like truth, is intrinsic to being.[20] But there is also something more to be said. The absolute being of God in its *triunity* — the coexistence of being, truth and goodness in the unity

[19] Ce n'est pas du concept formel ou subjectif que je déduis la réalité objective de l'être; une telle déduction serait une pétition de principe. L'être est donné dans la pensée et par la pensée; mais s'il est donné dans la pensée, c'est qu'il est en soi ... Je le perçois comme une réalité qui m'informe, comme une règle ou une loi qui me domine' (*ibid.*, p. 111). Again: 'L'être nécessaire est donc perçu en lui-même, par conséquent il est. J'arrive à son existence sans nulle déduction, mais par une intuition immédiate. Cette instance ne se prouve pas, elle se constate' (p. 171).

[20] *ibid.*, p. 159.

of one and the same essence — has its counterpart or reflexion in created beings, though most clearly so of course in intelligence.[21] Here the Christian creed reinforces and clarifies the insight of philosophy by the light of supernatural revelation, teaching that the three 'primordialities' of being are hypostatized as three distinct 'persons'. This implies that there are no grounds whatever for separating faith from reason in the way that traditionalism and fideism envisage. To divorce theology from philosophy is to impair the credibility of both.

Having once established that being is directly disclosed to us in thought the philosopher's next task is to show exactly how this comes about. He must go on to consider being not as it is in itself but as apprehended by us *in the mind*. Thus his next inquiry is the nature of truth. Now on ontologist principles it is clear that truth is a matter of essences, not of existants; or in other words, things are known under that aspect of them which is universal and necessary. To try to extract the general from the particular is vain, for knowledge of the particular itself depends upon knowledge of the general, which alone is intelligible. But if we can form no idea of the particular *as such* how is it that finite objects can be known by us at all? Because, says Hugonin, their empirical element is given in perception, whereas their rational element, which is anterior to the empirical, is conveyed by the ideas we already have of them in their essences. It is from this rational element alone that the empirical takes its meaning. Thus Plato and Augustine are right as against Aristotle and Aquinas. For the Platonist tradition has properly maintained the reality, or objectivity, of the ideas which comprise the substance of thought, so making possible genuine science or unified knowledge and yielding the certitude of truth as distinct from the fluctuating impressions of the senses. Platonism therefore directs us away from the blind turnings of both Lockean empiricism and Fichtean idealism: in the latter indeed the subjective principle is so inflated as to become constitutive of all reality. Only an ontologist metaphysic explains how we come by concepts having an existence independent of us; a philosophy resting on individual experience certainly fails to do so. That our moral ideas, at least, cannot have had their origin in sense must be obvious to all.

Hugonin, then, finds himself at odds with St Thomas. In fact the great scholastic, though always displaying singular clarity and penetration when dealing with philosophical issues, did not, Hugonin thinks, have philosophy as his main interest. He made no attempt to work out a metaphysic of his own, but was content simply to adapt the new Aristotelianism to the needs (as he saw them) of Christian theology, which was his real concern. Though unlike Aristotle, St Thomas holds (with St Augustine) that ideas pre-exist

[21] The idea that the 'trinitarian' character of ultimate reality can be established by natural reason was, as we have already noted, much favoured among certain Catholic thinkers at this time. Bonald holds it, as too do Lamennais (in his later works), Buchez and Hermes.

in God, inasmuch as the divine essence contains within itself the essences of all things. But it also is his view that ideas as they exist in God are not the same as those which present themselves to our minds, and he falls back on a quite different principle of intelligibility by which sense-experience and the intrinsic light of individual reason play the determining roles. Hence St Thomas and his expositors repeat Aristotle's mistake of seeing universals only as the product of intelligence activated by sensation. As a result Thomism fails in the end to offer any assurance of truth as immutable and eternal.

The strength of ontologism in Hugonin's eyes is that while avoiding the errors of empiricism it also escapes the pantheism into which idealist doctrines so easily slip. For on Hegelian principles ideas are no more than historically conditioned and therefore ever-varying aspects of the Absolute, so that all truth is essentially relative to the evolutionary process itself. What is true in one age may hence become false in the next. Error and even evil are simply the limits which a ceaseless 'becoming' continually transcends.

But Hugonin was also critical of Rosmini, who in his opinion had conceded too much to Kant. He had indeed a high regard for the Italian thinker, whose views he discusses at length, but he makes the point that ontologism, like other philosophies, may well mean different things to different minds and that only in the form developed by Malebranche is it wholly acceptable. Rosmini's attempt to relate Augustinian Platonism to the critical philosophy was, he thought, a good deal more ingenious than convincing: Plato and Kant were poles apart. Rosmini held, with Kant, that to think is to judge and judgment completes the synthesis of sense and understanding.[22] Kant, along with idealists generally, failed, when trying to explain the nature of knowledge, to distinguish the idea in its basic intelligibility from the knowing subject himself and the conditions under which the latter exists. Ontology, Hugonin urges, posits a reality that is absolute, uncreated and wholly independent of the perceiving mind. Rosmini, on the other hand, allows the notion of a truth which somehow is created by the subject, thus undermining the objectivity of truth. But if truth is really to be known it must be 'given' with the living reality of god. This fundamental principle can brook no compromise with Kantian subjectivism and agnosticism.[23]

[22] *Ontologie*, i, pp. 311f.
[23] cf. Foucher, pp. 186f. It has been questioned whether Rosmini really was an ontologist. He was unattracted by Malebranche's theory of knowledge as 'vision in God' and accords it some rough handling. A thinker of unquestionable originality, his own system, outlined first in *Nuovo saggio sull'origine delle Idee* (1830) and elaborated in his *Sistema filosofico* (1845), is so subtly nuanced as to render exact classification difficult. He himself repeatedly rejected the description of his views as ontologist. Malebranche's great mistake, in his judgment, was to suppose that one could pass from the merely indeterminate idea of *being* to that of God in all his living reality. The deity, the Italian philosopher thinks, is known only by way of a 'representative idea', such as is not in any sense primal or innate but the outcome of philosophical reflexion. Whether God actually exists, therefore, is something to be demonstrated, and he himself resorts to the classical

Hugonin's ontologism is thus entirely in line with Malebranche's and firmly rooted in the Augustinian tradition. So for all the respect in which he held St Thomas Aquinas as a theologian he felt in no way bound to follow him as a philosopher. Further, the notion that Thomism is a form of ontologism in disguise seemed to him quite untenable. Yet his own successor at the Sorbonne, Jules Fabre d'Envieu, although a convinced upholder of ontologist doctrines, did believe a reconciliation between the two philosophies to be possible, as he himself undertook to show. The difficulty which many felt about ontologism was that, despite its protestations to the contrary, it had about it an unmistakably pantheistic look. Thomism did at all events avoid this pitfall. But Fabre's own opinion, sincerely maintained, was that there is a good deal more of the Platonist in St Thomas than is usually realized and that no compelling reason can be adduced why a Thomist should not feel himself at ease even among ontologists.[24] He had as a former Jesuit himself received training in Suarezian Thomism, but had been subsequently influenced in an ontologist direction by a fellow-Jesuit, Jean-Pierre Martin, a man who, although publishing nothing, was looked on in his own circle as something of an oracle in philosophical matters.[25] When Fabre left the Society he took the opportunity to reply to a recent book by another Jesuit, Henri Ramière, a staunch Thomist, entitled *De l'Unité dans l'enseignement de la philosophie au sein des écoles catholiques* (1862), in which the author delivered a sharp attack on the whole ontologist position. At the time he was preparing his own *Cours de Philosophie* (1863), but he at once set about answering his Thomist

proofs, the ontological in particular, in order to effect this. Gioberti, we may note, was under no illusion in the matter of his compatriot's alleged ontologism. Hugonin, who in any case was more theologian than metaphysician, was probably right in thinking the Rosminian doctrine at least as much idealism as a form of ontologism.

[24] The ontologists were in agreement with the Thomists that it is inadmissible to speak of a 'Christian philosophy', if by that is meant a philosophy peculiar to Christianity and the exclusive property of the church, as traditionalism, particularly when presented by the *Annales de Philosophie chrétienne*, was tireless in urging. Thus Hugonin very emphatically states: 'Nous ne pensons pas qu'il y ait une philosophie chrétienne, c'est-à-dire une philosophie fondée par Jésus-Christ en dehors des lumières purement naturelles, une philosophie qui soit le domaine exclusif de l'Église, qu'elle ait mission d'enseigner, comme elle a mission de prêcher l'Évangile, dont elle ait érigé les principes en dogme de foi. La foi et la grâce guerrissent la raison; mals elles ne la remplacent pas. Donc une philosophie chrétienne n'est et ne peut être qu'une philosophie qui prépare à la foi et à la théologie. Il est déplorable de voir l'abus qu'on a fait depuis quelque temps de ce mot *chrétien*, combien les esprits superficiels se laissent séduire par les expressions dont ils ne cherchent même pas le signification, et comment un mot jeté au hasard peut donner naissance à une grande controverse, dans laquelle les plus grands intérêts sont engagés et parfois compromis' (*Ontologie*, i, pp. 387f.).

[25] See J. Burnichon, *La Compagnie de Jésus en France, histoire d'un siècle*, iii, pp. 140–61. Martin, who seems to have been largely self-taught, exercised a considerable influence on French ontologist thinking, mainly through personal intercourse, since his writings circulated only in manuscript. Five of the propositions censured by the Holy Office in 1861 are said to have been extracted from them. In 1850, on the authority of his superiors, he was inhibited from teaching certain opinions listed in seventeen propositions. cf. Burnichon, *La Compagnie*, iii, p. 594.

opponent in an explicit *Défense de l'Ontologisme contre les attaques de quelques écrivains qui se disent disciples de Saint Thomas.*

Fabre begins by calling to mind what the ontologist philosophy really says, as distinct from the misinterpretations of its adversaries. If the learned Jesuit is looking for unity in philosophical teaching let him drop the Peripatetic principle of *nihil est in intellectu quod prius non fuerit in sensu* and return to St Augustine's belief in the objective reality of ideas as the intelligible types of all existing things, types which have their necessary and eternal ground in the absolute being of God. Indeed St Thomas, when rightly understood, can be seen — so Fabre argues — to belong himself to the Augustinian tradition, despite his Aristotelian borrowings; for he holds, with Augustine, not only that God contains in himself the ideal patterns or archetypes of all creatures but that our human understanding draws its own light from the divine reason itself, which for us is the reason of our reasonings and the very foundation of knowledge.

Nevertheless from the ontologist's point of view there are weaknesses in St Thomas which it would be folly to overlook. And foremost among them is of course the empiricist theory of knowledge which he derives from Aristotle. He does not appreciate, what Malebranche was so insistent upon, that it is impossible to rest the concept of God on experience merely of finite objects. Yet Aquinas's statement, for example, that since God is revealed through his creatures he cannot himself be the primary object of knowledge,[26] difficult though this must be for an ontologist to accept on the face of it, is still capable of being construed in an ontologist sense. For what it really signifies is a reflective or rationalized knowledge of God, not that immediate and spontaneous apprehension of him which St Thomas himself admits to be natural to all men. Again, it is true that the philosopher-saint — whose true vocation, one should remember, was that of a theologian — holds that any direct perception of the divine essence which the soul may attain to is a supernatural *enablement*, the gift of grace. Yet Fabre stresses that ontologists of every shade of thought would agree that the knowledge of God's inner being or essence, the source itself of the divine perfections which we speak of as his attributes, cannot be reached through our natural resources alone. What they claim, rather, is that it is only *in God* that we discern the rational principles of things, the highest of which, indeed the one that illuminates all others, is the idea of God himself as pure and sovereign Being. However, for a *supernatural* understanding of the divine nature, as expressed in the dogma of the trinity, revelation is necessary. Contrasted with this the 'natural' or extrinsic knowledge of God with which the ontologist is especially concerned could be described, in a word Fabre borrows from Martin, as *extuitive*. The intuitive vision of God is enjoyed only by the blessed. St Thomas's

---

[26] *Summa theol.*, p. i, qu. 88, art. iii.

teaching always merits the closest attention, but on this point, Fabre thinks, he is open to correction in the light of the older and more consistent tradition that the primary evidence of divine existence is the actual presence of necessary truth within the soul. Ramière, like other opponents of ontologism, has misconceived the doctrine he impugns and is in fact in error in supposing it to have been condemned by the Vatican in 1861.

The End of the Debate

Fabre's argument is an interesting one, if not altogether convincing as an interpretation of Aquinas; but it certainly did not bring the ontologist debate to an end. Ramière himself answered it in the *Revue du Monde catholique* (1862–3), contending that the 1861 decree was directed at 'moderate' ontologism no less than any other kind and that Fabre's supposed distinction between the 'inward' (*intime*) and the 'outward' (*extime*) essences of God was a pure verbalism. Fabre, undeterred, countered in *Réponse aux lettres d'un sensualiste contre l'ontologisme* (1864), in which he cited the instance of two Roman priests, Antonio Rignano, a Franciscan, and Carlo Vercellone, a Barnabite, both of them consultants of the Holy Office, who had actually published treatises on plainly ontologist lines, and who in so doing had run into no difficulties.[27] He also pointed out that Propaganda itself had sponsored an edition by Vercellone of a hitherto unpublished work of Gerdil's. Such evidence left no doubt in Fabre's mind that the Roman censure was not directed against all forms of ontologism, although a series of articles by the German Jesuit Josef Kleutgen in the Mainz periodical, *Der Katholik*, aimed to demonstrate that the censured propositions quite definitely had the current ontologism in view. The latter in turn evoked a pseudonymous *riposte* in a work entitled *Orthodoxie de l'ontologie*, which appeared in 1869.[28] Pantheist and rationalist errors, the author agreed, were to be condemned, and even Malebranche's teaching must be considered suspect from the Vatican's point of view. But contemporary ontologism, such as Hugonin's or Fabre's, which had simply re-emphasized the teachings of Bossuet and Fénelon, was immune. Indeed it was based upon three principles which could not be faulted and which Rome did not prohibit. The first was that we have a direct intuition of God, not in his essence but in his attributes, and not by identifying our human existence with the divine but by the presence of God himself to the soul as the light of our human understanding. The second affirmed a direct intuition on our part of the eternal types of God's creation, while the third admitted a no less direct knowledge of contingent beings in their individuality. Whether or not these three principles were censurable would

[27] The former with his *Il principio protologico dell'umana intelligenza o il concetto dell' 'Itinerarium mentis ad Deum' di San Bonaventura* (1863), the latter in *Dottrine filosofiche di San Agostino* (1863).
[28] The author used the *non-de-plume* of 'Jean Sans-Fiel'. He had already published (1865) a *Discussion amicale sur l'ontologisme*.

depend on whether they were ambiguous and in particular whether they contained a latent pantheism. But ontologists like Hugonin expressly rejected any tendency in that direction. On the question of perception a clear distinction had been made between the sensible, the intellectual (i.e. perception of the particular or contingent), and the rational or universal, the last alone requiring an intuition of the infinite, made possible by the action of the absolute itself upon the human mind. Thus for the 'moderate' ontologist there were two modes or channels of intellectual illumination, the (one — in the full sense — rational, the other empirical. As a statement of the ontologist case this pseudonymous book was in fact as lucid as could be expected.

A proposal was introduced at the Vatican Council of 1870 to condemn ontologism, or at least the doctrine of a 'natural' vision of God, but it failed to gain acceptance; insufficient time remained, it was felt, for discussion of the subject. The real reason for the decline of interest in this type of philosophy is however to be found less in official opposition than in the revival of Thomism then gathering pace and soon to receive the blessing of the highest authority. It is appropriate at this point therefore to afford it some consideration.

The Beginnings of the Thomist Revival

Ontologism and neo-Cartesianism, much open to criticism though they may have been, did at least uphold the rights of reason alongside the claims of faith; rights which traditionalism, especially when armed with the ironic mockery of a Lamennais, had come near to denying altogether. Yet their success in loosening the grip which the traditionalist doctrine had maintained for over a generation on the minds of Catholic intellectuals in France was only partial,[29] and after the overthrow of the Second Republic the attractions of authoritarianism, as presented by such organs of opinion as Louis Veuillot's *Univers* and the little less influential *Monde catholique*, could not be said to be fading. Nevertheless — and somewhat paradoxically, it may be thought — an attitude of mind whose appeal seemed to depend on the extent to which it denigrated mere reason, was gradually to produce a reaction in favour of mediaeval scholasticism. Hitherto traditionalists and fideists alike had agreed on the rejection of Aristotelianism, and with it at any rate the metaphysics of St Thomas Aquinas. For Aristotelianism meant non-Christian rationalism, an unsuitable foundation for a Christian philosophy in any genuine sense of the word. But with the turn of the half-century Thomism, which had never lacked supporters, began to acquire new prestige as the crowning intellectual glory of that distant mediaeval world in which Catholic faith and order were still untroubled by the subversive forces of Protestantism and its noxious

[29] cf. E. Chastel, *L'Église et les systèmes de philosophie moderne* (1852), pp. 154f.

offspring, the secular Enlightenment. Thomist philosophy, that is, could be seen as the historic symbol of Catholic cultural unity. Viewed thus it appeared as the most fitting instrument, on the intellectual side, for the ecclesiastical conservatism which now turned increasingly to Rome for encouragement and direction.

In Lamennais's *Essai* of 1817 the Restoration had found an eloquent and persuasive voice. Nothing nearly so impressive was to make itself heard in the days of Louis-Napoléon, but Barbey d'Aurévilly's *Les Prophètes du passé* (1851), slight enough in itself, was symptomatic of a growing trend in Catholic thinking. For the cry now was 'Back to the middle ages', of which the Angelic Doctor had been so conspicuous an ornament. It was a curious twist in historical perspective, for which, moreover, a single writer was in no small degree personally responsible, Giacchino Ventura di Raulica (1792–1861), at one time a strong traditionalist and a friend and disciple of Lamennais. A noted Roman theologian, canonist and preacher, he delivered the oration at Pius VII's funeral and enjoyed the personal confidence of both Leo XII and Gregory XVI, although his earlier writings were strongly coloured by Lamennais's ideas and for this reason provoked some controversy.[30] Later however came disillusionment with the whole Mennaisian doctrine and the relations between the two men were finally severed. At the time of Pius IX's election he openly sympathized with liberal aspirations in the papal states, but after the pontiff's flight to Gaeta he left Italy and sought asylum in France where — having in the meantime largely abandoned his liberalism — he came to enjoy the favour of Napoleon III. As provincial of the French Theatines Ventura lived in Paris until his death in 1861. His main, though uncompleted, literary work was his *Philosophie chrétienne*, published in the same year.

The year Ventura settled in Paris saw the publication of his *Raison philosophique et la raison catholique, ou démonstration philosophique des principaux dogmes catholiques* (1851), which, with its sequel, *La Tradition et les semipélagiens de la philosophie, ou le semi-rationalisme dévoilé*,[31] sets out fully the position he now had reached. At the same time it is clear that although he had come to think of himself as a Thomist he had not entirely abandoned traditionalism. Certainly no true Thomist could have accepted his theory of knowledge. Our ideas, he says, are of two kinds; the notions we form of material things from the images created by sense-experience, and our concepts of non-material or spiritual entities, above all God and the soul. That

---

[30] e.g. *De methodo philosophandi* (1828). Ventura brought out an Italian translation of Maistre's *Du Pape* in 1825 and shortly afterwards a commentary on Bonald's *Législation primitive*.
[31] *La tradizione e i semipelagiani della filosofia ossia il semirazionalismo svelato* (Milan, 1857). On Ventura's ideas generally see A. Cristofoli, *Il pensiero religioso del P. Giacchino Ventura* (1927), and for his part in the nineteenth-century Thomist revival G. Albino, 'Contributo del P. Ventura al rinascita del tomismo nel secolo 19', in *Regnum Dei: Collectanea Theatina*, v (1949), pp. 260–8, should be consulted. See also pp. 115f. above.

the latter can be regarded as the product of reason alone is impossible, since of divine existence we have at the most, humanly speaking, no more than an instinctive apprehension. It follows therefore that God must himself be the source of all knowledge of spiritual and moral truth, by way of an original revelation which has been transmitted verbally from generation to generation. Thus language must be seen to have a permanent and indispensable role. Nevertheless — for at this point Ventura somewhat modifies the traditionalist theory —the function of reason is not so much that of communicating revelation as of demonstrating by its own light the truth of what tradition has preserved and of deducing from the premises of faith the theological conclusions implicit in them. What it cannot do is to discover any really new spiritual truths. Hence faith is necessarily anterior to the work of reason.

Ventura's 'traditionalist' Thomism moreover admits no serious debt to Aristotle. In fact he dislikes Greek metaphysics in general, as indeed any other philosophy of *mere* reason. Truth, he holds, is in all important respects *given*, whether as a 'natural' disclosure before Adam's fall, or as a 'supernatural' one after it, both revelations alike being embodied in the Bible and the Christian creed. Thus on the face of it Ventura's neo-scholasticism of 1851 remains substantially in accord with what he was saying back in the eighteen-twenties, except that he has now rejected Lamennais's idea of the *raison générale* along with those vestiges of Cartesianism — particularly the notion of innate, 'embryonic' ideas — still retained by Bonald. Fundamental to his whole way of thinking is the distinction he draws between the 'inquisitive' or speculative function of reason and its 'analytic' or demonstrative function, or alternatively between 'Catholic' and 'philosophical' reason. Doctrines relying on inquisitive reason, as history repeatedly shows, have been a constant source of error. The divorce between philosophy and theology which reached its culmination in the sixteenth century has been especially disastrous. Modern unbelief — in part the legacy of Descartes — must be attributed to a radically false philosophical method, that of trying to found certitude upon individual inquiry instead of the universal testimony of mankind. Philosophy is not a *search* for truth, as Malebranche misleadingly taught, because truth is already known. It also is useless to expect to prove God's existence and attributes or the soul's immortality or the divine sanction of the moral law by abstract speculation. On the other hand, the demonstrative function of philosophy, by which reason is used to elucidate and verify logically the truths of revelation, both natural and supernatural, is another matter altogether. This reached its apogee in the middle ages, the high noon of Christian thought and culture, with St Thomas Aquinas as its great exemplar. For the *Summa theologica* yet remains the profoundest and most comprehensive systematic statement of Christian teaching ever attempted. And the basis of St Thomas's doctrine is divine revelation, all else being derived from it by discursive reasoning.[32] No doubt the great doctor made use of Aristotle here and there, but his dependence on the pagan thinker was minimal.

Lamennais and Bonald, Ventura considers, did a useful work in criticizing Descartes, whom they rightly depicted as essentially a product of the Protestant Reformation and a major influence behind the baneful negations of eighteenth-century thought. They also warned their age of the futility of all individualistic speculation. But there they stopped short, failing totally to appreciate the stature of Aquinas. Lamennais ignored him, while Bonald denigrated him – along with scholasticism generally: 'a reasoning mechanism', he dubbed it – out of sheer ignorance. Traditionalism of the Mennaisian kind was unsatisfactory not least because it omitted to point the way back to where an authentic Christian philosophy could all along have been found.

Ventura's account of St Thomas, especially in *De la vraie et de la fausse philosophie*, published in 1852,[33] was scarcely that of seminarist orthodoxy and its shortcomings did not go unremarked, even though allowance might be made for the fact that his work was mainly addressed to a popular audience. However, no official objection was registered. But the fact is that the more ample statement of his views contained in the latter volume does nothing to modify the impression created by its predecessor. A notably severe critic was a layman, Charles de Rémusat, who examined Ventura's book in a long article in the *Revue des Deux Mondes* for 1 March 1853. In his opinion the attempt to synthetize traditionalism with Thomism was a mistake and sprang from a serious misinterpretation of the whole scholastic method. The mediaeval mind did not regard human reason as in some way inherently defective and in need of supernatural support, but as the natural possession of all men and the organizing principle of experience. As such it was a reflexion of the divine mind itself. Reason, in this sense of the word, as much of the argument of the *Summa contra Gentiles* in particular is concerned to show, is primarily a faculty or instrument, not a mere handing-down of a body of settled truths. Even in the *Summa theologica* there is no minimizing of the capacity of natural reason out of regard for revelation. If revelation includes also certain truths of reason it is as a divine provision to render them more accessible to the generality of mankind. Human understanding has in practice been impaired by the fall and is thus in need of the enlightening Word of God; but St Thomas treats the whole problem with discriminating care. Theology, he makes clear, has its proper subject-matter and therefore

---

[32] 'Ontologie, anthropologie, religion, fins dernières et même philosophie de la nature, tout se déduit par raisonnement du dogme révélé . . . par le génie purement discursif d'une raison croyante fixant son regard sur la Révélation' (*Raison philosophique*, 2e conférence. Cited Foucher, *La Philosophie catholique*, p. 243).

[33] A defence of the author's criticisms of Bonald, the book was written in answer to a letter from Bonald's son, Vicomte Victor de Bonald.

exists as a science in its own right. But it does not preclude the possibility or the necessity of philosophy as such. Rémusat holds it against Ventura, as against all exponents of the traditionalist doctrine, that by devaluing human reason one only ends in encouraging scepticism. In any case how does one differentiate between rival systems of philosophy without recourse to the very faculty which traditionalism affects to distrust? Finally, the account which the author of *La Raison philosophique* gives of the ancient philosophies is such as to raise doubts, from the historical angle, of the soundness of his interpretations of them. Even his knowledge of Thomism, Rémusat thinks, would seem to indicate a by no means exhaustive acquaintance with the original text.

These criticisms, as one peruses Ventura's work today, appear in the main justifiable. How far, then, can we seriously claim him as an inaugurator of the scholastic revival of the later nineteenth century? The answer is that he undoubtedly helped to overthrow the prejudice against scholasticism which traditionalists, fideists and ontologists alike had done so much to create. It had become something of a habit among many Catholic intellectuals, sons of the romantic movement, to dismiss it as so much arid rationalism, unappealing in itself and unavailing in face of contemporary science and philosophy. Ventura succeeded at least in presenting St Thomas in a new light, perhaps not an altogether 'white' one, but of a colour to render it not unattractive at a time when conservative and reactionary forces were gaining ground in church as in state. During the earlier years of the Second Empire the prevailing mood was authoritarian, and Catholics were not alone in their fears of the social dangers latent in the 'philosophical reason', the subversive spirit of restless inquiry. The temper of the age demanded unity and stability, both social and intellectual, and looked to authority, ecclesiastical as well as political, for the assured guidance it felt to be needed. And Thomism, a voice from the distant Catholic past, began to sound less like the rationalization of faith than an attempt to harness reason to it. Faith, that is to say, in prescribing the conclusions left to reason the task of producing the demonstration. The mediaeval world-view was essentially unitary; debatable points were only marginal. Certainly no individual system of thought would then have been tolerated which overtly questioned the basic principles. The mind's horizons were bounded by orthodoxy; heresy and infidelity were inadmissible. St Thomas Aquinas, most conspicuously, accepted the authority of faith and had subjected his own philosophy, Aristotelian in content though it was, to a use that could itself be recognized as an extension of the authoritarian rule. Thomism, in short, was to be seen not simply as a speculative system but the formally articulated teaching of the Catholic church.

Another factor contributing to the revival of scholasticism was the growing interest in the thought and culture of the middle ages on purely historical grounds. This indeed had had its beginnings, fanciful enough at times, in the romanticist enthusiasm of earlier decades, but with the emergence of a more serious and disciplined approach to the past curiosity ripened into solid knowledge. Here too the influence of Victor Cousin proved of importance. The history of philosophy, to which some monographs of his own had made a respectable addition, was now becoming an investigation in its own right. Not himself a mediaevalist, he readily encouraged the study of mediaeval thought by others, particularly in his capacity as chairman of the philosophical section of the Academy of Moral Sciences. Among the fruits of this patronage was Hauréaù's *Philosophie scholastique* (1850), a work of pioneering scholarship.[34] Further, it was as a direct result of Cousin's friendly concern that Charles Jourdain brought out his *Philosophie de St Thomas* in 1858. Thus an historical interest in scholasticism helped prepare the climate for a renewed attempt to reconstruct Christian philosophy itself upon a firmly Thomistic foundation.

Added support for the neo-scholastic movement came from the Jesuits. They had all along been opposed to traditionalism, as in the instance of Rozaven's criticisms of both Lamennais and Bautain.[35] And Rozaven's example was followed by the French Jesuits as a whole, in regard not only to traditionalism but to ontologism as well. Thomism, as seen in the usual Suarezian perspective, was likewise upheld by Père Chastel, along with a repudiation of traditionalism, whether Bonaldian or Mennaisian, scarcely less final than that of his fellow-Jesuit.[36] He notes in particular the influence on Lamennais of Maistre's pessimistic authoritarianism, the outcome of which had been, as he thought, a virtual surrender to irrationalism, since the intelligence was bidden to embrace truths which it could not hope really to understand. It was an impasse the only escape from which lay in a return to the teachings of St Thomas.[37] In *De la Valeur de la raison humaine*, which came out in 1854, Chastel again insisted on the essential agreement of Lamennais's ideas with Bonald's, whose inconsistencies he rather gleefully exposes. Another Jesuit publication that did much to stimulate interest in mediaeval thought was Kleutgen's *Die Philosophie der Vorzeit* (1860–3), a French translation of which appeared in 1868. The merit of this book was that it by-passed the all-too-familiar seminary manuals to go back to the original texts, but its aim was no less defensive than expository – to demonstrate the superiority of the traditional Christian philosophy, of which the middle ages had wit-

[34]Hauréau, it is true, paid no attention to Aquinas, who in his estimation had made little advance upon Albert the Great, from whom his ideas were for the most part derived. The earlier work was superseded however by his *Histoire de la Philosophie scholastique*, published in 1872, a general survey which even today has not lost its usefulness.

[35]For Rozaven's views on Bautain see Ingold, 'Lettres inédites du P. Rozaven', in *Bulletin critique*, xxiii, pp. 194 and 353.

[36]cf. his *L'Église et les systèmes de philosophie moderne* (1852). Chastel had especially in mind Bonnetty's *Annales de Philosophie chrétienne*.

[37]*L'Église et les systèmes de philosophie moderne*, p. 195.

nessed the fullest development, to all modern enterprises of the sort, whether traditionalism, Hermesian rationalism, or neo-ontologism, French or Italian. Kleutgen was also critical of Ventura, whose theory of knowledge he found tainted with traditionalist assumptions.

Finally in this connexion we should mention the influence, in France as well as in Italy, of the *Civiltà cattolica*, organ of the Roman Jesuits, which in 1850 embarked upon a career that has not yet ended. One of its two founders, Taparelli d'Angelo — the other was Carlo-Maria Curci — was a man of considerable intelligence and learning, if not an original thinker, but his real concern was ecclesiastical rather than philosophical. What he strove for was intellectual unity among Catholics under the centralizing aegis of the papacy. As a one-time admirer of Lamennais his early sympathies had been with traditionalism, but the conviction grew in him that only Thomism was fully consistent with Catholic dogma while at the same time being reconcilable with what was best in current philosophical tendencies, particularly French eclecticism. His teaching at the Jesuit college in Rome established his reputation as a Thomist and the pages of the *Civiltà* gave him a propaganda platform. Like Ventura, Taparelli looked on modern philosophy as essentially 'inquisitive': analytical, critical and preoccupied with the question of individual certitude. Its effect would be intellectually anarchic, dangerous to faith and socially subversive. A sound use of reason would, on the contrary, be 'demonstrative', proceeding from either universal axioms or supernaturally revealed truths. Thomism, in offering precisely such a method, was genuinely Catholic and socially beneficial. If the age, he believed, was ever to recover intellectual balance and moral cohesion it must once again give ear to the teachings of the thirteenth century.

Thus the transition from traditionalism and ontologism to neo-scholasticism — given the ecclesiastical atmosphere then developing — was natural and perhaps inevitable. Henceforth for Catholics the realm of speculative thought no less than that of faith was to be subject to a centralized authority. Such clearly was the real intent and significance of Leo XIII's encyclical *Aeterni Patris*, issued in August 1879. In this the new pontiff called upon the bishops 'to restore the golden wisdom of St Thomas', alike 'for the defence of the Catholic faith, the good of society and the advantage of all science'.[38] It was to implement this restoration that Leo founded the Roman Academy of St Thomas in October 1879, set up a commission to produce a new critical edition of the saint's works and (in 1880) ordered the establishment of an Institut Supérieure de Philosophie as a centre for Thomistic studies in France. Eventually, in 1890, the Angelic Doctor was accorded the patronage of all Catholic universities, academies, colleges and schools throughout the world. Scholasticism had to all intents been canonized as the official philosophy of the Roman Catholic Church.

[38] *Acta S. Sedis*, xi (1879), p. 114.

9

MARET AND GRATRY

Victor Cousin's 'Spiritualisme éclectique'

It is appropriate at this point in our survey to take a look at the 'spiritual electicism' of Victor Cousin and his school, for although Cousin and his disciples were certainly not Catholics their doctrine was widely regarded as underpinning Christian theism and therefore as consonant, at the most fundamental level, with Catholic faith itself. In fact, for many years during the first half of the nineteenth century, eclecticism appeared as a rival to Catholic philosophy for the allegiance of that younger generation of intellectuals which felt no attraction either to the materialist theories of the older *idéologues* or to Comtean positivism, while at the same time remaining aloof from any commitment of dogmatic Christianity. It was a rivalry all the more weighty no doubt for its being based on the University, the Napoleonic foundation by which all secondary and higher education throughout France had been centralized under direct state control.[1] And of the University Cousin, who presided over the École Normale Supérieure, was himself rector, so that throughout the period of the July Monarchy his teaching, which enjoyed the blessing of officialdom, acquired the status and prestige of an orthodoxy. As such it exercised a preponderant influence upon the entire national educational system. Himself nurtured on Rousseau and Condillac, he had held a professorial post at the Sorbonne from 1815, apart from an interval of suspension for political reasons, and under Louis-Philippe his promotion had been rapid: a councillor of state, a member of the Académie Française, a peer of France, director of the École Normale, and finally minister of public instruction and head of the University in the Thiers government. His personal influence and authority were such therefore as to secure for his opinions the widest possible dissemination. For close on twenty years he was the most potent force in French public education.[2] With the accession to power of Louis-Napoléon, however, he forfeited

[1] The system had long been an object of clerical odium. Lamennais, for example, had denounced it as 'this monstrous edifice' and 'a monument of Bonaparte's hatred for future generations' (*Œuvres complètes*, vi, p. 308). Montalembert spent much of his life and energy in combatting it.

[2] He was a man, it has been said, determined to get on, to make his way in the world, to reach the top. As he himself confessed, 'Il est vrai, j'aime à faire du bruit'. Of a restless,

his position and spent the remainder of his life in retirement building up the splendid library which he bequeathed to the Sorbonne. Even so his prestige as the *beau idéal* of bourgeois intellectualism lingered on.

Cousin adhered firmly to the axiom that philosophy has no other basis than human reason. Certainly he believed that it had no right to ground its conclusions in religious authority. Yet although in this sense a free-thinker he liked to consider himself as also a Christian, and he thought a *rapproche-ment* possible between Christianity and modern philosophy — a concordat, as it were, in the intellectual sphere analogous to that established by Bona-parte in the political.[3] But his direct influence in the theological field was very limited, even if indirectly it did turn out to be of some consequence. He readily conceded the dangers of an individualistic or purely critical view of reason such as the previous century had fostered, just as he affirmed the basic moral and spiritual truths on which the life of man had always been held to rest, and he understood his own philosophy as essentially *spiritual-iste*. This standpoint he adopted at the outset of his career and he never afterwards considered himself to have departed from it in any significant respect. A diversity of influences had contributed to its definition: Descartes, Rousseau, Kant, Maine de Biran, Royer-Collard and the Scottish philosophy all supplied something. But perhaps the most important period of his life, for its bearing on his intellectual development, was that marked by his successive visits to Germany, first in 1817 and 1818, and again in 1824. For in Germany he came under the spell of Hegel; and it was a fascination which few then could resist. Nevertheless — to quote Hegel himself — the fish Cousin had caught in the great philosopher's pond he soused in a sauce of his own!

Cousin's doctrine, as expounded in the famous lectures of 1828 published under the general title of *Introduction à l'histoire de la Philosophie*, is avowedly eclectic and at the time had the obvious virtue of making the best of all philosophical worlds. Moreover, although he can hardly be said to have produced a fully-rounded system of his own his views as a whole are a good deal more than a mere patchwork of disparate elements. He himself claimed that eclecticism, at least on his terms, was itself systematic. 'One must discover truths', he wrote, 'in the errors that surround them; . . . and this one cannot do unless one has a measure of appreciation, a principle of criticism — unless one knows what is true and what is false in itself. And this one cannot know unless one has oneself made a sufficient study of

questing, impressionable and even somewhat histrionic disposition, he was gifted with a remarkable fluency of utterance and had the arts of the rhetorician at his fingertips. His best-known and most characteristic work has the title *Sur le fondement des Idées absolues du vrai, du beau et du bien*. Published in 1836, it was a revised version of a lecture-course given by him as early as 1818.

[3] In his youth he had been a great admirer of both Chateaubriand and Mme de Staël.

philosophical problems and of human nature, its faculties and their laws . . .
Only then comes the turn of historical analysis.'[4]

Cousin maintained that for the vast majority of men faith is a necessity.
He affirmed, in Hegelian style, the three principles of God, the human
spirit and nature, but insisted that the God of the moral conscience is no
abstract deity or solitary monarch, but a God, rather, who is 'at once true and
real, substance and cause, infinite and finite all together'. 'Indeed, unless God
is everywhere he is nowhere.'[5]

The 1828 lectures were the first really comprehensive statement of his
ideas, although two years earlier he had brought out a volume of *Fragments
de Philosophie contemporaine*, which already gave fairly clear indication of
the nature of his thinking as an attempted reconciliation of the various
philosophical systems by selecting from each its most permanently valuable
components. In this respect he drew a parallel between philosophical science
and representative government, which similarly involves a balance of interests. Philosophy he defines as the self-understanding of human thought,
superior to religion in as far as it is the rational statement of what in religious
imagery is given only symbolically. The historical movement of reason he
sees as determined by a series of oppositions and their successive resolutions,
in which the antithesis of finite and infinite is fundamental, while the weakness of individual reason he would overcome by his concept of an 'impersonal reason'. His 'ternary' principle he finds reflected in Christian trinitarianism: God, he argues, should be understood as both infinite and finite,
along with the relationship that subsists between them. In his absoluteness,
that is, God is infinite, but in his rational self-consciousness finite, the third
'person' signifying the spiritual bond which unites the two. Creation, finally,
was achieved not *ex nihilo*, as in orthodox theology, but from the inner
being of the divine and by virtue of an inherent necessity of the divine nature.
The Hegelian inspiration behind all this — determinism, immanentism, the
identification of the real and the ideal — is undisguised. Religion and
philosophy we are told are 'deux sœurs immortelles'.[6]

[4] *Fragments de Philosophie moderne* (ed. 1855), p. 228. Cousin early on adopted Leibniz's
principle that philosophical systems are wrong in what they deny but right in what they
affirm. A completely *new* system, in fact, was not feasible.

[5] In 1825 Cousin entered into correspondence with Lamennais, both writers seeking
to express their opinions in a form likely to prove mutually congenial. Thus Cousin urged
not only the Christian but the *Catholic* character of his own philosophy, as conforming
with the Vincentian canon: *quod ubique, quod semper, quod ab omnibus*; while Lamennais
for his part saw fit to mitigate his attacks on individual reason, the *particular* role of which
he freely admitted. This happy agreement between the two authors did not, however, prove
durable. cf. B. Saint-Hilaire, *Victor Cousin, sa vie et sa correspondance* (1895), ii, pp. 4–27.

[6] It is only fair to note, however, that the Hegelianism of Cousin's 1828 volume had
undergone some modification. The 'spiritual' character of the eclectic philosophy was to
be underlined by such doctrines as, e.g., the soul's independence of the body, personal
immortality and the truth of absolute values as distinct from the relativism of empirical
knowledge. The autonomy of ethics, as based on natural reason, was to be stressed, but

Indeed to the traditionalist school Cousin's spiritual eclecticism appeared as nothing else than a form of historical determinism according to which the development of thought follows a course dictated by its own immanent logic, even though its contingent and temporary forms may in time drop away and what remains become a permanent possession of the human mind. It was a metaphysic which in the eyes of Catholic critics eliminated the supernatural entirely, pointing the conclusion that the Christian creed is simply the product of historical conditions and that what is of lasting value in it derives from the progressive movement of 'impersonal reason'. Certainly through his plan of promoting the hitherto neglected teaching of philosophy in the *lycées* and colleges Cousin intended to make use of the national educational system to disseminate this new ideology. But Catholic opposition alike to the state monopoly in education and to 'Cousin-ist' ideas found increasingly vigorous expression in the religious press, in episcopal charges, in parliamentary debates and in popular pamphlets such as abbé Cabet's *Le monopole universitaire destructeur de la religion et des lois* (1841) — an ill-judged publication, as it happened, by which sober Catholic opinion was not a little embarrassed. Cousin however was extremely reluctant to become involved personally in the controversy, being anxious rather that the University philosophy should not be thought anti-Catholic or even neutralist towards religion. His own feelings, as we have said, were quite to the contrary. His enthusiasm for German idealist doctrines even began to be noticeably tempered. What he wanted to be understood as advocating was the type of 'spiritualism' set out in *Du vrai, du beau et du bien*, a rationalism, that is, which he believed to be in the great tradition of Descartes and the seventeenth century, Christian in impulse but fully consonant with the political and social idealism of the day.[7]

Outlines of a Christian Metaphysic

One of the earliest of Cousin's Catholic critics was his own former pupil Bautain, who could thus claim with justice to speak of his master's system with 'inside' knowledge. Much of what he writes in his *Philosophie du Christianisme* has the eclectic teaching directly in view, even though Cousin himself is not named.[8] A theism based on purely rational considerations, he maintains, will have pantheism as its inevitable outcome.[9] And pantheism is 'an enemy becoming daily more formidable'. Its ancestry is ancient,

not to the exclusion of the idea that the theological doctrine of rewards and punishments in a future life can bring to morality a powerful practical reinforcement.

[7] It was at Cousin's own suggestion and under his supervision that a composite *Manuel de Philosophie* by three of his disciples, E. Saisset, J. Simon and A. Jacques, came out in 1846.

[8] See, for example, *Philosophie du Christianisme*, letters 27–9.

[9] 'La question est tout entière entre le théisme pur, basé sur la foi, et le panthéisme, produit nécessaire de la raison séparée de la foi' (Bautain, *Philosophie*, ii, p. 82).

stretching back through Scotus Eriugena to the gnostics of the second century, but it has of late been resuscitated in Germany as the philosophy of the absolute and now from across the Rhine it has rapidly begun to affect Gallic minds, albeit in diluted strength. On the idealistic confusion of God and man, Bautain thinks, the destiny of Christian civilization itself may well be said to depend.[10]

Bautain, in the eighteen-thirties, was already a well-known philosophical theologian, but a similar attack on eclecticism came not long after from a man who at the time was a quite obscure parish priest, abbé Henri-Louis-Charles Maret (1805—1884), *vicaire* of Saint-Philippe du Roule in Paris, whose *Essai sur le panthéisme dans les sociétés modernes* appeared at the beginning of 1839. In this he assailed in the name of a genuinely Christian philosophy what seemed to him the unmistakable tendency of 'eclectic spiritualism', despite its author's claim to be preserving an essential Christianity. Bautain's indictment of it had been right, for pantheism it was. Maret was a new-comer without academic distinction, but his book was at once recognized as the work of a forceful thinker. A native of Lozère, he had attended the seminary of Issy — where he had come to know Lacordaire — and was later enrolled at Saint-Sulpice. It is said that as a youth he was an avid student of the eighteenth-century *philosophes*, although they seem never to have shaken the convictions implanted by his pious upbringing. Ordained priest in 1830, he embarked on a pastoral career, but the archbishop of Paris, Mgr Affre, aware of his intellectual abilities, encouraged him to write. Maret was troubled by what he saw as the growing antagonism between Catholic Christianity and the contemporary outlook, fearing especially the danger to faith from the type of idealist philosophy then being impressed on youthful minds through the Université. It was mainly the impact of his book on Archbishop Affre which led to his appointment in 1841 as professor of dogmatics at the Sorbonne, a post in which he soon built up a reputation as a highly stimulating teacher.

Maret's *Essai* was manifestly inspired by Bautain's *Philosophie du Christianisme*, as also to some extent by Lamennais.[11] The charge of pantheism which he brings against the eclectic doctrine rests, he holds, on two of its admitted principles: the unity and identity of substance and the 'variable' character of truth. He then reviews the history of pantheism and undertakes a systematic refutation of its tenets. Like Bautain Maret contends that any purely rational view of God will end by equating him with the universe

---

[10]*ibid.*, p. 95.

[11]Maret was also interested in the work of Ballanche and Buchez, and was a subscriber to Eckstein's *Le Catholique*. His knowledge of German idealism drew chiefly on French sources, Barchon de Penhoen for Hegel, and Jean Ancillon for Fichte and Schelling. But he did spend a year in Munich where he came to know both Görres and Döllinger. No doubt he was able to sense for himself the German philosophical climate.

itself, so abolishing the distinction between divinity and humanity. Further, the identification of mind and matter really means that the spiritual is eliminated. The tone of Maret's apologetic, however, is not aggressive, nor does he engage in personal attacks, although the teachings he criticizes include not only Cousin's but those of the Saint-Simonians and Lamennais's later writings.

But what of his own position? It is clear that he has a good deal of sympathy with both the traditionalist and ontologist positions,[12] and he denounces the attitude to truth which sees therein no more than a human creation changing with times and circumstances. On the contrary, truth is one and immutable, indeed is being itself, 'that which is'. Catholicism originated in a divine revelation and teaches that its truths are preserved in this world by a living and infallible authority. Further, it ascribes to 'that society which is the depository of truth and the divine word the characteristics which distinguish it from all that is other than itself and allòw all men to recognize upon its brow the seal of God'.[13] Sometimes a Bonaldian note is audible: man's knowledge of the truths necessary to his life has been *given* him, although the term 'revelation' is to be taken in a very broad sense:

We believe that ideas and language have been disclosed to man. It is the revelation which St John speaks of, that lightens every man coming into the world and is the real source of reason. This primal and natural revelation, which all sound psychology authenticates, is in perfect harmony with the teaching that represents religion to us as born of a revelation and as conserving and developing itself by that revelation. Thus there is a revelation in the natural order as in the supernatural; there are natural truths and supernatural ones, both equally from God. The first make up the domain of natural reason, the second that of divine faith.[14]

The point Maret wishes to drive home is that once reason is identified with individual speculation truth is relativized and distinctions become blurred. The threshold of pantheism will have been crossed.

The effect of Maret's *Essai* on the eclectics themselves was one of indignation. Cousin did not reply to it, but Émile Saisset, who after the master was the school's leading representative, attacked it in an article, 'La philosophie du clergé', in the *Revue des Deux Mondes* (May 1884). He began with a general survey of clerical attitudes over the preceding decades: Lamennais, an out-and-out traditionalist, had urged the radical impotence of reason; Bautain had considerably modified this condemnation, and now abbé Maret was assuring his readers that the human intellect had sufficient scope to attain the knowledge not only of the moral law but of God himself. Unfortunately the abbé was still tainted with the traditionalism he seemed to want to disclaim, making acceptance of the Christian creed the condition of all progress in the

[12] See especially the second edition of the *Essai*, pp. 96—103.
[13] *ibid.*, p. 98.
[14] *ibid.*, p. 99, note 1.

realm of thought. In other words, reason left to itself was in the dark and could only stumble into error.

Nevertheless Maret's book had many favourable reviews in the current periodicals and was translated into German, Italian and Spanish. Catholic readers welcomed it as a timely piece of apologetic and the author's Sorbonne professorship seemed an appropriate reward. His first literary undertaking in his new post bore the title *Theodicée chrétienne, ou comparaison de la notion chrétienne et de la notion rationaliste de Dieu,* and was largely a sequel to his previous work, and no less polemical than didactic. Theology is contrasted with philosophy, on the thesis that philosophical thinking is profitable only when placed at the service of religion. Between theodicy as an enterprise of pure reason and one that can be qualified as Christian a clear distinction needs to be drawn. Indeed no proof of God is possible outside the context of religious faith and under the authority of Catholic doctrine. Thus at the outset a definite concession is made to traditionalism. Yet when it comes to the actual forms of proof Maret is content to martial the familiar scholástic arguments quite in the manner of Mgr Frayssinous. His sole reservation is that we are not in a position to understand their true bearing and cogency. This he contends is evident from the superiority of St Augustine's reasoning — with revelation behind him — to Plato's or Aristotle's. Even St Thomas's Five Ways he dismisses as no more than 'a pale reflexion of Augustinian ideas'. Thus he arrives at Descartes, whom he treats with great circumspection. That the author of the *Discourse on Method* was the father of modern rationalism he will not have, even if he feels bound to deplore the fact that so outstanding an intelligence had 'wholly neglected tradition and the element of belief which belongs to the constitution of reason'. The Cartesian theodicy is then examined at length and is shown to rest on the assumption that the idea of the infinite is native to the human reason. It is only because man has a natural apprehension of God and of his own relation to God, and therewith a complete assurance of the existence of other beings, that he can proceed by the light of supernatural faith to develop really convincing arguments.[15] Descartes's own example illustrates this, for he too in his philosophical reflexion was enlightened by the Christian beliefs in which he had been nurtured.

But if faith is necessary for a proper grasp of the proofs of divine existence still more so is it when we try to understand God's own nature and his purposes for mankind. Here obviously rationalism fails, if only because, in order to render divinity intelligible, it has to assimilate the divine to the universe itself. Christian theology however, in insisting on God's sovereign perfection, must exclude from his being all the multiplicity and diversity, the temporality and successiveness of the visible world, teaching on the contrary that he is one, absolute and eternal. Yet the God even of Christian metaphysics does not suffice for religion, and theology has to bring to philosophy the truths of reve-

---

[15] *Theodicée chrétienne,* p. 177.

lation. At this point therefore the theologian in Maret takes over from the philosopher and what the reader is left with is the orthodox trinitarianism he might have found in any seminary manual. So too with Maret's account of creation *ex nihilo*, which he opposes to both dualism and pantheism on the ground that each in its own way denies the divine perfection. The Christian doctrine may be difficult to grasp conceptually, but at least it does not contradict what by the conviction of faith is God's essential nature.

On the constructive side, then, Maret is uncontroversial and unoriginal; his personal views emerge only when he criticizes contemporary thought, though in the main the *Théodicée* takes up a more rationalistic position than does the earlier *Essai*. This impression is confirmed when one turns to his *Philosophie et Religion: dignité de la raison humaine et nécessité de la révélation divine*, published twelve years later. His evident shift of attitude away from traditionalism may well have been spontaneous, but it would not be unfair to detect in it also a certain responsiveness to the changing theological climate. Traditionalism had by now lost its former appeal and, as we have seen, ontologism and scholasticism stood to offer greater attractions. In this new book Maret rejects any philosophy built on sensualism, since sense-experience, through its relativity and contingency, is powerless to explain the necessity and absoluteness of our fundamental ideas. Neither will he accept psychologism (or 'conceptualism', as he calls it), for although this theory may rightly attribute the origin of such concepts as those of being, unity and identity to the constitution of the mind itself it cannot tell us how we arrive at the notions, say, of genus and species, which depend on data outside the mind, or at our moral ideas, which again are not simply of our own creating, or, finally, at the metaphysical ideas of infinity and perfection, which certainly cannot be represented as the product of the finite mind and its experiences. The only alternative is to conclude that they come from God himself, or are the reflexion of God within us by the light of his divine Word. In short, Maret now seems to join the company of the thinkers we discussed in our last chapter. The work which rounded off his apologetic efforts, *La Vérité catholique et la paix religieuse. Appel à la raison de la France*, did not appear until 1884, shortly after his death. In it he once more attacked current philosophical tendencies inimical to Christianity and entered a renewed plea on behalf of revealed religion, at the same time repeating his conviction that there is no necessary incompatibility between the church and modern society.

Although our main concern here is with Maret as a philosophical thinker his career as a churchman, signalized by his sustained opposition to the growth of ultramontanism and the definition of papal infallibility, also deserves notice.[16] Moreover he was deeply affected by what he felt to be the gravity of the social problem presented by the state of the industrial working-

---

[16] See G. Bazin, *La Vie de Mgr Maret* (1891). This three-volume work includes Maret's own *Mémoires*.

class. It was in order to rouse Catholic opinion on this matter that together with the cultural historian and philanthropist Frédéric Ozanam he established a new liberal journal, *l'Ère nouvelle*, in which after the manner of the ill-fated *L'Avenir* he urged the necessity of a *rapprochement* between the church and democracy. It was not enough, be believed, for Catholic political action to be concentrated on the struggle for freedom in education; a *parti catholique* ought also to work for the amelioration of working-class conditions, an aim challengingly set forth in the new journal's prospectus.[17] Henri de Lacordaire at first took over the editorship, but his own doubts as to the virtues of social democracy led to his resignation shortly afterwards. Maret, who replaced him, continued however, with Ozanam's help, to press the need of a Christian social movement with a specific programme of reform.[18] Unfortunately for the two enthusiasts the French bishops made their disapproval obvious. Subscriptions fell off disastrously and the paper was obliged to cease publication after an existence of barely a twelvemonth. Maret subsequently declared his support of Louis-Napoléon and in 1853 was rewarded by nomination as dean of the theological faculty at the Sorbonne. From then on he was closely associated with the imperial government and on friendly terms with Napoléon III himself. In 1860 he was appointed to the see of Vannes, but Pius IX, who disliked both his liberalism and his Gallicanism, refused confirmation, with the result that he had to make do with the bishopric of Sura *in partibus infidelium*. On the other hand his influence with the government continued undiminished, his voice carrying special weight in nominations to the episcopate. Nor were his academic responsibilities in any way neglected: he made a point of securing on his staff the best men available, among them Bautain, Freppel, Lavigne, Hugonin and Gratry. He also succeeded in winning recognition of the Sorbonne faculty by the Vatican, thus securing it an ecclesiastical status it had not hitherto enjoyed. But his efforts to do as much for the École des Carmes ended in failure, despite protracted negotiations.

A staunch Gallican, Maret was sharply critical of such ultramontanist zealots as Louis Veuillot, as too of bishops whose enthusiasm for papal autocracy could only be explained, he judged, by their ignorance of both theology and history. He was dismayed at the prospect, during the later sixties, of the forthcoming Vatican Council, the purpose of which, in common knowledge, was to be the definition of the pope's infallibility. On the eve of the Council he published the two volumes of his *Du Concile générale et de la paix religieuse*, followed by a defence of the views there stated under the title *Le Pape et les évêques* (1869). Together they presented a clear and forceful

[17] Bazin, *La vie.*, i, pp. 231f. See also J.-B. Duroselle, *Les Débuts du catholicisme social en France 1822–1870* (1951), p. 295. See below, pp. 207f.

[18] cf. Duroselle, *Les Débuts*, p. 316. Other collaborators included Charles de Coux and Charles de Sainte-Foi, both of them in earlier days followers of Lamennais.

exposition of the old Gallican principles with the somewhat heroized figure of Bossuet always in the background. The result was an outburst of controversy, as he himself must have foreseen. Yet although he dealt harshly with works like Mazarelli's *De auctoritate romani pontificis in conciliis generalibus* mere polemic was not his aim; his tone is courteous and his argument underpinned with a formidable array of historical references. His main contention is that the papal authority does not depend on infallibility; indeed ecclesiastical sovereignty is not to be identified with any form of absolutist monarchy, but must be qualified by the aristocratic principle. This means that for the infallible exercise of the church's *magisterium* there has to be joint action by both the pope and the bishops. In himself the supreme pontiff has no singular and exclusive character of infallibility, though the expression 'papal infallibility' may be allowed in general parlance. The pope alone has the right to consult the whole church and to summon the bishops for solemn deliberation, but it is the decisions made in union with the episcopate which have the charism of infallibility. Maret held however that the chair of St Peter is indefectible and that the supreme pontificate would always be found to have upheld Catholic truth, whatever the errors or personal failings of any single pope.

The fact is that with the years the Gallican theory had been losing ground in France, not least among the bishops themselves, its traditional defenders, and the cold reception accorded to Maret's book only encouraged the ultramontane party in their resolve that the time for authoritative definition of the infallibility doctrine had arrived. It is noteworthy that at the Council the *schema* 'De Ecclesia' was largely concerned with Maret's arguments, which he vigorously maintained to the last. Yet when the decree was finally promulgated he, unlike Döllinger, submitted, intimating his decision in a personal letter to Pius IX (October 1870). In the following year he issued a solemn declaration repudiating his recent publications as 'contrary to the constitution "Pastor Aeternus" and to the definitions and decrees of the preceding councils and the Roman pontiffs'. In 1882, two years before his death, a titular archbishopric was conferred upon him.

Gratry's 'Dialectical' Theodicy

Ontologism represents one form of the 'rationalist' reaction to Mennaisian traditionalism, Thomism another. Yet both were themselves 'traditionalist' in the more usual sense of harking back to the doctrines of former times, in the one case to St Bonaventura and Malebranche, in the other to St Thomas and the school-philosophy which in the eyes of perhaps the majority of Catholic teachers had always presented the most satisfactory account of the relations of faith and reason. We come now to another attempt to fashion a Christian metaphysic wholly opposed to Mennaisianism in its belief that the intelligence has rights of its own in face of the claims of revelation, but containing also elements of voluntarism and mysticism in a way that anticipates the type of Catholic thinking to emerge in the closing decades of the century with the work of Ollé-Laprune and Blondel. We refer to the Christian philosophy of Alphonse Gratry, a priest of the Oratory whose achievement has been described as of its kind 'the most characteristic and complete — albeit unfinished in respect of its initial plan — which was to appear in the French Catholic world of the nineteenth century'.[19] Not that it is altogether easy to classify, despite Gratry's unquestionable facility as a writer.[20] Its aim was one of synthesis, or at least of reconciliation — to bring together, as far as possible, the conflicting tendencies in Catholic philosophy which had arisen during the previous half-century and even to find common ground with Cousin's spiritual eclecticism. But romanticist and fideist strains are also present, for as a young man Gratry came under the spell of Bautain at Strasbourg and for some years was a member of his circle. In spite of this variety of influences, Gratry should however be seen as a thinker in his own right, with an originality of outlook no less distinctive than that of the author of the *Philosophie du Christianisme*, with whom he is usually linked. One commentator even goes so far as to dismiss Gratry's teaching as little more than an unacknowledged reproduction of Bautain's.[21] This is a mistake, as we hope to make clear. As for the absence of acknowledgment of a debt which in itself is obvious enough, too much should not be made of it. Gratry may not himself have been wholly conscious of its extent, and in any case the ecclesiastical censure of Bautain's views meant that any express invocation of his name might well have struck the younger man as an imprudence which the service of the truth they both sought could hardly be supposed to require.

Born at Lille in 1805, August-Joseph-Alphonse Gratry received his earliest education in part at home — he was always deeply attached to his mother — in part at the *lycée* of Tours. At the age of fifteen he went to Paris to attend the famous Collège Henri IV, where he showed himself an eager and able student; but as he relates in his fragmentary *Souvenirs de Jeunesse* he disliked the irreligious atmosphere of the place no less than its moral laxity, and he was glad to leave it for the École Polytechnique in 1825. His stay there, though, lasted for no more than a year; the abstract nature of his studies bored him, and he wanted to read and think for himself in his own way. His autobiography describes his conversion to Christianity: as a schoolboy he once underwent a dreamlike experience in which he suddenly was overwhelmed by a sense of the futility of life as lived by the mass of man-

[19] Foucher, *La Philosophie catholique.*, p. 197.
[20] Thiers commented, when the question was broached of Gratry's election to the Académie: 'Il n'est pas un philosophe. Est-ce comme prédicateur qu'il se présente?' (A. Chauvin, *Le Père Gratry*, 2nd ed., 1911, p. 192). In this as in other respects he more than a little resembles Newman.
[21] W. M. Horton, *The Philosophy of the Abbé Bautain*, p. 81 note.

kind. 'O God', he cried aloud, 'explain to me the mystery. Make me to know the truth. I vow to dedicate my life to it.' But his actual return to Catholic practice seems mainly to have been brought about by a friend. In 1828 he moved to Strasbourg to study under Bautain, though he never really became a disciple; Bautain's fideism he could not quite bring himself to share and in any event he was unwilling to submit himself to the intellectual tutelage of any single mind. The break between them occurred in 1840 when Gratry was appointed rector of the Collège Stanislas.[22] A few years later he went to the École Normale as chaplain, a post in which he was able to exercise consider-able personal influence, *incroyants* as Catholics freely acknowledging his high qualities of character no less than his intellectual gifts.[23]

Nevertheless difficulties arose between himself and the École's director, Étienne Vacherot, a man of keen intelligence and reputable scholarship but whose coldly logical cast of mind was alien to Gratry's own warmth of tem-perament. At the time Vacherot was strongly drawn to Hegelianism, and in 1884 began work on his weighty *Histoire de l'école d'Alexandrie*, the third and final volume of which appeared six years afterward. Though a long way from being a Catholic he professed a deep respect for the Christian religion and was especially interested in the influence of Hellenistic philosophy upon early Christianity, which he saw as a matter for dispassionate historical in-vestigation. His own view was that during the first three centuries of its history Christianity had undergone a continuous change of form, dogmatic fixity, necessary for a potentially universal institution, having been achieved by means of Greek metaphysics enshrined in the decrees of general councils. Vacherot recognized that the early church Fathers had successfully resisted the more overt attempts to dissolve Christianity in Hellenism, but the course of doctrinal development had been dictated by influences alien to Chris-tianity's original character. From first-century Jerusalem to fourth-century Nicæa was a far cry.[24]

Vacherot's thesis is one which since his day has become familiar, but at that time and in Catholic France it looked like a new and subtle form of anti-Christian rationalism. His own philosophical opinions approximated to those of Cousin in the earlier phase of his thought: the inspiration and basic concepts were Hegelian, in particular the idea of the reconciliation of op-posites in a new and transcendent synthesis, though a less easily definable quantity of Spinozistic pantheism was also present.[25] Gratry's position was

---

[22]He was ordained to the priesthood in 1832.

[23]See Cardinal [Charles] Perraud, *Le Père Gratry, sa vie et ses œuvres* (1900), p. 3.

[24]*Histoire critique de l'école d'Alexandrie*, i, pp. 168—230, 296.

[25]Vacherot subsequently abandoned his Hegelianism for positivism. His *De la Religion*, published in 1869, reveals how far he had by then progressed along the road to unbelief. This work has little use for the speculations of the Cousinist school. Intellectually speaking religion, the author thinks, has no future, for faith can never be a permanent substitute for demonstration, though Vacherot testifies his admiration for many of the theological writers

now somewhat invidious: the author was a senior colleague of his, yet he had no doubt that the book itself demanded a reply. This he undertook in 1851, with a publication entitled *La Sophistique contemporaine*, in the shape of a series of open letters addressed to Vacherot himself. But his action caused something of a scandal and embarrassed the whole university. The upshot was Gratry's resignation, although the issue between the two men never became a personal quarrel.[26]

The occurrence proved a turning-point in Gratry's life. The following year, in pursuit of his idea of a community of priests dedicated to study, he sought to re-establish the Oratorians in France, a proposal which the Holy See approved. But in view of the rather compromising Jansenist and Gallican associations of the Oratory of St Philip Neri in the past the new congregation was renamed the Oratory of the Immaculate Conception. Besides Gratry himself its membership included Adolphe and Charles Perraud — the latter afterwards a cardinal and Gratry's biographer — and Henri Perreyve (whose own biography Gratry was to write), with the former *curé* of Saint-Roch, Père Pététot, as its superior. Gratry's years as an Oratorian proved to be the most fruitful of his career, although with his reclusive disposition and somewhat undisciplined habits his personal suitability for community living became more and more apparent. But it gave him the leisure and opportunity to embark on the comprehensive task of Christian apology which he had long planned. This, as he now saw it, would have to assume a double role: on the one hand, to bring together religion and modern science in a relation of mutual support, and on the other to confront the growing social problem created by industrialism. Regarding the former, Gratry's own early mathematical training led him to use the term science in a more restricted way than Bautain had done. Not just the sum of rational knowledge in all fields but, to be precise, *natural* science was in his judgment the form of secular knowledge currently presenting the most serious problem for the Christian teacher. On the social issue — 'How', he asks, 'can men be brought to love one another?' — Gratry's ideas could hardly be considered very radical, for here he was himself something of a Cousinist and socialism appeared as

of his day who, he concedes, are an honour not only to the Church of France but to the nation's literature (*De la Religion*, p. 135). Gratry's abilities he particularly acknowledges, but rhetoric is no match for consistent thought and laborious research (p. 149). The greatest threat to religious belief will increasingly come from history and psychology. Supernaturalism in any guise is untenable (p. 240).

[26] Gratry had shown his manuscript to Vacherot before publication, although the latter declined to read it. Vacherot however did admit certain errors of fact in his own work, such as a mistranslation of a passage from St John of Damascus, and was scrupulous enough to call in all the unsold copies of the volume containing them so that the relevant pages could be suppressed. See Perraud, *Le Père*, pp. 49f.; also H. Chauvin, *Le Père Gratry: l'homme et l'œuvre d'après des documents inédits* (2nd ed., 1911), c. vii. But Gratry's book, while exposing some minor defects in Vacherot's scholarship, betrays the fact that Gratry himself was not fully aware of the problem posed by the development of doctrine in the patristic period.

much a menace to Christianity in the political sphere as did positivism in the intellectual.

Gratry's overall aim is to portray Christianity not as a fugitive from the advance of modern science and philosophy but as the real spiritual dynamic behind all intellectual progress. Christian theism, he argues in the philosophical treatises he published at intervals during the fifties, is the ground and guarantee of reason and the necessary light for all constructive thought, and hence the safeguard against scepticism and pantheism alike. Only on the basis of religion can science itself discover its proper direction and identity, so recognizing the limits inherent in its own methods. To attain its ends it must first possess a sense of the infinite and a knowledge of the divine purpose for mankind disclosed in the eternal gospel.

Gratry's system is expounded in three works: *La connaissance de Dieu* (1853), *Logique* (1855) and *La connaissance de l'Âme* (1858), dealing in turn with knowledge of God as the starting-point of the whole metaphysical enterprise, knowledge of the soul in its relation to God and to the physical body, and knowledge of man's own understanding and will; in short, with theodicy, psychology, logic and ethics. Theodicy is to be seen as primal: the existence of God must be affirmed and demonstrated before anything else. The age has lost confidence in reason[27] and is faced now with starkly alternative options: either to believe in an infinite and perfect Being, the unchanging foundation and support of all things, or to accept the world as mere contingency without ultimate meaning. The great majority of men give no serious thought whatever to the momentous issue which life thus poses, whereas those with a genuine religious faith can also draw satisfaction from knowing that many of the finest minds in history have shared their convictions. Yet to quote the authority of great names from Plato to Leibniz is not sufficient; proof of some kind must be forthcoming, and Gratry sees here the need for an altogether new procedure. The deductive method, for which the conclusion is already latent in the premises, has failed and will have to be replaced by the inductive or 'dialectic', which uses the known in order to discover the unknown. It alone can bridge the gulf separating the relative from the absolute.

Gratry holds that there is a knowledge of God which is both intuitive and rational. It was the capital error of traditionalism to have denied this. Language and the common belief have a pedagogical role, but mankind's fundamental ideas are the product of the reason which every normal individual possesses.[28] If a revelation has been vouchsafed us from above

---

[27] 'La raison est en péril' (*La connaissance de Dieu*, Introduction, p. 1). 'Nous croyons que c'est rendre un très mauvais service à la religion que de pousser au scepticisme philosophique ... Ruiner la raison, c'est défoncer le sol pour empêcher l'edifice religieux d'y tenir ... Il faut rétablir parmi nous la légitime autorité de la philosophie et de la raison' (*ibid.*, pp. 32, 44).

[28] Reason 'ne peut pas tout, même dans l'ordre de la vérité naturelle ... Mais elle peut quelque chose; elle a sa certitude propre; elle trouve, elle démontre avec certitude et con-

reason has an indispensable part in acknowledging it, a fact which any Christian *philosophy* has to admit from the start. On the other hand Descartes was wrong in attempting to erect his *cogito* into an absolute; thought cannot be isolated from that *being* which is anterior to it and its necessary condition. But in its essence being is personal and what ontologists mean when they use the word is far more than an abstraction covering a barely hidden pantheism.

Yet how can reason effectively substantiate faith in a transcendent God? In the first place it has to be understood that rational argument, if it is to carry conviction, requires a moral preparation, indeed an attitude of prayer:

> If there are proofs of divine existence these must be available to all men ... Hence in order to ensure their utility we have to seek their origin and substance in some common, everyday activity of the human spirit ... Now this common, everyday activity of the soul, — mind and heart, intelligence and will, — is nothing other than the universal fact of prayer. And I mean by prayer, in philosophy, what Descartes intimated when he said 'I feel myself to be a limited being who aims at and aspires unceasingly to something better and greater than what I am myself'. Prayer is the movement of the soul from the finite to the infinite.

To this type of proof, in the end an appeal to spiritual experience, all others are more or less assimilable, according to their degree of explicitness, clarity and solidity.

We should observe at the outset that Gratry discounts Descartes's theory of innate ideas. Ideas have their roots in the world about us. What *are* innate are our sense of the infinite and the constitutive principles of reason, which as Leibniz has shown are basically twofold: that of *identity*, or non-contradiction — necessary to all deductive reasoning, though by Hegel virtually denied — and that of *transcendence*, or sufficient reason — the principle of causality. The first ensures the coherence of our thinking and is of obviously fundamental importance; the second is able to advance knowledge by *explanation*. The word 'transcendence' Gratry uses deliberately to signify that all explanation lies ultimately beyond finitude in that 'infinite' which is both qualitative and quantitative, as implying not only limitlessness but absolute perfection — *id quo maius cogitari non potest*, in St Anselm's phrase. An effective theodicy must therefore be inductive or 'dialectical', indicating transition from the limited to the unlimited, or from the 'like' to the 'unlike' (or 'other'). Every finite and imperfect being has to be transcended if the ultimate reality of Being itself is to be affirmed. It is a procedure essentially different from that of deduction, which moves only within the circle of the known, or from 'like' to 'like'. Induction extends the mind's horizon, moving on from particular facts and experiences to the universally valid law of truth. Its utility has been amply proved by modern science, but

naît jusqu'à un certain point plusieurs vérités naturelles, comme l'existence de Dieu, ses attributs, la liberté morale et la spiritualité de l'âme' (Gratry, *La connaissance*, ii, p. 231).

in metaphysics and ethics, where its first great exponent was Plato, who directed men's gaze away from the illusory realm of sense to the real world of the eternal Ideas, it is no less necessary and fruitful.[29] In theodicy it offers a type of proof different from that of the classical arguments, but fundamentally these too depend on it for such cogency as they have.[30]

In applying induction to metaphysical problems Gratry believed himself to be clearing a new path in philosophy, leading perhaps to a reconciliation between religion and the natural sciences. But he attempted something much more risky when he identified the 'dialectical' method with the principle of the infinitesimal calculus, an idea which most likely had its roots in his youthful mathematical studies at the École Polytechnique.[31] His aim was to show that in mathematics the concept of the infinite, while corresponding to no genuine reality, is not simply a product of the human brain but is a manifestation of the divine reason itself. In mathematics and metaphysics alike, that is, we recognize the infinite by stripping the finite of its limits. His argument, however, came in for damaging criticism, in particular from Émile Saisset who dealt with the question at the strictly rational level and regardless of mystical sentiment.[32] No doubt Saisset was right, but to appreciate what Gratry was trying to say allowance must be made for the romanticist feeling for the infinite which governs his entire outlook, which he himself describes as 'the universal attraction for every soul of the sovereign Good', the unremitting appeal of 'the divine light soliciting the human soul to recognize it'.[33] Apart from this instinctive feeling for the divine and the 'dialectical' procedure which grows out of it reason is no more than the instrument for clarifying ideas and deducing conclusions. It operates as it were only within a closed circle. But given man's basic sense of the divine one sees how the process of knowledge is able to advance from 'likeness' to 'difference'.[34] It is because the mind is naturally directed to finite things that some higher impulse is needed to raise it to the plane of the truly spiritual. It is in this impulse — something which Plato himself recognizes — that the Christian believer becomes aware of the inward solicitation of divine grace. But response to it implies nothing less than *conversion*, both intellectual and moral, inasmuch as there is no real upward

[29] Gratry stresses however that by a logic of induction more is implied than mere Baconian 'tâtonnement empirique', the results of which are too meagre, he thinks, to provide a fully rational basis for natural law.

[30] See *La connaissance de Dieu*, ii, pp. 51—72 and 136—171. cf. *Logique*, i, pp. 170—98.

[31] His reasoning is set out at length in *Logique*, ii, pp. 183ff.

[32] *Revue des Deux Mondes*, 1 Sept. 1855. cf. abbé de Broglie's remark (*La Quinzaine*, 1 Nov. 1894, 'Le Père Gratry, polytechnicien, philosophe et apologiste'): 'La plupart des philosophes spiritualistes repousseraient également une assimilation entre l'infini mathématique essentiellement divisibles en parties et la simplicité de l'Être divin.'

[33] See *La connaissance de Dieu*, ii, c. 5, 'Rapports de la raison et de la foi'.

[34] Gratry, *La connaissance*, i. p. 373.

movement of the intellect without an accompanying renewal of its moral force. *Qui facit veritatem venit ad lucem.*

Like St Thomas, Gratry distinguishes two levels of degree in man's knowledge of God. But whereas for the Thomist the distinction is simply that of reason and faith, faith being understood as the counterpart and complement of reason, Gratry envisages a more subtle relationship of mutual penetration.[35] Reason, he holds, is primarily analytical and critical, but it also has a constructive role of generalization and synthesis. This comes of its power of transcendence, of moving out from the known to the unknown.

But where precisely the line is to be drawn between the natural and the supernatural Gratry is evidently not prepared to say. It is enough to claim that faith and reason are interactive, the former taking the lead. 'I count on grace alone to conduct reason to the limits of reason.'[36] Moreover reason itself in the final resort is not a purely discursive or speculative faculty but a spontaneous assent or recognition, almost a kind of faith. And if reason is already as it were *compenetrated* by faith then faith itself can be said to have a 'natural' dimension which makes any real discontinuity between it and reason impossible. It is because of this that supernatural belief, the product of an express divine revelation, is not felt by us to be an alien and heteronomous element in our lives. Even St Thomas speaks of the soul's *natural* desire to see God and be made one with him. In *La connaissance de l'Âme* Gratry turns with evident relief from metaphysics to psychology. 'May I leave', he says, 'the abstract realm of science and say with Malebranche, "Henceforth I wish to occupy myself with morality and religion alone." From now on I desire to meditate only upon the soul and its future, humanity and its destiny, on earth and in heaven.'[37] These fields certainly were more congenial to him temperamentally. In spiritual matters, he believed, the head is a less sure guide than the heart. Not however that the metaphysical concern is absent from the new work, which was planned as something more than a mere treatise in experimental psychology. For Gratry views man as essentially a spiritual being whose nature is fulfilled only when its moral needs are adequately met.

The book falls into five sections: the soul of man as compared both with God and with the body; its faculties; its transformation through sacrifice; and its immortality. The arguments set out in the author's previous works are of course presupposed, God's existence now being assumed in order that man himself may be studied in the light of it. Human nature is presented as tripartite — animal, rational and spiritual — spirituality forming man's bond of union with the divine. But Gratry's aim is to show that this last — the spirit — is a 'natural' faculty or capacity of which the science of

---

[35] cf. especially La connaissance de Dieu, ii, pp. 171–278.
[36] *ibid.*, p. 359.   [37] Preface to second edition, p. XVII.

psychology should take due account; indeed apart from it the lower faculties cannot properly be understood. The soul, that is, is primarily *spirit*, a potency created by God in his own image and continuously sustained by the power of his word, through which alone it attains its perfection. Like its maker it comprises a 'trinity' of being, conceivable perhaps as a series of concentric circles, the affective, the intellectual and the volitional. The first, however, in which the personality has so to speak its 'centre', is more subconscious than conscious, a kind of impersonal self-within-the-self; though our whole reflective and spiritual life draws its strength from it. As regards *language* Gratry finds in it a parallel with the body, in that both are indispensable to the soul's functional life. Without language thought itself, which is the mind in action, cannot develop. But the traditionalists are right in claiming that it is the vehicle also of that 'common reason' by which human society is able to subsist.

The form of the common reason is in the first place given to each of us from without. A sort of ready-made rationality is imposed upon the individual reason struggling to the birth.[38]

As union of mankind in a single social whole is the object of God's will, speech is the divinely created tool with which to fashion it. But words can imply a good deal more than they actually say: hence the power of the poet and the orator. For they carry with them overtones of the infinite, and the mind that is spiritually awake will apprehend in what they convey to it not merely their ordinary significance but the divine 'light' in which all things have ultimately to be seen.

When he goes on to consider the soul's faculties Gratry at once makes clear how different will be his own procedure from the empiricist rationalism of either the Scottish or the electric schools. A place, that is, will have to be found for men's religious intuitions as such. This means that the mind is to be studied not simply in its bodily relations but in its orientation toward the God whom it spontaneously and continuously seeks.[39] For as Gratry sees it the goal of the moral life is to transcend not only the egoism of the senses but that of reason itself, so as to attain to what Pascal calls the 'order of charity'. And that can only be achieved by sacrifice alike of sensuality to reason and of reason to love; although such sacrifice is finally possible only by divine grace, which is never withheld. Yet the actual moral effort required must be our own.

Sacrifice is the free act of a loving and courageous will such as desires to transcend self in order to reach God and to rediscover itself in God. To transcend self or to remain in it — therein is the whole question, the whole history, the whole drama of the moral life.[40]

[38] *La connaissance de l'Âme*, i, p. 120.   [39] *ibid.*, pp. 223–7.

[40] It is interesting to compare what Gratry says about moral self-transcendence with the views expressed by Lucien Laberthonnière in 'Le dogmatisme moral' (*Essais de Philosophie religieuse*, pp. 40ff.)

And the goal of life here, when achieved, is an earnest of that which is to come. Gratry at this point re-examines the usual arguments for immortality and offers an explanation of why to so many minds they fail to carry conviction. The reason, he thinks, is moral: men do not know the meaning of 'fullness of life' even here. For the kind of life they generally choose is directed not towards Being but towards non-being, extinction, *le néant*. Such souls are already half dead and thus, without realizing why, feel themselves *destined* for death. They do not believe in life simply because they do not know how to live. Those, though, who do know may be said to *anticipate* immortality in all their actions, so that they already in a sense possess it. But if there is a life after death the problem inevitably arises of its *milieu*. It is a question, Gratry admits, that ought not to be shirked. For what men hope for is life in the true meaning of the word and not the merely shadowy and abstract existence which often enough is all that the metaphysicians seem to envisage. His own answer is striking. By contrast with the restlessness and flux of this life, which Gratry compares to the perpetual motion of the heavenly bodies, immortality will be a condition of stability, of understanding, love and self-fulfilment, in which discontent and striving will have ceased. Yet its *place* will be here in the world we know, though a world renewed and transformed.[41] For then God will be all in all and his purposes realized, as the scriptures prophesy.

The Gospel and Human Progress

Gratry's ambitious design of a completed system of Christian philosophy was never quite accomplished. It should have comprised two further treatises dealing with moral and natural philosophy.[42] His failure after 1858 to carry his plan through is attributable partly to the difficulties that arose in his relations with the Oratory, but partly also to his need of some more practical interest, especially the social question, about which he had long felt concern. Polemic too was to engage him, whether in answering Renan's *Vie de Jésus* or in his resumed campaign, signalized by *Les Sophistes et la critique* (1864), against the Hegelianizing of Schérer and Vacherot. But one undertaking which did in its way forward his main intellectual task was a Sorbonne lecture-course published in 1868 as *La Morale et la loi de l'histoire*. In this, with acknowledgments to Vico's *Principles of a New Science*, he tries to present a philosophy of history, if in language essentially theological.[43] He starts, that is, with man's sin and fall, while interpreting his

[41] *La connaissance de l'Âme*, ii, p. 371.
[42] cf. *La connaissance de Dieu*, Introduction and foreword to the second edition. But part of the second volume of *La connaissance de l'Âme* contains a lengthy section on ethics.
[43] In his *Scienza Nuova*, which appeared first in 1725, Giambattista Vico argued that a study of human psychology is the necessary preliminary to an understanding of history. The true history of the human race is that of its progressive mental states. cf. O. Klemm, *G. B. Vico als Geschichts-philosoph und Völkerpsycholog* (1906).

history in terms of an evolutionary progress inspired by the principles of the gospel. Man himself, Gratry again reminds us, is a denizen of three worlds: the world of nature, the world of society and the world of the Spirit, to each of which he has specific duties summed up in the words of Scripture. His duty to nature is in the command that he should be fruitful and multiply, and replenish the earth and subdue it; to society, that he was put upon the earth to govern it with order and justice; to God, that he should seek first that divine righteousness on which all other goods depend. But man being what he is these commandments are unlikely to find simultaneous ful-filment and he must learn to advance by successive stages: his conquest of nature as a necessary beginning; his continual struggle for a just social order; and his new life under divine grace, by which alone will all his pre-ceding efforts reach fruition.

Gratry's vision is utopian, with its prospect of a final amelioration of the human condition here on earth — 'circles of progress, the march of humanity towards a life ever more abundant'. But the law of this progress is the principle of justice, as without justice there is neither true science nor liberty. On it indeed depends the knowledge and love of God himself, for the way to God lies in obedience to his precepts. Progress therefore, as history demon-strates, is basically a matter of morality as understood and practised by the individual. At the same time it is the individual's involvement with the race that gives to virtue its larger meaning. The thought of man's ethical advance over the ages is 'what appeals to the intelligence and to the heart, to individuals and to peoples. It is the desire that elicits the heroic forces which lie hidden in the human soul'.[44] Thus the gospel, as the ideal ethic, is the real power behind the humanitarian ideals of liberty, equality and fraternity. And the gospel, Gratry reminds his readers, is the gift of God. Society like the individual rises above the mere life of the body, above that even of scientific reason and law, in response to the call of an absolute spiritual perfection. 'All motion forcefully declares the actual presence of God. *A fortiori* all progress declares still more forcefully the actual presence of Him who is at once powerful, wise and beneficent, free, perfect and infinite.'[45]

La Morale et la loi de l'histoire was a popular success. Its theme of human progress accorded with the mood of the times. Even readers suspicious of progressivist ideas when served up in a Condorcetan form were mollified by the argument that it is by God's own providence that man is destined for a splendid terrestrial future. For Gratry's philosophy, which had roots not only in the gospel but in the Saint-Simonianism of his youthful imagination, was one of optimism. Like so many of his contemporaries he believed firmly in the capacity of science to better the human lot and in the gradual renewal of political institutions through the spirit of liberty. He was in fact as little disposed to criticize the dogma of progress as was Auguste

[44] *La Morale et la loi de l'histoire*, i, p. 49.   [45] *ibid.*, p. 281.

Comte himself. The difference between the two men lay in the former's conviction that the condition of progress is the general acceptance of the Christian moral ideal and thus, in the long run, of the creed which supports it. For the truth Christianity proclaims is that of man's redemption, and this in the temporal order is bound to carry with it the re-creation of human society. It is because man has not been left to his own sole resources but has within him a God-given spiritual dynamic that he can look with confidence to some realization of the Heavenly City here on earth. History, in Gratry's view, already affords sufficient evidence that the Christian religion will continue as in the past to be a controlling factor in the development of Western civilization. The thesis of Gibbon and others that it was a main contributory cause of the decline of the Roman empire he rejected, nor would he tolerate the view that the middle ages were a time merely of intellectual darkness awaiting the dawn of the Renaissance and the sunrise of the Enlightenment. On the contrary the intellectual revival of the fifteenth century and after, especially the scientific movement, had, he believed, its source in the twelfth and was itself of ultimately Christian inspiration.[46] He held also, in opposition to most Catholic opinion, that it was the same inspiration that really motivated the Revolution of 1789, which for all its mistakes and excesses should be seen as a characteristically modern fruit of France's ancient faith.[47]

On the social issue Gratry remained loyal to the convictions voiced in his *Catéchisme social par demandes et réponses sur les devoirs sociaux* of 1848, a little work first published, we may note, in the year of the *Communist Manifesto*.[48] Indeed he increasingly had come to view the moral aspect of life in social terms. Like Armand de Melun, Maurice Maignen and other like-minded Catholics of his day, he was seriously troubled by the social effects of industrialism as these were now manifesting themselves, in France as elsewhere, in bad working conditions and low wages, and he favoured the setting-up of workers' associations as a means of mitigating them.[49] Anxious also about oppression in Poland and Ireland, he founded in 1867, along with Hyacinthe Loyson,[50] the International League of Peace, although his efforts in this as in other such respects had little effect on the prevailing conservatism of the Catholic outlook.[51]

---

[46] *ibid.*, pp. 250–3.   [47] *ibid.*, p. 139.

[48] It was reprinted in 1871 under the title *Les Sources de la régéneration sociale*.

[49] cf. *ibid.*, ii, pp. 277f.

[50] Charles (Hyacinthe) Loyson (1827–1912), at the time a Carmelite friar, left the Roman church on the eve of the Vatican Council, partly on account of the difficulties caused by his participation in the 1869 Peace Congress. He married in 1872. A liberal strongly opposed to the ultramontane doctrine and policy, he later became a sympathetic observer of the *crise moderniste* though himself playing no active part in it. See A. Houtin, *Le Père Hyacinthe* (3 vols., 1920–4).

[51] See Vidler, *A Century of Social Catholicism*, p. 77.

Gratry's last years were disturbed by his fear of the growing strength of neo-ultramontanism and in particular the outcome of the proposed Vatican Council. He realized well enough that the synod's chief purpose would be the definition of papal infallibility, the result of which, as it seemed to him, could only be the isolation of the church from the rest of Christendom and the eventual alienation of the secular world from Catholicism altogether — especially in view of the *Syllabus* of 1864 — thus overthrowing everything which it had been his life's aim to achieve. Regrettably, perhaps, he was induced to enter the arena of current controversy by Mgr Dupanloup, a man ever spoiling for a fight, and in his open letter to the cardinal archbishop of Malines, who was generally recognized ás one of the leaders of ultramontane opinion, he not only instanced the sort of problem which the infallibility definition would almost certainly create but denounced the 'school of lies and errors' which ignored such established facts of history as the declared heresy of Pope Honorius.[52] One may admire Gratry's integrity and concern for truth while allowing that ecclesiastical politics was not his proper element and that his intervention in the great debate did him less than justice. But once the definition was promulgated he like Maret made a complete submission. The whole episode told upon his health and left him a bewildered and unhappy man. Retiring to Switzerland for a rest he died there early in February 1872.

On any showing Alphonse Gratry is to be counted among the most influential Catholic thinkers of his century, alongside Newman and Johann Adam Moehler. A liberal, yet also in some respects a reactionary, his ideal, as thinker and churchman, lay in the seventeenth century and he resisted the philosophical tendencies of his own age. But he fully realized the importance of science and the need for religion to come to terms with it, seeing the whole field of knowledge, empirical and spiritual, as ultimately one and grounded in a transcendent absolute. That he succeeded in any measure in reconciling the diverse positions in contemporary Catholic thought is doubtful. The truth is that Gratry's philosophy, with its combination of mystical and scientific elements, is a distinctively personal one that today has no more than an historical interest. As such it may be seen principally as a link between the voluntarism of Maine de Biran and Bautain on one side and that of Ollé-Laprune, Blondel and Laberthonnière on the other. But although a detailed study of his work has never yet been published, no survey of nineteenth-century Catholic thought would be adequate which omitted to assign him a distinctive place.

[52] See E. Ollivier, *L'Église et l'État au concile du Vatican* (1877), ii, pp. 55ff.

10

AN ANSWER TO POSITIVISM

In Defence of Faith

During the eighteen-sixties and -seventies the need of an apologetic to meet the challenge of science, or more correctly the type of philosophy that had come to be associated with science, was increasingly felt by the more far-sighted among Catholics. The thinkers indeed whom we so far have been considering all wrote with a more or less apologetic aim in view, trying to present Christian belief not only as a body of divinely revealed truths but as the only really adequate interpretation of nature, man and society even at the level of natural reason itself. Bonald early in the century had sought to do precisely this, on the grounds that mankind's fundamental ideas are all God-given. So too in their differing ways did Lamennais and Lacordaire, Buchez and Bautain, Maret and Gratry.[1] They were always aware of having in the long run to meet the opponents of faith, whether the rearguard of the eighteenth-century *philosophes* or the followers among their own compatriots of the German idealists, Hegel especially. But the seventh and eighth decades of the century show up, in France as in England, as a time of particular stress for religious believers, traditionalism, fideism, intuitionism, ontologism and neo-scholasticism all laying claim to be the authentic Christian philosophy and as such the best fitted to protect the younger generation from the growing peril of infidelity. Gratry, as we have just seen, argued that a Christian meta-physic is itself *scientifically* based and need have no fear therefore of the advance of science in the natural order, while at the same time staking his conviction that reason has its limits and that knowledge of the supernatural, as his reply to Vacherot's *De la Religion* makes clear, demands more than merely a logical methodology.

Hostility to Catholicism as to Christianity in general now took the forms mainly of positivism, including a positivistic account of human history, and materialism. Of these ideas the leading exponents were Renan, Vacherot, Littré and Taine, men who moreover had scant regard for 'liberal' Catholics

---

[1] Other apologetic treatises worth listing here would include A. Genoud, *La Raison du christianisme* (1834) and *La Divinité du Jésus Christ* (1842); T. Foisset, *Catholicisme et Protestantisme* (1846); J. Gorini, *La defense de l'Église* (1854); Mgr Parisis, *Les Impossibilités, ou les libres penseurs désavoués par le simple bon sens* (1857); and E. Hello, *Renan, l'Allemagne et l'athéisme au xixe siècle* (1858).

of any brand, whom they accused either of double-talk or of blindness to the falsity of their own position. In Renan's view, for example, the Catholic church had set its face so resolutely against the aspirations of the modern world that any attempt to liberalize it was but to plough the waves.

The Inquisition [he wrote] is the logical consequence of the whole orthodox system; it summarizes the Church's mind. For the Church, were it able to, would bring back the Inquisition; and if it does not do so it is only because it cannot ... I understand the orthodox, I can understand unbelievers, but not the neo-orthodox.[2]

Vacherot likewise sees the issue as a clean-cut choice between Catholicism and free-thinking democracy.[3] Yet Catholics were for the most part still hardly awake to the gravity of the positivist attack. Conservatives were more intent on stamping out Gallicanism and liberalism than in facing new challenges from without, however serious. Thus Pie of Poitiers, the outstanding ultramontane among the bishops, could see as the chief enemy only Victor Cousin and his school; writers such as Taine and Renan were merely the epigoni of eclecticism and likely to be forgotten within a couple of decades. On the other hand the liberal Catholics were becoming more and more disturbed by the mounting pressure of anti-Catholic influences on public opinion and some, like abbé Cognat for instance, openly blamed the die-hards within the church itself. But the appearance in 1863 of Renan's *Vie de Jésus* came as a shock to Catholic susceptibilities throughout France and the numerous replies which it evoked kept orthodox pens busy for some years. Whether or not this notorious book was ever satisfactorily answered, the anti-Christian stance of periodicals like the *Journal des Débats* and the *Revue des Deux Mondes* was in no way modified.

If it is one thing to denounce current tendencies, it is another to reverse them. The liberal Catholics considered that false philosophies should be met with reasoned argument, but the great majority of the clergy, preoccupied as always with the question of church schools, as well as from an indifference bred of ignorance, remained apathetic, while their favourite journal, the ultramontane *Univers*, whose editor Veuillot always took bigotry for a sign of grace, never failed to pillory liberalism as treachery to the Catholic cause.[4] The Oratorians under their superior Pététot might have shouldered the apologetic task, but to the great disappointment of Gratry, whose own relations with the congregation were becoming increasingly difficult, as also of his

[2] See the article 'Du libéralisme clérical', reprinted in *Questions contemporaines* (1868).
[3] On the relations between church and state in France during this period see A. Debidour, *L'Église catholique et l'État sous la iiie République*, i (1906), which is fully detailed, though strongly anticlerical in outlook; as also G. Hanotaux, *Histoire de la France contemporaine* (1903). E. Lecanuet's *L'Église de France sous la iiie République*, vols. i and ii, is of great value.
[4] Popular apologetic — what there was of it — was altogether feeble. Lecanuet speaks of its 'complete sterility' as regards either philosophy or biblical exegesis. Seminary training concentrated on personal devotion and pastoralia, but on the intellectual plane offered no stimulus. See Lecanuet, *La Vie de l'Église sous Léon XIII* (1930), pp. 242f, 316f.

able colleague H. de Valroger, the work went by default.[5] Thus in 1863 the latter felt himself driven to admit that 'in our poor Church of France's present deplorable state a priest who wants to devote himself entirely to the ecclesiastical sciences is a man beyond the pale'.[6] In fact Gratry and his friends were fast discovering that in ecclesiastical circles a reputation for liberal-mindedness and concern for the intellectual needs of the church in a changing world were absolutely no recommendation. The spirit of the new Vaticanism was becoming too potent.

The École des Carmes did its best in face of the prevailing apathy and suspicion, but its teaching staff, as is clear from abbé Isoard's *Le Clergé et la science moderne* (1864), were only too well aware of the difficulties of their position. The theological faculty of the Sorbonne under Maret was similarly isolated. The fact that its professors were state-appointed and that it enjoyed no official recognition at Rome were fatal defects in the eyes of the *Univers*, quite apart from the inclusion in its membership of a number of well-known liberals. Of the bishops, Darboy of Paris and Dupanloup of Orléans realized the need for a better educated clergy and did what they could to promote clerical studies. But not all shared their conviction. Cardinal de Bonald, archbishop of Lyons, for example, could ask: *Des savants, que voulez-vous que j'en fasse?*[7]

Nevertheless three writers in particular call for mention at this point expressly because of their concern on the present issue, though also because two of them at least were to have a decisive influence upon Léon Ollé-Laprune, whose career and teachings will be the subject of the greater part of this chapter. They are abbé Meignan, who later became archbishop of Tours and a cardinal,[8] Frédéric Ozanam, historian and philanthropist, and Elme Caro, a philosopher of the eclectic school who strongly upheld the case for theism against the fashionable naturalism and positivism.

Guillaume Meignan (1817–1896), a liberal of the Dupanloup variety, had received his education in Germany and was familiar with the tendencies of contemporary German thought. By interest a biblical student and author of a book on the messianic prophecies in the Old Testament (1856), he recognized that a new-style apologetic, historically grounded, had become necessary. Moreover if the educated rejected Christianity for intellectual reasons the masses did so for social. Both sections of society would have to be penetrated, yet the clergy remained at a disadvantage both for their political conservatism and their ignorance of the new directions in science and in scholarship. He even arranged for a young priest named Vollot to attend a course at the

[5] See *Lettres à T. R. P. Pététot, par les PP. de Valroger et Gratry* (1887).

[6] Quoted A. Houtin, *La Crise du clergé* (1907), p. 40.

[7] Houtin, *La Crise*, p. 240.

[8] See H. Boissonnot, *Le cardinal Meignan* (1899). cf. A. Houtin, *La Question biblique chez les catholiques de France au xixe siècle*, 2nd ed. 1902, pp. 206–12.

university of Tübingen with a view to passing on his knowledge to the Paris seminarists, but the result was not encouraging: a timid and fussy orthodoxy was quite unable to take the biblical question seriously. Meignan's own views may have been somewhat temporizing – Loisy considered him an opportunist[9] – but he understood well enough that a critical approach to the Bible was a necessity for the modern apologist.[10] Houtin, while indeed accusing him of an inconsistency by no means always inadvert, thought him the best biblical apologist of his age in France.[11]

Antoine-Frédéric Ozanam (1813–1853) was of the generation of young Catholics who in the wake of the religious and ecclesiastical revival of the Restoration years heralded by the *Génie du Christianisme*, saw as their mission that of rallying to the church of their ancestors minds alienated alike by rationalism and the Revolution. It was through the influence of abbé Noirot at the Lyons *lycée* he attended as a boy – a man incidentally whom Victor Cousin went so far as to describe as 'the premier teacher of philosophy in France' – that he first became conscious both of a personal religious commitment and of a sense of cultural mission to his fellow-countrymen. He had a wide acquaintance among the leading spirits of his day – the ageing Chateaubriand, Ampère, Ballanche (whose ideas especially impressed him), Lamennais, Montalembert, Gerbet, Lacordaire – and was an early recruit to the cause of liberal and social Catholicism, although at the same time sharply opposed to the Saint-Simonianism to which a good many young Catholic idealists were attracted.[12] It was his realization of the deepening gravity of the social problem which led him while still a youth to found a philanthropic organization destined to have a great future, the Society of St Vincent de Paul, which by 1861 had no fewer than four thousand branches or *conférences* under a *Conseil générale* in Paris and administering an annual budget of five million francs. Ozanam was also among those who persuaded the archbishop of Paris, de Quélen, to institute sermon-lecture courses at Notre Dame with Lacordaire as the inaugural speaker, and he himself set out to influence public opinion through the columns of the *Correspondant*, the *Tribune catholique*, the *Univers* and the *Revue européenne*, to all of which he had become a notable contributor.

[9] *Mémoires pour servir à l'histoire religieuse de notre temps*, i, p. 40. It was Meignan who ordained Loisy to the priesthood. See also pp. 249–51 below.

[10] In his younger days he was outspoken: 'Le christianisme', he said in 1848, 'c'est un vivant qu'on a voulu attacher à des morts . . . il était temps que cette révolution se fît' (cf. Boissonnot, *Le cardinal*, p. 150).

[11] Houtin's comments are as usual caustic, amusing and unfair.'Sceptique presque autant qu'un cardinal de la Renaissance', he remarks, [Meignan] 'ne songeait pas à refaire sa réputation d'orthodoxie compromise dans le libéralisme' (*La Question*, p. 212); to which Lecanuet (*La Vie*, p. 34) replies: 'Il est sceptique se l'on veut dire qu'il possède une philosophie profonde de la vie, qu'il compte très peu sur les hommes et beaucoup sur Dieu.'

[12] 'Pour nous, Français, esclaves des mots', he wrote in 1838, 'une grande chose est faite: la séparation de deux grands mots qui semblaient inséparables, le trône et l'autel' (quoted by A. Thureau-Dangin, *Histoire de la Monarchie de Juillet*, iii, p. 443).

Though appointed in 1839 to a professorship in commercial law at the university of Lyons, his real interests clearly lay in the field of history, and in 1844 he succeeded Fauriel in the chair of *littérature étrangère* at the Sorbonne, where he was to make a name for himself as a pioneer in the study of comparative literature. Always however his guiding motive was apologetic. As early as 1829 he had conceived the ambitious idea of a 'Demonstration of the Catholic religion from the antiquity of its historical, religious and moral beliefs', the scope of which would be nothing less than a religious history of mankind illustrating the social benefits of religion in general and of Christianity in particular, a theme summarized in an article of his in the *Revue européenne* in 1835 with the title 'Le progrès par le christianisme'. He also planned a magisterial *Histoire de la civilisation au moyen âge*, covering the period from the fifth to the twelfth centuries and culminating in the age of his hero Dante, which again was intended to demonstrate the potentialities of Catholicism as a civilizing force. But the scheme fell short of completion. *La Civilisation du ve siècle* provides a general introduction to the subject, dealing with the close of antiquity and the barbarian invasions of the empire, whilst representing the church as the custodian of what could be salvaged from the wreck and hence the educational basis on which the slow process of rebuilding civilization was able to rest. His subsequent study of the rise of the Gothic culture, *Études germaniques*, formed part of the same design and carried on the same apologetic purpose. But the crown of his literary career was undoubtedly his work on Dante, in whom he saw the finest flower of a Christian and Catholic civilization. Ozanam's learning, highmindedness, purity of motive and depth of conviction gained him the esteem even of those who, like Renan for example, in no wise shared his beliefs.[13]

Elme-Marie Caro (1826—1887), an eclectic of the 'spiritualist' school of Cousin, was not a practising Catholic, but he nonetheless was a vigorous defender of Christian theism. Educated at the Collège Stanislas, he held teaching posts at various lycées until his appointment as *maître de conférences* as the École Normale in 1858. Six years later he was elected to the professorship of philosophy there, but was always more of a moralist than a metaphysician, and a talented writer rather than an original thinker. He possessed a brilliant gift of exposition, being in the best sense a *vulgarisateur*. It was to his teaching and example that his pupil Ollé-Laprune always confessed a profound intellectual debt. In 1874 he was admitted to the French Academy, mainly on the strength of his *Idée de Dieu et ses nouveaux critiques* (1864) and *Le Matérialisme et la science* (1868), although what is probably his best work, *Le Pessimisme au xixe siècle*, did not appear until 1878. To all open-minded Catholics his apologetic writings were the more welcome as coming from a source that could not be identified with clericalist causes.

[13]See F. Méjecaze, *Frédéric Ozanam et l'Église catholique* (Lyons, 1932); E. Labelle, *Frédéric Ozanam. Une âme de lumière et de charité* (1939): N. de Rooy, *Frédéric Ozanam* (1948).

Léon Ollé-Laprune

Outstanding among Gratry's immediate followers, although never actually a pupil of his, was a layman, Léon Ollé-Laprune, a great admirer of the Oratorian tradition who fully shared Gratry's conviction that if truth is indivisible there can be no real antagonism between the principles of faith and the rational methods of philosophy. In fact he never ceased to urge that the philosopher who in fulfilment of his truth-seeking vocation has pursued it with his 'whole soul' will discover that Christianity alone affords the complete intellectual satisfaction which is the end of his quest. But the proviso, *avec l'âme toute entière*, was all-important. Ollé-Laprune could not doubt that knowledge of the truth depends upon moral integrity and that real certitude is not a matter of the intellect alone. Man *acts* as well as knows, his knowing being inseparable from his acting; for it is his destiny not only to amass information, whether theoretical or technical, but to establish himself as a moral entity. Otherwise he will have failed: *Il n'est pas dans l'ordre.*[14] His perfection is not complete, that is, until goodness is combined with knowledge. Humanity itself demands the full consistency of the rational with the moral, of science with faith. Ollé-Laprune further claimed that the reconciliation of religion and science is entirely possible within the framework of Catholicism and under the authority of the church. He tried in his own writings to present a coherent philosophy which would be no less 'rational' for presupposing the truth of the Catholic creed and the *magisterium* of the Roman papacy. He would not allow that it could be said of him that he was a philosopher *although* a Christian, or a Christian *although* a philosopher. On the contrary, he insisted that his philosophy had its focus and fulfilment in Christianity and that his Christianity would not have had the same breadth or stability without the philosophical reasoning that buttressed it.

Léon Ollé-Laprune was born in Paris on 23 July 1839, of middle-class parents comfortably circumstanced. At the Lycée Bonaparte (later re-named Condorcet) his intellectual promise was confirmed when in 1858 he headed the list of entrants at the École Normale. There his studies turned to philosophy, but as the *agrégation* in that subject had not at the time (1861) been re-established he instead took his degree in letters, although specializing in philosophy. When he did sit for it in 1864 he was awarded second place, after Alfred Fouillée. His first teaching post was at the *lycée* of Nice, but he soon exchanged it for one at Douai. After three years at Versailles he moved to the Henri IV in 1871, and finally, in 1875, was appointed *maître de conférences* at the École, a position which he held for the remainder of his all too short life. Meantime he had begun his career as a writer with a monograph on Malebranche.[15] Devout though he was he seems never to have felt a call to the

---

[14] *La Certitude morale* (2nd ed.), p. 348.
[15] *La Philosophie de Malebranche*, 2 vols., 1870. The opening chapter, 'Les origines de la philoso-

priesthood, being inspired rather by Ozanam's conception of a lay apostolate, and in May 1872 he married.

Ollé-Laprune's lectureship at the École Normale, occurring as it did during a period of strong anti-clerical and indeed anti-religious feeling, was in some quarters criticized as socially undesirable. But his erudition, native ability and dedication as a teacher surmounted all prejudice, at least within the institution itself. That he was a convinced Christian and a fervent Catholic could not obscure the fact that he was a first-rate classical scholar and a philosophical thinker no less rigorous in his standards than those who professed the way of 'free' thought only. His personal character too was such as to win him the widest respect, as was plainly evidenced by an incident in 1880. While on holiday at a small coastal resort in the south of France he put his signature to a protest against the proposed dissolution under the recent Ferry decrees of a local community of Carmelite friars.[16] His action however was reported in Paris, the consequence being that he was suspended from duty for a year. But throughout he had the loyal support of his students, who addressed to him an open letter of sympathy and respect drafted by Jean Jaurès, the future socialist leader.[17] His pupils admired him not only for his learning but for the sense he conveyed of personal involvement in all that he taught while at the same time never permitting his academic instruction to become the vehicle of religious propaganda. Well grounded in Plato and Aristotle, Augustine and Aquinas, and a specialist in Malebranche and Leibniz, he could also claim first-hand acquaintance with Kant, Fichte and Schelling and in fact to be abreast of most contemporary writing in the philosophical field. The year 1880 saw the publication of his two doctoral theses, a Latin dissertation on Aristotle's ethics[18] and the volume bearing the title *De la Certitude morale*, perhaps the most characteristic and permanently interesting of his works. In this he argues that moral truths are as acceptable to reason as are those of science. The evidence of course may be less obvious, but the mind grasps them quite as clearly and firmly. But to this conviction of his we shall be returning in a moment.

On resuming his official teaching in 1882 he began with a series of addresses on contemporary scepticism, in which he took the opportunity to outline a philosophical system of his own, 'in harmony', he considered, 'with common sense and the requirements of science'. Subsequent courses dealt

phie de Malebranche', had previously been printed in the *Correspondant* (10 May 1869), a periodical to which he became a frequent and much-valued contributor.

[16] Religious communities were mainly affected by the highly controversial Article 7, directly intended to eliminate their role in education. Congregations failing to secure government authorization were to be suppressed, while even such as survived were subject to penal taxation. See Lecanuet, *La Vie*, pp. 95ff.

[17] cf. G. Goyau (ed.), *La Vitalité chrétienne*, pp. xxiif.

[18] *de Aristotelae ethices fundamento*. His *Essai sur la Morale d'Aristote*, based on this, appeared a year later.

with the nature of philosophy (1883–1884), reason (1884–1885), the theory
of causation (1885–1886), truth (1886–1887), the meaning of life (1887–
1888), perfection (1888–1889), the basis of ethics (1889–1890), the existence
of God (1890–1891) and the idea of providence (1891–1892). Thus to all
appearances his career was simply the uneventful routine of an academic,
with total absorption in teaching and writing. The 1884 course was published
in book form as *La Philosophie et le temps présent* (1890) and that of 1888 as *Le
Prix de la vie* (1894). A further work, *Les Sources de la paix intellectuelle*, came out
in 1892. During his last years he lectured at the École on 'Contemporary idols
in philosophy'. 'The crisis of morality', 'Cause and law' and 'Reason and
rationalism'.[19] At the time of his death in February, 1898 he had begun a new
series on metaphysics.[20] Four years previously he had sought membership of
the Academy of Moral Sciences, applying to the philosophy section on the
grounds of his professional teaching and published writings, but he met with
opposition and his application failed. No philosopher in the proper sense of
the word, so his critics maintained, could so consistently and openly identify
himself with the Catholic creed and ecclesiastical authority as did he. His
friends then urged him to transfer his claim to the ethics section, but this he
characteristically refused to do. He would enter the Academy in the role of
philosopher *tout court* or not at all. In December 1897 his perseverance was
rewarded with his election in place of Vacherot. Another distinction was the
cross of the Légion d'Honneur, conferred on him on the occasion of the
centenary of the École Normale. When he died at the age of fifty-eight, and at
the height of his career and powers, he was probably the most highly-
regarded Catholic layman in France.

Moral Certitude

Ollé-Laprune, we have said, regarded himself as at once philosopher and
Christian. He believed that it was his Christianity which made him a philosopher, while philosophy gave his faith depth and quality, so that in himself
at least the two characters were inseparable. He certainly would not allow
that the Catholic in him was in any respect a discredit to the philosopher or
the philosopher a peril to the Catholic.

[19] The 'Reason and rationalism' course was published by his friend Victor Delbos in 1907.
Other posthumous volumes include short studies of Vacherot (1898) and Jouffroy (1899), and
a collection of articles and addresses, some not hitherto printed, edited by Georges Goyau under
the title *La Vitalité chrétienne* (1901). The latter contains a notable paper on 'La vie intellectuelle
du catholicisme en France au xixe siècle', which first appeared in *La Quinzaine* on 1 December
1895.
[20] He was also now addressing general audiences, such as that assembled under the auspices
of the Comité de Défense et de Progrès social in 1895, the year in which he greatly impressed
the Saint-Sulpice seminarists with a lecture on the clergy and the contemporary intellectual
situation. First published in the *Revue du Clergé français* on 1 July 1895, this was reprinted in
La Vitalité chrétienne (pp. 158–82).

Philosophy [he wrote as early on as 1870] is essentially an examination and an effort: an examination of the ideas one has in one's mind, and an effort to see clearly. To examine is not to doubt, whatever some may say. Because I may have had the good fortune not to have my heart and mind empty of God, am I, in spite of the sincerity, the freedom, even the boldness of my speculations, to be refused the name of philosopher? I declare that I do not understand either the necessity of being tortured by doubt or of having coldly to make *tabula rasa* of the intelligence in order to be a philosopher ... There is no question, in philosophical examination, of isolating the reason within itself; there is no question of creating a void around it ... If one has the Christian faith in one's heart would it not be altogether an odd thing, in order to pursue the philosophical method in all its rigour, to have first to cast aside this deep inward certitude, to extinguish its light, to deprive oneself of its aid? The answer, once again, is No; philosophy is not to be bought at that price.[21]

Ollé-Laprune was the more convinced of it because of a conception of philosophy's proper task to which he adhered all his life. For its object, he held, is essentially man's own being and destiny. The genuine thinker, accordingly, will first look into himself, to discover the reality that is there.

To think is to find oneself alone with an object: to consider it, to study it, to penetrate it, while at the same time drawing from the depths of one's own being the means of pronouncing what that object is and what it is worth ... And what is laid hold of in this way is being.[22]

Philosophy, then, is nothing less or other than the science of being, of being *qua* being; but its principles are dynamic and directional as well as constitutive and static. For what metaphysics really does is to reflect man's own nature and needs; needs and a nature, however, which are not to be explained in terms merely of the lower levels of his being. To the charge that his view was 'anthropomorphic' he was content to reply that in the order of creation we know nothing higher than man himself and that when we talk about truth we can do so only with reference to our own understanding: it cannot be other than truth *for us*.

This explains Ollé-Laprune's readiness to endorse the affirmations of commonsense — truth as it strikes the ordinary man. Moreover his own approach to philosophy was always more constructive than critical. He knew his Kant well enough, but his natural interest was in human thought and experience for what they are more than in the abstract function of reason as such. Again, his mind was not of a speculative bent, nor was he a system-builder: what concerned him most were *facts* — specific problems and conditions. For the notion of the 'pure' philosopher he had little regard.

Ollé-Laprune himself was not only a Catholic but an ultramontane with it.[23] In December 1894 he visited Rome with his family and was received by

---

[21] *La Philosophie de Malebranche*, ii, pp. 249–52.
[22] *La Philosophie et le temps présent*, p. 162.
[23] 'Je suis Catholique', he once confessed, 'dans le sens très précis et rigoureusement exact du mot. Je suis d'esprit et de cœur Catholique, et le vrai et complet Christianisme est là pour

Pope Leo XIII in private audience. Deeply impressed by Leo personally, he wrote on his return the article 'Ce qu'on va chercher à Rome', which appeared in the *Quinzaine* for 15 April 1895.[24] Here he takes the most exalted view of the papal authority. 'On all sides Rome is turned to, Rome is listened to, and what the Pope does, what the Pope says, echoes throughout the world.' The papal utterance is a force at once of preservation, of liberation and of inspiration. Not only is Rome a bulwark against error, she frees the church from attitudes that have become outdated and unserviceable and points to new horizons. In every department of life, political, economic and social as well as scientific and philosophical, the supreme pontiff speaks with a voice that is not only wise and stimulating but infallible. Much of the article, it has to be said, is couched in a tone of pious rhetoric that a Catholic of today would scruple to use. Thus are we told:

In her [i.e. the church's] head — not indeed impeccable, but infallible — she sees the representative of God Himself, the universal Doctor, the Master of minds and souls, the voice of Authority *par excellence,* promulgating truth and law, declaring what should be believed and what should be done and resuming in his person, though himself a mortal man and a sinner like all other men, the immortal and indefectible power of the Church, which is to say, of Christ — which is to say of God.[25]

Worse, Ollé-Laprune deplores what he calls the 'indocility' of certain Catholics towards the papal authority. Rome, he says, disturbs and alarms them. Either she has done too much — in the realm of politics, for example — or else not enough, as in the social sphere; while in matters of philosophy and even of religion her teaching, so it is objected, has misled the faithful. Such criticisms he deplores as the outcome of pride. Presumably he was here censuring liberal Catholic opinion of the kind denounced in the *Syllabus* of 1864, for which, strangely, he finds words of excuse. If, like Newman, whom he greatly admired, he is to be counted among the precursors of Modernism it must be clearly understood within what narrow limits this is so.

La Certitude morale contains the essence of Ollé-Laprune's religious philosophy. It made its appearance at a time when the vogue of rationalism and positivism had begun to wane. To have attempted to present the case for religion in a rationalistic or 'scientific' form would therefore have miscalculated the current mood. As Georges Goyau put it: 'Hymns to science and reason, the divinities of the preceding epoch, left the new generation cold; it had not enough faith to believe even in these idols.'[26] Ollé-Laprune's starting-point is the principle that a man's thinking is always in some degree a

moi. Je crois ce que croît l'Église Catholique romaine. Je n'ai aucune arrière-pensée, aucune réserve, aucune hesitation dans ma soumission à l'infaillible autorité de l'Eglise et de son chef infaillible, le Souverain Pontife. J'accepte toutes les définitions du Concile du Vatican' (from a letter to Charles Secrétain, quoted by Lecanuet, *La Vie,* p. 497).

[24] See *La Vitalité chrétienne,* pp. 245—94.

[25] *ibid.,* p. 252.   [26] *ibid.,* p. xxxiii.

personal responsibility, and that the quest of truth involves the *will*. The pressure of habitual attitudes, accepted opinions, inherited prejudices has to be consciously resisted. True free-thinking acknowledges the volitional element in the activity of reason itself:

The act of judging, is it or is it not an act of the will? Descartes, who says that it is, makes no distinction between *assent* and *consent*. For us, however, everything that we say concerning the role of the will implies precisely this distinction.

In itself, then, assent is not consent. Not indeed that one declares a thing to be true merely because one wishes it to be so: the act of will is not identical with the rational *judgment* by which one pronounces something to be true or false. For in itself judgment is not a free act but rather the 'given' condition which makes assent possible: one affirms or denies legitimately when it is seen that one *must* affirm or deny. Judgment, that is, cannot deny what is *seen* to be the case, which strictly speaking is a matter of *knowledge*, and knowledge in itself does not depend on the will. Nevertheless because our mental faculties constitute a unity, interpenetrating one another, it follows that the will is implicated in an act which *per se* is purely intellectual. Thus assent is involuntary, whereas consent is not. Consent means *acceptance* of the truth:

It is not the act itself of affirming or denying, for that is something, so to say, dictated by the truth. It is the soul's response to that higher voice.

Hence truth is not merely recognized, but received, welcomed and loved.[27]

The will, then, has a part in all knowledge. It prepares the mind to see and judge properly, keeping it attentive and persuading it to accept the truth. To induce oneself to adhere to the truth, of whatever order, is a genuinely moral act, a function of the moral life. 'Among the conditions required for the full and legitimate exercise of the reason the moral occupy first place.' And this pre-eminently is the case with moral truths themselves, which relate to man's entire personal being, and which demand a practical response:

Moral truth is not given merely to look at; it is not an object purely of contemplation. Essentially practical, it requires of us a practical assent, and if we fall into the habit of refusing this the liveliness of our first impressions diminishes. As the measure of the responses to the interior call becomes weaker and less satisfactory, so the appeal itself becomes less forceful ... There is a light which shines in the mind, but one has to make use of it, otherwise it becomes feeble and seems to go out.

It is of the very nature of truth in this realm that the soul should embrace it and receive it wholly, the heart consenting as well as the understanding assenting.

An intelligence like man's, subject to the law of work and to the necessity of being

[27] *La Certitude morale*, pp. 64f.

able to attain its object only by a more or less lengthy and difficult series of discursive operations, cannot judge properly without the intervention of the will, which sustains the attention and appears to become part of the act of assent itself. As between the true and the false it has to make the kind of choice which in moral matters is itself essentially moral.[28]

For choice it truly is when the reasons by which the mind is enlightened are not enough to compel assent. 'It is then that the will has to decide.' Moral truths have too an element of obscurity about them which renders faith both possible and necessary. In order to be known, they have to be *done*.

Complete certitude is personal. It is the total act of the soul itself embracing by a free choice no less than by a firm judgement present truth as light and law, as an object of contemplation and love, of respect and obedience.[29]

In this way, then, an act of judgment becomes an act of *faith*. Faith does not imply renunciation of reason, but it does mean that in the moral sphere the abstract understanding cannot be our sole guide. Besides, faith includes trust, which again is a personal factor.

Trust is of the nature of love. It presupposes two terms between which an accord freely comes about. The object works through its appeal, and the power of its attraction seems irresistible. But if, on the other side, the will is inactive, nothing is achieved. Such is the character of all things *moral*.[30]

Constraint certainly has no place here; it is attraction which constitutes the law of the spiritual as of the physical world — so long as it is a free attraction.

Love, genuine love, freely and willingly given and received, unites souls one with another, and then, in turn, to the true and the good. Obligation, or moral necessity, is the character of the new order in which rule dominates the will without forcing it.

Thus faith rests on consent. To affirm anything with insufficient reason is mere credulity, but to do so with good reason is wisdom. The virtue of faith however lies in its surmounting obstacles by 'a noble and generous effort'.[31]

But is all this compatible with the intellectual objectivity which the very notion of truth would seem to require? Ollé-Laprune does not deny the need for objectivity. Moral and religious truths are the subject of knowledge as well as faith. In affirming the existence of God, the freedom of the will and the immortality of the soul rational criteria must be satisfied, even though one may, with Plato, distinguish the demands of the 'wise' from those of the merely 'clever'.[32] We do not *create* truth even in the moral order, and in the

[28] *ibid.*, pp. 67f.   [29] *ibid.*, p. 79.
[30] *ibid.*, p. 96.   [31] *ibid.*, p. 98.
[32] *ibid.*, p. 289. Ollé-Laprune was by no means lacking in sympathy with the neo-scholastic movement. But he insisted that it should involve much more than a mere parrot-like repetition of St Thomas's own phrases. cf. *La Vitalité chrétienne*, p. 275.

end it is possible without contradicting reason to refuse to admit such truth. The God of religious faith and the moral consciousness, like our own freedom and immortality, are not to be found simply in the conclusion of a syllogism. But the importance of these beliefs lies in the fact that although the abstract reasoning alone cannot convince us of their truth they nevertheless are central to the whole question of human destiny and hence to any genuine science of man. No doubt the effort and responsibility of achieving a rationally grounded faith may be too much for any given individual, but the individual does not stand alone: beside him, independent of him and superior to him is the universal reason, *le bon sens public*, articulated and interpreted by the teaching authority of the Catholic church.[33]

Ollé-Laprune's next volume, *La Philosophie et le temps présent*, again leads up to an affirmation of the existence of God as 'He who is'. Yet it is the least overtly theological of all his works. Religion is referred to simply as a fact of human experience which like other such facts is a proper subject for philosophical inquiry.[34] The book's central concern is the moral responsibility of the philosopher *qua* philosopher. There is no knowledge of truth apart ultimately from the will to realize the good; nor, at the highest level, is there any order of truth that does not carry with it practical implications.

The moral act is truly known as such only if, for him who studies it, it is also something other than a subject for study. To have a real and the living idea of it one must have it within oneself, through intimate experience of the reality itself.[35]

In other words, one is 'to go to the truth with one's whole soul', to take hold of what *is*, so far as possible, 'in being oneself all that authentic nature and right reason require one to be'.[36] Philosophy therefore is not a mere intellectual entertainment, as the contemporary 'aesthetic' or 'dilettante' school were suggesting. Yet neither is it purely a science. As a serious *moral* enterprise it proceeds by both imagination (using symbols) and reason (using concepts). It is essentially exploratory, tentative and personal, and its forms may as well be literary as abstract and systematic.

The work which appeared two years after the foregoing, *Les Sources de la paix intellectuelle*, was aimed at those who, like Paul Desjardins for example, sought moral unity within the nation — in effect the reconciliation for all practical purposes of radicals and Catholics — on the basis of a minimal consensus of ethical principle beyond which opinion should be free.[37] In the

[33] *La Certitude morale*, p. 405.   [34] *Le Philosophie et le temps présent*, p. 281.
[35] *ibid.*, p. 258.   [36] *ibid.*, p. 344.
[37] Desjardins, founder of the non-sectarian *Union pour l'Acion morale*, was one of a group that came to be known, in the early 'nineties, as *les néo-chrétiens*. Disillusioned with the hope that science alone could provide a sufficient basis for the moral life of modern society, they looked to Christianity to supply the needed ethic, provided its dogmas — though not its ecclesiastical organization — were quietly jettisoned. Many Catholics were impressed. See Lecanuet, *La Vie*, pp. 457f.

divided state of French public opinion at the time such a solution had obvious attractions, but Ollé-Laprune, the committed believer, was ready with a warning of its dangers. Fundamentally it was reductionist and sceptical, and the unity of outlook which it desiderated would be bought only at the price of a loss of confidence in truth itself. For society to have cohesion there has to be a certain basic community of ideas, and superficially at least these will appear to be relatively few. But truth has depth: more is involved than at first comes to light, and if the minimum is really to serve it will not remain minimal indefinitely. To begin with, four principles at the very least would have to be secured: 1. An established *fact* in any field of knowledge is no longer open to question; 2. A proven contradiction cannot be removed; 3. Discussion is precluded when all assertions are accepted as true; and 4. Moral integrity is primal, meaning that what is opposed to morality, either self-evidently or through its consequences, is to be rejected. In other words, facts are to be respected, absurdity avoided, the truth believed in and morality upheld. Ollé-Laprune's intention, however, is not merely to lay down a few truisms. He was convinced that once principles like these are accepted the force of reason is such that simple agreement on a working morality is bound to lead in the end to a much fuller meeting of minds. It is the ethical starting-point that matters. Establish unity there and the final outcome will be Christianity.

The claim is an audacious one, implying that the Christian creed provides the 'natural' response to man's inherent moral need. The soul of Western man truly is, in Tertullian's famous phrase, *naturaliter christiana*. Begin with a commonly accepted residuum of truth, draw out its inferences, both theoretical and practical, sustain your effort with a good will, and there can be but one consequence. And what this is forms the substance of Ollé-Laprune's last major work published during his lifetime, *Le Prix de la vie*. The question here raised is nothing less than the meaning and value of human life itself. Of supreme importance, it is to be approached with the greatest seriousness. Consider it, he says, in all its range, at the lowliest level and the highest, and it is plain that life consists in a twofold movement of acquisition and restitution, of accumulation and expenditure. To live is to receive what life has to offer and at the same time to pass it on to others, for we take in in order to give out again. Such is the law of our being. But human life, as the most highly organized form of existence known to us, has a quality proper to itself. Man must live as man and not as the beasts, for his life has a specific character and worth deriving from his unique intelligence. The fulfilment of that life cannot depend on science alone, of which the modern world has made a god, otherwise the vast majority would simply fail to realize their own humanity. There must therefore be a goal accessible to all, namely moral good. The moral life, in short, constitutes the vocation of man as man. Where it is followed there is hope; where it is denied, practically if not nominally, there can only be despair. But it cannot be lived by the individual in isolation; each of us has received from others, or from society at large, the greater part of what is necessary for living, so that to render something in return is a moral obligation.[38] But the ground of obligation is the law of love, and the law of love carries us into the realm of the spirit, of religion.

It is Christianity's sublime originality to have proclaimed this commandment in a way hitherto unknown, resting it upon its true foundation, and to have reinforced it by the sublime example of the sacrifice of the Cross.

The fundamental reason for Ollé-Laprune's insistence that philosophy must finally yield to religion is the moral flaw in man's own nature, which makes it impossible for him to fulfil his human vocation completely. For between what man can achieve of himself and what God requires of him there is a fatal gap. Through sin the primal man lost sanctifying grace and his original state of righteousness. Thus his present state is one not of nature but of defect of nature; his integrity is gone, its place taken by *concupiscence*, inordinate desire.

Reason is not destroyed, but it is obscured. Free will is not extinguished, but it is weakened and attenuated. Man is capable of both natural knowledge and natural virtue. But that whereof he is incapable, wholly and radically, is supernatural good.[39]

The Christian gospel, however, offers redemption.

By the grace of salvation — grace liberating, restoring, healing, which the Saviour has won for us — we return to grace; and this second state is glorious. The Man-God is a marvel surpassing all else . . . The sin of one man lost us: Jesus Christ saves us; and he saves us in suffering and dying for us. The solidarity which renders us participants in Adam's fault makes us partakers also of the merits of Jesus Christ. By the righteousness of one are all men justified. Christ is the new Adam and the true author of life.[40]

Humanity has therefore no cause for despair, even though no man can be saved against his will; for the more he feels his own insufficiency the more likely is he to admit his need of God. *Cum infirmor tunc potens sum.*

Fin de Siècle

The Italian Modernist, Giovanni Semeria, remarked of Léon Ollé-Laprune that when the history of the Christian philosophical movement of the time came to be written his name would be 'among the first and most illustrious'.[41]

---

[38] *Le Prix de la vie*, pp. 277f.
[39] ibid., pp. 352f. Ollé-Laprune distinguishes of course the orthodox Catholic doctrine of the fall from the Jansenist.
[40] ibid., pp. 355f.
[41] *Gente che torna, gente che si muove, gente che s'avviva* (1901), p. 22. The best study of Ollé-Laprune is still Blondel's (*Léon Ollé-Laprune: l'achèvement et l'avenir de son œuvre, 1923*).

Yet Ollé-Laprune was only a shining instance of a number of such 'new' Catholics; men strictly orthodox, indeed ultramontane, but open nevertheless to the increasingly 'socializing' tendencies of their age. With the most brilliant of his disciples, Maurice Blondel, we shall be dealing in the next chapter. It remains for us here to take a look at three or four other writers who belonged to his circle and espoused his ideals.

George Fonsegrive (1852–1917), who spent the greater part of his professional career at the Lycée Buffon, — he would most probably have been given a chair at the Collège de France but for the intervention of Renan — was the author of philosophical works of a technical character and of some important articles on philosophical subjects in the current journals, notably the *Revue philosophique* and the long-surviving *Annales de Philosophie chrétienne*.[42] But it is for his writings as a Catholic moralist in the field of political theory and social ethics that he is best remembered: *Catholicisme et démocratie* (1896), *Le Catholicisme et la vie de l'esprit* (1899) and *La Crise sociale* (1901). Like Ollé-Laprune Fonsegrive conceived his role as that of Christian philosopher, although he did not perhaps find it so easy to win an audience. While conservative Catholics took him for a rather dangerous 'progressivist', to his academic colleagues he has only a clericalist with a 'mediaeval' outlook; and in any case he lacked Ollé-Laprune's natural gifts as a teacher. His philosophical treatises are abstract and scholastic in style, although he had no interest in the contemporary neo-scholastic movement itself. He was most influential as a polemist and his connexion with *La Quinzaine*, which he edited from 1897 to 1907, when it ceased publication, registered a sustained attempt to 'acclimatize French Catholics to the modern', as he himself put it. He consistently advocated a repudiation of economic individualism in the name of a new 'social' Catholicism. But with the movement for social justice there must also, he held, go scientific advance and further progress towards democracy, the three being inseparable.[43] Catholics therefore must be frank in their acceptance of the republic, learning to judge contemporary issues on their own merits. Religious dogma is unchangeable — Fonsegrive was no theological liberal and he was unattracted by Blondel's immanentism — but in secular affairs each man has to reason in the light of his own knowledge and moral conviction. Certainly politics ought not to be approached in a sectarian spirit. Catholic opinion, that is, should be flexible, eschewing an imposed conformism and realizing that it will often be right for it to align itself with those who do not admit its spiritual basis. A Catholic upbringing is a priceless

[42] The former include an *Essai sur le libre arbitre* (1887), *La Causalité efficiente* (1893) and *Essais sur la Connaissance* (1909). His *Évolution des Idées dans la France contemporaine, de Taine à Péguy* — an admirable survey of the period with which it deals — was published posthumously in 1920. Fonsegrive's historical studies have retained an interest which his original work has lost.

[43] *Regards en arrière* (1908), p. 8.

thing, but it does not depend on segregation and narrowness of outlook.[44]

Fonsegrive's younger *confrère*, Georges Goyau (1869—1939) strove for similar ends. He entered the École Normale with a first place in 1888, thirty years after Ollé-Laprune's identical distinction, and with his studies in Roman history won a name for himself as a classical scholar. But as an ardent Catholic he could not stand aloof from religious issues, especially the relation of church and society. The public pronouncements of Leo XIII on the social problem, *Rerum novarum* particularly, stirred him deeply. He was also convinced that French Catholicism needed to awaken from its ancient dreams of monarchy and accept the republic freely, difficult though this might appear in the prevailing political conditions. Support of the *ralliement* he therefore deemed essential.[45] In 1891, under the pseudonym of 'Léon Grégoire', he published *Le Pape, les catholiques et la question sociale*, extolling the new Vatican social doctrine, and subsequently a volume of *Quinzaine* articles under the collective title *Autour du Catholicisme social*.[46] Much of Goyau's time was spent in Rome at the French School of Archaeology, which he had joined in 1891, but he frequently visited Germany and Austria and made a detailed study of the religious situation in the German-speaking lands. *L'Allemagne religieuse*, the five volumes of which appeared during the decade 1898 to 1908 is in fact his main literary achievement. With the ending of the Concordat in 1906 Goyau at first took his stand with such of his co-religionists who were willing to recognize the *associations cultuelles* to be set up under the new law,[47] thus placing himself alongside those whom its opponents dubbed 'les cardinaux verts'.[48] But when the pope denounced the law Goyau immediately sub-

---

[44] Fonsegrive was also a novelist, writing under the pseudonym of Ives Le Quebec. His *Lettres d'un Curé de campagne* (1894), *Lettres d'un Curé de canton*, (1895), *Le Journal d'un évêque* (1896), *Le Fils de l'esprit* (1905) and *Le Mariage du docteur Ducros* (1911) all deal with clerical life and topical matters relating to the situation of the Catholic church in France. On Fonsegrive's work generally see *George Fonsegrive* in 'Cahiers de la Nouvelle Journée' (1928) and P. Archambault, *George Fonsegrive* (1932).

[45] He expressed his views with decision, albeit anonymously, in a pamphlet, *Être républicain ou n'être pas*, written in collaboration with Bernard and Jean Brunhes (1891).

[46] Among his later writings on the social question, *Catholicisme et politique* (1923), *Orientations catholiques* (1925), *Pages catholiques socials* (1926) and *L'Épanouissement du credo* (1931) are especially noteworthy.

[47] The *associations cultuelles* provided for under Article 18 were to serve the purpose of controlling 'the expenses, the upkeep and the public exercise of religion' and were to consist of local residents, the number of members varying according to population. Thus effective regulation of church affairs at the local level was transferred to the laity, who would now have a say even in the ordering of worship. This provision, which aroused bitter though by no means universal hostility on the Catholic side, was repudiated by Pius X, who condemned the entire Separation Law in his encyclical *Vehementer* of 11 February 1906, declaring its terms to be contrary to the constitution of the church as founded by Jesus Christ. For the full text of the law see Debidour, *L'Église catholique.*, ii, pp. 577ff.

[48] An allusion to the green uniform of the Academicians, a number of whom were among the signatories of a petition addressed by twenty-three leading laymen to the French bishops requesting acceptance of the law as it stood. Goyau was not himself elected to the Academy until 1922. A year before his death he was chosen as its permanent secretary.

mitted to the pontiff's judgment, ill-considered though it was. His later career does not concern us here, but his literary effort in the Catholic cause was un-flaggingly sustained — as a writer he was prolific — and for eleven years (1927–1938) he held the chair of the history of missions at the Paris Institut Catholique. He died in 1939, a revered figure, not only among churchmen. Henri Bremond was wont to speak of him as 'notre Ozanam'; while Pope Pius XII called him 'a soul of light'.

Victor Delbos (1862–1916), after Ollé-Laprune the third figure in what we may call the Ozanam succession, was, like Ozanam himself, a historian of ideas.[49] He first taught at the *lycées* of Limoges and Toulouse before going on to the Henri IV in Paris and finally to the Sorbonne, where he occupied a chair from 1902 until his death during the first world war. His membership of the Academy of Moral and Political Sciences dated from 1911. Not himself of any marked originality as a teacher, he nevertheless was able to expound the ideas of others with an unusual degree of insight and objectivity. His reserved and self-effacing disposition, coupled with the fact that he was personally unconnected with any particular philosophical school, no doubt enhanced his scrupulous impartiality. A loyal friend of Maurice Blondel's, his general neutrality in the current philosophical debate was something wholly distinct from his convictions as a Christian and a Catholic.[50] For what most deeply motivated him was his concern for the 'existential' issues of man's actual nature and destiny, issues upon which Christianity alone, with its faith in the transcendent, seemed to cast an effectively practical light.

No survey of Catholic thought during these *fin de siècle* years would be com-plete, however, without some notice of the work of Ferdinand Brunetière (1849–1906), who in his day was not only the leading literary critic in France but a man also with a profound regard for social order and for the traditional attitudes which he saw as its true foundation. An Englishman might think of him as by anticipation a kind of Gallic T. S. Eliot. From his early youth he was an avid reader with an unusual capacity for assimilating ideas. He decided to make literary criticism his *métier*, joining the staff of the *Revue des Deux Mondes* and focusing his attention on the contemporary literary scene. In 1886 he was given a lectureship at the École Normale, at a period of his life when his outlook was largely dominated by Darwinism and the philosophy of Schopenhauer. By 1893 his reputation stood high enough to

---

[49] His chief works on the history of philosophy are: *Le problème moral dans la philosophie de Spinoza et dans l'histoire du spinozisme* (1893), *La Philosophie pratique de Kant* (1905) and a survey of contemporary French philosophy published posthumously in 1919. His book on Maine de Biran (*Maine de Biran et son œuvre philosophique*) did not appear until 1932. See J. Wehrlé, *Victor Delbos* (1932). Émile Boutroux judged him to be 'a scholar of the first rank, and an historian and critic of a penetration and balance universally recognized'.

[50] He it was who compiled the *notice* on Blondel in the *Annuaire des anciens élèves de l'École Normale Supérieure* for 1917 (pp. 47–69).

secure his election to the French Academy, and in the following year he assumed the directorate of the *Revue*. But his restless, searching intelligence could not long remain attached to his earlier ideals. Keenly interested as he was in metaphysical and ethical questions, positivism held him for a while until he succumbed to the attractions of Buddhism and oriental mysticism. Gradually, though, the traditional faith of his native land exerted its appeal and in 1894 he was received in audience by Pope Leo XIII, an occasion memorialized by him in 'Après une visite au Vatican', published in the *Revue des Deux Mondes* on New Year's Day, 1895. In this the one-time positivist voiced his disillusion with the unfulfilled promises of science, which, for all the trust the modern world so readily placed in it, was neither a complete explanation nor a reliable guide to the conduct of human life. What men need is an authoritative ethic such as only religion can impose. And of religion Catholicism provides the one satisfactory embodiment, its virtue being that it alone amid the shifting sands of current opinion can supply a basis for a morality which is both clear and firm. The very coherence of society itself thus requires Catholicism as a necessary part of its fabric. Brunetière's argument, so reminiscent of the traditionalist doctrines of Bonald, came as a surprise to the *Revue*'s readers, since previous editorial policy had not as a rule been of a kind to warm Catholic hearts.[51] It was construed as a forthright indictment of that brash confidence in scientific progress which was the activating spirit of orthodox secularism.

Brunetière was clearly an *engagé*, a man with a mission. Of a dogmatic temperament even in regard to purely literary matters, his concerns were invariably propagandist and polemical. One after another of his numerous publications — for like Goyau he was a tireless writer — revealed the growing force of his Christian conviction. *La Renaissance de l'idéalisme* (1896), *Le Besoin de croire* (1898) and *Les ennemis de l'Âme française* (1899) led up to *Les Raisons actuelles de croire* (1900), in which he openly announced his formal adherence to Catholicism. He admitted no qualifications: *Ce que je crois, allez le demander à Rome.*

Yet Brunetière's standpoint remained consistently that of an intellectual. Religious feeling as such, despite the emotional impetus which finally carried him into the bosom of the Catholic church, seems to have played only a small part in his conversion. So far however as his academic career was involved he paid a price for his change of mind. Posts at the Sorbonne (1899) and the Collège de France (1904) which might have been his went to others. In addition he upset conservative Catholics by assuming the leadership of the 'cardi-

---

[51] Of the *Revue des Deux Mondes* under Brunetière's directorship Lecanuet writes: 'Depuis lors, la *Revue* non seulement ne contiendra pas un mot qui puisse blesser nos croyances, mais ses lecteurs y trouveront des études historiques ou sociales inspirées par un véritable esprit chrétien ... En somme pendant une dizaine d'années, la *Revue de Deux Mondes* devint presque une revue apologétique' (*La Vie de l'Église sous Léon XIII*, p. 249. On the effect of Brunetière's article see also *ibid.*, pp. 461f.).

naux verts' in urging acceptance of the resented *associations cultuelles*, although he subsequently bowed to the papal decision and advised his followers to do likewise. But by now his health was failing and a stroke deprived him of the power of speech. With his premature death the French church lost an able and determined servant and partisan.

In the field of religious philosophy Brunetière's writings — *Science et Religion* (1895), *Discours de Combat* (1899—1903)[52] and *Sur les chemins de Croyance. Première etape: l'utilisation du positivisme* (1905) — were well-argued and hard-hitting, in a style reminiscent of the traditionalists of the early years of the century. As the latter denounced the individualism of the Enlightenment so the former saw in the naturalism and positivism of his own day a new cause of social disintegration.[53] The views of such men as Taine and Littré could only lead, he considered, to the eventual collapse of any real basis of moral judgment. Freedom needed the counterpoise of authority if society is to survive, and France had flourished only under authoritarian government. The prevailing scientism, dilettantism and scepticism were undermining the nation's faith and self-confidence. Brunetière's defence of the moral and social values of Catholicism is impressive and for a time proved influential in its dogmatic and argumentative way, but on the whole his apologetic failed to retain its interest, although his standing as a critic and man of letters allows even today of no serious detraction. Nor should it be forgotten that the mere fact of the conversion to Catholicism of so prominent an intellectual and *incroyant* was of undoubted encouragement to French Catholics at a time of grave stress in their church's history.

[52] Two further series with this title were published in 1907.
[53] Brunetière rejected Protestantism for the same reasons as did Bonald, while as for democracy it both flattered and fostered the vices that history demonstrates to be the most inimical to social welfare.

11

MAURICE BLONDEL AND THE PHILOSOPHY OF ACTION

L'Action

'My original intention was to establish a philosophy which was autonomous, but which nevertheless, from the rational standpoint, conformed to the most minute and rigorous demands of Catholicism'. Such in his own words was Maurice Blondel's aim in publishing at the age of thirty-two the work which was to place him among the foremost philosophical thinkers of his time.[1] The title he gave it was simply *L'Action*, although his sub-title explained it as an 'Essai d'une critique de la vie et d'une science de la pratique'.[2] In his student days he was astonished to discover that philosophical speculation, even in Catholic eyes, proceeded 'as though man's real state was a purely natural one, upon which Christianity could be superimposed like a wig, so to say'. A Christian philosophy of this sort, he judged, 'would not succeed in gaining a hold on the minds even of those still faithful to their baptismal vows, and even less of those who, though nurtured in Christianity, benefit from it only by breaking with it or actually opposing it'. This 'patchwork' type of approach struck him therefore as wholly inadequate. One would simply have to start all over again.

Maurice Blondel was born at Dijon on 2 November 1861, of an old Burgundian family whose successive generations had produced lawyers, physicians and public servants. His father, Henri Blondel, who had himself (like his brother) carried on the family's legal tradition, was a man in easy circumstances, with properties in the country as well as a town house at Dijon. The estate at Saint-Seine-sur-Vingeanne was especially dear to the young Maurice, whose love of nature − and he had a considerable knowledge of natural history − was first stimulated there. Inherited means also gave him a

---

[1] 'Lettre-préface pour une réédition de *L'Action*', in *Études blondéliennes*, i (1951), pp. 16f. Blondel has been described as 'probably the most important French philosopher since Descartes' (Katherine Gilbert, *Maurice Blondel's Philosophy of Action*, 1924, p. iii). In France at least his reputation has been equalled in this century only by Bergson and J.-P. Sartre, neither of whom is a 'philosopher's philosopher' in the sense that could be claimed for Blondel.

[2] The first edition appeared in 1893, but the author refused to allow a reprint and copies of it eventually became rare. The two-volume work bearing the same title which was published in 1936−7 represents an extensive recasting of the original. The treatise of 1893 was re-issued in 1950, the year after its author's death, as the first volume of his *Premiers écrits*.

freedom from material concern which was undoubtedly a boon in later life, when he was incapacitated by blindness. He received his secondary education at the Dijon *lycée*, where he first read the works of Leibniz and Maine de Biran, both of whom were to be a strong influence on the development of his own thought.[3] It was here too that he made up his mind to become not a lawyer or *fonctionnaire* but a professor of philosophy. At any rate it was with this latter ambition in mind that he left Dijon in his twenty-first year for Paris and the École Normale. There he stayed till 1885, with Émile Boutroux to instruct him in philosophy and Ollé-Laprune as his general director of studies, both of whom fully appreciated his bent and capabilities. Friends among his contemporaries at the École included Victor Delbos, André Pératé (afterwards Custodian of Versailles) and Johannes Wehrlé, who though he subsequently entered the priesthood retained a warm sympathy with Blondel's views and supported him loyally during the years of controversy. Taking his *agrégation* in 1886 — although not with marked distinction — he went on to teach at the *lycées* of Chaumont, Montauban and Aix-en-Provence, and for a short while at the Collège Stanislas. In 1889 he was given leave to present a doctoral thesis.

His day-by-day thoughts during these years (1883—1894) have been preserved in the *Carnets intimes* published in 1961. At one time he considered becoming a priest, but the project had its difficulties:

To devote oneself to others is the rule common to all men, just as Christianity is the universal remedy. But how? Is it to be in intellectual conflicts, in the *mêlée* of ideas? Then I shall end by becoming a priest. Or in hand-to-hand fights, in the political and social fray? There the cassock is a scarecrow. It compromises you and you compromise it. Your personal action is incommoded and restricted.

But the intellectual life too had its drawbacks. He goes on:

It is true that I am speculative rather than active: I have some ideas of my own, but will they ever acquire the semi-scientific precision needed to make them efficacious? And especially where I am concerned, who have not the gift of defining an ideal, would not an intellectual life tend to become a moving phantasmagoria of interlinked forms whose indefinite contours overlap and penetrate one another? Is it not action alone which defines ideas?

Yet whatever his career was to be it would demand a life of Christian service. Abstract work, he confessed, tired and depressed him — 'it is contrary to our nature, to all nature'. Nevertheless the philosophical vocation held him, and in 1895, two years after the publication of *L'Action*, he was given a lectureship at the university of Lille. But he did not stay there long, and at the end of the

[3] His Latin doctoral thesis of 1893 was on Leibniz: *De vinculo substantiali et de substantia composita apud Leibnitium*. Copies of it were printed, but for private circulation only. His *Le 'Vinculum substantiale' d'après Leibniz et l'ébauche d'un réalisme supérieur* was published in 1930. A reprint of the original Latin dissertation, edited with an introduction and French translation by C. Troisfontaines, was issued in 1972.

following year he assumed the post at Aix which he was to hold until 1927, when ill-health enforced his retirement. It was in 1896 also that he married.

To return however to *L'Action* itself. Blondel had been working on it for some years, making repeated new drafts. At last in November 1891 he settled down to the seventh and final version. Some eighteen months later it was completed and presented at the Sorbonne. But from the very start he had encountered problems. The subject itself was rejected out of hand when first proposed: the *idea* of action might perhaps have been allowed, but not action *tout court*. Only after he had gone to some trouble to explain what he really had in mind was his proposal grudgingly admitted. Similar prejudice was met with when the work was finished. Boutroux, who as his supervisor had read through the manuscript, was aware of what the examiners' attitude was likely to be and advised his young friend to call on them privately so as to give them a chance 'to blow off steam' (as he put it) before the formal and public *soutenance de thèse* due to take place on 7 June 1893.[4] At the latter Blondel acquitted himself with honour, through a long and sometimes heated discussion. One of the examiners, Paul Janet, accused him of obscurity in thought and style alike: 'It takes me an hour to read one of your pages', he complained, 'and then I fail to understand it.'[5]

Janet's strictures were by no means unmerited. Most of *L'Action's* readers have found the writing dense and indeed Blondel's whole approach to his subject opaque. Some words of his in his own defence ought therefore in fairness to be quoted.

Style [he says] should be a precision instrument which renders the whole feeling, and nothing but the feeling, of the inevitable difficulty of things. Whatever one does one can never make certain ideas easily accessible; they require an initiation analogous to that of higher mathematics. It is also true that one can never hope to succeed in preventing impatient and presumptuous minds from wanting to grasp, and believing that they have penetrated, everything without competence ... If I wrote out certain parts of my work six or seven times, it was not for the pleasure of remaining obscure. I sincerely tried to diminish the difficulties which arose from the imperfection of the expression, and I am distressed not to have succeeded better. And yet I did not hope, nor did I wish, to make all the obstacles disappear. Style is not only a passage open to others, giving them access to our thought; it is also a protection against hasty judgements. The right thing would be to understand neither too soon nor too late.[6]

But obscurity was not the only ground of objection. Several of Blondel's academic critics disliked his overtly religious standpoint,[7] with the result that

[4] cf. Bourbon di Petrella, *Il pensiero di Maurice Blondel* (1950), p. 21.

[5] cf. J. Wehrlé, 'Une soutenance de thèse', in *Études blondéliennes*, i pp. 79—98. See also E. Masure, 'Le témoignage d'un théologien', in *Les Études philosophiques* (new series), i (1950) pp. 54f.

[6] *Études blondéliennes*, i, p. 88 (cited by A. Dru and I. Trethowan, *Maurice Blondel: the* Letter on Apologetics *and* History and Dogma, 1964, p. 41.)

[7] Thus Séailles, another of Blondel's examiners, objected to what he considered a doctrine 'toute pénétrée d'esprit conservateur, de préoccupations orthodoxes, de fidelité à la lettre des dogmes et aux préceptes d'une Église'. See R. Aubert, *La Revue nouvelle*, x (1949) p. 107.

the professorship to which the acceptance of his thesis would normally have
entitled him was not forthcoming, the Lille lectureship being the outcome of
Boutroux's good offices. For some while Blondel felt ill at ease and frustrated,
as his journal reveals.[8] By now in his thirties, he seemed to have got himself
no proper place in life.

What, then, did he set out to do in this celebrated but taxing work? It is
clear, first of all, that he intended it not as an essay in apologetic theology but
in pure philosophy. And like his master Ollé-Laprune he was convinced that
philosophy is not a mere intellectual pastime, pursued for its own sake. Without direct relation to life it is barren, and life at its deepest level is inseparable
from the great issues posed by religious faith. The volume's subtitle, 'Essai
d'une critique de la vie et d'une science de la pratique', is significant: Blondel
was writing as both a philosopher and a Christian. Philosophy in his view
could not dissociate itself from 'existential' questions, as we today would call
them, without destroying most of its value. And as a Christian he believed
that human existence has a 'supernatural' as well as a natural meaning. Not
indeed that the supernatural can be the discovery of reason alone; were that
the case 'supernature', so-called, would itself be part of nature. Yet if supernature is a reality it is bound to have effects discernible within the order of
nature. What philosophy will reveal when applied to the structures of human
existence is that man *naturally* aspires to an end *beyond* nature. Not that it can
demonstrate the supernatural, as still less present it, but it can show that the
hypothesis of supernature is one which meets the needs of man's being at the
deepest level, needs which 'natural' reason by itself does not satisfy. The
philosopher's starting-point, accordingly, should be human life in its concrete
actuality — *action*. Not simply *thought*, that is to say, — to begin with the 'idea'
of action would be to entangle oneself at the outset in logical abstractions — but
the total activity of man as man, ranging from the practical concerns of every-
day life to the highest flights of philosophy and science. In short, philosophy's
task is the problem of man's existence in its whole 'spiritual' aspect in order
to discover as far as possible what this implies in regard to man himself, its
subject. Thus in Blondel's terminology action is man's spiritual existence as
manifested in every phase of his being. Investigation of it, however, must
reach back beyond all specific articulations of the understanding and the
will, to the point indeed where they both have a common origin in the
primal *élan* of spirit itself, since it is there that all human activity has its
source and from it derives its strength, — 'Ce dernier fond où, sans moi,
malgré moi, je subis l'être et je m'y attache'.[9]

[8] See, for example, *Carnets intimes*, (1961), p. 496. A second volume, covering the years 1894
to 1949, was published in 1966.

[9] *L'Action*, p. vii. Human *action* means more than activity in the usual sense, and involves a
continuous interdependence and reciprocal relationship of thought, activity and being. In his
later work Blondel is at pains to show how thought and activity are united in being.

On Blondel's philosophy as a whole much has been published in recent years. Among the

The inquiry therefore necessarily demands much more than the description of psychological phenomena. Blondel's successive studies of such phenomena are, as it happens, remarkably penetrating; but simply to describe is not his purpose. Certainly he is not interested in discussing the subjective needs of individual types, or in suggesting how such needs can be met. Nor, on the other hand, does he seek to round off his investigation with an appeal to some postulated supernatural power or authority to whose dictates reason has no choice but to submit. 'Extrinsicism' of this sort he consistently repudiated. On the contrary, his whole concern is to maintain that human action is autonomous, not heteronomous, by demonstrating the demand of the supernatural implicit in every act of will, whether conscious or unconscious. In other words, the will's ultimate satisfaction is *intrinsic* to the very nature of human volition. It is this which Blondel means by the determinism of action, and the purpose of his work is nothing less than to expose this determinism to close analysis through every stage of its course. His objective also decides his method, which may be characterized as dialectical. 'Yes or no', he asks at the very beginning of his work, 'has human life a meaning? Has man a destiny?'

I act, but without knowing what action is. I have not wished to live, nor do I know precisely who I am or even whether I am. I hear it said that this appearance of being which acts in me, these trivial and fugitive acts of a mere shadow, nevertheless carry within themselves the weight of an eternal responsibility ... Shall I say, then, that I have been condemned to live, condemned to die, condemned to eternity? But how and by what right is this possible, if I have not willed it? The problem is inevitable, and man resolves it inevitably. And the solution, whether right or wrong, is at one and the same time both voluntary and necessary, and each of us carries it out in his own actions. That is why one must study *action*. The very meaning of the word and the wealth of its content will be disclosed little by little.[10]

And he adds: 'It is the role of the logic of action to determine the chain of necessities that compose the drama of life and lead it inevitably to its *dénouement*.'

Human existence itself thus is shaped by an immanent dialectic and embodies a metaphysical principle. The resemblance here between Blondel and Hegel can hardly fail to be noted: Blondel has even been called a 'Christian Hegel'.[11] To each of them the self-consciousness of the subject

works the present author has found the most valuable are: P. Archambault, *Initiation à la philosophie blondélienne en forme de court traité de métaphysique* (1941); B. Romeyer, *La Philosophie religieuse de Maurice Blondel* (1943); H. Duméry, *La philosophie de l'Action* (1948) and *Blondel et la Religion* (1954); M. Ritz, *Le Problème de l'être dans l'ontologie de Maurice Blondel* (1958): H. Bouillard, *Blondel et le Christianisme* (1961); and C. Tresmontant, *Introduction à la métaphysique de Maurice Blondel* (1963). Dru and Trethowan, *Maurice Blondel*, provides the best introduction in English. Blondel's interpreters are not always in agreement as to his meaning.

[10] *L'Action*, pp. viii.

[11] On the German influences upon Blondel's thinking see J. J. McNeill, *The Blondelian Synthesis: a Study of the influence of German philosophical sources on the formation of Blondel's method and thought (1966).*

implies the self-consciousness of the universe. For the latter, a single idea involves the totality of thought; for the former, a single act of will has infinite repercussions. Blondel's philosophy also resembles Hegel's in being a philosophy of mediation, except that for the Catholic thinker both the expression of thought and the product of will are never adequate to the potentialities of either.[12] There is within us always more than we conceive, a basic truth which philosophy must accept. The ultimate ideal of knowledge and attainment alike may be perfect unity, complete adequation, but it is an ideal beyond man's reach, and a *de facto* mediation has to suffice for that immediacy which he is ever striving for. It is recognition of this, whether conscious or not, which decides the whole Blondelian procedure. Our thought is always reaching out after something that in reality we are not or do not possess. Between life as it is and life as we conceive it or will it there is a gap; action is never commensurate with its 'idea' or project. On the one hand we have actual living and thinking in all their unreflective spontaneity; on the other, the systematizations of science and philosophy. But the latter can never become a substitute for the former. Apart from life as men live it there can be neither philosophy nor science, since science and philosophy are themselves no more than modes of reflexion upon life. But although knowledge is not a succedaneum for living, or systematic thought an alternative to the unreflective activity of our actual existence, they are nevertheless of prime importance. For all reality is in principle their province, and there is nothing the mind does not aspire sooner or later to comprehend.

'Action' is thus a fundamental datum underlying every conscious question or deliberate undertaking. Without having 'wished to live' man is ineluctably caught up in the drama of living.

The problem is inevitable, and man resolves it inevitably. But whether the solution be right or wrong, it is at once both *willed and necessary*, as something implicit in every man's acts. Hence the need to study *action*. The real meaning of the word and the wealth of its content will by degrees become apparent. It is good to put before man all that his life demands of him, with all the force of affirmative belief, in the courage to act.[13]

What is required therefore is no mere *a priori* and abstract definition of action but a stage by stage unfolding of its concrete reality. In the least of our acts there is a 'hidden depth', the spring of an expansive dynamism whose logic it is the philosopher's task to delineate. But by detailing the phenomenology of action he will be allowing the facts to speak for themselves and so reveal their inward implications, a procedure to which Blondel afterwards gave the name *méthode d'immanence*. All action, that is, discloses an immanent creative principle, an intrinsic design or tendency, the meaning of which it is

---

[12] See J. Flamand, *L'Idée de médiation chez Maurice Blondel* (1969).
[13] *L'Action*, p. viii.

possible to decipher. At the same time it does not denote unlimited freedom. If it is to become the object of knowledge it must disclose a logic that can be presented in rational terms. The charge that the philosophy of action is an attempt to justify irrationalism is therefore entirely unfounded.[14] What Blondel is seeking is a logic determinative of man's very existence and of which all other logics — the Aristotelian and the Hegelian among them — are but partial expressions.

Blondel's argument so far, then, is clear enough: man's attempt to give adequate expression to the dynamism of his mind and will always ends in failure. There is more in him than he can ever properly externalize and objectify. In Blondel's own words, man 'cannot prove himself equal to his own demands upon himself. Never does he succeed, on his own resources, in putting into the product of his willing all that is really implicit in volition'.[15] The distinction here drawn between the 'manifest will', or *volonté voulue*, and the 'basic will', or *volonté voulante*, is for Blondel a cardinal one. By the latter he means that 'ultimate depth' in which 'outside of myself and in spite of myself I submit to being and cleave to it'. Which means that man's fundamental potentiality, lying as it does beyond the distinction between reason and will as such, is the real and constitutive power of his nature. The *volonté voulante* is for ever trying to realize in the *volonté voulue* the plenitude of its own latent forces. But the dynamism of the *volonté voulante* cannot find utterance apart from the mediation of the rational will. Yet the ends which reason and will are able actually to effect are always limited; not one of them, however far-reaching, is capable in itself of deploying the whole wealth of energy inherent in man's being; the *volonté voulue* always falls short of its goal. But this very failure is the spur to further enterprise, to renewed efforts to secure the adequation of purpose to attainment. The result of human activity may thus be likened to a series of ever-widening circles whose one centre is the basic will or energy which is the root of all action. The life of the individual, the family, political society, indeed every sphere or medium in which man seeks to realize his ends, fall within their scope. For in the pursuit of these ends man knows no stopping-place; the necessity of action continually drives him on. Yet every end, once attained, is always and inevitably less than what the rational will originally envisaged and the struggle has to be resumed. What the dialectic of action shows us is the evolving pattern of these successive but unfulfilled aims. It also compels us to recognize the fact of an ultimate choice which it cannot itself determine. For whether the infinite it-

---

[14] Blondel had earlier (1888) coined the term *pragmatisme* to designate his philosophy, quite unaware of the use of the word in America by C. S. Peirce. When however it became evident that in France his own doctrine was being assimilated to American 'pragmatism' as expounded by William James he repudiated the description. See *Bulletin de la Société française de philosophie* (1908) pp. 293f. Pragmatism in the sphere of religious philosophy received explicit statement in E. Le Roy's *Dogme et Critique* (1907).

[15] *L'Action*, p. 338.

self or some merely finite end is to become for us 'the one thing necessary' — and this, no less, is the issue — is something which abstract reason alone is powerless to decide, because any such decision is necessarily and essentially personal. But philosophy does point to the *demand* for the transcendent which is immanent in every phase of action.

Yet because of this cleavage, this 'fissure ouverte', in all human action which no finite good can bridge, response to the immanent *super*natural can be effected only by a deliberate act of moral self-surrender or 'conversion' — a *sortir de soi*. There is no self-betrayal in such an act, though, since genuine affirmation is bound to exact negation of some kind. 'Mortification alone brings about the contradiction of non-being, and by a sort of metaphysical experiment creates the reality of our own being.'[16] Have we then to accept the *heteronomous* as the law of that being after all? Blondel's answer is that some measure of heteronomy, of what apparently is alien to us, is in fact the necessary condition of any true autonomy. But the heteronomous here is *only* apparent, because the ends of action, as has been stressed, are never completely achieved in the natural order. Blondel admits that the term supernatural is on the face of it a strumbling-block to reason. 'Is it not true that when a philosopher is confronted with such an unknown quantity his reaction is simply to ignore it, or else, more resolutely and frankly, to deny it?' In so doing however he would be wrong: to deny or ignore a datum of experience is contrary to the spirit of philosophy. 'Far from invading a reserved domain, one must show that any such invasion is impossible and that it is precisely because of this impossibility that a necessary relation exists between the natural order and the supernatural.' The role of the understanding, Blondel insists, is to investigate the absolute independence as well as the necessity of the supernatural order.[17] Thus to talk of the need for a personal conversion is in no essential way to question the inherent determinism of action, which is always identical with the logic of the *volonté voulante*.

Blondel opens his detailed account of the dialectic by considering whether the problem it poses, that of human destiny itself, can merely be shelved. Why, one may ask, be so serious about the whole business? Why not take life simply as it comes? The 'dilettante', as Blondel calls him, with the examples of Renan and Maurice Barrès in mind, will try anything for the sake of immediate satisfaction but commit himself to nothing, since for him no real moral issue is involved.[18] Nevertheless his supposed non-commitment is delusive: he in fact is entirely committed to *self*, which he virtually deifies. Deliberate refusal

---

[16] *Ibid.*, pp. 145f.   [17] *ibid.*, p. 389.
[18] *ibid.*, p. 9. cf. *L'Action* (1936–7 ed.), ii, p. 418, where Blondel argues that dilettantism, although especially characteristic of the eighteen-nineties, represents a persistent attitude of the human mind. In the later work he has his eye on the 'humanism' of André Gide's *Nourritures terrestres* — 'un livre de dépouillements', as he dubbed it.

of commitment, Blondel points out, is *per se* commitment, not-to-will is itself an act of will. Thus the question whether life has an overall meaning still stands, inasmuch as to the sceptic the 'nothingness' of life is a significant 'truth of being'. If what the dilettante says about the necessity of non-commitment is valid then the implications of his view, negative though they are, are themselves serious and must be taken seriously. 'Le départ est forcé, mais vers quel but?'

The idea of negation, however, at once introduces the pessimist, who thinks, with Schopenhauer, that he can and should will *nothing. Le néant*, it is now said, is the true end of action.[19] Yet is not the attempt to annihilate the will also an act of will? Because the will-not-to-be involves volition pessimism presents the same inherent contradiction as dilettantism: negation is itself an expression of intent. The suicide testifies by his very act to the existence within him of a 'secret hope' on the strength of which he repudiates life and the world as they are. In any case we have no real conception of and thus no true option for sheer nothingness.

The action which seems to aim at it is composite and hybrid ... In getting to the metaphysical root of pessimism one discovers that in the annihilation of the will which it demands of man there is a conflict of urges: one which carries the will forward to a great idea and a profound love of being, and another which delivers it over only to desire, curiosity and obsession with phenomena.[20]

Hence the conclusion to be drawn is that action, in itself, implies being, that 'there is something which exists', and every attempt to deny or avoid it is futile.

The inherent challenge of action has then to be faced. But what does it entail and what is its object? In its most elemental form it is bare sense-experience. Yet even at this level inconsistencies and incoherences occur that have to be resolved if our immediate environment is to become intelligible. The result is the organization of experience into an increasingly elaborate and sophisticated scheme of objective knowledge, — science. But this very objectivity, which aims of course to include the subject himself, still *depends* on him. For although science assumes the nexus of cause and effect, it is actually the creation of self-consciously free intelligence.

From the primary sense-impression which appears simple only because it is confused and of necessity inconsistent is the need for science born. But positive science does not find within itself the unity and cohesion which it takes for granted without explanation. Just as in pure sensation there is already the awakening of a curiosity without which sensation itself would be non-existent, so positive truth requires the

---

[19] The second edition of *L'Action* makes no overt reference to J.-P. Sartre, but Blondel regards pessimism as well as dilettantism as a common frame of mind, and indeed to be especially characteristic of twentieth-century philosophy. cf. *L'Action*, ii, p. 68, note *a*.

[20] *L'Action* (1893), p. 30.

mediation of an act, the presence of a subject, apart from which or whom there would be no positive truth.[21]

But if 'object' implies a subject and 'phenomena' a knowing mind, solipsism can be counted out. The individual, however, is not an isolated centre of knowledge; his intelligence draws sustenance from its whole environment, of which it is at once the focus and the reflexion. Indeed the mind's power of assimilation seems limitless. Nor can action confine itself to the life of the individual; inevitably it passes over to the external world, in which its intentionality, at whatever risk to itself, perforce seeks expression and self-realization.[22] It is because any and every act involves engagement with the world around us that individual action necessarily becomes social. In fact it is only by the indiviual's commitment to society and the *don de soi* which this demands that true personality develops.[23]

Blondel's dialectic now traces the process of action from its beginnings within the closed circle of pure individuality through all the varying forms of interpersonal relationship. And it is at once clear that man seeks not co-operation simply but in a real sense union. He desires to embrace a being like himself who will both make good what he lacks and draw him out of himself, while at the same time enabling him to achieve full self-identity. He wants 'a help meet for himself' and a love responding to his love. In this way is the family created, since it is in children that the longed-for but ultimately impossible unity of two separate lives is attained. Yet even the family is far from self-sufficient and social feeling demands larger embodiment in state and nation, although these are not mere extensions of the family but something new and *sui generis*. What precisely it is that constitutes national individuality is of course a question for the historian, and one whose answer calls for deep insight into and sympathy with a people's communal ethos and spirit: often enough the reasons given to explain nationality are only abstract and superficial. Nor in the social order is the nation itself the final end, for beyond it is the world of humanity as a whole, where again we find something original and irreducible, although feeling for it springs in the first instance from the simple love of one's own country. But with regard to humanity it is compassion rather than a sense of strength that operates.

The law of egoism, active and conquering, in some way contradicts or reconsiders

---

[21] *ibid.*, p. 101.

[22] In the second edition of *L'Action* Blondel puts his meaning very succinctly: 'Cette sortie de l'opération naissante hors de sa matrice originelle est pour elle l'indispensable moyen de se préciser, de s'enrichir, de se soumettre à la norme salutaire dont elle tirera le sens et la réalisation du vouloir profond et de la fin secrètement poursuivie' (ii, p. 179). The entry of action upon the world of partial achievement carries with it, says Blondel, the risk of perversion and failure, but also the possibility of discovering the ultimate significance of all human activity.

[23] *L'Action*, p. 200.

itself so as to include what at first seemed repellent. . . . Man aspires as it were to wed humanity and to unite with it in a single will.[24]

In short, the reach of the *volonté voulante* always exceeds the grasp of the *volonté voulue*. But because of it man is led inexorably on to what at last must prove a decisive choice. Love of humanity has real meaning only in so far as it implies a universal moral ideal, an entirely disinterested concern for the good. But at this point human action meets the limits which finitude always sets upon its actual achievements. For there now lies before it a world of spiritual or religious reality of which man cannot take possession by his own sole effort. No doubt a 'humanistic' religion of some kind is possible, but it is of an inferior order — 'superstitious action', Blondel calls it: man tries to satisfy his need of the infinite by identifying it with this or that finite object, thus succumbing to magic and myth and attaching himself to cults which in their grossest form are simply idolatrous.[25] Yet it is by such means that he hopes to gain the mastery over powers which altogether transcend his own world. True reverence, genuine awe of the 'holy', have no part in this enterprise, for men turn to false gods not because they believe in them but because they are afraid. No such effort can succeed, however, for once more man's drive outdistances its fulfilment.

What has always been latent in action now becomes increasingly apparent.

It is impossible not to recognize the insufficiency of the entire natural order and at the same time to experience no ulterior need. Yet it is impossible to discover in oneself the means of satisfying this need. We confront something which is at once both necessary and impracticable.[26]

Blondel sees the impulsion of action towards the infinite as twofold. On the one side we are, so to speak, drawn upward from above (*par en haut*); on the other the feeling grows on us that the supposedly solid ground beneath us is no longer firm: our self-confidence is undermined (*par en bas*). We thus begin to understand how the basic will at the root of our being is also somehow independent of us. We are placed in this world, although we did not ask to be; we act, although not simply by our own free volition. We sense ourselves to be in the grip of a force which moves us to seek the impossible, namely a synthesis of our deepest nature with our only partial and imperfect achievements. Yet why should this be the case? What, or who, made us so? The answer to these questions raises the whole issue of *transcendence* as 'the one thing necessary' (*l'unique nécessaire*) to bridge the gap between the *volonté voulue* and the *volonté voulante*. It is an issue man cannot avoid, even if he would. Ought

[24] *ibid.*, pp. 257f.
[25] cf. *ibid.*, p. 307: 'Le fétiche, c'est l'objet visible et mystérieux, incompréhensible et accessible, menaçant et protecteur qui résume le divin comme si le fini pouvait devenir la réalité meme de l'infini.'
[26] *ibid.*, p. 319.

he not, then, to recognize it and face it openly? To allow himself, in the end, 'to be supplanted by God'?[27]

The truth is, Blondel contends, that God has all along been at the root of the will's dynamism. In other words, he is *implicit* in the determinism of human action itself as the cause and source of all that one is and does. But the question is whether or not man recognizes this — whether the 'divinity' he looks for is 'without God and against God' or 'by God and with God'. 'It is in face of being, and only in face of being, that the law of contradiction applies in all its rigour, and freedom comes into play in all its force'[28] — merely a more abstruse way of saying what the plain man already understands and believes:

The quite simple manner in which the popular consciousness conceives the problem of human destiny as a choice, personal to each of us, between good and evil, between the order of God and the temptations of egoism, reflects the profoundest drama of the interior life.[29]

Thus the determinism of action, which *seems* to deny our liberty, turns out to be dependent ultimately on that supreme liberty of choice which confronts us in 'the one thing necessary'.[30] This freedom, that is, is not an unlimited and therefore essentially vacuous autonomy, but the specific option of accepting or refusing the transcendent which also is immanent in us.

How the transcendent is immanent in our experience is, Blondel holds, for philosophy to show. For even if there had been no divine revelation in history, no deliberate gift to man of the means whereby he may 'live the life of God himself', reasoned consideration of the problem brings before us the alternative of choosing or not choosing to identify with a reality which is at once wholly desirable, inaccessible and free; a choice moreover the very possibility of which is to be seen as the basic condition of all human activity. To put the matter in even more elementary terms, philosophy itself leaves room for God in presenting us with at least the *idea* of God as a hypothesis demanding consideration. What it cannot do is actually to verify this hypothesis; only man himself — the 'whole man', and not only his critical reason — can

[27]'Ainsi, par le méchanisme de la vie intérieure, nous voici conduits en face d'une alternative qui résume tous les renseignements de la pratique. L'homme, par lui seul, ne peut être ce qu'il est déjà malgré lui, ce qu'il prétend devenir volontairement. Oui ou non, voudra-t-il vivre, jusqu'à en mourir si l'on peut ainsi parler, en consentant à être supplanté par Dieu? ou bien prétendra-t-il se suffire sans lui, profiter de sa présence nécessaire sans la rendre volontaire, lui emprunter la force de se passer de lui, et vouloir infiniment sans vouloir l'infini?' (*ibid.*, p. 354).

[28]*ibid.*, p. 356.

[29]p. 357. cf. p. 254.

[30]'Ainsi, en dernière analyse, ce n'est pas la liberté qui s'absorbe dans le déterminisme; c'est le déterminisme total de la vie humaine qui est suspendu à cette suprême alternative: ou exclure de nous toute autre volonté que le nôtre, ou se livrer à l'être que nous ne sommes pas comme à l'unique salutaire' (p. 356). See M. Renault, *Déterminisme et liberté dans 'L'Action' de Maurice Blondel* (Lyons, 1965).

make the specific life-choice that will do so. The role of philosophy, and it is a highly important one, is to indicate the conditions which render the choice *rational*. Hence a religious faith that claims to offer the fulfilment of human action should be able to demonstrate its consistency with the exigencies of an independent metaphysic.

The whole process of action makes it plain therefore that from the very depths of his being man *needs* what he himself cannot create. If he is to possess what all along his activity has been leading him towards he must submit himself to a Will which is not his own, a seemingly paradoxical conclusion nevertheless forced upon us, Blondel insists, by reason itself, quite apart from 'supernature' and grace. But what the 'one thing necessary' is in its positive reality can be known only through revelation, which in Christian teaching is focused on an historical event. Concerning this of course philosophy has to remain silent; it can say why the supernatural is necessary, but not what concrete form it will assume in human experience, a question that theology alone can answer. While in content, then, the dogmas of faith are beyond discovery by human reason, — God must be within reach of the humblest, must be seen to offer a universal salvation conveyed to mankind through sacramental means — and although a study of human action has disclosed that no achievement of the *volonté voulante*, no affirmation of the moral conscience alone, can fully embrace the divine, yet at the same time God is he who invests human action with its fundamental meaning, he who is immanent in all that we do and strive for whilst at the same time transcending even our highest intellectual and moral aspirations.

L'Action would have left no doubt in the mind of any unprejudiced reader that Blondel, like his master Ollé-Laprune, took his stand firmly on the ground of orthodox Catholic doctrine. But with Pascal and St Augustine as particular sources of inspiration it was clear too that he dissociated himself from the current neo-Thomist intellectualism.[31] Moral certitude is to be reached neither by purely rational argument nor by an arbitrary assertion of the subjective will-to-believe. On the contrary it must represent an experience of the 'whole man'.

We do not find being and life simply in what is to be thought or believed or even practised, but in what is effectively done.[32]

Again:

Pure understanding is never enough to move us, because it does not grasp us totally. In every act there is an act of faith.[33]

---

[31] On Pascal's influence see D. M. Eastwood, *The Revival of Pascal* (1936), c. VII. For Blondel's own thoughts on St Augustine see his essay in the composite volume, *Saint Augustin* in the series 'Cahiers de la Nouvelle Journée', xvii (English trans., *A Monument to St Augustine*, 1930).

[32] *L'Action*, p. 427.

[33] *ibid.*, p. IX. cf. pp. 405f.

Indeed it was the alleged 'irrationalism' of Blondel's philosophy which first aroused criticism, initially from the pen of Léon Brunschvicg in the supplement to the *Revue de Métaphysique et de Morale* for November 1893. Brunschvicg objected that *L'Action* was an overt plea for the practice of Catholicism and felt bound to record 'a courteous but firm opposition' to it 'in the interests of reason and of that idea of immanence which for modern rationalism is the basis and condition of all philosophical criticism', a comment which at once elicited a reply from Blondel himself defending the properly rational and philosophic character of his work.[34] In approaching the religious problem it had been his aim, he declared, actually to reassert the role of reason as against what had long been the markedly contrary tendency in religious thought in France. His own method was itself one of *immanence*.[35]

On the Catholic side it can only be said that the significance of *L'Action* was not quickly appreciated. One or two favourable notices appeared in Catholic periodicals, but it is evident that Blondel's procedure had by some readers been misunderstood, as when the editor of *Annales de Philosophie chrétienne*, Charles Denis, congratulated him on having tried 'to free apologetics from its old methods of argument and to lead it on to purely psychological ground'.[36] It was in order to clarify his real position on this issue that he wrote the articles which appeared some months later (January to July 1896) in the same periodical under the title of *Lettre sur les exigences de la pensée contemporaine en matière d'apologétique et sur la méthode de la philosophie dans l'étude des problèmes religieux*. This work, which despite its relative brevity occupies a distinctive place in Blondel's *œuvre*, is of an importance to merit discussion in detail.[37]

The Method of Immanence

The *Letter on Apologetics* (as we may more conveniently describe it), although it has properly to be read in the light of *L'Action* itself, to which it serves as a kind

---

[34] *Revue de Métaphysique et de Morale*, January 1894, pp. 5—8. See *Études blondéliennes*, i, pp. 100—4.

[35] 'Simplement en suivant l'évolution continue de nos exigences rationnelles, j'arrive donc à faire jaillir de la conscience, au dedans, ce qui paraissait, à l'origine de ce mouvement, imposé à la conscience, du dehors ... En s'appliquant à l'action, la raison découvre plus qu'en s'appliquant à la raison même, sans cesser d'être rationnelle. Et si je parle de surnaturel, c'est encore un cri de la nature, un appel de la conscience morale et une requête de la pensée, que je fais attendre' (*Revue de Mét. et de Mor.*, Jan. 1894, p. 7).

[36] September 1895. A month earlier a writer in the Benedictine *Mois bibliographique* had hailed the book 'comme l'une des œuvres philosophiques les plus hautes qui ait paru depuis un siècle, œuvre de très haute portée, d'une conception puissante, originale, très philosophique et à la fois très chrétienne.' Another very sympathetic Catholic review was that of A. de Margerie, dean of the theological faculty at Lille, in *Annales de Philosophie chrétienne* (December 1895).

[37] It was reprinted, along with *Histoire et Dogme* and other pieces, in 1956 (*Les premiers écrits de Maurice Blondel*, ii). An English version is included in Dru and Trethowan, *Maurice Blondel*. It is to this that the page-numbers in the following section refer.

of appendix, provides what is probably still the best introduction to its author's religious philosophy as a whole. An authority on Blondel has not hesitated to acclaim it as his masterpiece.[38]

Blondel's point of departure is the unsatisfactory state of contemporary religious apologetic. In a book published many years afterwards entitled *Le Problème de la philosophie catholique* (1932), he describes the attitude to Christianity of a large number of young men at the time of *L'Action*'s appearance as one of total rejection.[39] They were not even willing to consider the Christian claim, 'as though a philosophy were automatically disqualified that took the trouble to consider a doctrine supposedly arrogating to itself the right, in the name of fact, to demand both the assent of the understanding and the submission of the will to an order of things the origins of which are totally external to life'.[40] To meet so radical an objection it was necessary to persuade them that in supposing the Christian demand to be based exclusively on 'something entirely extrinsic and arbitrary' they were profoundly mistaken. Yet it had to be admitted that the Christian faith, all too often, was presented in such a way as to warrant this impression. Blind-turnings on the apologetic road have then to be marked up, and the various forms they assume Blondel proceeds to review *seriatim*. Sometimes, he points out, it is a matter simply of bad philosophy, or pseudo-philosophy — resort to the wrong kinds of argument. At other times however it involves a misapplication of scientific knowledge, in which case it must be realized that the time is past when mathematics, physics or biology could be thought to have any direct bearing on philosophy.

There is no more continuity between scientific symbols and philosophical ideas than there is between the qualities perceived by the senses and the calculations based on these same data of intuition.[41]

Or again there is the appeal to historical fact. This certainty is not without weight; yet whatever the *historical* value of such evidence 'it is the conclusion of reason and faith that they are not apodeictic as regards the order of revelation'; consequently 'it is not within the competence of philosophy to indicate the existence of the supernatural in actual fact'. It is all very well to refute the negations of rationalism, but that done is it enough to examine the history of the great 'Christian' fact unless the philosopher's *reason* is right for conversion? Apologetics must show that the *supernatural* interpretation is a necessity.

The moral and psychological approaches are the next to come in for criticism. Blondel admits that for many minds they are cogent, but their force is

---

[38] See H. Duméry, *Blondel et la Religion* (1954), p. 1.

[39] Dru and Trethowan, *Blondel*, pp. 11f.

[40] 'Un condisciple m'objectait: "Pourquoi serais-je obligé de m'enquérir et de tenir compte d'un fait divers survenu il y a 1900 ans dans un coin obscur de l'Empire Romain, alors que je me fais gloire d'ignorer tant de grands événements, contingents dont la curiosité appauvrirait ma vie intérieure?".' (*ibid.*)   [41] *ibid.*, p. 131.

subjective, convincing only those 'who are moved by considerations of a sort which is not strictly philosophical'. In effect this type of argument 'merely exploits the witness of the soul which Tertullian called "naturally Christian"', and fails altogether to dispel the objections of those who accept Christianity simply as 'a superior but still human form of morality and doctrine'. A different kind of argument, and one now frequently put forward, is that which would defend Christianity, and Catholicism in particular, on the grounds that it alone offers a fully satisfactory interpretation of life. 'It claims to prove that Christianity *alone* satisfies all the artistic, intellectual, moral and social requirements of mankind.'[42] The difficulty here however is that despite its obvious attraction it affords no clear definition of the relations of the natural order to the supernatural. Can one just *assume* 'the identity of Catholicism with life'? Is it really evident that the Catholic religion is so admirably adapted to human needs that its laws are those precisely of humanity itself? Or that its dogmas make an exact response to man's natural wants? And what in any case of the life that is 'closed and alien to the supernatural' and hence cannot, or declines to, recognize its need? Finally there is the traditional scholastic-type apologetic, with its simple logic: (a) Reason proves the existence of God and suggests at least the possibility that he has revealed himself. (b) History shows that he in fact has done so and vindicates the authenticity of scripture and the authority of the church. Thus (so it is maintained) Catholicism is established on 'a truly rational and scientific basis'. But the difficulty here is that the argument takes for granted an outlook which is not at all that of the average modern man, although his viewpoint has to be accepted for what it is and if an apologetic is to be effective today it must deal in an unprejudiced way with things as they are.

To lay down without more ado the basic doctrinal affirmations of the thirteenth century is not only to stop up all access to those who think in terms of our own time but also to make a hopeless attempt to recover for one's own mind an equilibrium which has been irretrievably lost ... To think in our day in precisely the same terms as five centuries ago is inevitably to think in a different spirit.[43]

What, then, is the appropriate method for the modern religious philosopher to pursue? The key-word, Blondel proposes, is *immanence*. In current thinking it has become a principle 'that nothing can enter into a man's mind which does not come out of him and correspond in some way to a need for development and that there is nothing in the nature of historical or traditional teaching or obligation imposed from without which counts for him, no truth and no precept which is acceptable, unless it is in some sort autonomous and autochthonous'.[44] Against this must be set the Christian and Catholic principle of the *supernatural*, an order of reality which is not only transcendent in the ordinary metaphysical sense but, in all strictness, *super*natural: i.e.

[42]*ibid.*, p. 142.   [43]*ibid.*, pp. 148f.   [44]*ibid.*, p. 152.

beyond the power of man to discover for himself while at the same time *imposed* on his thought and will. A genuine apologetic is therefore committed to both principles.

But is this possible, it may be asked? Can there by any real connexion between philosophy and Christianity when the one seems necessarily to exclude the other? Blondel believes that the antithesis thus stated is essentially false, as the *méthode d'immanence*, 'which compels us to be equally faithful to philosophy and orthodoxy'. will demonstrate. But that method, it should be clearly understood, does not state or imply that a man can find *in and of himself* all the truths requisite to his life and that his salvation is ultimately his own work. Any such notion would prejudge the very question at issue: 'and what is good and useful as a preparation or as a means becomes ineffective and dangerous, to say no more of it, if it is taken to be a satisfactory end'. Nevertheless both faith and reason teach that the supernatural must be humanly accessible.

So without there being *real* continuity between the sphere of reason and that of faith, without in any way bringing within the determinism of human action the order of supernature, which is always beyond the capacity, the merits and the demands of our nature or any conceivable nature, it is legitimate to show that the development of the will constrains us to the avowal of our insufficiency, leads us to recognize the need of a further gift, gives us the aptitude not to produce or to define but to recognize and to receive it, offers us, in a word, by a sort of prevenient grace, that baptism of desire which, presupposing God's secret touch, is always accessible and necessary apart from any explicit revelation, and which, even when revelation is known, is, as it were, the human sacrament immanent in the divine operation.[45]

This means that human life is a drama in which every man, whether or not he realizes it, is brought face to face with the issue of salvation. The supernatural gift may of course be either accepted or refused: the conscious will is here free; but refusal is contrary to the natural needs of the soul itself, 'for if our nature is not at home with the supernatural, the supernatural is at home with our nature'. The issue is one which only practical action can resolve: philosophy comes to a halt at the threshold of that vital act in which alone human and divine, nature and grace, can unite. Merely to acknowledge the principle of the divine gift is not enough; life has actually to realize it.

The relation between religion and philosophy now begins to show more plainly. If apologetic is to be genuinely philosophical it must address itself to all men regardless of their individual differences. One no longer has the right, in trying to be simultaneously philosopher and believer, to start with the tacit assumption of faith and then later produce it openly as if newly discovered, any more than, contrariwise, one can keep one's beliefs 'at a discreet distance from one's own thinking'. Religion as *faith* is not to be substituted for philosophical *reason*, but neither on the other hand are the two to be permanently se-

---

[45] *ibid.*, pp. 162f.

parated. Rather have they to be united without being confused. When the nature and role of philosophy are correctly assessed the apologist will thus be able to indicate 'both a religious development for philosophical thought in its entirety and a human development for the religious consciousness', even indeed for the understanding of Christianity itself.[46]

Blondel's aim in this work was to establish the principles of a fresh apologetic able to meet the difficulties of the modern enquirer while at the same time upholding the integral truth of Catholic supernaturalism. Whatever his success may have been in convincing non-believers, his views were not seen in a uniformly favourable light by fellow-Catholics. This was at once evident from the strictures of a young Dominican critic, a certain Père Schwalm, who in the September 1896 issue of the *Revue Thomiste* set out to expose 'the illusions of idealism and their dangers for the faith' by loftily castigating the author of the *Letter* for his intellectual pride and youthful presumption! Other objectors also were quickly on the scene. Blondel was accused variously of 'Kantism', fideism and naturalism: of Kantism because of his alleged subjectivism, of fideism through his supposedly anti-rationalist voluntarism, and of naturalism for maintaining — or so it was argued — that the supernatural is in some way deducible from the natural. Although these criticisms were hardly self-consistent they amounted in sum to the objection that the so-called 'method of immanence' entailed also a *doctrine* of immanence; that the Blondelian religious philosophy was in fact merely a pseudo-Christian immanetism, according to which the entire content of Catholic doctrine, including the idea of God himself, is in essence the product of the believer's own inner consciousness. Yet Blondel had himself stated categorically that philosophy recognizes the supernatural only in so far as the idea of it is immanent in our experience and that it certainly cannot produce or even demonstrate it. 'Man', he insisted, 'has his share in everything and his sufficiency in nothing.' Why therefore *L'Action* should have been attacked in this manner by the author's fellow-Catholics was surprising and bewildering. However, as Blondel admits, he for many years to come avoided entering into controversy personally, 'on weighty advice'.[47] The *Letter* had indeed been delated to the Holy Office, but on the express instruction of Leo XIII no action was taken against its writer.[48] Maurice Blondel was, in fact, never to incur any official censure, and it is said that Leo's successor, Pope Pius X, who pronounced a total condemnation of Modernism, assured the then archbishop of Aix that he was convinced of the philosopher's orthodoxy and

[46] *ibid.*, p. 170.
[47] cf. *Le Problème de la philosophie catholique*, p. 46. In time Blondel himself found reason to modify a number of passages in the *Letter*, but it is clear that in substance he adhered to his original positions.
[48] cf. Dumery, *Blondel*, p. 4 note. See also G. Fonsegrive, *Le Catholicisme et la vie de l'esprit* (1899) pp. 64f.

charged the archbishop to tell him so.[49] Long afterwards Pius XI, when receiving Blondel in private audience, expressed the hope that his students might be inspired by his own spirit. Pius XII likewise commended his work generously.[50]

History and Dogma

Yet on one occasion, early in the new century, Blondel did contribute briefly but impressively to current theological debate. At the time the so-called Modernist crisis, precipitated by the appearance of Alfred Loisy's books, *L'Évangile et l'Église* and its still more provocative sequel *Autour d'un petit livre*, had become of major concern not only in France but at Rome. The question which in particular had attracted Blondel's attention was the bearing of dogma upon historical research. Loisy's critical and apologetic writings, of a remarkable boldness and originality, had brought the issue into clear focus. For what he was saying in unmistakable terms was that dogma had nothing at all to do with scientific history and that the theologian should keep to his own territory and leave the historian to his. On the other side of course was the traditional view that all matters involving doctrine are to be studied in the light of doctrine and judged in accordance with its principles. Sacred history could not in the nature of the case be subjected to 'impartial' investigation. To Blondel, however, it seemed that a false antithesis was being set up, and in an attempt to resolve it he published, during the January and February of 1904, a three-tier article in Fonsegrive's *Quinzaine* with the title *Histoire et Dogme: les lacunes philosophiques de l'exégèse moderne*.[51] Both contestants, Blondel observes, claim to speak in the name of historical accuracy and the facts of tradition, as well as in the interest of faith; yet each reproaches the other with endangering religion alike in spirit and in the letter. The position is abnormal and unnatural — 'there cannot be two Catholicisms' — but it will continue as long as two 'incomplete and incompatible' viewpoints are simply juxtaposed. For whilst it is true that historical facts are the foundation of the Catholic faith, they do not of themselves engender it or fully justify it.[52]

Blondel designates these incomplete and incompatible solutions as, respectively, 'extrinsicism' and 'historicism': opposing errors, 'but of the same kind, based upon similar habits of mind, suffering from analogous philosophical lacunae, and aggravating one another by their conflicts'. The former has no

[49] See K. Gilbert, *Maurice Blondel's Philosophy of Action* (1924), p. 4.
[50] See Paul E. McKeever, 'Maurice Blondel: Figure of Controversy', in *American Ecclesiastical Review*, 1952, p. 444.
[51] Vol. lvi, pp. 145–67, 349–73, 433–58. See *Les premiers écrits de Maurice Blondel*, ii, pp. 149–228. The whole essay is reproduced in translation in Dru and Trethowan, *Blondel*, pp. 219–87.
[52] Dru and Trethowan, *Blondel*, p. 223.

real room for historical *science*, and indeed is interested in history only for apologetic purposes, i.e. in testimony of miracle. 'The Bible is guaranteed *en bloc*, not by its content but by the external seal of the divine: why bother to verify the details? It is full of absolute knowledge, ensconced in its eternal truth: why search for its human conditions or its relative meanings?' The contrary view — the historicist — is represented by the critical work of Loisy, although he is nowhere named in the article. Its aim, plausible enough in itself, is 'to consider the facts for their own sake, and, instead of looking for dogma and its abstract formula in history, to look for history and history alone even in regard to dogma, which will then come fully alive again'.[53] But can historical inquiry ever prove the truth of supernatural faith? In any case, what are the 'facts'? 'Real history is composed of human lives; and human life is metaphysics in act.' The historian is bound to see past events in the light of interpretative criteria, since 'in default of an explicit philosophy a man usually has an unconscious one'. Faced by Jesus Christ and his historical achievement the critic cannot avoid asking what his intentions and actions could really have been and what he was in himself, as also how his initial design and its tremendous historical consequences are related.[54]

But if extrinsicism and historicism alike imply a divorce between dogma and history — thus in large measure nullifying the special truth which each of them stresses — by what principle can the separation be overcome and a true synthesis obtained? The answer, Blondel holds, lies in a proper understanding of the meaning of *tradition*, which is neither a fixed deposit nor a progressive introduction of novelties, but *une expérience toujours en acte*. It is in fact 'the collective experience of Christ verified and realized within us', and as such is the effectively mediating principle between history and dogma. For dogma is to be seen as less the result of treating a sacred text dialectically than the expression of a reality constantly tested in experience. In this sense tradition is scripture's 'mistress' rather than its 'servant'. As a power which, at least on the surface, conserves, it is fruitful, at a deeper level, of an experience that is continually renewed. What in the end therefore is explicitly formulated has all along been implicit in the life of faith itself.[55]

Père Laberthonnière's Moral Dogmatism

It had been a disconcerting experience for Blondel, in trying to produce a new and more philosophical type of apologetic, to discover that the effect of his

---

[53]*ibid.*, pp. 229, 232.   [54]*ibid.*, pp. 237, 244.

[55]After *Histoire et Dogme* Blondel published little until the nineteen-thirties, when he brought out in quick succession the series of volumes on which he had for many years been working and which constitute a trilogy: *La Pensée* (1934), *L'Être et les êtres* (1935) and the much-revised second edition of *L'Action* (1936–7). These were followed, after the second World War, by *La Philosophie et l'esprit chrétien* (1944–6) and the posthumous *Exigences philosophiques du Christianisme* (1950). Blondel died in 1949 at the age of 88. His correspondence

views was mainly to arouse suspicion among Catholics themselves. He was convinced that he had been misunderstood, but the bitterness of the criticism he at times encountered was enough to discourage him from further publication. He soon found however that he had an eager and talented follower in a young teacher at the Oratorian college of Juilly, near Paris. In fact Père Lucien Laberthonnière had already anticipated Blondel's general cast of thought in his own published writings,[56] and from the moment L'Action appeared he became an open partisan although the originality of his own ideas was in no way dimmed. He was in truth as admirable a disciple as a great philosopher may hope to come by — sympathetic and penetrating yet independent and clear-headed. He was also a much better writer than Blondel.[57] Indeed it was even said that he had succeeded in translating Blondel into French, as well as being qualified, as a trained theologian, to present the philosophy of action in a more theological form. His reward for so doing was to bring upon himself the ecclesiastical censure which the more abstruse lay thinker escaped.

A year older than Blondel — he was born at Chazalet, in Berry, in October 1860 — Laberthonnière was educated at the Bourges seminary and joined the Oratorians in 1886, his appointment as professor of philosophy at Juilly soon following. In 1897 he became director of the École Massillon in Paris, but returned to Juilly three years later as superior of the congregation. Unhappily his career in education was terminated in 1903, when state authorization of the college was withdrawn under the law of 1901, although it meant that he was now able to devote himself entirely to philosophical study. In 1905, at the height of the Modernist controversy, he took over the editorship of *Annales de Philosophie chrétienne*, retaining it until 1913, when the Index obliged him to

has also now been published, of particular interest being that with Auguste Valensin (1957) and L. Laberthonnière (ed. C. Tresmontant, 1961). René Marlé, *Au cœur de la crise moderniste* (1960), contains an important collection of letters relating to Modernism.

[56] For example, in the essay 'La philosophie est un art' in *Essais de Philosophie religieuse*, pp. 3–15, where he writes: 'Il faut considérer la philosophie non comme une science faite qui se trouve dans les livres, mais comme l'effort conscient et réfléchi de l'esprit humain pour savoir, pour atteindre les raisons dernières, pour trouver le sens véritable des choses, de façon, en définitive, à tirer le meilleur parti possible de l'existence. Philosopher, c'est donc chercher à vivre pleinement ... Mais cela, est-ce de l'action ou de la spéculation pure? C'est l'une et l'autre, et c'est l'un autant que l'autre. Ce travail ne peut se faire réellement que si l'on y met son âme toute entière.' The essay dates from 1891, when it appeared in *L'Enseignement chrétien*.

[57] Fr Tyrrell's opinion of *L'Action*, expressed in a letter to von Hügel dated 7 September 1900, is forthright: 'One cannot sufficiently regret', he writes, 'that so epochmaking a book should be practically buried in the obscurity of its style — buried, that is, to those who stand most in need of it and are accustomed to that familiar terminology of the schools which has passed into every modern language.' But he adds: 'I steadily refuse to admit that everything Blondel has said could not be said with transparent simplicity' (M. D. Petre, *Autobiography and Life of George Tyrrell*, 1912, ii, p. 92). It is this lucidity that Laberthonnière achieves.

suspend further publication.[58] Two of his own books had already been condemned in 1906.

Laberthonnière answered some of Schwalm's criticisms of Blondel's *Lettre* in an article, 'Le problème religieux', in which he stressed the necessary correlation of faith and life.[59]

To have faith, a faith living and complete, is to possess God. But we can possess God only by giving ourselves to him, and this we can do only because he first gives himself to us. Faith is therefore to be seen as a union of two loves rather than as a combination of two ideas. It is not an abstract conclusion but a vital action.

It is in this way that the synthesis of natural and supernatural is actually achieved, not as a mere juxtaposition but as a mutually 'vivifying penetration'. God does not enter into us from outside; he comes to us from *within*, being closer to us than we are to ourselves. Whatever kind of truth it may be which we have to live out in action if our destiny is to be realized, whatever spiritual aid we may require or moral condition develop in order to attain it, it does not become *ours* unless we ourselves succeed in making it an inward possession.[60]

It is this practical attitude to Catholic doctrine which Laberthonnière calls *moral dogmatism*: The understanding of divine revelation demands every available resource, no doubt; history, tradition and authority are all necessary. But they are only the means to an end, not the end itself. They witness to and safeguard divine truth but the external must always serve the internal. The essence of what we call supernatural is the union of God and man, the extension of the divine life into humanity.[61]

Philosophy itself is a basically moral discipline. No mere intellectual technique or abstract systematizing, it is the mind's consciously reflective effort to comprehend the real meaning of human existence and promote what is best in it. The moral life, it could be said, is metaphysics in practice. 'Those who believe in God, freedom and immortality – as likewise those who do not – are applying metaphysics.'

[58] In the same year the Holy See expressly forbade him to publish anything more, an inhibition to which he meekly submitted for the rest of his life, although after his death his manuscripts were edited for the press by his friend Louis Canet.

Among the most important of these posthumous works are his Cartesian studies and the *Esquisse d'une Philosophie personaliste* (1942). Moreover, although not allowed to publish he was permitted to teach. Thus he founded an Association for Religious Studies with the aim of bringing Catholics together to discuss problems of faith. He believed strongly in the desirability of church unity and may be looked on as a precursor of the ecumenical movement, though he was convinced that a new relationship among the churches depended first and foremost on the renewal of their own outlook by the spirit of the gospel. On Laberthonnière's teaching and opinions generally see M. d'Hendecourt, *Essai sur la philosophie du Père Laberthonnière* (1947). Also D. M. Eastwood, *The revival of Pascal. A Study of his Relation to Modern French Thought*, c. VIII and P. Beillevert, *Laberthonnière: l'homme et l'œuvre* (Oratoriana) (1972).

[59] *Essais de Philosophie religieuse* (1930) pp. 157–90.

[60] *ibid.*, p. XVI.   [61] *ibid.*, pp. XXIV–IX.

Laberthonnière's views, more patently even than Blondel's imply a rejection of scholastic intellectualism.[62] To prove religion true may be very desirable, but what in this context does proof really mean? Ordinarily

it is to show how one truth follows from another. Yet can supernatural truth follow from natural in the way that the properties of a geometrical figure necessitate each other? Evidently not, for were it otherwise there could be no *super*nature. The supernatural is in its essence free and differs from the natural *non solum principio sed objecto*.

In one sense of course, the objective, faith simply connotes the sum of revealed truth — the creed; in another, the subjective, it means *adherence* to revealed truth — 'embodying it in one's life, living supernaturally'.[63] To believe as a religious man believes is therefore something quite other than to understand the connexion between abstract ideas and to combine them in a rational system. The practical solution of the problem of validity in this realm is in fact so little of a speculative matter that any attempt to turn revealed truth into a *science* is an irrelevancy. For faith through and through is subjective, personal and individual. Obviously in many areas of life to think at all is to think as all men do; but to *believe*, as often as not, is to believe only for oneself, since to believe is to live and none can live other than *as* himself. Compared with rational speculation therefore faith is of a different order, not only because grace is needed for its realization but because basically it is a matter of the will. The great Christian mystics — an Augustine, a Teresa of Avila, the author of the *Imitatio Christi* — indeed all for whom to *think* is not to fall back on abstractions and empty formulas 'suspended in mid-air', have said again and again in their diverse ways that it is only *within* himself that man truly finds God and that everything else is but a means to discover him there. Accordingly it is in the life of prayer that one becomes increasingly aware of one's innate longing and appetite for the divine.[64]

The relation between the exteriority and the interiority of revelation Laberthonnière explains thus. Organisms receive their nutriment from outside themselves, but their growth and development are intrinsic. Similarly were there nothing of the supernatural already within us 'revealed' truth could never become truth *for us*, because it would not really be a response to any need of our own. Apart, then, from this internal 'grace' an external disclosure would have no meaning. In any case it is not enough for the divine word to be uttered, it has also to be heeded.

The sun shines for the whole world; nevertheless you cannot enjoy its light if you do not open your eyes ... Without implicit faith and a good will neither revelation nor miracles nor reasoning of any kind will produce light in the soul nor lead it on to explicit belief.

[62]*ibid.*, p. 186. 'On ne peut être à la fois intellectualiste et chrétien que par un compromis en vertu duquel, parce qu'on veut admettre en même temps des contraires, on est comme forcé de vivre en partie double et de séparer la spéculation de la pratique.'
[63]*ibid.*, p. 160.   [64]*ibid.*, pp. 169f.

In the essay entitled 'Le dogmatisme moral' Laberthonnière defines dogmatism as the affirmation of being, thus distinguishing it from scepticism or agnosticism, which imply negation. But dogmatism itself may be true or false, and false dogmatism can assume a number of forms. In the end however it is always marked by the claim to self-sufficiency: in other words, the object affirmed is exploited for one's own ends. False dogmatism rests on a misconception of the very nature of being, explaining it in terms of either sensationalism or idealism, but invariably as something external and objectified. By contrast true dogmatism is personal and moral. Being, that is, is essentially *subject* and cannot be grasped by sense or thought alone.[65] For what is *felt* is simply a state of mind, just as what is *thought* is no more than an abstract concept or mental generalization.

But if knowledge of being is vital and not merely theoretical it must largely depend, Laberthonnière argues, on what we are ourselves; and what we are ourselves depends in turn on the ends we pursue. What therefore we *will* to be is all-important. Again, though, there is a choice confronting us: willing can be either externalized or internalized. In the one case we found our being on things outside us — the world and its manifold objects; in the other, we first seek reality within ourselves. For if reality is primarily subject and not object it is only *as* subjects that we can have any authentic knowledge of it. The process of knowing is thus basically ethical. Man does not affirm himself, in the unity and permanence of his subjectivity, through the completeness of his abstract understanding but in acts of the moral personality motivated by the love of God. For in true self-affirmation he also affirms God, even though no affirmation of God is possible apart from God, who is the sustaining principle of man's own existence, whether he recognizes it or not.[66] Thus Laberthonnière follows Blondel's method of immanence quite faithfully: we desire God and seek him because we ourselves are *of* him; he is our omega because he is at the same time our alpha; or as St Augustine says, we exist only because God exists in us.[67] A 'certitude' which has any other foundation than this is illusory.

That knowledge of the ultimate reality is basically 'concrete' and personal Laberthonnière regards as a first principle of any genuinely Christian philosophy. In a little book published in 1904, *Le réalisme chrétien et l'idéalisme grec*, he develops his view along the lines of a radical contrast between Christian realism and Greek idealism.[68] Christian monotheism, he maintains,

[65] 'L'être n'est ni une chose sentie ni une chose pensée. Il nous est devenu impossible de le concevoir sous forme d'objet' (*ibid.*, p. 82).

[66] 'Puisqu'il existe un ordre surnaturel, puisque tout en fait ... est appelé à vivre surnaturellement, c'est que Dieu agit par sa grâce sur le cœur de tout homme et le pénètre de sa charité; c'est que l'action même qui constitue fondamentalement notre vie est en fait comme informée surnaturellement par Dieu. Si donc on suit l'expansion et le développement de l'action humaine, on devra voir apparaître, et s'épanouir, ce qu'elle recèle en son fond. Même méconnu Dieu est toujours là' (*ibid.*, p. 171).

[67] *ibid.*, p. 69.

[68] A new edition by L. Canet of both this and the *Essais* was published in 1966.

has little in common with Greek. For Hellenic philosophy God is a supreme Idea, the constitutive reason of things. For Christian theology, on the other hand, he is a supreme Person, living and acting. Instead therefore of a divinity who is to all intents the order of nature itself faith cleaves to a personal being whose essential character is expressed in moral action.[69] With Aristotle, who marks the culmination of Greek thought in its speculative aspect, God is conceived not as a power of action merely but as *pure* act (*actus purus*), eternally realized and self-fulfilled, and hence incapable of achieving anything more. All possibility of *becoming* is *ex hypothesi* excluded. In Christian thinking, however, the words 'power' and 'action' have a quite different sense. Power is no longer a passive condition but an active purpose. God, we may say, is the eternal action of an eternal life, not an idea or essence fixed in an eternal repose.[70] The reality of the world is the outcome of this divine power and purpose. God is not present to the world simply as an ideal or example or final cause, but really and actively as its efficient and perpetually concurrent cause. Further, as everything exists only by the action of God the Greek dualism of matter and intelligible idea, of the world and God, is eliminated. The divine potency is in the last analysis the love by which God gives himself to as well as produces the multiformity of being which we call nature. 'Love is thus principle, means and end. It is the ultimate reason, rendering account of all things, illuminating all things, explaining all things.' God is not, as in Aristotle, the Idea of ideas, or an essence proceeding from other essences by logical sequence: he is the Being of beings, the Life of lives, he who exists and lives of himself and from and by whom all other beings exist and live also. Where the Greeks sought to conceive the world *sub specie aeternitatis* Christianity apprehends God *sub specie temporis*. In fine, if Greek philosophy is in the full sense of the term an idealism, then equally Christian doctrine is a realism.[71]

---

[69] *Le réalisme chrétien*, pp. 65f.   [70] *ibid*., p. 69.

[71] The personal friendship between Blondel and Laberthonnière survived the Modernist crisis for a good many years, but eventually the viewpoints of the two men so far diverged that they gave up corresponding. The former disliked controversy, whereas the latter would not abandon a fight when the cause was still at issue. Blondel, whose pacific disposition sometimes bordered on timidity, considered the priest hot-headed; Laberthonnière judged the layman to have become subservient to an authority whose visage he himself liked less and less. 'Vous dîtes: il y'a qu'à prendre cela à sa charge et à se faire martyr interieurement', he wrote (February 1920). 'Mais être martyr c'est porter témoignage. En quoi portez-vous témoignage si votre silence et votre attitude sont telles que souffrant intérieurement, vous ne laissez rien paraître de la protestation qui jaillit de votre conscience? Ceux d'en haut ne demandent qu'une chose: qu'on paraisse au moins les approuver. Et si pour obéir il faut en effet paraître approuver quand on ne les approuve pas, ce sera jusqu'au bout le mensonge élève à la hauteur d'une institution' (Blondel and Laberthonnière, *Lettres philosophiques*, pp. 251f.) He also thought Blondel was leaning too much towards the officially-sponsored neo-Thomism.

12

ALFRED LOISY AND THE
BIBLICAL QUESTION

Catholics and the Problem of Biblical Criticism

Throughout the greater part of the nineteenth century the state of biblical
studies among French Catholics was one of unrelieved poverty. The clergy in
general were ignorant of the Bible, such knowledge as they had, especially
of the Old Testament, being confined mainly to what could be gleaned from
their breviaries. For the average Catholic indeed the scriptures were simply
a book of devotion. Seminary manuals dealing specifically with the Bible
were few, since Bible study for its own sake formed only a small part of the
curriculum. Mgr Le Camus, bishop of La Rochelle from 1901 to 1906, reveals
that it took up no more than one hour a week and that the responsibility for
conducting it might fall to any member of the staff regardless of his qualifications. He himself tried to remedy this condition of affairs in his own diocese,
where it still persisted, but he won little support from his clergy.

Nevertheless the pressure of the critical movement in Germany was bound
sooner or later to make itself felt in Catholic France, as it also did, if tardily
and somewhat painfully, in Protestant Britain; and the reaction, naturally
enough, was in the first instance one of alarm. In 1860 Mgr Guillaume
Meignan, later archbishop of Tours and a cardinal, had sounded a warning
note. Catholics would have to be convinced of the danger which threatened
and so forced out of their settled mood of complacency and indifference.
'We cry Fire! telling the sleeping inhabitants that their house is ablaze so
as to get them to join us in putting out the flames.'[1] He repeated his monitions
ten years later in the Vatican Council, pointing out the great need Catholics
had for guidance in a matter of such complexity and difficulty.

The modern sciences of archaeology, history and philology [he declared], with their
ever-continuing progress, complicate the situation. It is no small problem to bring
the conclusions of science into harmony with the sacred text. Instructed laymen
and learned priests are plainly disquieted and confess their embarrassment. Must
they interpret questions of chronology, for example, in the same way as those
touching faith and morals? Can one not leave them to the latest explanations of
science rather than to the out-dated interpretations of the Fathers? On all sides the
demand is for a definite rule concerning the relations of the biblical revelation with

[1] *Le Correspondant*, 25 February 1860 (quoted Lecanuet), *La vie*, p. 318.

science. The answers of learned Catholics are obscure and hesitating. The latter are afraid of being condemned by the Roman Congregations, a fear which ends in preventing them from doing anything to refute the neo-critics, who loftily proclaim the incompatibility of science and the faith. Error thus has every chance to spread abroad.[2]

Unhappily the Council had no time, and probably little inclination, to delve into problems of this nature. Meignan himself, in his continuing concern, wrote to Leo XIII in 1881 saying that it had simply to be recognized that the French clergy were for the most part not sufficiently instructed to confront Protestant and rationalist biblical critics with their own weapons and that the seminaries only rarely possessed a professor capable of refuting the type of error now being imported into France from across the Rhine. From the stand-point whether of philosophy, history, archaeology or natural science they were altogether ill-equipped for the task. 'Neither preachers nor lecturers nor catechists are in a position to discuss with any competence the questions which today preoccupy educated men and trouble their consciences.'[3]

The establishment of Catholic universities brought some improvement, and with the pontificate of Leo XIII a new regard for serious biblical study became evident. Even so the question of the right attitude to adopt towards historical criticism at once threw up problems. For some the whole issue was seen as simply that of an unyielding defence of traditional beliefs, in which case the difficulty of explaining such points as Jonah's survival in the whale's belly was bound to lead to 'rationalizing' absurdities.[4] But the ultra-conservatives were unabashed: the principle of the complete inerrancy of scripture in all things had to be maintained. The more moderate conservatives, on the other hand, admitted that the advance of scientific knowledge demanded some revision of received notions, provided it conformed with official church teaching. Yet they too, while ready to make concessions on specific issues, saw any consistent application of the critical method as a stumbling-block to faith. Their distrust of it arose not only from what they regarded as its consistently negative conclusions but, and more fundamentally, from the philosophical presuppositions which, as they thought, underlay it. German scholars, so Meignan claimed, were actuated not so much by a scientific interest as by a spirit of irreligion born of pantheism, positivism and social-

[2]H. Boissonnot, *Le Cardinal Meignan* (1899), p. 294.
[3]*ibid.*, p. 345.
[4]cf. A. Houtin, *La Question biblique chez les catholiques de France au xixe siècle*, 2nd ed. (1902), pp. 117f. Albert Houtin (1867—1926), himself a priest, was given a teaching post in history at the *petit séminaire* of Angers in 1894. This he resigned some years later through differences with his superiors caused by an article of his on the early history of the diocese of Angers. He settled in Paris in 1901, serving as an assistant curate but also acting, from 1904 to 1909, as ecclesiastical correspondent of the radical journal *Le Siècle*. He laid aside his soutane in 1912. The two volumes of his autobiography, *Une Vie de prêtre. Mon expérience (1867—1912)* (1926) and *Mon Expérience, ii* (1928, ed. F. Sartiaux), provide much caustic comment on ecclesiastical affairs. But his bias is excessive.

ism.[5] He himself was the author of a multi-volume work entitled *L'Ancien Testament dans ses rapports avec le Nouveau et la critique moderne* (1889–96), but although his standpoint was on the whole traditionalist he was not uncompromising where it seemed necessary. Thus in his *Prophéties messianiques* of 1856 he had insisted that the story of the Garden of Eden was historic fact and any attempt to allegorize it was stigmatized as 'dangerous, ill-founded and useless', but in a revised edition of the same work published in 1895 he takes the view that 'one must not look to the first chapters of Genesis so much for an exact history of the origins of the world and of the human race as for the religious interpretation of that history'. To speculate about the location of the earthly paradise and other such topics is in fact 'to run the risk of losing sight of the inspired author's purpose and to reduce his teaching to the limits of a mere question of geography and topography'.[6]

Another moderate among conservatives was the Jesuit, Joseph Brucker (1845–1926). He too recognized that a blanket rejection of all criticism was futile and that the method, at least in principle, would have to be accepted. The question as he saw it was to determine on purely scientific grounds 'both the value and the precise scope of the documents on which the faith of the Church rests', an investigation which was perfectly proper and one which the church encourages. The trouble was that the critics too often were content with untested hypothesis or mere conjecture. Worse, the 'great majority of them, and notably those who lay down the law in scientific circles', were rationalists admitting neither revelation, inspiration nor the supernatural.[7] This was the real ground of conflict. It was illusory therefore for Catholic scholars to suppose that they could ever succeed in coming to terms with a method of Bible study based on assumptions so essentially alien to their own. For rationalist critics would themselves never allow that Catholic studies could be impartial or genuinely scientific. In fact the very attempt on the part of 'liberal' Catholics to fall in with Protestants and rationalists was a profound mistake. You do not, he said, burn down a man's house in order to light it up.

However, for us it is not a case of all or nothing. We shall seek to determine in complete loyalty what can or ought to be accepted among the findings of criticism.[8]

Also among the conservatives, though again not himself a diehard 'literalist',

[5] *Le Correspondant*, 25 June 1889, p. 1028.
[6] *Les Prophéties messianiques*, p. 421. cf. Houtin, *La Question*, pp. 206ff. Lecanuet says of Meignan that 'il regarde de haut toutes les batailles, profondément attaché à sa foi, mais indulgent, bienvaillant, évitant de se montrer sévère et de condamner, quand l'Église elle-même a refusé de porter sa sentance' (*La Vie.*, p. 323).
[7] *L'Église et la critique biblique*, pp. 27f.
[8] cf. the same author's *Questions actuelles d'Écriture Sainte* (1895). At the time of the Modernist crisis Brucker was director of the Jesuit periodical *Études* and showed no mercy towards Loisy or even Lagrange.

was one whom even Loisy once described as 'the great Catholic apologist of the Bible', Fulcran Vigouroux (1837–1915),[9] a Sulpician and one-time professor at the seminaries of Autun and Issy, who in 1890 was given the chair of Holy Scripture at the Paris Institut Catholique in Loisy's place and who eventually became first secretary of the papal Biblical Commission. The author, in collaboration with another Sulpician, N. Bacuez, of a *Manuel biblique* published in 1879, he later edited the five volumes of the *Dictionnaire de la Bible*, a work of reference which has been criticized by Catholics themselves for its concern with relatively trivial factual details whilst ignoring biblical theology.

Towards the end of the century it was nonetheless coming to be realized by a few at least among the French clergy and the more educated laymen that traditional ideas about the inspiration of scripture, as on the date, composition and historicity of its component books, could not be maintained in face of the critical procedures applied to both Old and New Testaments by a succession of eminent German scholars: Eichhorn, de Wette, Ewald, F. C. Baur, Kuenen, Wellhausen and many others. Reactions varied, of course; some feared what the consequences of criticism for faith might turn out to be, while others welcomed it as the means to a new kind of exegesis, spiritually more fruitful because intellectually more satisfying. Among the first of such 'progressives' was the Assyriologist, François Lenormant (1837–1883), son of Charles Lenormant, the famous Egyptologist, who, ironically enough, had been forced to resign his chair at the Sorbonne for having professed views 'too favourable to the Catholic Church'.[10] François had been brought up, as Houtin observes, in both the principles of science and the purest Catholic orthodoxy,[11] and his earlier writings — he felt almost from the outset of his career an obligation to assume the apologist's role — were in no respect innovating. But in a work the first volume of which was published in 1880 under the title *Les Origines de l'histoire d'après la Bible et les traditions des peuples orientaux* he opted for a more accommodating attitude to criticism.

I firmly believe [he wrote], in the divine inspiration of the sacred Books and I assent with entire submission to the doctrinal decisions of the Church in that respect. But I know that these decisions extend inspiration only to what interests religion, as touching faith and morals; that is, only to supernatural teachings contained in the writings. As far as other matters are concerned, the human character of the biblical writers is found throughout. Each one of them has put his personal mark on the

---

[9] Loisy (*Mémoires*, i, p. 189) later speaks of him in disparaging terms — as 'aussi terne dans ses méfaits que dans son style'. Marcel Hébert, however, thought him learned and scrupulous and ready to open the door to criticism, for all his orthodox zeal. cf. *Revue de Belgique*, 1904, p. 176.

[10] See J. T. Burtschaell, *Catholic Theories of Biblical Inspiration since 1810: a Review and Critique* (1969), p. 63.

[11] Burtschaell, *Catholic Theories*, p. 105.

style of his book. In regard to the physical sciences they had no exceptional insights; they followed the common opinions and even the prejudices of their times.[12]

The opening chapters of *Genesis*, he pointed out, are to be seen as embodying 'a tradition the origins of which are lost in the night of the most remote ages, and which all the great peoples of Asia possessed in common, with some variation'. The uniqueness of the biblical account lay 'in the absolutely new spirit which animated [the] narration, even though its form has remained in almost every detail the same as that of the neighbouring peoples ... The exuberant polytheism which filled these stories among the Chaldeans has been carefully eliminated, in order to introduce the most severe monotheism. Singularly gross expressions of naturalistic notions have become the cloak for moral truths of the highest and most spiritual order'.[13] Lenormant's book was still unfinished at the time of his death and four years later was placed on the Index, along with Ledrain's *Histoire d'Israel*.[14]

Abbé Paul de Broglie (1834—1895), professor of apologetics at the Paris Institut Catholique and brother of the historian, the Duc de Broglie, took up a similar position. The Bible was not an authority in purely scientific matters. Where nothing relevant to dogma, morals or religious history was involved details 'borrowed by the inspired author from traditions or profane documents' were not to be considered covered by the guarantee of inspiration. *Obiter dicta* — to use Newman's term — frequently occur in the sacred books and the history itself is not necessarily set down in precise form.[15] Error in doctrine would, however, have been incompatible with divine inspiration. As to criticism there was no need whatever to view the assertions of German scholars as the truths of an established science. 'We cannot remain Catholics and not admit the Church's control over opinion, above all where the Sacred Scriptures are concerned.' But no censure, he thought, should attach itself to the prudent in their efforts to combine sound science with a reasonable theology.[16] Such too, in general, was the attitude of a number of other moderates, like Father John Hogan, subsequently president of the Boston (Massachusetts) seminary, Mgr Duilhe de Saint-Projet, rector of the Institut Catholique at Toulouse, Mgr Pierre Batiffol, also of Toulouse, and the Assyriologist, abbé François Martin.

Among the bishops the most forward-looking was undoubtedly Eudoxe-Irénée Mignot (1842—1918), bishop of Fréjus and afterwards (from 1900) archbishop of Albi, a close friend of both Loisy and the Anglo-German Baron

[12] *Les Origines de l'histoire*, i, pp. viif.

[13] *ibid.*, pp. xvi—xix.

[14] Likewise condemned, though surprisingly so in the eyes of many even conservative Catholics, was Henri Lasserre's translation of the gospels, on which he had laboured for five years and had received the congratulations of Leo XIII himself. cf. Lecanuet, *La vie*, pp. 343ff.

[15] *Questions bibliques* (ed. C. Piat) (1904), p. 19.

[16] Lecanuet, *La vie*, p. 329.

Friedrich von Hügel. Mignot, who has been called 'the Erasmus of Modernism', had a greater knowledge of the actual state of biblical studies in Germany and Britain than probably any other high ecclesiastic in France, a distinction which, especially later, was to lead to his increasing isolation. His view, broadly, was that the mind of God in revelation is disclosed progressively and that there had been times even in the biblical period when the divine voice was more clearly audible than at others. The great biblical teachers appeared at the appropriate moments and must thus be seen in the context of the revelational process as a whole.[17] Jesus himself, in respect of his ordinary knowledge and understanding, spoke as a man of his own time.

He took the facts before him, the current ideas, and used them to instruct his followers, He never went beyond the science of his day, never rectified a historical, philosophical or literary error. He generally remained on the doctrinal level of his hearers, using their religious convictions, and even their mistakes and prejudices, in order to elevate them, as he used their observations of the colours of the sky in order to predict the morrow's weather.[18]

On the subject of biblical inspiration Mignot sounded a cautious note. We no more understand it, he warned, than we understand the presence of God in the natural order or grace in the supernatural. The actual operation of God escapes us always. 'We see only the outcome of it and mark it as in the vision of Horeb.'[19]

Finally, although most of the exegetical work of the eminent Dominican scholar Marie-Joseph Lagrange (1855–1938) falls outside of the period with which the present volume deals, we should not omit to note the founding by him of the École Biblique (Saint-Étienne) at Jerusalem in 1890. Its members, carefully selected,' were dedicated', as it has been said, 'under the authority of the Church, to an ideal both of intellectual reconciliation and of religious enlargement, in light and in freedom'.[20] Lagrange's aims were those of promoting the sound linguistic and historical study of the Bible without any overt apologetic purpose. Every discipline relevant to biblical research — philology, archaeology, epigraphy and so forth — was employed. The school's organ was the *Revue biblique*, the first issue of which appeared in 1892, its object, as stated in its programme, being to provide 'a fuller exegesis and a broader horizon' than older periodicals had done, by making use of the new data afforded by modern scientific research. Although definitely a conservative Lagrange enjoyed Loisy's respect in no small degree, even if the latter did think it a pity that he should have spent 'the best part of his life

---

[17] *Lettres sur les Études ecclésiastiques* (1908), pp. 252, 284f.

[18] ibid., p. 261. See also *L'Église et la critique* (1910). Mignot was among the contributors to Vigouroux's *Dictionnaire de la Bible*.

[19] *Le Correspondant*, 10 April 1897.

[20] Lecanuet, *La vie*, p. 332, who also made the comment: 'Regrettons en passant que les évêques français ne soutiennent pas, comme ils le devraient, ce foyer scientifique de premier ordre.'

covering the biblical texts with a layer of erudition so thick that no one could perceive the difficulties they raised for the official theology'.[21] Yet Lagrange himself was sometimes made uncomfortably aware of the proximity of the Index and in 1912, during the aftermath of the Modernist scare, he had to relinquish control of the École Biblique.

Towards a Scientific Exegesis

All discussion of the biblical question in nineteenth-century Catholicism must eventually focus on the work of Alfred Firmin Loisy. Much has been written about him – his role in the Modernist movement, his scholarship, the sincerity of his vocation as a priest, indeed the reality of his personal faith even in his early days as a teacher at the Institut Catholique. Yet he remains a somewhat enigmatic figure and no really satisfactory study of his character and achievement has yet been published.[22] What will concern us here is simply his contribution to Catholic biblical science during the last two decades of the century and the apology for historic Catholicism outlined in the most celebrated of his 'petits livres rouges', L'Évangile et l'Église, first published in 1902.[23] Immanuel Kant once predicted that if religion ever came to depend on 'the critical knowledge of ancient languages' then the man who possessed it would 'drag all the orthodox believers, in spite of their wry faces, wherever he may choose'.[24] Loisy began his academic career by equipping himself with such knowledge, with the full intention moreover of using it in the pursuit of scientific ends. But he could hardly have set about his task at a less auspicious time or in a more discouraging atmosphere. The Church of France, still for the most part unreconciled to the Republic, seemed to have drawn in upon itself. Its prevailing mood was one of defensive nervousness, suspicious of 'liberalism' whether in politics or theology, while Rome herself, now largely identified with the standpoint of the Civiltà cattolica and the Univers, showed no inclination, even under the supposedly open-minded Leo XIII, to promote

[21]Mémoires, ii, p. 99. Lagrange's own attitude to Loisy was one of regretful disapproval. See his M. Loisy et le Modernisme (1932). On Lagrange as a scholar cf. J. Chaine (ed.), L'Œuvre exégétique et historique du Père Lagrange (1935).

[22]The primary sources of information about Loisy's career are the three volumes of his own Mémoires pour servir à l'histoire religieuse de notre temps (1930–1), Choses passées (1913) and Quelques lettres sur des questions actuelles et sur des évènements récents (1908). Alfred Loisy: sa vie et son œuvre, by A. Houtin and F. Sartiaux (ed. E. Poulat) (1960), is of importance, but should be read with an understanding of its ex parte approach. See too F. Heiler, Alfred Loisy (1857–1940): Der Vater des katholischen Modernismus (1947) and E. Poulat, Histoire, dogme et critique dans la crise moderniste (1962). Loisy's religious sincerity is defended by A. R. Vidler in A Variety of Catholic Modernists, chs. 2 and 3. On the same subject, R. de Boyer de Sainte Suzanne, Alfred Loisy: entre la foi et l'incroyance (1968), should also be consulted.

[23]The 'little red books' was his description of the long series of small octavos issued by Émile Nourry, the last of which appeared in 1937.

[24]See F. von Hügel, Essays and Addresses in the Philosophy of Religion, 2nd series (1926), p. 27.

anything resembling that freedom of scholarly inquiry which the Protestant world had in the main come to accept as normal. Seminary teaching in particular was in little better condition than it had been half a century before. Traditional views on all subjects had to be upheld, and a student's chief virtue was docility, with the example of Ernest Renan always to be quoted as an awful warning.[25] As regards the Bible official Catholicism, no less than popular, was rooted in fundamentalism.[26]

Alfred Loisy was born in 1857 at Ambrières, a village in the *département* of the Marne. Of farming stock, he too might have worked on the land but for his rather weakly physical constitution and his early promise of intellectual ability. Instead he was marked out for the priesthood — with his willing consent — and despatched in 1872 to the *collège ecclésiastique* at St-Dizier. Soon afterwards his religious feelings were stirred by a retreat conducted at the school, and when he entered the *grand séminaire* at Châlons in the autumn of 1874 it was as a student both devout and diligent; although even at that time the authorities there deemed him a little lacking in the proper spirit of deference to church tradition. He himself relates, in fact, that from 1875 onwards he was in a state of 'perpetual anguish'.[27] Willing to believe Catholic doctrines true, the question nevertheless repeatedly recurred to him whether they really were so.[28] He communicated his doubts to his spiritual directors, but they dismissed them as merely an excess of scruple. He did his best to cultivate religious sentiments, although if we are to take his later admissions literally his misgivings persisted. At all events his entry on the subdiaconate in June 1878 was to be described by him afterwards as consummating 'the great mistake of my life'.[29] Not that his seminary training meant entire repression of his intellectual curiosity, for it was at Châlons that he first learned something about the liberal movement in French Catholicism. But on the whole the effect of it was negative.

In 1878 he left Châlons to finish his ordination course at the newly constituted theological faculty of the Paris Institut Catholique.[30] The founding of the Institut as a centre for advanced clerical study was very largely the achievement of Mgr Maurice d'Hulst (1841—1896), who in 1880 became its

[25] See Appendix III, p. 295 below.
[26] cf. Loisy, *Mémoires*, i. p. 22.
[27] *Choses passées*, p. 34.
[28] 'Je regardais l'incredulité comme un péché grave et comme un malheur' (*ibid.*, p. 60).
[29] 'Même à cet instant critique', he later recalled, 'je ne songeai pas à prendre le parti le plus sûr, qui était de rentrer dans le monde. Je croyais, je voulais croire que la religion catholique était l'absolue vérité ... Cela ne m'empêcha point de passer sans sommeil toute la nuit du 29 au 30 juin 1878, qui était le jour fixe pour l'ordination ... Quand vint le matin, j'étais brisé. Je n'avais plus la force de penser, mais la volonté subsistait, inflexible. Je voulais appartenir à Dieu, au Christ, à l'Église' (*Choses passées*, pp. 45f.). It is to be noted that the reference to ordination as 'la grande faute de ma vie' does not appear in the *Mémoires*.
[30] At the time it was known as the Catholic University. The subsequent change of name was necessitated by a law of 1880.

rector, holding the office for the remaining sixteen years of his life.[31] His career there was not always plain-sailing however, since the idea of a genuine Catholic *university* was no more acceptable to ultra-conservatives in the French capital then than it had been at Dublin in Newman's day, and both the historian Louis Duchesne and the young Loisy, when he too became a member of the Institut's staff, were to cause him trouble. Loisy came in contact with Duchesne (1843–1922), then d'Hulst's professor of church history, in his first year as a student. At the time of his appointment in 1877 Duchesne had already aroused suspicion in some minds as 'un prêtre plus que libéral et d'esprit peu ecclésiastique'.[32] The son of a Breton fisherman, he had been ordained priest in 1867 and had afterwards studied archaeology in Rome. His doctoral thesis of 1877 on the *Liber Pontificalis*, in which he dealt trenchantly with certain papal records, was delated to the Roman authorities by Freppel, although the candidate himself, warned of the danger, took the precaution of sending his work to the secretary of the Index before submitting it and of undertaking there and then to make such amendments as might be required — an act, it has to be said, very characteristic of him: fine scholar that he was, ecclesiastically he always played for safety. ('A good sailor', observes Loisy, 'he took in his canvas as the storm arose'.) Nevertheless his Institut lectures on church history caused offence in some quarters, as also did his *Bulletin critique*, a periodical founded by him in 1872. The superior-general of Saint-Sulpice even forbade his own students to attend any more of Duchesne's courses. A crisis was reached in 1882 when the latter published his *Origines chrétiennes*, a work that came in for vehement criticism because of its admission of the principle of organic doctrinal development. As a result he was given a year's leave of absence. Three years later, following another dispute, this time over his exploding of the cherished legend of the apostolic foundation of certain of the episcopal sees of ancient Gaul — that of Sens notably — he was dismissed by the Institut's governing body, the council of bishops. D'Hulst, solicitous for the good name of the Institut itself, felt that no other course was open to him. Luckily Duchesne was appointed to the chair of Christian antiquities at the École des Hautes Études, and eventually to the government post of director of the French School in Rome, where he stayed until his death in 1922.[33]

---

[31] Maurice Le Sage d'Hauteroche d'Hulst, an aristocrat and staunch monarchist, had been assistant priest at Saint-Ambroise in Paris, before becoming literary secretary to Cardinal Guibert, archbishop of Paris, and then, in 1875, vicar-general of the Paris archdiocese and archdeacon of Saint-Denis. On d'Hulst's career see Cardinal Baudrillart, *La Vie de Mgr d'Hulst* (2 vols., 1921) and C. Cordonnier, *Mgr d'Hulst* (1952).

[32] Baudrillart, *La Vie de Mgr d'Hulst*, i, p. 361.

[33] In 1911 he was elected to the French Academy, but next year the Italian translation of his great *Histoire ancienne de l'Église* was placed on the Index. He received numerous academic honours, but never a cardinal's hat. See C. d'Habloville, *Grandes figures de l'Église contemporaine* (1925), pp. 1–77. Loisy says of Duchesne that he 'did more than anyone to initiate a scientific movement in French Catholicism', but he is hardly to be classed with

Duchesne's influence on Loisy was far-reaching, although its effect was not immediately evident as Loisy's time at the Institut was only short and for a while he served as a country priest. But in May 1881 he returned there in answer to Duchesne's pressing appeals. The work allotted him was that of teaching elementary Hebrew, but he also began to specialize in Assyriology. At the close of 1882 he started attending Renan's lectures at the Collège de France on the textual criticism of the Old Testament, an experience which to all intents was his first introduction to the scientific study of the Bible,[34] but as he states in his *Mémoires* he made no effort to get to know Renan personally and never even spoke to him. He admired the old agnostic's scholarship but thought his general position false and that he had been wrong to leave the church.

Thus I instructed myself at his school in the hope of proving to him that all that was true in his science was compatible with Catholicism sanely understood.[35]

All the same Loisy never allowed it to be said that his faith had been undermined by 'rationalist critics'.[36] The Bible, itself, he insisted, had been 'the first and principle cause' of his intellectual evolution: it was because he read it seriously that he became a critic of it.[37]

In 1883 Loisy began the preparation of a doctoral thesis in theology at the Institut on the inspiration of Holy Scripture, but abandoned it on the advice of d'Hulst himself who feared that its publication would cause scandal. A second dissertation was therefore submitted later, this time based on a lecture-course dealing with a 'safe' subject on purely historical lines.[38] In 1890

the Modernists, who believed in theological renovation and ecclesiastical reform. Indeed Loisy himself says that Duchesne always had a 'horror of what is called modernism' and in his public utterances never for a moment questioned the church's dogmas (*Mémoires*, ii, p. 278). But it is certain that despite his reticence in these matters his private opinions admitted a good deal of scepticism. Thus in a letter of 18 January 1900 to Marcel Hébèrt, at the time director of the École Fénelon, he expressed the view that 'religious authority rests upon its tradition and the members of its personnel who are the most devoted — and also the least intelligent', a state of affairs which he doubted to be capable of either change or reformation. Poulat however regards him as a 'precursor' of Modernism (*Histoire*, p. 19) cf. also J.-B. Duroselle, *L'Évolution culturelle, l'Europe du xixe et xxe siècles (1870–1914)* (ed. M. Beloff et al., 1962) where he is referred to as 'the founder and master of Modernism'. Loisy's final comment on him is: 'Un savant très solide et un croyant plutôt superficiel' (*Mémoires*, i, p. 106).

[34] *Mémoires*, i, p. 98.
[35] *ibid.*, p. 118.
[36] The charge that it had been appears in, e.g. J. Rivière, *Le Modernisme dans l'Église* (1929), p. 96, M. J. Lagrange, *M. Loisy et le modernisme*, pp. 236f., and L. de Grandmaison, *Jésus Christ* (1932), ii, p. 292. cf. *Mémoires*, iii, pp. 83f.
[37] *Mémoires*, ii, p. 16.
[38] *Histoire du Canon de l'Ancien Testament*, published in 1890. It was followed a year later by a similar volume on the canon of the New Testament, neither volume evoking any serious criticism. But the appearance in the *Revue des Religions* for 1892 of a series of articles on the Chaldean myths of Creation and the Deluge, in turn succeeded by his 1893 lectures on the opening chapters of Genesis, proved more disturbing. Once again the superior-general of Saint-Sulpice informed his students that certain courses at the Institut were forbidden to them.

he was appointed professor of Holy Scripture at the Institut and at once drew up a comprehensive programme of teaching covering the whole field of biblical study and making use of modern critical methods. He also started a bi-monthly review, *L'Enseignement biblique*, by means of which the substance of his lecture-courses could be made available to the clergy at large, and especially, as he hoped, the younger among them.[39]

The year 1892 saw the death of Renan, and Mgr d'Hulst, with the best of intentions, judged fit to mark the occasion with a retrospective article on the celebrated scholar in the pages of the *Correspondant*. His aim was neither to condemn nor to point a moral but to look at his subject impartially and to praise where praise seemed due. From the Catholic standpoint Renan unquestionably had apostatized, but the reasons for his apostasy, d'Hulst suggested, were not entirely blameworthy. Had the difficulties which the Bible assuredly poses for an inquiring intellect been dealt with by his seminary teachers in a frank and reasonable way the break with the church might never have come about. In any case the doctrine of inspiration need not necessarily be presented in a rigidly traditional form. D'Hulst's argument, though in itself trite enough, was then quite unfamiliar to pious Catholics and caused no little astonishment to many of his readers. Moreover the *Univers* attacked him with its wonted vigour and accused him outright of substituting 'rationalism' for faith.[40] D'Hulst, in face of the mounting criticism, tried to explain himself in a second *Correspondant* article, at the same time endeavouring to defend Loisy too, even though, as his own statements disclosed, he had no very clear grasp of what the latter's position really was. The question, he suggested, is not whether the Bible contains authentic history but whether everything which appears to be historical comes under the guarantee of inspiration. God indeed is ultimately the author of scripture, but he makes use of human media, who, though inspired, preserve a relative independence. Opinions on the matter within the church varied. On the one side were those for whom the Bible contains and can contain no error whatsoever; on the other, an *école large* (as d'Hulst called it) which would confine inspiration to matters strictly of faith and morals. Between the two were such as held a mediating position, an *école moyenne*; and without expressly saying so he clearly implied that this standpoint was his own, whereas Loisy belonged to

[39] The periodical ran for two years and comprised twelve issues, with one more outside the series. See Houtin and Sartiaux, *Alfred Loisy*, pp. 54–7, 311f.

[40] Baudrillart, *La vie*, ii, p. 139; and for a full account of the article see pp. 145–57. In the previous October Loisy had at his own request been interviewed by Mgr Meignan, now archbishop of Tours and on the eve of becoming a cardinal. The advice the wary prelate gave him was to practise caution. Criticism had never been admitted in the church and any attempt to dispel the profound ignorance in which the clergy, on this subject, were sunk, would be a risky procedure. 'Our theologians are ferocious; they put us on the Index for nothing ... Let us then be the advocates of tradition – des avocats sincères, toujours sincères ... But one must above all avoid compromising oneself' (*Choses passées*, pp. 116ff. cf. *Mémoires*, i, pp. 224ff.)

the *école large*. All three points of view were, he thought, to be tolerated within the church.

Unfortunately the outcome of the article was anything but eirenic. Traditionalists immediately demanded its condemnation by Rome, and d'Hulst became seriously alarmed for the future of his institute. As earlier Duchesne had had to be sacrificed, so now it was to be Loisy's turn. The rector, in all conscience, was in a dilemma, for he had no wish to lose his brilliant young professor; but the Institut itself, he judged, had the prime claim upon his care. The article had a further consequence in the publication of Leo XIII's encyclical *Providentissimus Deus* in November 1893.[41] No one was actually named in the papal document, but the very restricted limits within which biblical scholars could regard themselves as free to move were plainly indicated. The books of the Bible were declared to contain nothing which was false, having in truth been set down *cum Spiritu Sancto dictante*, and those who presumed to teach otherwise were said either to have perverted the nature of divine inspiration or else to have made God himself the author of errors. To these pronouncements d'Hulst and the rest of the theological faculty at once testified their complete submission. Loisy himself, so far from registering dissent, even sent a personal letter to the pope assuring him of his loyalty to the church's teaching and in particular the contents of the encyclical.[42]

The fact was, however, that d'Hulst had seriously misrepresented Loisy's real views. As the latter saw it the problem was not simply one of defining the limits of inspiration, but something altogether more complex and subtle. Accordingly he ventured to state his own opinion in an article in the *Enseignement biblique* of 10 November 1893 — the periodical's final issue, as it turned out. Previously given as a lecture at the Institut, 'La question biblique et l'inspiration des Écritures' was also to be Loisy's swan-song there.[43] To the theory — supposedly of the *école large* — that the Bible's inspiration was confined to its teaching on faith and morals, he objected that neither the Fathers of the early church nor the mediaeval doctors had held that scripture contained passages that were not inspired, and that both Trent and the Vatican Council envisaged no such distinction as that which had now been put forward.

The Church has never thought of the Bible as a mosaic in which fragments of human error were put side by side with fragments of divine truth. On the traditional assumptions there is no room for error in the Bible.

But scripture had to be looked at from the historical and critical angle as well as the theological. For more than a century it had been dissected by

---

[41] *De studiis sacris.* See *Acta Sanctae Sedis*, xxvi (1893–4, pp. 269–92). cf. Lecanuet, *La vie*, pp. 356–60.

[42] *Mémoires*, ii, pp. 311f.

[43] It was reprinted, with additional notes, in *Études bibliques*, 3rd ed. (1903), pp. 139–69.

rationalist and Protestant critics and its origins discussed, and the question
to which this treatment had led was not at all the same as that which
theologians concerned themselves with.

The issue is no longer of whether the Bible contains errors, but rather that of the
truth which it embodies.

Criticism had arrived at certain conclusions which it regarded as assured:
namely, that the Pentateuch, as it has come down to us, is not the work of
Moses; that the opening chapters of *Genesis* do not present an historical
account of human origins; and that the several books of the Old Testament,
and the various parts of each, are not, historically speaking, of a homogeneous
character: the Old Testament, as likewise indeed the New, had been freely
edited, so that 'a certain liberty of interpretation is therefore the legitimate
consequence of the liberty which obtained in its composition'. Finally, the
history of the religious teaching convered by the Bible discloses a considerable
measure of development in all its constituent elements: *viz.* its ideas of God,
of human destiny, of the moral law. It is hardly necessary to say, then, that
for an independent and scientific exegesis of the sacred books, at least in all
that touches on matters of scientific fact, they do not rise above the common
notions of antiquity, notions which have left their very clear mark on the
biblical writings and even on biblical teaching.

A few months after his dismissal the former professor of Holy Scripture
at the premier Catholic university of France found himself in the post of
chaplain at a junior girls' school run by Dominican nuns in the Paris suburb
of Neuilly. It was to be his last ecclesiastical charge and for the next five
years he scrupulously carried out its duties. But these were not arduous and
they afforded him abundant leisure for study and writing. Furthermore, the
task of preaching and catechizing at an elementary level prompted him to
reflect upon some of the larger issues raised by religious belief generally and
the Catholic creed in particular. Thus his thoughts turned increasingly to
apologetic problems and especially the need for a more trenchant type of
apology based on a critical understanding of the origin and early development of Christianity — an apology which was eventually to take shape in
the famous *L'Évangile et l'Église*. But with this side of Loisy's work we shall
deal later. For the moment it is his exegetical interest which must continue
to hold our attention.

In 1894 he brought out the first edition of a volume of *Études bibliques*, a
second and third, revised and enlarged, appearing some years later, in 1901
and 1903 respectively. This for the most part consisted of papers which had
first seen print in the *Enseignement biblique* and other periodicals; but the
1903 edition was designed to carry a lengthy prefatorial essay furnishing a
summary statement of ideas which the author had already expressed elsewhere. To avoid controversy, however, this at the last moment was suppressed,

so that the book when published began at page ninety-seven. Privately circulated copies which do carry the preface indicate plainly enough the development which the author's views had undergone since 1892.

The first chapter discusses the critical method as applied to the Bible as a whole. The church's definitions, Loisy argues, are concerned with scripture only in its theological aspect; they have nothing to do with criticism or questions of historicity, a distinction which was to become for him a firm principle. Not that he thought the historical can have no theological significance: he was saying only that history as such cannot negate theological affirmations any more than theology can reasonably reject the conclusions of historical science.[44] History presents events simply in their externality: what religion discerns in them is a matter for faith. The next two chapters, the one dating from March 1892 and the other from November 1893, dealt with the problem of biblical inspiration, the second of them comprising the paper referred to above. To say that a biblical writing is inspired is not to claim divine verbal dictation. Inspiration is, rather, a 'divine aid for the purpose of furnishing the Church with a kind of *répertoire* of religious and moral teaching'; this aid being such that 'it is impossible to determine in [the sacred writers'] works what comes solely from God and what solely from man'. One has no right therefore to expect from the Bible 'positive agreement with all the results of all the sciences, natural and historical'. The representation of the most essential truths, 'notwithstanding the certitude of faith', cannot but be 'relative and imperfect, enclosed as it is in the symbols which figure forth those truths only by analogy, without expressing them adequately'. Hence to 'propound in the name of the church a teaching which, on many points, is proved to be false by an impartial science' can only be dangerous.

Of the remaining items in the book one reproduces an article on the first eleven chapters of *Genesis*, originally published in 1893,[45] while another examines the question of the Mosaic authorship of the Pentateuch: to contest the traditional view does not diminish the work's historical authority, but rather sets it in its true light.[46] A third criticizes Renan's ideas on the messiahship: the value of the messianic hope depends not on its precise historical form 'but on the invisible spirit which impels it forward, even — and above all — when it would seem that events ought to have crushed it'.[47] A final chapter discusses the symbolical character of the Fourth Gospel.[48]

[44]'De même le critique ne peut ni ne doit définir la signification historique. Le principe de critique ne lui permet pas de formuler des conclusions de foi. Nul principe du théologien ne l'autorise à formuler des conclusions d'histoire' (*Études bibliques*, 3rd ed., unpublished preface, p. 36).

[45]*Enseignement biblique*, 7, pp. 1–16.

[46]*Revue du Clergé français*, 15 February 1899, pp. 526–57.

[47]*Revue d'Histoire et de littérature religieuses*, 1898, pp. 385–406.

[48]*Revue du Clergé français*, 1 November 1899, pp. 484–506.

In September 1899 Loisy was taken seriously ill and had to resign his chaplaincy. On recovery he moved to Bellevue, without employment, but the following year was given a lectureship at the École des Hautes Études, a department of the Sorbonne. This post, which he retained until 1904, secured him both academic status and a livelihood independent of ecclesiastical sources. Meantime his articles in the *Revue du Clergé français* and the *Revue d'histoire et de littérature religieuses* continued to appear, usually under a pseudonym – 'A. Firmin', 'Étienne Sharp', or 'Isidore Desprès'. In October 1900 he began in the former journal what he intended as a sequence of three articles of a non-technical character on the religion of Israel,[49] but his first contribution was immediately censured by the archbishop of Paris, Cardinal Richard, and the subsequent instalments were left unpublished until all three were issued in volume form in 1901,[50] a year which also saw the publication of a further collection of review articles under the title *Les Mythes babyloniens et les premiers chapitres de la Genèse*. But although the archbishop had condemned Loisy's book Rome, as it happened did not, a fact which afforded its author some encouragement. In 1902, accordingly, he brought out a third volume of critical papers, treating principally of Johannine problems, under the general heading of *Études évangeliques*. A few months later, on 30 October, the papal Biblical Commission was formally constituted, an event which not a few interpreted as indicative of a more open-minded policy with regard to biblical studies. At any rate it was widely accepted that the Commission's aim was to promote rather than retard such studies.[51] It was at this time too – surprisingly enough, in the circumstances – that Loisy's candidature was canvassed for a French bishopric, first of Monaco and then of Tarentaise, even though, in the outcome, the episcopal purple was not to be his, since the Vatican simply would not hear of it. But he himself entertained no real hopes of his success. As he told von Hügel: 'Il est trop probable que je resterai, entre mes deux trônes, assis par terre.'

History and Apologetics

We have said that Loisy's duties at Neuilly afforded him time and opportunity to reflect on some of the broader questions of religious belief, and it was during this period that he published a number of papers, under the thin disguise of 'Firmin', upon such themes as the nature and definition of religion, the idea of revelation and the concept of development in Christian doctrine. But he also planned a major work of religious philosophy to be called *Essais d'histoire et de critique religieuses*, which would include a discussion of the

---

[49] *Revue du Clergé français*, pp. 337–63.
[50] A second and considerably enlarged edition was published in 1906 (English trans. by A. Galton, 1910), and a third, yet further enlarged, in 1933.
[51] cf. Lecanuet, *La vie*, pp. 373f.

general character of Catholicism and indicate the lines on which, in his own view, it might find a new measure of intellectual justification.[52] But this was not the first time his thoughts had turned to the apologetic problem as it appeared in the light of contemporary scholarship and philosophy. As far back as July 1883 he had composed an imaginary dialogue between a 'young scholar' — was Renan perhaps his model? — and a personification of the church, in which the latter is made to speak thus:

I must allow that my teaching, immutable in its principles and its end, can and should be modified in its form and perfected in its exposition, in order that it may the better respond to the needs of the generations which it must bring to God. Perhaps my doctors in this century have been inferior to their task and have not understood that it was permissible for them to abandon the old formulas — that they ought indeed almost to forget them — in order to preserve for the world the very substance of the truth which is entrusted to me. God will, I hope, give me men apt for their work, and you will no longer be able to accuse me of ignorance.

But the *jeune savant* insists that 'it is not your formulas that you must translate for us into a speech intelligible to the men of our age; it is rather your ideas themselves, your absolute affirmations, your theory of the universe, the conception you have of your own history, that you must renew, rectify and reconstruct'.[53] Doubtless there already was not a little of Renan in the young Loisy, but he was also overtly critical of him, as too of the liberal Protestant Auguste Sabatier, and in fact of the whole 'secularist' or non-Catholic case against the Catholic embodiment of Christianity. Yet his approach was always and quite consistently that of the scientific historian, enjoying as of right complete freedom of inquiry in his own sphere.

Of the 'Firmin' articles the first was on Newman's idea of development.[54] Loisy had some time before this been reading Newman 'with enthusiasm', judging him, as he told von Hügel, to be 'the most open-minded theologian to have existed in the Church since Origen'. He now was convinced that Newman's theory was superior to either Harnack's or Sabatier's, inasmuch as for the English divine Christianity was like a living person, changing often, as living persons do, but never losing its identity. Thus it was a Catholic thinker who had first introduced 'a broad and genuinely scientific conception of the history of dogma and of Christian development, under which all the legitimate conclusions of historical criticism can find shelter'. Unfortunately the idea of development as Newman presented it had still not taken possession of theology and continued to have no place at all in official Catholic teaching. Yet it may fairly be said to be 'in possession of tradition', in that the whole history of the church provides evidence in favour of the theory. 'Catholic theology has had in Newman the great doctor which it has stood

[52] *Mémoires*, i, pp. 441–3.   [53] *ibid.*, pp. 118–25.
[54] *Revue du Clergé français*, 1 December 1898, pp. 5–20.

in need of; what he perhaps has lacked is disciples.' But although Loisy admits to having derived great stimulus from Newman he denies that he actually took the notion of development from the famous *Essay*. Certainly his own evolutionary view of it differed widely from the cardinal's and in spite of his relative depreciation of them owed far more to both Harnack and Sabatier, as well as to the critical writings of biblical scholars like H. J. Holtzmann and Johannes Weiss.[55]

The second article, 'La théorie individualiste de la religion',[56] is concerned with the liberal Protestant standpoint embodied in a work like Auguste Sabatier's *Esquisse d'une Philosophie de la religion*. It argues that liberal Protestantism entirely fails to understand the social character of Christianity and that in effect it denies the truth of a supernatural revelation. Catholicism, on the other hand, precisely because in its historic aspect it is a living institution, is bound to undergo change. 'Dogma would be petrified in the Church, and not alive, were it to be identified absolutely with its theological formulation and this in turn declared to be wholly immutable.' The difficulties which Catholicism presents to the historian have in fact arisen from the very necessities of its life; but much more than Protestant individualism can it give the believer an objective assurance of truth. A similar argument is used in the paper on the 'definition of religion', in which the spontaneously social character of religion is again stressed.[57]

That which throws a man at the feet of God, impels the mind to conceive him and the conscience to invoke him is the universal need that is manifested not only in the exercise of man's highest faculties but in the whole order of human life.

The idea of revelation, which is the subject of the next article,[58] Loisy concedes to be more problematic, but he criticizes Sabatier for reducing it to a mere 'psychological phenomenon'. On the one hand revelation may be thought of as man's consciousness of God; on the other however — when considered in itself and as to both its cause and its end — as the manifestation of God to man, 'a manifestation which transcends man in its origin, content and objective alike'. Accordingly a distinction has to be drawn between 'truth' and 'doctrine', the former being the divine reality which is disclosed over the ages, the latter the formulation of that reality made under the conditions obtaining at the time and therefore subject to change with time. To regard the abstract propositions of theology as the 'essential and indispensable element' in revelation, to be passed on from generation to generation 'like a

[55] For Loisy's personal explanation of his attitude to Newman see *Mémoires*, i, pp. 359–78. The editor (Bernard Holland) of von Hügel's *Selected Letters, 1896–1924* (1927) was probably correct in saying that Newman's works 'fell in with and accelerated the line of thought that Loisy was already pursuing' (*Selected Letters*, p. 16).
[56] *Revue du Clergé français*, 1 January 1899, pp. 202–15.
[57] *Revue du Clergé français*, 1 June 1899, pp. 193–209.
[58] *Revue du Clergé français*, 1 January 1900, pp. 250–71 ('L'idée de la Révélation').

set lesson in which, for whatever reason, nothing is to be altered', is a complete misconception. What needs to be understood is the *immanent* operation of the divine transcendence. Religion is 'first and foremost the action of God in man or of man with God'.

It is man who seeks, but it is God who moves him to do so. It is man who perceives, but it is God who enlightens him. Revelation is realized in man, but it is the work of God in him, with him and by him. The efficient cause of revelation is supernatural like its object, in that both cause and object are God himself. But God acts in man and is known by man.

Thus religion is never simply a doctrine: it is a reality before becoming a theory, a spirit before becoming an idea, a life before becoming a formula. The theory reveals but one face of the reality, just as the idea is only an imperfect expression of the spirit or the formula an inadequate manifestation of the life.

Loisy's consistent argument is therefore that the necessary conceptualism of theology is never to be confused with religion, a truth which becomes increasingly apparent, he holds, when the morphology of religion and religious institutions is brought under scrutiny by the critical historian, who also is in a position to observe how far the subsequent theological development may have misrepresented the original spiritual impulse. His final article, 'Les preuves et l'économie de la Révélation',[59] dealing with the questions of miracle and prophecy, renders his own position unambiguously clear. Miracle is not a mere prodigy of nature but a 'sign', a manifestation of God to the eye of faith — an interpretation of the miraculous which goes back at least to St Augustine. As for prophecy it is not exact prediction of future events but a proclamation appealing, rather, to the 'intimate and constant harmony of ideas and facts in a religious movement progressively realized under the guidance of Providence'. It is in this sense that the Old Testament prepares for, announces and figures forth the New. Genuine religion, Loisy concludes, is something experienced, lived, and it is in such living experience that its true proof lies. So far from this view of it being opposed to the church's authority it presupposes it. 'A religion which ceased to be a Church or a Church which relinquished its authority would exist only in appearance.'

The general standpoint of all these articles, then, is the view that the Christian religion is a vital experience whose articulation and forms of expression necessarily undergo change, its unity being secured within the framework of a continuing institution. Hence the life of faith will persist so long as the church itself does not become petrified in a rigid traditionalism. That forms which had unquestionable utility in the past may very well have lost it today is an assessment of things wherein historian and reformer can find themselves on common ground.

[59] *Revue du Clergé français*, 15 March 1900, pp. 126–53.

The 'Firmin' articles, for all their varied interest, were no more than a partial disclosure of Loisy's opinions at this stage of his career. A much fuller and more systematized statement of them existed in a manuscript also dating from the Neuilly years which was never published as a whole,[60] although parts of it supplied material for the 'Firmin' series.[61] This was the work, begun in July 1897 and completed a little short of seven months later, on 1 January 1898, to which he gave the unassuming title 'Essais d'histoire et de critique religieuse'. He records that the first sketch of it shows that its 'fundamental and dominant idea' was neither more nor less than reform of the entire intellectual system of Roman Catholicism, an undertaking to which historical criticism, philosophy and sociology would all contribute. It was, he admits, a bold venture, quite beyond the capacity of one man alone or even of several in the space of a single generation.[62] For what he envisaged was a full-scale defence of Catholicism based on a recognition of the very radical modifications in traditional positions which the historical critical method would inevitably demand.

In his foreword Loisy stated that a science of religion was taking shape *outside* Catholicism and in a spirit opposed to it. To neutralize this dangerous influence, which no external authority could prevent from reaching the more intelligent members of the public, it was necessary for just such a science of religion to be created *within* the church and in a spirit favourable to Catholicism. His own work he presented not as 'a learned apologetic' but merely as 'a single essay in which history, philosophy, theology and apologetics are combined in very moderate doses'; though above all as 'a sincere expression of the contemporary religious problem' in so far as the author himself had been able to grasp it.

The scope of the *Essais* therefore was as far-ranging as their aim was bold. The opening chapters dealt with various theories of religion generally and of

[60]The *livre inédit*, in the Paris Bibliothèque Nationale, exists in two different forms and in separate mss. The first is entitled 'Essais d'histoire et de critique religieuses' (N.a.f. 15634) and is a sort of general apologia for Catholicism. In a note at the end Loisy says that he considers it unsatisfactory, which doubtless is why he re-cast it as, secondly, 'Essais d'histoire et de philosophie religieuses' (N.a.f. 15635) (originally 'La crise de la foi dans le temps présent', a title crossed out in the ms). Louis Canet produced a three-volume typescript (N.a.f. 15636–8) of this latter work with appended notes giving details of the use of certain passages in articles in the *Revue du clergé français* and in *L'Évangile et l'Église*. In the 'Avant-propos' Loisy points out that he has written under the stimulus of recent liberal Protestant authors, notably Harnack, Auguste Sabatier, Wellhausen and H. J. Holtzmann.

[61]*Mémoires*, i, p. 448.

[62]*ibid.*, p. 443. He adds: 'Mais je ne me sentais pas complètement isolé; je ne me promettais pas un succès immédiat; je ne savais pas quand ni comment je publierais mon essai ... Je n'ignorais pas les difficultés de l'entreprise; mais de celle-ci je voyais et j'éprouvais très vivement, pour le sécurité de ma propre conscience, la nécessité. Ce que je ne prévoyais pas, c'est que cette entreprise dût presque fatalement me mener hors du catholicisme.' To no one did he show the final revision of his work. For a detailed account of the *livre inédit* see *Mémoires*, i, pp. 445–77.

Christianity in particular. This section, in the nature of an introduction, was
followed by a more detailed discussion of the character of religion and the
idea of revelation. Then came chapters on Hebrew monotheism, Jesus and his
teaching and the evolution of the church both as an institution and in respect
of its doctrine and worship. The remaining chapters were concerned with the
problem of Catholicism as the author then saw it. The Catholic religion was,
he said, 'reproached more or less openly with keeping men in a state of
permanent minority; of doing injury to the autonomy of the individual conscience by the principle of absolute submission to the Church, to that of
science and reason by its irrational and contradictory dogmas, and to that of
the family and of political society by the meddlesome activities of a supposed
spiritual power having jurisdiction over every manifestation of human life
and action'. Such adverse judgments were not indeed founded simply on
'misinterpreted appearances or on ignorance of what contemporary Catholicism is'; but they were, all the same, to be regarded as mistaken insofar as no
distinction was drawn by them between what is essential and indispensable
and what merely accidental and accessory — 'questionable, perhaps, and even
regrettable', but nonetheless reformable.

The gospel account of Jesus, Loisy pointed out, was in no sense a biography.
This was true of the synoptics as well as of the fourth gospel, the latter being
above all 'a Christology with which are associated certain traditional elements
the number and significance of which are more or less in dispute'. The
synoptics are not without historical authority, but they are not histories.
More remarkably, Loisy had now come to view the mission of Jesus himself
in the historical perspective of ancient Jewish apocalyptic — some years,
that is, before the publication of the important second edition of Johannes
Weiss's *Die Predigt Jesu vom Reiche Gottes* (1900)[63] or Albert Schweitzer's
Von Reimarus zu Wrede (1906). The gospel, appearing when and where it did,
was bound to be conditioned by its own time and circumstances: 'The Jewish
exterior is the body of which the Gospel is the soul.' And Jesus' own mind
was dominated by the *parousia*, or the Messiah's imminent coming again in
glory, an expectation fully shared by his followers. But if Jesus' prospect of
the future was so foreshortened what was to be made of the orthodox and
traditional claim that he was the conscious and deliberate founder of the
Catholic church, with its hierarchy, dogmas and sacraments? Were he seen
to be merely the victim of his own grandiose illusions would not Catholicism
have been deprived of the whole basis of its authority? 'Unbelieving rationalism' was well content of course to draw this conclusion, whilst 'theological
rationalism' simply took fright. Both however, in Loisy's opinion, entirely
misconceived the facts. Had it really been Jesus' intention to inaugurate a
doctrine or school or sect, let alone the immense fabric of historic Catholicism,

[63] The first edition had appeared in 1892, but as hardly more than a pamphlet.

he quite evidently did not adopt the measures necessary to ensure lasting success. He would actually have shown himself 'less clever than Mahomet'. But 'Jesus did not pursue such a project, nor did he flatter himself that he could succeed by means of a deceptive dream. He lived his project and his dream at the same time . . .'

L'essentiel de son rêve était la substance de sa vie . . . What had he to do with our abstractions, and why demand of him that he should know instead of believe, in a matter in which science had nothing to say and faith everything? . . . Just as Jesus was bound to believe himself to be the Messiah and to present himself as such to the Jews of his time in order to be in this world what he had to be, so he was bound to conceive his own future and that of his work under the same messianic form, were he to do here below what he had to do. The hope which he entertained was not an error, it was the only living way in which he could envisage the future, given what for him was the present.

Hence the idea of the *parousia*, with all that belonged to it, was the concrete symbol of what came after: faith in the Master's resurrection, so ardently embraced by his disciples; the conviction that Jesus, although he endured death, was still alive for his adherents and present among them, and that he really gave himself to them in the eucharist; and the growth of the church throughout the world and the continuous progress of the soul over the centuries. 'It was the symbol of all that we have seen, and also of what we do not see. For we do not know the aspect which the kingdom of God will present from the plane of eternity, nor how the reckoning of the divine justice and goodness will be drawn up behind the veil of this world.'

Subsequent chapters treating of the church, dogma and worship were to some extent reproduced — though in Loisy's judgment less satisfactorily — in *L'Évangile et l'Église*, and so we may defer consideration of them until we come to the later work; but we should note in passing the author's defence of the hierarchical principle:

The Church has heads who are not heads, but the slaves of their functions . . . The hierarchy is a means of assuring the unity of the Church;

and of the papacy:

The pope likewise exists only in order to synthetize and unify the action of the hierarchy;[64]

as too his belief that the church must sooner or later change from a political to a moral power, with a role which is spiritually educative rather than coercive. Regarding the church's dogma it has to be said that Christianity

[64]'Il n'entre dans la pensée d'aucun catholique ni dans l'enseignement de l'Église que tout l'effort du catholicisme doive tendre à rehausser la dignité pontificale, enrichir la curie romaine, accroître son influence politique, et procurer des sujets obéissants au successeur de Saint Pierre' (*Mémoires*, i, p. 462).

cannot confine itself to a single moment or phase in the process of doctrinal self-expression. New forms will have to take the place of those that have become obsolete. It is absurd to describe the church's dogmatic formulations as immutable: 'The word "immutability", sometimes employed, is not more applicable to dogma than to the Church herself. In the world in which we live nothing is immutable, and where there is most life there also, within the harmonious unity of growth, is the maximum of change.[65]

Of the remaining chapters that on the 'Intellectual regime of the Catholic Church' may in some respects have been the most interesting. Although the church admits in principle the autonomy of the various sciences outside her own immediate field of theology, there is, Loisy thinks, one which she had so far never looked on as free: that, namely, of her own origins, or the science of biblical criticism, which treats of the sacred books not as the documents of revelation but simply as historical sources. If Catholic exegesis has in modern times been static it is because it has, in fact, been condemned to immobility. But exegesis is neither theology nor apologetics, being only a matter of history. The result is that theology and criticism are now antagonists; for theology has been opposed to every move in the direction of a scientific exegesis, or to any effort intended 'to introduce into Catholic science the historical knowledge of the Bible'. Nor, alas, has this been all. It is impossible to formulate a new hypothesis or conclusion on an important point in either science or history 'without running up against the barrier of theological opinion'. Recent philosophy, in shaping its conceptions of the world and of man, has regard only to the state of knowledge as it is today. It has nothing to learn from theology, which embodies the science of the past. Yet it is this same contemporary science that theology itself should take account of if it is to bring about the changes needed to recommend itself to the real world of men. When however, Loisy observed, a young Catholic thinker of distinction like Maurice Blondel tries to introduce a new style of philosophy more appropriate to the church's actual apologetic requirements he is denounced at Rome. One conclusion, though, can be drawn:

The progress of the sciences in these last centuries has in some measure been brought about in spite of the Church, or at least in spite of the official representatives of its theology, who have led the Church, as far as they were able to do so, into an opposition which has had the most deplorable results; more so, perhaps, for theology than for science, the development of which has, moreover, been altered in consequence — driven as it has been, by resistance and oppression, into the path of revolution.

[65] *ibid.*, p. 463. The chapter ends with a passage which the author did not include in *L'Évangile et l'Église*. It contains the following sentences: 'La spéculation dogmatique ne peut jamais être arrêtée définitivement sur un point quelconque des sujets qu'elle embrasse ... Il se peut que la théologie des siècles prochains soit plus reservée que celles des siècles passés, qu'elle ait moins de confiance dans la valeur permanente des formules, qu'elle trouve sa lumière dans l'obscurité de la foi plus que dans les fragiles constructions du raisonnement. Cette sagesse sera même un progrès ...'

'*La Crise moderniste*'

Many readers of his memoirs must have regretted that Loisy did not see fit, or find occasion, to publish 'Essais d'histoire et de critique religieuse' as a whole and in its original draft. Although he afterwards described it as 'dense, and rather wordy in places', it constituted, on his own admission, 'a veritable *Summa* of what should have been Catholic Modernism'.[66] But the work did not appear and thus the *affaire Loisy*, which precipitated the Modernist crisis, was postponed for a while. Not however for long. The moment at which Loisy felt it appropriate to publicize his views on matters going far beyond questions of biblical exegesis soon arrived when Adolf Harnack, professor of church history at the university of Berlin and an out-standing liberal Protestant scholar, brought out a series of popular lectures which he had delivered before a large audience during the winter semester of 1899–1900. Harnack's book, which bore the title *Das Wesen des Christen-thums*, had an instant and unprecedented success.[67] Its intrinsic interest and importance, together with its author's personal reputation in the world of scholarship, prompted Loisy —after some hesitation – to reply to it, drawing largely on the material which already existed in the *livre inédit*. Not that Harnack's opinions had aroused much curiosity in France, at any rate among Catholics; but Loisy had already in his published writings, as well as in the *Essais*, made a point of criticizing the liberal Protestant position, and now saw an opportunity not only for returning to this criticism but – what was closer to his heart – of voicing his opinions, somewhat obliquely it might be, on issues deeply affecting Catholicism itself. *L'Évangile et l'Église*, the most keenly discussed of all the Modernist publications – the book which the English Jesuit Father Tyrrell later referred to as 'the classical exposition of Catholic Modernism'[68] – was his answer. Of modest bulk, it came out in November 1902.[69]

Loisy set out to refute Harnack by accepting the latter's critical premises while dissenting totally from the historical and theological conclusions which he had professed to draw from them. The Catholic scholar's guiding principle could have been stated in a sentence: if theology is to take due account of history it must allow history to speak for itself. The presuppositions of

[66] *ibid.*, p. 477.

[67] Within a short time the volume had sold in tens of thousands of copies and was trans-lated into several foreign languages. The French version was published by Fischbacher in May 1902. The English translation by T. B. Saunders, called *What is Christianity?*, appeared in 1901.

[68] *Christianity at the Cross Roads* (1910), p. 92.

[69] Loisy disclosed his intentions only to his friends, Baron von Hügel and the archbishop of Albi, Mgr Mignot. The latter, who read the manuscript before publication, expressed himself 'fort satisfait'. 'Je ne pense pas', he added, 'que l'on puisse vous condamner, et, tout au contraire, cette publication vous placera au premier rang des critiques chrétiens' (Loisy, *Mémoires*, i, p. 133).

personal or indeed traditional faith cannot be allowed to 'trim' the facts.[70]

What, briefly, had been Harnack's argument? His procedure, in seeking to determine what the essential content of Christianity amounts to, was, as he himself said (and as Loisy carefully noted) to 'employ the methods of historical science, and the experience of life gained by studying the actual course of history'. The historical critic had thus to remove whatever was merely adventitious even where it formed part of the evangelic tradition itself. Jesus' own message, that is, had to be separated from its 'Jewish limitations', such as the apocalyptic idea of the Kingdom as a trans-temporal event already immanent. For as he saw it 'the Kingdom of God comes by coming to the individual, by entering into his soul and laying hold of it'. Understood in this way his teaching finally reduces itself to two elements: 'God as Father and the human soul so ennobled that it can and does unite with him.' The gospel was intrinsically an appeal to the individual conscience: Jesus 'had never anyone but the individual in mind, and the abiding disposition of the heart in love'. As for his conception of himself, Harnack was convinced that it was determined by his sense of his own singular relation to God, exemplified in the synoptic text — taken as authentic: 'No man knoweth the Son, but the Father; neither knoweth any man the Father, save the Son' — a saying which Loisy on critical grounds regarded as no more likely to have been the *ipsissima verba* of the Lord than similar utterances in the fourth gospel. Because of this felt relationship, Harnack held, Jesus could well, according to the ideas current at the time, have thought of himself as the Messiah. But 'sonship' to God is really something open to all men. The Christological dogma, based as it was on the Messiah-image, has therefore no warrant. The gospel is not a theoretical system of doctrine, and in fact the whole outward and visible institution of the church, claiming divine dignity, has no evangelic foundation at all. 'It is a case not of distortion but of total perversion.'[71] Protestantism in its modern and revised form, was a return to the original truth of Jesus' own message. The Reformation had begun the process of restoration, but its work was abortive and had to be completed by means of knowledge which the Reformers did not possess.

Loisy in his reply at once takes Harnack up on the very point of his appeal to history, arguing that he failed to pursue the historical method consistently. Had he done so he would have seen that the Catholic church arose out of the gospel by a process of development in which there is a clearly discernible identity of direction. To emphasize the fact that his own procedure would remain strictly that of an historical investigator Loisy included in the second

---

[70] Loisy was well aware that his proposed defence of the church 'impliquait l'abandon des thèses absolues que professe la théologie scolastique touchant l'institution formelle de l'Église et des sacrements par le Christ, l'immutabilité des dogmes et la nature de l'autorité ecclésiastique' (*ibid.*, p. 168).

[71] *What is Christianity?* English trans. pp. 6, 56, 63, 262.

edition of his book a preliminary chapter on the gospel sources in order to show that the gospels are themselves the mirror of Christian belief as it had shaped itself by the time of their composition. Viewed thus 'they will no longer be a dangerous trial to the faith of our contemporaries'.[72] The really essential thing in Jesus' teaching seems to have been his proclamation of the imminent Kingdom and the urgent need for men to prepare for it in penitence. As Jesus conceived it it was not an inward condition of the soul, or 'the fate of the individual within the world', but a future involving 'the renewal of the world, the restoration of humanity, in eternal justice and happiness'. Not indeed that this expectation required any disciplinary prescription or economic programme: the gospel in its historic form was sublimely indifferent to merely human concerns.

[It] contains no formal declaration for or against the constitution of human society in the world as it is ... The gospel of Jesus is addressed to the whole man to snatch him from the conditions normal to the present life.

Nor has it entered the world as 'an unconditional absolute doctrine summed up in a unique and steadfast truth'; rather did it appear as a living faith the evolution of which proceeds from the same interior power that has since enabled it to endure, although always influenced by the environment in which it originated and has subsequently developed.

The role of Jesus Christ himself is primarily to be explained in the eschatological terms appropriate to his age and circumstances. He believed himself to be the Messiah whose function it was to inaugurate the Kingdom. Such too was the interpretation of the primitive church, which saw the vindication of his Messiahship in the resurrection. If he thought of himself as 'Son of God' he did so in accordance with this same Messiah-image.

The idea of the divine Sonship was to be linked with that of the Kingdom; it had no definite signification, as far as Jesus was concerned, except in regard to the Kingdom about to be established.[73]

This doubtless was not the meaning which the expression came to acquire later, but it was the principle or germ of it, in the same way that the gospel was the principle or germ of the church. As for the resurrection, all the historian can do is to recognize the strength of the apostles' faith, in that it became the activating force of all that they did. What the nature of the event itself was cannot however be determined. As a physical fact, that is, history is unable to affirm it, even though the inconsistencies in the narrative are not in themselves a compelling reason for denying it.

As to the church itself Loisy's aim is to demonstrate, contrary to Harnack's thesis, that between it and the gospel there is no antagonism of principle.

[72] *L'Évangile et l'Église* (5th ed., 1930), p. 15.
[73] *ibid.*, pp. 64, 89.

'The Church is as necessary to the Gospel as is the Gospel to the Church', for they really are one.[74]

The Church can fairly say that, in order to be at all times what Jesus desired the society of his friends to be, it had to become what it has become: for it has become what it had to be to save the Gospel by saving itself.

The church of Rome in particular grew up as 'the providential centre of Christian evangelization', the papacy having shown the same circumstantial inevitability as the Catholic church itself.

The popes were perforce what they were and what they became, in order that the Church might be still the Church and continue to represent Christianity and the religion of Jesus.

In truth the whole ecclesiastical organization, whatever temporary faults it may exhibit, has been unavoidable.

Thus to reproach the Catholic Church for the development of her constitution is to reproach her for having chosen to live, and that, moreover, when her life was indispensable for the preservation of the Gospel itself.[75]

The concluding chapters, on dogma and worship, were to prove the most controversial. As Loisy saw matters neither the church's developed doctrine nor its sacramental cult bore any direct relation to Christ, a judgment in plain contradiction of the traditional view. 'The fact is that the development of dogma is not in the gospel, and could not be there.' But it did not follow that the dogma had not proceeded from the gospel, or that the gospel had not lived, as it lives still, in the dogma as well as in the church. Theological doctrines are not 'truths fallen from heaven', to be preserved by religious tradition in the precise form in which they first appeared.

Divine though they may be in origin and substance, in structure and composition they are human; the historian sees them as the intellectual interpretation of religious facts. It will, moreover, be with them in the future as it has been in the past. Reason never ceases to ask questions.

Hence

The efforts of a healthy theology should be directed to a solution of the difficulty, presented by the unquestionable authority faith demands for dogma, and the variability, the relativity, the critic cannot fail to perceive in the history of dogmas and dogmatic formulas.

Finally, there had also to be a cultus: history knows of no instance of a religion without a ritual. As Christianity became separated from Judaism it created its own rites, of which the two principal were baptism and the

---

[74] 'Jésus annonçait le royaume et c'est l'Église qui est venue' (ibid., p. 153).
[75] ibid., pp. 142, 150, 152.

eucharist. These sacramental signs were practically necessary, and in their shaping became what the conditions of the Christian institution demanded. That paganism may have made its contribution is irrelevant, since any such element 'ceased to be pagan when accepted and interpreted by the Church'. 'The important question is whether the adaptation has served the spread and preservation of the gospel, or whether the gospel itself has been lost in it.'[76]

On its appearance *L'Évangile et l'Église* was welcomed by not a few Catholics, von Hügel in particular being warm in its praise. But the storm soon broke. The integralists of the *Univers* and *La Vérité française* attacked it bitterly.[77] Its author, who always claimed that he knew nothing of philosophy, was accused variously of Kantism, Hegelianism and rationalism. Even the progressives were disturbed: his refutation of liberal Protestantism had been splendid, but they were not blind to the fact that his use of the critical method cut deeply into the fabric of traditional Catholicism. The *Revue du Clergé français* sensed that he had tried to prove too much. The Jesuit Léonce de Grandmaison, a man whom Loisy respected, reviewed the book at length in *Études*,[78] his tone being moderate if critical, but the clerical reaction as a whole was expressed by abbé Gayraud, a die-hard conservative, when he proclaimed that 'the only result of criticism will be to render necessary and legitimate efforts dubious ... Let us stand firm on the ground of our tradition. The Christ-God established the Church: that is the sum of Christianity; otherwise it is nothing but an idol of the Hellenic spirit, and Catholicism idolatry'.[79] Another priest-publicist, abbé Oger, a professor at the Soissons seminary, declared roundly that 'to analyse the mystery of faith is to annihilate it'. What was needed, in answer to 'criticism', was a return to 'integral and intransigent Catholicism, in the true supernatural sense of that word'.[80] Not many therefore could have been surprised when the volume was condemned by the archbishop of Paris, whose action was supported by a number of other diocesan bishops. According to the archbishop *L'Évangile et l'Église* was 'calculated seriously to disturb the belief of the faithful in the fundamental dogmas of Catholic teaching, notably the authority of the Scriptures and Tradition, the divinity of Jesus Christ, his infallible knowledge, the redemption wrought by his death, the Resurrection, the Eucharist, the divine institution of the Episcopate and the Sovereign Pontificate'. Harnack himself, the personal target of Loisy's attack, never replied to his opponent.[81]

[76] *ibid.*, pp. 200f., 205, 233.
[77] For a detailed discussion of *l'affaire Loisy* see Poulat, *Histoire*, pp. 125–61.
[78] 20 January 1903, pp. 145–74.
[79] Poulat, *Histoire*, pp. 126f.
[80] *ibid.*, pp. 147f.
[81] Commenting however on the argument of *L'Évangile et l'Église* in the *Theologische Literaturzeitung* of 23 January 1904 he remarked that he was often incapable of recognizing his own thought in the form which Loisy gave it. 'I have the feeling that the inquisitorial

Loisy was advised by Mignot and other friends to clarify his views — and presumably to reassure his critics as to his orthodoxy — by issuing a sequel or supplement to *L'Évangile et l'Église*. The upshot was the publication of *Autour d'un petit livre*, in the form of a series of letters — never actually sent — to prominent French churchmen.[82] The addressees were not named but their identities were not in doubt and included both the sympathetic and the hostile. The tone adopted however was markedly sharper than in the preceding volume — Houtin described its successive chapters as 'remplies de malices très fines' — and even in his preface the writer showed himself in no mood for conciliation. ('The spectacle of disinterested scholars seemingly hunted like dangerous animals is hardly one to add to the glory of the Church of France!') Clearly Loisy was no longer now concerned with Harnack's Protestantism. The issue was that of Catholicism itself and he was not disposed to be diplomatic.[83]

The first letter (addressed to one of the writer's former teachers at Châlons, abbé Ludot) concerns the aim of his *petit livre*. Biblical criticism is to be seen as a science, with its proper autonomy. The ministry of Jesus therefore must be placed in historical perspective. The development of ecclesiastical institutions, of doctrine and of worship, must likewise be assessed historically. The biblical question comes in for more direct treatment in the second letter (to Cardinal Perraud, bishop of Autun). The literary history of the Bible has been a long and complex one and raises many problems for the critic. These the theological tradition as such is incapable of solving; and the difficulty is enhanced by the fact that the religious outlook which the scriptures reflect is by no means uniform. The critical scholar must feel free to study the data as they exist, without theological presuppositions. Were he to submit to anterior theological direction he would be guilty of insincerity. The third letter (to Bishop Camus of La Rochelle) concentrates on the criticism of the gospels in particular. Account must be taken, it is pointed out, of the work of 'progressive idealization, and of symbolical and dogmatic interpretation' that has 'operated on the facts themselves'.

method is the worst of all for grasping what has been said. Is it that the Latin does not understand the German, or the Catholic does not understand the Protestant? Are our respective ways of thinking and our language foreign to him at this point?' (p. 59). cf. Loisy, *Mémoires*, ii, pp. 235, 416, 418ff. Ernst Troeltsch, on the other hand, was much more appreciative of Loisy's standpoint, while the effectiveness of his critique of the liberal Protestant position was recognized at the time by some who, like Gabriel Monod, for example, themselves adhered to it. cf Loisy *Autour d'un petit livre*, pp. 287ff. The eminent New Testament scholar, Maurice Goguel, confessed that '*L'Évangile et l'Église* est peut-être le livre qui m'a le plus clairement ouvert les yeux sur la faiblesse de la conception de Jésus et de l'histoire du christianisme primitif à laquelle a abouti la critique liberale du xixe siècle et qui m'a fait nettement sentir la nécessité de reprendre l'ensemble du problème sur des bases nouvelles' (*Revue d'histoire et de philosophie religieuses*, 1930, p. 199).

[82] 1st ed., 1903; 2nd ed., slightly enlarged, 1904.

[83] Loisy had intimated his submission, in somewhat equivocal terms, to Cardinal Richard early in February 1903. This he felt he had to do if he was to remain in the church.

But the most weighty item in the series, the letter addressed to Mignot, tackles the central issue of the divinity of Christ. Here Loisy has to insist on the distinction, which by now he had come to regard as unavoidable, between 'the Jesus of history' and 'the Christ of faith', though he is no less insistent that nothing which can be said of the former necessarily contradicts what may be believed of the latter. The historical Jesus is Jesus the *man*, bound to his time and environment.[84] The *Christ*, on the other hand, is the expression and symbol of a faith which reaches out beyond material circumstances. In a letter intended for his friend abbé Klein, Loisy then seeks to show that the church is of divine foundation in that it is the embodiment and continuation of the gospel itself.

The Church, in all truth, continues the Gospel, in maintaining before men the same ideal of justice to be realized and in seeking fulfilment of the same ideal of blessedness. It continues the ministry of Jesus, according to the instructions which he gave to his disciples, in such a way as to prove itself to rest upon Christ's clearest intentions.

Nevertheless the church's dominical institution is a matter essentially of faith: historical evidence cannot demonstrate it. Facts are one thing, but their formulation as religious doctrine is another — a distinction that becomes still more apparent when discussion turns to dogma (as in Loisy's next letter, to Thureau-Dangin). Basically it is man's sense of his relationship with God.

What is the Christian revelation, in principle and starting-point, if not the perception in the soul of Christ of the bond which unites Christ himself to God, and of that which binds all men to their heavenly Father? The apprehension of these ties is a form of human knowledge, and it is as such only that it can be communicated to men.[85]

The concluding letter (to the director of Saint-Sulpice) deals with the sacraments, arguing that the decrees of Trent are essentially theology and not history, and that the apostles themselves attribute the institution of the sacraments to the Risen Christ, thus bringing them also within the apostolic tradition of faith, the gradual development of which has to be co-ordinated with the moral and intellectual evolution of mankind.

With *Autour d'un petit livre* Loisy's opinions as a Catholic 'modernist' were made unmistakably plain. He was calling for a reform of the traditional theological teaching in the name of scientific knowledge. But controversy, so far from being allayed, was only stimulated, and it was evident that Rome herself would soon have to act. Leo XIII died on 20 July 1903, and with his demise the interval of Vatican 'liberalism', which his personality and policies had for a while secured, passed away. The new pontiff, who assumed the title of Pius X, soon gave warning to the clergy that the 'insidious manoeuvres of

[84] cf. *Autour d'un petit livre*, p. 133.   [85] *ibid.*, pp. 159, 196.

a certain new science which adorns itself with the mask of truth' would not
for much longer be tolerated. On 16 December 1903 the Holy Office issued a
decree placing five of Loisy's works upon the Index. They comprised, besides
L'Évangile et l'Église and its sequel, an elaborate commentary on the fourth
gospel which he had but recently published.[86] Yet he accepted the condemnation with seeming patience, intimating to Cardinal Merry del Val that
he 'received with respect the judgment of the Sacred Congregations' and
that he himself condemned in his writings 'whatever they might contain
which was reprehensible'. But he also made it clear that his submission
to the Holy See, like that to Richard, was purely disciplinary. 'I reserve',
he added, 'the rights of my conscience, and do not intend, in inclining
before the judgment delivered by the Holy Office, to abandon or retract the
opinions which I have put forward as a historian and critic.'[87] Such qualified
obedience did not however satisfy Rome, and although in a second communication he declared his acceptance of 'all the dogmas of the Church' and
repeated his own condemnation of whatever was censurable in his writings,
this protestation too fell short of what the Vatican expected. It was a case
simply of *Succede quod adorasti, et ador quod incendisti*, and this Loisy's conscience as a scholar forbade him to do. Yet the anticipated excommunication
did not occur and his position became more and more equivocal. He believed
it possible, in spite of the authorities' express repudiation of both his conclusions as a critical exegete and of his historicist apologetic, that he could
continue to serve the church alike as scholar and as priest. Thus on 12 May
1904 he wrote in his journal: 'Je veux rester prêtre et savant, *res dissociabiles*.'
But it is evident from other private thoughts which he confided to it that he
was fast losing touch with Catholic and indeed Christian doctrine altogether.

Christ [he mused] has even less significance in my religion than in that of the
liberal Protestants: for I attach little importance to the revelation of God the
Father for which they honour Jesus. If I am anything in religion, it is more pantheist-
positivist-humanitarian than Christian.[88]

The wonder is that in the circumstances he should still have continued to
exercise his priestly function of saying Mass. One cannot but feel that during
these years his loyalty to the institutional church, purely as such, was stronger
than his belief in anything resembling the orthodox creed. The excommunication was not in fact pronounced until 7 March 1908.

Meanwhile the *crise moderniste* had come to a head. The reform movement was not confined to France. In England its protagonists were von
Hügel and George Tyrrell; in Italy Don Romolo Murri, the Barnabite Giovanni Semeria, Ernesto Buonaiuti — an indefatigable publicist for the
cause — and the Senator and man of letters, Antonio Fogazzaro. Germany

[86] *Le Quatrième Évangile* (1903; 2nd, revised edition, including the Johannine Epistles, 1921).
[87] *Mémoires*, ii, p. 313.   [88] Houtin and Sartiaux, *Alfred Loisy*, pp. 128f.

too was not without a representative in Hermann Schell. In France, besides Loisy himself, Laberthonnière, we have seen, came under censure, as later did the mathematician and philosopher, Edouard Le Roy, with his controversial *Dogme et Critique* (1907). But Modernism as a movement lacked coherence. What Loisy said of it was at bottom true: 'Il y a autant de modernismes que de modernistes'; and the attempt of its opponents to trace its diverse tendencies and objectives — critical, doctrinal, political, social — to a single philosophical principle, usually dubbed Kantian agnosticism, was no more than a polemical ploy.[88] The fact is that there were very many who wished for some kind of modernisation of Catholicism, but their interests and presuppositions varied widely. Hence for the most part their efforts were uncoordinated. Moreover neither Loisy nor Tyrrell was a man to find it easy to cooperate with others. The former in particular, a solitary by temperament, remained an individualist working always by preference on his own. Von Hügel had more of the qualities of a movement leader, and the same may be said of Buonaiuti. Numerous Modernist periodicals made their appearance, though usually sustaining only a brief existence. The opposition, on the other hand, knew its own mind, at least after a negative fashion. Pius X had neither the learning nor the understanding to become the patron of a new reformation, in however mild a degree. His view of the church, essentially that of his predecessor but one, was of a beleaguered city with foes on every side. There could be no accommodation therefore with those within its gates whose own sympathies seemed to lie with the enemy without. In such an atmosphere the condemnation of Modernism, in whatever measure or disguise, thus became inevitable. The decree of the Holy Office, *Lamentabili sane exitu* — a syllabus of errors reminiscent of that of 1864 — was published on 3 July 1907. It listed sixty-five propositions culled from the writings of both Loisy and Tyrrell, though with an eye also on Le Roy's theory of dogma. They were errors, it declared, being 'daily spread among the faithful'; and one of the first to be cited was the view that biblical exegesis is an autonomous science, independent of theological control. But the fate of the Modernists was finally sealed with the publication of the encyclical letter *Pascendi dominici gregis* early in the following September.[90] It purported to offer a systematic account of the whole Modernist programme, based on the now fixed assumption that the latter stemmed from an agnostic

[88] See Appended Note below on Americanism.

[90] On 18 November Pius X issued a *motu proprio* in which he held all Catholics to be bound in conscience to accept the decrees of the Biblical Commission without exception, not only those already promulgated but future ones likewise. Further, any person daring to contradict the teachings of *Lamentabili* and *Pascendi* was automatically excommunicated (*Acta Sanctae Sedis*, xl (1907), pp. 723–6). A month later, at a secret consistory of cardinals, he launched another attack on the Modernists, accusing them of deliberately seeking to undermine the faith and papal authority (*A.S.S.*, xli (1908), pp. 21–4).

or immanentist philosophy.[91] The pope's language was often intemperate: the course of speculative thought since the middle ages, for example, was dismissed as 'the ravings of philosophers', whilst the Modernists themselves were denounced as traitors to the church, 'thoroughly imbued with the poisonous doctrines taught by her enemies', and 'lost to all sense of modesty'. Not surprisingly the authors thus censured regarded such pronouncements as a travesty of their views. Loisy referred to it as 'a fantasy of the theological imagination' and denied emphatically that there was any Modernist sect or party or even school of thought in the church. On both documents he commented acidly in two more 'petit livres rouges', *Simples réfléxions sur le Décret du Saint-Office 'Lamentabili sane exitu' et sur l'encyclique 'Pascendi dominici gregis'* (1907) and *Quelques lettres sur des questions actuelles et sur des événements récents* (1908). In the former he pointed out how the Vatican persistently distorted his meaning by exaggeration in order to justify its act of condemnation, and in the latter he assembled a collection of letters written by himself to various persons over the recent years, a correspondence which reveals clearly enough, one would think, what his aims and attitudes had been and leaves no real doubt of his personal sincerity. But by this time his own Modernist period was concluded and the two volumes mentioned, along with *Choses passées* five years later and, eventually, the *Mémoires*, are only a retrospect and a postscript. He himself was soon afterwards appointed to the chair of the History of Religions at the Collège de France — the same post, he probably recalled with some ironical satisfaction, once held by Renan. In 1927 he retired to his little property at Ceffonds on the Marne, dying there in June 1940, as the German armies were for the third time in his life invading the France he devotedly loved. And although the Catholic church, which he also loved and by his talents had tried to serve, had long since repudiated him, he seems to the end to have thought of himself as in some manner still a priest.[92]

Appended Note: Americanism

Modernism would appear to have had no following in the United States of America, unless exception be made, somewhat doubtfully, of William Sullivan, the Paulist.

---

[91] Much speculation has arisen as to the precise authorship of *Pascendi*. Some observers attributed it to the Jesuit theologian Louis Billot, others to Umberto Benigni or the Benedictine Lorenzo Jansenns. On the evidence it now seems that Père Joseph Lemius, O.M.I., was mainly responsible for its drafting. (See J. Rivière, 'Qui rédigea l'encyclique "Pascendi"?') *Bulletin de littérature ecclésiastique*, Toulouse, April-September 1946, pp. 143−61). cf. Vidler, *A Variety of Catholic Modernists*, pp. 15f.

[92] The inscription which he directed to be placed on his gravestone reads:

Alfred Loisy
Prêtre
Retiré du ministère et de l'enseignement
Professeur au Collège de France
Tuam in votis tenuit voluntatem.

(On Sullivan see J. Ratté, *Three Modernists*, 1968, pp. 259–336.) But a tendency of thought originating in America, and hence nicknamed 'Americanism', was condemned by Leo XIII in an encyclical letter, *Testem benevolentiae*, of 22 January 1899, mainly on account of the sympathetic interest which it aroused in France. In so far as Americanism is capable of any exact identification it merely sought to press upon Catholics the need for the church to re-assess the forms of its action in the modern world and in particular to come to terms with democratic aspirations. Thus when Mgr John Ireland, archbishop of St Paul, Minnesota, with whose name it was chiefly associated, visited Paris in 1892 he declared, in the presence of a distinguished audience, that 'the Church in America is the Church of the people. Our priests, our bishops, are all devoted to the people . . . The American people likes to see the clergy occupying themselves with all the interests of the country. They feel they are neces-sarily a social force'; and he continued: 'Our hearts beat always for the Republic of the United States. In the past it was said that the Catholic Church would not reconcile itself with the Republic and that the free air of America would be fatal to it'. (See P. Dabry, *Les Catholiques republicains* (1905), pp. 263f.) The action of the Vatican, however, was brought about by the publication in 1897 of a French translation of a *Life of Father Hecker*, the founder of the Paulist order, by one of its members, Walter Elliott. The translation was made and edited by abbé Felix Klein of the Paris Institut Catholique, a friend of Loisy's. Klein was enthusiastic in his praise of Hecker. 'Humanity', he wrote, 'transforms itself and demands a new apostolate. The apostle has come. In Father Hecker it has found the ideal priest for the new future of the Church' (Lecanuet, *La vie.*, p. 569). But the book was attacked by the Jesuits and the conservative *Vérité*. Although the Vatican forbore to place it on the Index a commission of cardinals was appointed to consider the matter, and when it reported adversely Leo formally pronounced against 'Americanism' as involving five specific errors: its rejection of external ecclesiastical direction as no longer necessary; its equation of natural with supernatural virtues; its criticism of religious vows as incompatible with Christian liberty; and its calls for new apologetic methods and a fresh way of approach to non-Catholics. In Loisy's judgment, however, the whole thing could be dismissed as 'a phantom heresy'. cf. A. Houtin, *L'Américanisme* (1904). On the movement in the U.S.A. see T. T. McAvoy, *The Great Crisis in American Catholic History 1895–1900* (Chicago, 1957).

POSTSCRIPT

Our survey opened with an allusion to a political event, Napoleon's concordat of 1802 with the Vatican. It may appropriately be closed, therefore, by referring to another, namely the terminating of that historic agreement by the Separation Law enacted by the government of the Third Republic on 9 December 1905. With the particular strains and tensions which led to the final breach we are not here concerned, although the wonder is that the relationship between the two powers had lasted so long. Nor does it fall within our purpose to detail the changes in the church's position in the nation which the law brought about, extensive as these were. The fact to be taken account of is, rather, that the Catholic church in France now for the first time had no standing in respect of the civil authorities, that it was a 'free church' answerable only to the Holy See. It had not itself sought such freedom, nor did it desire it; its new status was thrust upon it by an anti-clerical and secularist administration glad to pursue any course that might end in eliminating religion from the life of the French people. Thus the church had no alternative but to make the best of it, and the schism between those who would and those who would not accept that government's terms, which some anti-clericals gleefully expected, did not occur, although at the time most Catholics regarded the law as a disaster. For the Vatican too took a gloomy view of the immediate prospect. The cardinal secretary of state, Merry del Val, expressed the opinion a few weeks after the bill's passage that the provisions of the new law were even more deplorable than those of the civil constitution in the days of the Revolution. Pius X himself, who could rarely grasp the significance of what lay beyond the limits of his own restricted ecclesiastical horizon, did not properly understand the situation in France and was to some extent actually out of sympathy with the French church, blaming it for its present misfortunes and doubting any possibilities for good which might yet be open to it.[1]

Yet the upshot was that the ancient church of the French nation had by the event been brought closer to Rome than ever before in its history, its whole organization being now subject to direct Vatican control. Thus at their

---

[1] On the Separation Law and its aftermath in the Church of France see Dansette, *Religious History of Modern France*, ii, Bk II, cc. 2–5.

very first gathering after the Separation, held in August 1906, the French bishops were forbidden to discuss either the method of episcopal election or the permanency of the appointment of parish priests, or indeed the basic principles of the future relations of the Holy See and ecclesiastical institutions in France. 'Proceedings were under the secrecy oath of the Holy Office, which meant that the pope was able to leave the wishes of the French hierarchy out of account without causing any great remark.'[2] Aided by the policies of a strongly anti-ecclesiastical civil authority the new ultramontanism, of which Pius X could well be seen as the living embodiment, had completely triumphed. The condemnation of Modernism but two years after the Separation, followed by that of Le Sillon,[3] made it clear that intellectually, socially and politically Rome no more welcomed contemporary trends than she did in 1864.

Nevertheless the opening decade of the twentieth century, like its counterpart in the nineteenth, witnessed a remarkable revival of Catholic sentiment among the French people, and notably so among young men of ability. As we have seen, the revival had begun some years before the turn of the century. The eighties — 'les tristes années quatre-vingt' — had been a time of virulent anti-clericalism in politics and a somewhat truculent atheism in philosophy. The deaths of Renan in 1892 and Taine the year after, like the election, also in 1893, of a new parliament, signalized the beginning of a change. It became evident that a new spirit was abroad which, at any rate in the cultural sphere if not in the political, was to persist over the ensuing years. Modernism itself was an aspect of it, a recognition on the part of at least some Catholic scholars and thinkers that the doctrinal expression of their faith called for adjustment to the intellectual and moral outlook of a world far different from that of Bossuet and Fénelon, let alone St Thomas Aquinas. It was an attempt at what, more than sixty years later, Pope John XXIII was to call an aggiornamento. But the climate of opinion in the church itself was not ready for it, or at least not for the kind of radicalism with which the leading Modernists were rightly or wrongly identified. Pascendi therefore was the Vatican's emphatic non possumus, and neo-ultramontanism and 'integralism' were to enjoy complete ascendency for a half-century to come. But although Modernism in its day failed, new conversions to Catholicism, or the reaffirmation of faith on the part of those who had never formally abandoned it, continued. In many instances the revival took the shape of a deepened personal conviction of the truth of Catholic doctrine, in others — despite the affaire Dreyfus — a revaluation of Catholicism as a force making for patriotism and social cohesion such as the France of the Third Republic, confronted with the rising power of imperial Germany, could not afford to lose.

[2]Dansette, Religious History, p. 250.
[3]See, e.g., A. R. Vidler, A Variety of Catholic Modernists (1970), ch. 8.

The way to revival was assisted by the new philosophical atmosphere created by the work of Henri Poincaré, Émile Boutroux, William James and above all Henri Bergson. Positivism and naturalism had not of course occupied the entire philosophical scene during the preceding decades, as the names of Ravaisson, Renouvier, Secrétan and Lachelier are sufficient to prove, for all of these taught philosophies of human freedom in declared opposition to the doctrines of Taine and Renan. But they had resisted determinist theories less by way of direct criticism than by pursuing their own independent lines of speculation. With Poincaré and Boutroux, however, naturalism was assailed upon its own terrain, thus incidentally winning the attention of a wider public than usually found its reading in metaphysical treatises. In his early *De la Contingence des lois de la nature* (1875) Boutroux showed by an analysis of the methods proper to science itself that as between one scientific discipline and another there is always a certain hiatus. An account of reality therefore which would be *scientifically* exhaustive could not be said to exist; an argument resumed and developed in his *Idée de la loi naturelle* of 1891. But it was Bergson, Boutroux's pupil at the École Normale, who appeared to have destroyed the very presuppositions of naturalism and so opened the way to a metaphysic of spiritual freedom. He himself was to claim as much in an often-quoted statement from a letter of his to the Jesuit Maurice de Tonquédec. 'In my *Essai sur les données immédiates de la Conscience* (1889)', he wrote, 'I stressed the existence of freedom. In *Matière et mémoire* (1896), I succeeded, I hope, in demonstrating the reality of the soul. In *L'Evolution creatrice* (1907), I presented creation as a fact. From this the existence should stand out clearly of a God freely responsible for creation and the generator of both matter and life, through the evolution of the species and the constitution of human personalities'.[4] However this may have been — and Bergson himself was admittedly neither Catholic nor Christian — it was claimed not without reason that he 'had transformed the conditions of philosophic thought in our epoch'.[5] At all events of Bergson's success with the general reading public there could be no question. Seldom has a philosopher won such popular esteem in his own lifetime, both as writer and lecturer. Thus his influence in favour of basic Christian theism is not to be underestimated. What Bergson's thinking appeared to have accomplished was the removal of the prejudice that only scientific knowledge is worthy of the name and that there is no road to understanding apart from that of the intellect. Intuition, in a word, can be accepted as an authentic means to truth. The effect of this upon two such representatives of the younger generation as Charles Péguy and Ernest Psichari was spiritually liberating.[6]

---

[4] *Études*, 20 February 1911. Quoted Dansette, *Religious History*, p. 317.
[5] E. Bréhier, *Histoire de la Philosophie*, ii (1932), p. 1025.
[6] Psichari was Ernest Renan's grandson. On Bergson's influence both in France and abroad

But when the younger generation did turn to Catholicism, or at least discovered in it a vitality hitherto unrealized, it was not, remarkably enough, among the Modernists that they beheld the embodiment of their ideal. On the contrary, what satisfied them was nothing less than Catholicism in its fully ultramontane guise, dogmatically rigid and absolutist. Not intellectual compromise or accommodation but the unfaltering statement of an authoritative creed was what they wanted. Their concern was with action, particularly social action, for which only religion in its most positive and traditionalist form could supply the desired impetus and discipline. Speculative and critical questions, issues of pure scholarship, had no appeal for them. Their mood, rather, was that of men seeking to equip themselves to meet a future full of splendid possibilities as well as great perils. Such a sentiment, in the years leading up to 1914, was indeed prophetic; and as it happened both Psichari and Péguy were killed in the still early days of the first world war, along with other young Catholic writers, Maurice Masson, Émile Clermont, and André Lafon, to name but three.[7]

As regards scholarship and constructive thought during the first decade or so of the present century it can be said that the *débâcle* of Modernism did not have a wholly negative result. Biblical exegesis certainly did suffer, since virtually every serious biblical student found himself an actual or possible object of suspicion. Some preferred to delay publication of their works until less troubled times, and in any case the censorship had become so rigorous that others were deterred from pursuing their studies further. Thus the 'Bibliothèque de l'Enseignement scripturaire' ceased publication after bringing out only a couple of titles, Batiffol's *L'Enseignement de Jésus* and Touzard's *Le prophète Amos*, although the *Revue biblique* managed to keep up its high standard as a technical journal, while the *Revue du Clergé français* was still able to print the occasional article which attempted to deal with biblical matters in a well-informed way. Scholarly work, if of a conservative order, was produced by M.-J. Lagrange — most eminent and prolific of all Catholic exegetes — Dhorme, van Hoonacker, Jacquier and others, some

see J. Chevalier, 'La métaphysique, son renouveau depuis le début du xxe siècle', in *Larousse mensuel illustrée*, February 1933.

[7] An inquiry undertaken by the magazine *L'Opinion* in 1912 found a growing concern of youth to be 'the awakening of the national consciousness, a taste for heroism, a feeling for humanity, a certain moral and religious attitude of mind, the call of the classical tradition, and political realism'. Victor Giraud, writing in 1913, considered that Anatole France alone would 'be definitely classed among the "negators" or sheer amoralists' (see E. Magnin, *Un demi-siècle de Pensée catholique*, 1937, p. 28). In fact one has only to recall the names of the outstanding French literary figures of the earlier years of this century — those of Charles Guérin, Paul Claudel, Francis Jammes, Paul Bourget, René Bazin, Henry Bordeaux and Louis Bertrand do not exhaust the list — to prove the point that Catholicism then, as a century previously, could once more show its capacity to provide the dynamic not only of religious but of cultural revival.

of it deliberately aimed at countering the extreme radicalism of Loisy. In patristics the studies of Lebreton, notably his *Histoire du dogme de la Trinité*, were of indubitable value, as too were those of Hemmer, Lejay and Jacques Tixeront, whose *Histoire des dogmes dans l'antiquité chrétienne* remains among the best general surveys of its kind. The erudite Duchesne continued his researches, if with discretion, while in the field of later church history mention is possible here only of the magisterial achievement of Henri Bremond, with his *Histoire du Sentiment religieux en France*, of Imbart de la Tour's work on the Reformation, and of Lecanuet's *Histoire de l'Église de France sous la iiie République*. Much sound scholarship went into the production of various encyclopaedias: the *Dictionnaire de Théologie catholique* (Vacant-Mangenot) notably, as also those dealing with archaeology and liturgy (Cabrol-Leclerq), ecclesiastical history and geography (Baudrillart) and apologetics (d'Alès). Vigouroux's *Dictionnaire de la Bible* reached completion in 1912.

In the field of religious philosophy Thomism dominated the scene. But as the Thomist revival progressed it wore less and less its earlier appearance of an archaistic reaction. A genuine attempt was made to recapture the spirit and not merely to recall the letter of the great mediaeval doctor's writings, as may be seen in the work particularly of A. D. Sertillanges and Jacques Maritain, although learned studies of scholasticism in its historical aspect were published by men like Maurice du Wulf of Louvain and the Dominican Père Mandonnet. Moreover, a continuing dialogue was felt to be needed between Thomism and contemporary thought such as the *Revue des Sciences philosophiques et théologiques* aimed at maintaining for a generation to come. Indeed the range and vigour of the neo-Thomist movement proved sufficient to raise the whole enterprise from the status of a mere seminary discipline to that of an academic subject with right of entry into the syllabus of a modern secular university. Finally, regarding theology proper, some allusion is due to the work, first, of the Jesuit Léonce de Grandmaison, founder of *Recherches de Science religieuse* (1910), who at a difficult time adhered to a consistently moderate and balanced viewpoint, if at the price of a certain blandness on the more fundamental and intellectually pressing issues; and secondly, of the Dominican Ambroise Gardeil, director of studies at La Saulchoir from 1894 to 1912, who with his two treatises, *La Credibilité et l'apologétique* (1908, second and revised edition 1910) and *Le Donné révélé et la théologie* (1910) — the latter especially — was to demonstrate that conservatism need not be a synonym for obscurantism. In the first he set out to investigate the idea of *credibility* as an element in or condition of the act of faith, particularly in relation to the task of the Christian apologist, an area of thought in which he disclosed some degree of sympathy with the Blondelian *méthode d'immanence*. The subsequent volume attempts to assess the nature and validity of theology as a formalization of supernatural revelation while keeping in mind the requirement that, although a 'science' in respect of its rational structure, it should always retain its contact with the immediate data of the religious life itself. It is a conclusion, in truth, which may be said to have been the activating principle of the best Catholic thinking throughout the period which has been the subject of our survey.

SAINT-SIMONIANISM

Saint-Simonianism had its efflorescence in France only after the death of its founder, Claude-Henri, comte de Saint-Simon (1760–1825), when for some years it exerted a potent influence on the minds of many eager young intellectuals. It even acquired religious characteristics, clearly anticipating the *religion d'humanité* of Auguste Comte, who in fact was a good deal indebted to it. Saint-Simon, it can hardly be questioned, was among the originators of modern socialism, despite his personal doubts about social equality no less than individual liberty. He also was a man of large ideas, even if his manner of conceiving them tended to the bizarre. 'The only possible aim for a thinker today', he declared, 'is to work at the reorganization of our systems of morals, of religion, of politics, – in a word, of our whole system of ideas from whatever angle we look at it' (cf. G. Weill, *Un précurseur du socialisme. Saint-Simon et son oeuvre*, 1894). In his early *Lettres d'un habitant de Genève à ses contemporains* (1803) he urged the need of transferring the spiritual authority of the clergy and the temporal powers of the aristocracy to scientists and agriculturists respectively. Such notions were a pointer to all his subsequent thinking. Political parties of every kind he came to look on as futile. The reactionaries – Bonald, Maistre and their train – themselves admitted, by their hostility to current movements, the need of a new social order. The moderates, so-called, were mere compromisers with no coherent doctrine of their own. As for the liberals, in former days so hope-inspiring, they were now but a spent force. The society of the future would draw its strength not from political programmes but from industrialization based on the application of the 'positive' knowledge of science. Nevertheless there could be no change in the social system without a prior change in property-relations. 'The law of property depends on the general conception of public utility, and as this conception varies so must the laws regulating the acquisition and use of wealth at any given time. There must be *a* law of property, but its precise form and scope are bound to vary, and it can be altered whenever it is thought socially desirable.'

Saint-Simon's most celebrated work was perhaps his last, *Le Nouveau Christianisme* (1825). In this his concern for the poor, who numerically constitute the bulk of society, is the presiding motive, but it contains much that is in the nature of a profession of religious faith. He believes in Christianity's divine origin, of which its sublime ethic is, he thinks, proof sufficient. He even goes so far as to affirm the divine origin of the Church, which from its ideal of universal charity is a major force for good in society. For what essentially the Christian church proclaims is the brotherhood of man. Unfortunately its social mission has been obscured by its preoccupation with 'mysteries' and a multiplicity of trifling observances. But if Catholicism is most obviously at fault in this Protestantism also is by no means guiltless. Obsessed as it has been with the New Testament beginnings of Christianity, it ignores the experience of history. What is wanted, Saint-Simon stresses, is a 'new' Christianity intent on promoting universal brotherhood through a form of human association in which the pursuit of purely private advantage will no longer obtain. Such a Christianity, needless to say, will be mainly a 'lay' religion: priests have an incorrigibly vested interest in maintaining their schemes of dogma and ritual. Certainly it will be from the laity that the 'theologian' of the coming age will be drawn. 'The best ... is he who gives the widest application to the fundamental principle of the divine ethic [i.e. the brotherhood of mankind]. The best of theologians will be the genuine pope, and God's vicar on earth' — an office for which, it may be tacitly inferred, Saint-Simon esteemed himself well qualified.

The Saint-Simonian gospel was afterwards preached by a small band of the Master's apostles, who in *Le Producteur* furnished it with a periodical organ and also issued a collective and authoritative *Exposition de la Doctrine* (cf. G. Weill, *L'École saint-simonienne. Son histoire, son influence jusqu'à nos jours*, 1896). The former, which was not altogether characteristic of the style of thought that the movement subsequently developed, was short-lived, but the latter is virtually a dogmatic treatise, supplementing and considerably enlarging the original teachings. Moreover, although Saint-Simonianism remained loyal to its founder's economic and social theories, its adherents' main emphasis was on morality and religion. 'The doctrine of Saint-Simonianism', they solemnly pronounced, 'should bring about in humanity *as a whole* a renewal comparable to that which was effected among *some peoples* by Christianity' (*Exposition de la Doctrine*, p. 368). Christianity had failed, they held, both by its partiality and by its 'neglect of the material setting of human existence'. But the Saint-Simonians were not content only with a theology: the renovation of society would demand, they judged, a social instrument in the shape of a fully organized community. Thus besides starting a new journal, *L'Organisateur*, to propagate the faith they set about establishing a *church*, with two of their number, B.-P. Enfantin and S.-A. Bazard, as joint pontiffs. This quasi-ecclesiastical structure was centred in Paris, but it had branches in the provinces at Toulouse, Montpellier, Lyons, Dijon and Metz. To the heads of these bodies apostolic letters were from time to time despatched, in true apostolic fashion, for instruction, exhortation and correction. Systematic preaching was encouraged and monetary gifts by the faithful unstinting.

THE NEW ULTRAMONTANISM AND THE FIRST VATICAN COUNCIL

Ultramontanism in nineteenth-century France passed through three distinct and in certain respects opposed phases. Maistre's papalism was the central theme of a reactionary political theory. The vaunted 'liberties' of the Gallican church he dismissed as spurious: all that was concealed under that high-sounding phrase was 'a conspiracy of the temporal authority for despoiling the Holy See of its legitimate rights and separating it from the church in France while paying lip-service to its authority' (*De l'Église gallicane*, ii, c. xii). But with Lamennais and his sympathizers the papalist doctrine signified the liberation of the church itself from the yoke of state control, on the principle that only under conditions of complete freedom could it discharge its divine mission to society. The July Revolution, in terminating the alliance between the altar and the throne, seemed therefore to offer fresh ground for Lamennais's own hopes of a libertarian papacy. It was the liberal Catholics' misfortune that the pusillanimous Gregory XVI should have placed his confidence in the policies of Prince Metternich rather than in the editorials of *L'Avenir*. The French clergy generally, if not the episcopate, were eager enough to look to a benevolent Rome for the defence of their interests.

Pius IX however was not the man to minimize what he believed to be the prerogatives of his august office out of deference to episcopal feelings. The ordinary clergy, as he soon let it be known, need not fear to look to him for sympathy and even aid against bishops too conscious of their own importance. Appeals to Rome from disaffected clerics would be treated in accordance with regulations framed for the purpose. The result of this policy was an immense enhancement of the pope's personal prestige, a development at once reflected and stimulated by a lay journalist, Louis Veuillot, editor to the *Univers*, a newspaper founded in 1830 but not hitherto conspicuous or influential. (Veuillot's biography was begun by his brother Eugène in 1899 and completed by his nephew François in 1904. In all matters it upholds the rectitude of its subject's actions. For a more balanced estimate see J. Morienval, *Louis Veuillot*, 1941.)

Born in 1813 at Boynes in the Gâtinais, Veuillot took to journalism as a career in his youth, became a convert to religion in 1838 during a visit to Rome and in 1843 assumed the editorship of the paper which made him famous, a post he held until his death in 1883, having in the meantime become 'a sort of spiritual director to the clergy from the beginning of the Second Empire onwards' (Dansette, *Religious History*, ii, p. 19). A man of extreme and even fanatical opinions, his journal was from the start an apple of discord in ecclesiastical affairs and could never be ignored even by the government. Gallicans and liberals detested it — Dupanloup characterized it as 'une plaie vive dans l'Église' — although in the eyes of its supporters it was 'a great Catholic institution', the suppression of which, in the words of one of them, 'would be a great public misfortune to religion'. The supreme pontiff himself was said to have remarked, 'Je lis l'Univers et je l'aime' (see Maurain, *La Politique ecclesiastique du second Empire de 1852 à 1869*, 1930, p. 172n.) and its editor could confidently rely on the Vatican's sympathy and support even though the pope might at times counsel 'moderation and mildness', virtues of which the pugnacious editor himself had little inkling. For Veuillot has been described not inaptly as an ecclesiastical Voltaire. Certainly his literary manners lacked nothing of the great deist's acerbity while his knowledge of history was as superficial. But for the nineteenth-century polemicist the cause was religious traditionalism in its most obdurate form. Of tireless energy and pertinacity, with abilities which not even his most resolute detractors could deny, Veuillot's self-dedication to what he deemed to be the interests of the Holy See became obsessive. The critics of papalism, however moderate, were never to be spared. He confessed himself to putting 'vinegar' into his ink, though not, he wryly insisted, poison (cf. P. de la Gorce, *Histoire du second Empire*, 1894, ii. p. 156). As a thinker he was shallow – the deeper aspects of any theological issue were beyond his grasp – but in practical matters he revealed a hard commonsense. As a controversialist he was a match for any adversary, even if his unscrupulous vilification of opponents was at times an embarrassment to the very persons he professed to serve.

The summoning of an œcumenical council of the church was first announced in June 1867 and in the following year it was formally convoked. The official statement said nothing about a definition of the papal infallibility, but it was widely understood that this was to be the assembly's main purpose. The 'French correspondent' of the Jesuit *Civiltà cattolica* expressed the confident expectation that this would in fact be accomplished, in the shortest possible time, simply by acclamation and with the minimum of debate, a view which the *Univers* enthusiastically endorsed. Actually the article was not by the *Civilità*'s French correspondent at all, the anonymous author basing his assertions on memoranda sent by the papal nuncio in Paris, Archbishop Chigi, to the papal secretary of state, Antonelli, who himself forwarded it to the editor of the *Civiltà*. But feeling in France, as a result, ran high. Gallicans and ultramontanes, liberals and authoritarians, infallibilists and anti-infallibilists (or 'inopportunists') were soon embroiled in bitter controversy, Veuillot mocking those in particular who, as he put it, 'wanted to give the Holy Ghost sufficient time to form an opinion'.

In 1869 Maret's *Du Concile général et de la paix religieuse* came out, upholding a basically Gallican position. Although conceding that the pope is by divine right head of the church, the bishops also by divine right share, he argued, his authority in the general government of the religious society. Maret was answered by Pie of Poitiers and by other diocesan bishops, as too by Archbishop Manning of Westminster – an out-and-out infallibilist – in the appendix to his *Œcumenical Council and the Infallibility of the Roman Pontiff*. Maret countered with *Le Pape et les évêques, défense du livre sur le concile général et la paix religieuse*, replying not only to his episcopal critics but to a series of articles in *Études* by the Jesuit Père Matignon. The ultramontane abbot of Solesmes, Dom Guéranger, made his contribution to the acrimonious debate with *De la Monarchie pontificale, à propos du livre de Mgr l'évêque de Sutra* (1870) – Sutra being the title of Maret's see *in partibus infidelium*. The liberal case was presented, although in studiously moderate terms, by the *Correspondant* of 10 October 1869, which saw in the proposed definition a radical departure from the church's ancient tradition, resulting in what would almost certainly be a papal despotism, however benevolent. It could not bring itself to believe that a general council, under divine guidance, would ever be found to commit itself to such a course. In any event the problem must arise as to precisely what conditions are necessary for a papal utterance to be recognized as infallible. Presumably too the scope of the definition would be retrospective, even in regard to acts which in modern times would be contrary to the laws of the state. The article also hoped that the council itself would in some way or other be settled on a permanent basis as part of the church's constituted order of government. The *Correspondant*'s pronouncement was widely looked on as the liberal party's manifesto and was at once denounced as such by both Pie and the *Univers*. To at least a section of ultramontane opinion it seemed paradoxical that a faction which in the earlier years of the century had been among the protagonists of the papalist doctrine in France should now emerge as its avowed opponents.

The views of the *Correspondant* reached only the better educated sections of the Catholic public at large. A letter addressed by the bishop of Orléans to the clergy of his diocese under the title 'Observations sur la controverse soulevée relativement à l'infaillibilité au prochain concile' gained much more publicity. His concern, he insisted, was not the theory of infallibility *per se* but the definition's timing: in his own opinion the promulgation of it was altogether inopportune. He then urged that the definition was actually unnecessary, as the church's *inherent* infallibility had been acknowledged for eighteen centuries; that Trent, in its wisdom, had deliberately shelved it; that it would create a new barrier between Rome and both the Eastern churches and Protestantism; and that it would antagonize secular governments, which would read it as a confirmation of the notorious *Unam Sanctam* of Boniface VIII. It further was evident, quite apart from issues of historical fact, that theological difficulties as to the proper conditions of an infallible act and of distinguishing between the pope's judgments as a private doctor and as head of the church could not easily be removed, since theologians themselves were divided about them. Finally it was bound to have the effect of reducing the status of the bishops in the eyes of the faithful.

The ultramontanist interpretation of Dupanloup's letter was that it repudiated the doctrine itself and was a calculated attempt to involve the whole question in further dispute. The liberals, on the other hand — and of course the anti-clericals — applauded him. But the bishop had also been unable to resist a thrust at his old adversary, the editor of the *Univers*, whom he accused of subjecting matters of faith to the caprices of sensational journalism. Veuillot answered him in characteristic vein, but in so doing provoked Dupanloup into an angry rejoinder in the shape of an 'Avertissement' addressed to the editor of the *Univers* personally (Veuillot himself gives it in full in his *Rome pendant le Concile*, 1872, pp. 551–83), in which he charged him with 'usurpations on the Episcopate' and with 'accusing, insulting and calumniating the brethren in the Faith', applying to him the opprobrious biblical term *Accusator fratrum*. The bishop of Orléans had now, too, to contend with another dedicated ultramontane in the person of Mgr Deschamps, archbishop of Malines, whose *L'Infaillibilité et le concile général* had just appeared (30 November 1869). The latter, whose tone was not unconciliatory, pointed out that when the sovereign pontiff declares or defines the faith he proclaims the truth only as divinely revealed in scripture and tradition, which he does 'sometimes by consulting the bishops; sometimes by convoking Councils; sometimes doing neither, when tradition is indubitable and springs to the eyes of all'. What use was there then in speaking of a 'separate' infallibility, as if the faith of the successor of Peter could ever be exclusively personal, or separate itself from that of all the centuries'? (See *Collectio Lacensis Conciliorum recentiorum,* vii, 1892, coll. 1286–95, for the full text of the archbishop's letter. cf. also Cuthbert Butler, *The Vatican Council 1869–1870*, ed. Cristopher Butler, 1962, p. 126). But although Dupanloup was the leading spokesman on the 'inapportunist' side he enjoyed the open sympathy and support of the archbishop of Besançon, Cardinal Matthieu, the archbishop of Paris, Mgr Darboy, the scholarly bishop of Grenoble, Ginoulhiac and a number of others in the French hierarchy. Dechamps' pamphlet was also the occasion of Gratry's *Lettres à Mgr Dechamps*, a *riposte* comparable, some even thought, to Pascal's *Provinciales*.

Throughout the seven months of the Council's session Veuillot took care to station himself at Rome, with Pius IX's full cognizance and approval. His lodgings became a centre for the collection and dissemination of news, none being better informed on what occurred both in and behind the Council than the editor of the *Univers*. By means of the papal secretaries who were authorized to instruct him he was in fact in constant communication with the supreme pontiff himself. His campaign against Dupanloup won him the pope's express commendation; and indeed the papal cause, as the more advanced ultramontanes saw it, had no more dedicated adherent or vocal apologist. Every papal utterance he seems to have regarded as divinely inspired. As he wrote from Rome, 'Does the Church believe, or does she not believe, that her Head is inspired directly by God, that is to say, infallible in his decisions regarding faith and morals? (*Rome pendant le Concile*, ii, p. 50). It was a view that went far beyond anything which a classical exponent of infallibilism such as Bellarmine had ever claimed. Yet Veuillot's attitude and methods not only pleased the curialists and the Jesuits but gained him popularity with the great body of Catholic opinion in France, whether clerical or lay, and although men like Salinis of Amiens or Gerbet of Perpignan might dissociate themselves from his political interests they supported his ecclesiastical policy without demur, even when they could have wished for more diplomacy in the propagation of it.

But abrasive journalism alone could not have secured the success of the new papalism against the *parti du diable* — in Veuillot's phrase — of anti-infallibilists and 'inopportunists': the influence of the religious orders also worked powerfully. Although the Jesuits and Assumptionists were well to the fore in this regard the Dominicans and Benedictines too had their zealots. In a *Defense de l'Église romaine contre les accusations du Père Gratry* (1870) Dom Guéranger, who had been mainly instrumental in substituting the Roman liturgy for the old diocesan forms, produced an answer to the Oratorian's case against the infallibility doctrine mainly on the latter's own chosen ground of history.

In the end, and despite all the controversy, the Council's deliberations took their foreseen course. No fewer than thirty-four plenary sessions were given over to the question of the pope's primacy and infallibility. The minority pressed their views bravely but unavailingly. Pio Nono himself, be it said, had the most complete confidence in the outcome. He, Gian Mastai, he declared, believed in infallibility, and as pope he had nothing to ask of the Council: the Holy Spirit would enlighten it (E. Ollivier, *L'Église et l'État au Concile du Vatican*, 1877, i, p. 535), though he evidently saw no reason why the Spirit's working should not be well publicized beforehand. The hot Roman summer passed slowly, tempers frayed, patience grew thin, and the anti-infallibilists could not but perceive their cause to be lost. *Il faut en finir* became the prevailing mood. On 13 June the Council voted on the entire *schema de Ecclesia*; 451 members registered *Placet*, 88 *Non placet*; while 62 gave a qualified approval, *juxta modum*. It was therefore referred back to the deputation (i.e. committee) *de Fide*, though only to re-emerge with an addition likely to cause the minority still further distress. For it was now to be proclaimed that the pope's decisions not only were irreformable *ex sese* but that they did not require the assent of the church (*non autem ex consensu Ecclesiae*). A last-minute attempt by Archbishop Darboy to secure the inclusion of some such phrase as *innixus testimonio Ecclesiae* failed: Pius's view was that it was too late. When the final and public voting took place on 18 July the opposition virtually collapsed. A Hungarian prelate, Haynald of Colocza, had urged a *Non placet*, but Dupanloup preferred a simple abstention, although a letter to the pope stating so gained no more than fifty-five signatures (see Ollivier, *L'Église*, ii, pp. 344f.). Thus the constitution *Pastor Aeternus*, which contained the infallibility definition, came to be adopted almost unanimously, if not precisely in a form to give satisfaction to the extreme infallibilists. Only two bishops returned a *Non placet* vote, whereas five hundred and thirty-three favoured it. While the actual voting was being conducted a thunderstorm burst over the Eternal City, which the impressionable interpreted as a portent, albeit one of ambiguous meaning. The Council never completed its deliberations, a crisis in international politics supervening, and it was adjourned *sine die*. Whatever else might have been judged to have foundered, the ultramontane cause had clearly triumphed.

ERNEST RENAN

With the exception of Hippolyte Taine no French writer of the second half of the nineteenth century exercised so pervasive an influence as did Ernest Renan. Both men have been described, not unfittingly, as 'the intellectual conscience of their age' (V. Giraud, *De Chateaubriand à Brunetière*, p. 184). Renan was a Breton, – he was born at Tréguier in 1823 – a man of immense intelligence and industry, but by temperament a romantic and a dreamer. For all his philosophical and historical learning he conveyed the impression of a dilettante, an intellectual *flâneur*. Destined for the priesthood when still a child, he was educated at the Sulpician *petit séminaire* of Saint-Nicholas de Chardonnet and subsequently at Issy and Saint-Sulpice itself, where his aptitude for oriental languages, which he studied under Quatremère and Burnouf, became evident. His intention to take Orders, however, was abandoned in 1845, when he had attained the age of 22, for the vocation he had come increasingly to feel was that of a pure scholar, free to pursue truth wherever it might lead him. But it was not only the idea of the priestly life which he then relinquished: he had ceased to believe in Catholic dogma altogether, the divinity of Christ and personal immortality included. He was virtually, in fact, an agnostic, although religion itself continued to hold his imagination.

In 1848 the appearance of his first book, an *Histoire des Langues sémitiques*, with which he gained the Prix Volney, established his reputation as a philologist. It was at this time too that he wrote *L'Avenir de la science*, although its publication was delayed until 1890, only two years before his death. *Études d'Histoire religieuse* and *Essais de Morale et de critique* followed in 1857 and 1859 respectively. He also embarked on archaeological work, first in Italy (1849–50) but later in the Near East (during 1860–1 and again in 1864), where he began his celebrated *Vie de Jésus*. Appointed professor of Hebrew at the Collège de France in 1862, he was tactless enough in his inaugural lecture to refer to Jesus as 'cet homme incomparable', and it was not long before his opinions caused such offence in Catholic circles that he resigned his post, in which he was not reinstated until the fall of the Second Empire in 1870. Elected to the Académie Française in 1879 in place of Claude Bernard, he eventually became Director of the Collège de France. The seven volumes of his *Histoire des Origines du christianisme* came out between 1863 and 1881. Other publications comprised *Questions contemporaines* (including the essay 'L'avenir religieux des sociétés modernes') (1868), *Dialogues et fragments philosophiques* (1876) (with a reprint of the author's 1860 paper, 'La métaphysique et son avenir'), and *Discours et conférences* (1887). His *Feuilles détachées*, the last of his writings, contained an 'Examen de conscience philosophique', his final testament as a thinker. On his death in 1892 he was accorded a state funeral. (Renan's *Œuvres complètes*, in an edition by H. Psichari, were published between 1947 and 1960. See also J. Chaix-Ruy, *Ernest Renan*, 1956.)

It is doubtful whether even the young Renan's faith was very profound. Religion appealed to him emotionally, as it did to Chateaubriand, and this disposition he never outgrew: the *Vie de Jésus* is a curious amalgam of rationalism and romanticizing pietism. The rationalism however, in a man of such acute intelligence, was bound to prevail and it is absurd to take literally his own asseveration that it was for 'philological reasons' he left the church. Renowned in his day as a historian and biblical scholar, it was his philosophical interest which really determined the direction of his mind. 'Je t'assure', he told a friend early in 1842, 'que qui n'a pas la foi ferme n'a qu'à s'y adonner' — to philosophy, that is — 'pour la perdre tout à fait. Jamais je n'avais eu tant de difficultés, et même tant de doutes positifs.' He also confessed that but for his study of Pascal his own beliefs would have disintegrated even sooner. Philosophy and faith, as he saw them, could not coexist within the same understanding. His early *L'Avenir de la science*, written when he was twenty-five, revealed 'un jeune homme vivant uniquement dans sa piété et croyant frénétiquement à la vérité', as also the sources from which this young intellectual had drawn his philosophic nourishment. They were many and various: Spinoza and Herder, Hegel and D. F. Strauss, Cousin and Sainte-Beuve, Chateaubriand and Auguste Comte were all among them. Yet despite his eclecticism Renan's characteristic tone of ironic detachment is evident throughout. Indeed the whole tendency of his subsequent thinking is already anticipated in this work, along with his far-ranging intellectual curiosity, his temperamental scepticism, the *finesse* of his distinctions, his disdain of mere pedantry and his innate romanticism. And like all its successors, it is marked by the elegance and subtlety of style by which Renan unfailingly charmed his readers. Paradoxically, he calls to mind Newman — a Newman, so to speak, *à rebours*. (For an interesting comparison of the two men see Jean Guitton, *La Pensée moderne et le catholicisme. Parallèles: Renan and Newman*, 1938).

The views adumbrated in *L'Avenir de la science* were developed in the various review articles which compose the *Études d'Histoire religieuse* and *Essais de Morale et de critique*. Acclaimed at first by specialists, his work gradually reached a wider public, and he himself became the object of Sainte-Beuve's facile pen-portraiture in *Causeries du lundi*. But with the book on Jesus notoriety also caught up with him. Its appearance was hailed by Edmond Schérer as 'one of the events of the century'. Repeated editions of five thousand copies were exhausted in the space of a few days. Within two years a hundred thousand copies had been sold and the work translated into nine or ten different languages. In the literary and religious history of nineteenth-century France it was rivalled in popularity only by the *Génie du christianisme* and the *Essai sur l'Indifférence*. Yet as a piece of critical scholarship it carries no weight, although it served to introduce French readers to an altogether new kind of exegesis, with its subject depicted in a human perspective and a *mis-en-scène* of historical realism. The supernaturalism of the orthodox interpretation is of course dismissed entirely, but the treatment is apt to be remote from the spirit of the gospel text: Jesus, the 'young Galilean', becomes a poetic, not to say a sentimentalized, figure. The book's interest lies in its author's attempt to deal with the Jesus-story in a manner different from that of traditional dogma or conventional piety.

Renan's attitude to Catholicism is one of nostalgia, partly ironic partly wistful. He regards it as something which the educated of his own century could no longer believe. It had once been admirable, desirable, even in a sense true. Its truth for some, might still hold: man always has need of imaginative sustenance, and

Catholicism still retains a residual power to enlighten and instruct the moral conscience. Again, unbeliever though he was, Renan was not imbued with anti-clerical zeal: he himself insisted that he had never known a bad priest. But for all its attractiveness and pragmatic worth the Catholic religion in an age of science could not, he thought, be taken for the truth. According to his own confession in *Souvenirs de Jeunesse*: 'Le christianisme suffit à toutes mes facultés sauf ma raison critique; il faut donc ou renoncer au catholicisme ou amputer cette faculté.' He could find no substitute, imaginative or moral, for a failure of rational conviction.

INDEX